# Design Tools for Evidence-Based Healthcare Design

The growing movement towards evidence-based health care design has largely emphasised a change of culture and attitudes. It has advocated for new ways of working, but until now it has not focused on equipping health care clients and their designers with the practical means to exploit the potential benefits of evidence-based architectural design.

Development of indicators and tools that aid designers and users of the built environments in thinking about quality enhances the design process to achieve better outcomes. Importantly, design tools can support managers and designers through end-user involvement and an increased understanding of what patients and staff expect from their healthcare facilities. They can facilitate the creation of patient-centred environments which improve user satisfaction.

*Design Tools for Evidence-Based Healthcare Design*:

- discusses the tools that are being used to achieve design quality and excellence within the context of NHS procurement systems such as PFI, ProCure21 and others;
- collates information that increases our understanding of these tools, in order to be able to make the best use of them;
- clarifies where, during the various stages of a building's life (from inception, design, construction, occupation and re-use), these tools should be used in order to derive the benefits possible from evidence-based design;
- provides in one place an authoritative reference publication that will act as an aide memoire, a user guide and manual for these design tools.

Illustrated with case studies from throughout the UK and beyond and written by a well-known expert in the field, this book will provide essential reading for anyone involved in healthcare design.

**Michael Phiri** is the author of nine books and over 50 technical reports. He is the Director of Healing Architecture Research at the University of Sheffield and a chartered architect with over 20 years' post-qualification experience in both private and public practice. He has research and teaching experience from Sheffield, York, Edinburgh, Heriot-Watt and Strathclyde Universities.

'Dr Michael Phiri has succeeded in a daunting task: bringing rigour and utility to the complex world of the design tools used to plan, design, construct and evaluate the physical infrastructure of healthcare in the UK and beyond. This book will be an essential companion to anyone involved in developing the health estate, and who wishes to know how the available tools link to the growing evidence base on healthcare building design.'

Jonathan Erskine, Executive Director, European Health Property Network, UK

'The emergence of Evidence-Based Design marks the evolution of contemporary creative practice from the ephemeral to a discipline at the core of health systems planning. Michael Phiri provides a valuable overview of the approaches, methods and tools available to those planners and architects formulating the future healthcare estate.'

Christopher Shaw, Senior Director, Medical Architecture and Chairman of 'Architects for Health', UK

'*Design Tools for Evidence-Based Healthcare Design* is a scholarly read that takes you on the journey of patient experience through the built environment, emphasising why the patient matters when designing a health facility.'

Steve Batson, Director, Bowman Riley Healthcare, UK

# Design Tools for Evidence-Based Healthcare Design

Michael Phiri

Routledge
Taylor & Francis Group

LONDON AND NEW YORK

First published 2015
by Routledge
2 Park Square, Milton Park, Abingdon, Oxon OX14 4RN

and by Routledge
711 Third Avenue, New York, NY 10017

*Routledge is an imprint of the Taylor & Francis Group, an informa business*

*British Library Cataloguing in Publication Data*
A catalogue record for this book is available from the British Library.

*Library of Congress Cataloging in Publication Data*
Phiri, Michael, author.
Design tools for evidence-based healthcare design / Michael Phiri.
p. ; cm.
Includes bibliographical references and index.
I. Title.
[DNLM: 1. Hospital Design and Construction--methods. 2. Evidence-Based Practice--methods. 3. Hospital Planning--methods. 4. Patient Safety--standards. 5. Quality Improvement--standards. WX 140.1]
RA967
725'.51--dc23
2014017172

ISBN: 978-0-415-59872-9
ISBN: 978-0-415-59873-6
ISBN: 978-1-315-74995-2

Typeset in Avenir
by Saxon Graphics Ltd, Derby

Printed and bound in Great Britain by
TJ International Ltd, Padstow, Cornwall

# Contents

# List of tables and figures

## Tables

# Figures

# Acknowledgements

Thanks are due to all those people and organisations which provided material, notably projects, illustrations and copyright permissions. These include Peter and Erica Bishop, Robert Etchell, Llewelyn Davis and Great Ormond Street Children's Hospital, Monika Purschke, Semir Zubcevic and the Health Team Albert Wimmer ZTgmbH, Andrew Link and CIC, David Low and the Department of Health Estates and Facilities.

# Foreword
# Sunand Prassard
## PPRIBA

In the early days of medicine the character of place was inseparable from the process of healing. In ancient Greece, for example, sick people spent time at the shrine of Asklepios, the god of medicine and healing, believing the place itself to have restorative powers in addition to those of the deity and the priests. This connection of healing with place, people and faith sustained itself up until the advent of science-based medicine.

The word hospital comes from the Latin *hospes* meaning guest, as does hospitality, both words combining shelter and caring. As a student of architecture I was taught that one of the very first buildings of the Renaissance was the *Ospedale degli Innocenti*, the Foundling Hospital in Florence by Filippo Bruelleschi. Though not a hospital in the modern sense, it is heartening for all who care about health care environments that a hospital was among the most significant works of architecture in history.

Several key buildings of the modern movement in architecture embody the belief that the design of the setting in which health care takes place can make a significant contribution to recovery and well-being. The Paimio Tuberculosis Sanatorium by Alvaar Aalto, the Zonestraal Sanatorium in Hilversum by Johannes Duicker and the Finsbury Health Centre, London by Tecton are among the best known. However, somewhere along the line in the evolution of this stream of thought a subtle shift came about which was to eclipse the relationship between place and healing. The functionalist strand in modernism came to dominate, focusing design on the clinical process rather than place. Among the drawings of the Finsbury Health Centre is a set of little axonometric views showing how patients would pass efficiently through examination booths. The arrangement is devised entirely to suit the doctor's working practices, with the patient seen as a passive body to be diagnosed and put right. While an explanatory drawing celebrates the centre's 'Cheerful Atmosphere', another points to its 'Orderly Design'. This was just before the war. In the less creative hands of some of the later architects of the NHS, formed just after the war, orderly design flourished while the atmosphere of health care buildings became increasingly clinical. The achievements of the in-house architects at the Ministry of Health, who numbered some 500 at their peak in the 1960s and early 1970s, were prodigious. They compiled a huge, world-leading literature on design data and guidance based on painstaking measurement, and they devised hospital templates that could be rolled out at scale. In hindsight this effort might be seen as an attempt to keep up with the dazzling advances of scientific medicine evidenced in its success in virtually eradicating communicable diseases, and in the reparative surgery of every damaged part of the human body.

It is natural that the design of health facilities should subject itself to standards of evidence and proof comparable to those in medical research. Yet this raises a problem, for the perception of the health care buildings and settings by the patient as well as the practitioner always involves three levels of judgement, whether consciously or not. There is a fully quantifiable level relating to how well the building is constructed, serviced and equipped – the domain of building science. There is a practical functional level relating to how well the building works – the domain of planning. Finally there is an almost entirely subjective or aesthetic level, relating to how the building affects the senses and emotions – the domain of architecture as an art. Two thousand years ago the Roman chronicler Vitruvius described these three domains of judgement as Firmitas, Utilitas and Venustas. Translated in the early seventeenth century as Firmness, Commodity and Delight by Sir Henry Wootton, these three levels of perception and judgement interact in complex ways. Subjective and objective get mixed up, and there is no room for that in medical research. Or is there?

The advent of 'patient focused medicine' in the 1970s and 1980s introduced the perception of the patient as a whole being with mind and body intertwined, and crucially as an active participant in her or his own treatment. This development created the space for a better appreciation of how the environment might interact with the diagnostic and therapeutic processes of modern medicine. The quality of space and place once again began to be considered as having as much importance as the accommodation of process.

So far so good, but the subjective inevitably poses the problem that assertions and facts are difficult to separate. A designer may be fully convinced of this or that approach, but they may simply be expressing an individual and untested

position, or perhaps an orthodoxy that has never been questioned. Such an approach may be shown to be brilliant in practice, or it may be a costly failure – how can we tell in advance?

In the last two decades a new factor has entered the realm of the construction, operation and management of health facilities – often called the accountability culture. In this culture, that which cannot be measured and accounted for is practically deemed not to exist. In this context factors that are easy to quantify, namely money, time, human and natural resources, tend to weigh more than factors such as customer satisfaction or design quality. In response a number of methods and tools have sprung up to try and capture some of the less tangible attributes of the health systems and settings alongside a more precise definition and positioning of the tangible attributes.

This book is the first comprehensive exposition of these methods. In laying out these tools clearly, devising a taxonomy to position them, and arguing for evidence-based design and assessment, Dr Phiri has done all involved in health care a valuable service. The division of the tools into the four categories of Compliance, Design Quality, Efficiency and Effectiveness and Sustainability is convincing and useful.

When a few of us were persuaded of the need to devise a tool, the Design Quality Indicator, that could guide clients, designers, constructors and building managers to assess and improve design quality, our motivation initially had more than a hint of "if you can't beat 'em, join 'em". Process KPIs were threatening to become the only evidence of project performance regardless of how good or bad the product might be. As it turned out, the Construction Industry Council's DQI, with its Vitruvius-derived, and I would argue timeless, structure, proved to be a highly effective map that enabled project teams to look at quality in the round, ensuring that all contributions were valued and driving improvement. In parallel the health care version of AEDET and its later evolutions, including ASPECT, added important evidence layers to the tool. This work was done by Professor Bryan Lawson and Dr Phiri, which explains the grasp displayed in this book, written as it is by someone who has been closely involved in devising the tools as well as using and analysing them.

All actors involved in creating the settings and systems for health care will do their job better by embracing an evidence-based approach. However, they also need to be able to understand and use practical and experiential knowledge and not rely on the academic and measurable, valuable though it is. Good tools will help us, but how we use them will matter more than what they are. Dr Phiri helps us with the former; the latter is up to us.

# 1 Introduction

The UK National Health Service design and procurement system now relies on a number of indicator tools built around a couple of key ideas. The first of these is learning from established practice and ongoing capital projects which feed knowledge back into new designs and the design process. The second is the notion of evidence-based architectural health care design, a process of basing design decisions regarding the built environment on credible and rigorous research to achieve the best possible outcomes.

The growing movement towards evidence-based health care design has largely emphasised a change of culture and attitudes and advocated for new ways of working. It has not focused on equipping health care clients and designers, and has resulted in a gap between aspirations for good and efficient design of health care buildings and the provision of the means to exploit the potential benefits of evidence-based architectural design. Design indicator tools not only aim to bridge this gap; they can also play a useful role in bringing together government clients, client bodies, contractors, design firms, local government and others to address issues of design and design quality, with improvements in quality a top priority of management today.

Concern with design quality increased in the 1990s following the UK government's introduction of new policies on construction procurement and infrastructure delivery vehicles in the public sector. The result of these policies was Private Finance Initiatives (PFIs) followed by Public Private Partnerships (PPPs), and various types of construct/operate delivery vehicles such as Build Operate Transfer (BOT), Design Build Operate (DBO) and Design Build Operate Transfer (DBOT). However, these execution modes did not always produce high quality health care facilities. More specifically, studies pointed to poor performance, inefficient project management, poor building quality and, above all, low levels of client and user satisfaction. As a result, the UK government demanded that the construction industry implement better work practices, with the objective of achieving high levels of building quality while initiating and funding the development of design tools and guidance (NHS Estates 1994, NHS Estates Design Brief Working Group 2002).

These measures by the UK government increased attention to the definition, measurement and monitoring of design quality in order to enhance the ability to create healing and therapeutic environments providing "function or **commodity, firmness** and **delight**"; in other words, "Well building hath three conditions, *commoditie, firmness and delight*", as indicated in *Principles of Architecture*, Wotton's translation of the ancient Roman architect Marcus Vitruvius Pollio's three principles or essential qualities for architecture – in Latin, "***utilitas, firmitas*** and ***venustas***" (Wotton 1624/2011). In modern times these Vitruvian ideals have been translated into functionality (a good building should be useful and function well for the people using it), impact (a good building should delight people and raise their spirits) and build quality (a good building should stand up robustly and remain in good condition) (Figure 1.1). Monitoring and establishing accountability for the quality of the built health care environment is crucial for quality improvement, raising standards and achieving excellence in the design of new health care buildings.

Development of indicators and tools to aid designers and users of the built environments in thinking about design quality enhances the procurement and design process to deliver good environments that promote healing. Such tools can support health care managers and designers through both end-user involvement and an increased understanding of what patients and staff expect from the built health care environment. Design tools can facilitate the creation of patient-centred therapeutic environments which improve user satisfaction.

The context for these tools is indicated by the evidence-base underpinning them, and by the total life span of the project from inception through to the end of the building's life cycle. The framework for the overall project process can be described by strategy, design, construction and operation; the key strategic and design issues relate to such things as improved health outcomes, impact on the community and so on, as well as the effectiveness of the roles and team expertise or skills to undertake the project work.

An evidence database essentially makes a link between structural and process measures of the estate and patient and staff outcomes. It is thus an essential tool in a system for measuring quality and safety in the health care estate. It indicates how the designed health care estate can impact on such things as length of stay, reduction of falls, rates of cross-infection, risks of clinical error and consumption of medication. It also shows very detailed results such as heart rates, sleep patterns, staff absenteeism and the like, and it can provide links to more qualitative measures such as patient satisfaction and staff recruitment and retention. The research in this field is international and extensive.

A database of such research for the Department of Health was started some years ago with funding from the old NHS Estates (Lawson & Phiri 2000). The database was updated annually until 2004 when NHS Estates was reorganised in the Department of Health (Lawson & Phiri 2003). We are now aware of around a thousand relevant items of research. The evidence suggests that factors that the architect/designer has control over can make significant differences to patient satisfaction, quality of life, treatment times, levels of medication, displayed aggression, sleep patterns and compliance with regimes, among many other similar factors. The database was cross-referenced to a similar literature search conducted in the USA by Professor Roger Ulrich's team (Ulrich et al. 2004, 2008). Ulrich's team looked for studies that were:

1.1 Ancient Roman architect Marcus Vitruvius Pollio's three principles or essential qualities for architecture in latin: "***utilitas, firmitas*** and ***venustas***"

- rigorous, in that they used appropriate research methods that allowed reasonable comparisons and discarded alternative hypotheses. The research studies were assessed on their rigour, quality of research design, sample sizes and degree of control (e.g. Ulrich 1984).
- high impact, in that the outcomes they explored were of importance to health care decision-makers, patients, clinicians and society.

Previously, Rubin, Owens and Golden 1998 had identified 84 studies (out of 78,761 papers) since 1968 that met similar criteria and rigorous standards of hard science. Reviewing the research literature in 2004, they estimated that they would find around 125 rigorous studies. Ulrich's team and Lawson's team found more than 600 studies.

> Since 1998, the increase in research related to the impact of the built environment on health care outcomes has increased at an exponential rate. There were 84 published studies at that time, and in 2004, the number grew to 600. Yet the debate continues about the reliability of this evidence to inform decisions about the design of health care environments. The interior designer can effectively use research as an iterative process throughout the design of a project, benefitting the decision making process. An exploration of the methods and tools that can be utilized have been described as well as some of the issues and pitfalls encountered as design professionals attempt to advance a research-based agenda.
>
> (Jocelyn Stroupe, President, AAHID;
> Health Care Interior Design Practice Leader,
> Cannon Design, March 2011)

We therefore have good reason to place high confidence in the Lawson and Phiri (2000, 2003) Sheffield database and believe we identified the overwhelming majority of work in the field internationally. It was published annually on the Department of Health Knowledge Portal (KIP) until 2004. Users of KIP regularly consulted the database and there have been lots of requests to make the database widely available to NHS Trusts, their consultants and others such as researchers in health care facility design and operation. The database has also been summarised in a Department of Health publication (Phiri 2006). Studies range in size and scope. Some are small and little more than anecdotal, while others are major longitudinal controlled investigations. Some are multi-factorial and some much more parametric.

Overall, however, there is now little doubt that all this adds up to a significant body of knowledge that can no longer be ignored in the design of new health care facilities and the management and upgrading of existing ones (Lawson 2002). Studies suggest that in general, designs complying with this evidence may be capable of repaying any small additional capital costs on an annual basis (Berry, Parker et al. 2004). Other analysis suggests that the total operating costs of secondary care buildings may normally be expected to exceed the capital construction costs in less than two years (Lawson & Phiri 2003). It is entirely appropriate that summaries of all the original research, together with very basic analysis, should be made available to those people who wish to check or question its validity. This is in line with normal practice that allows others to judge the value of research for themselves and to go back to primary sources. However, it is recognised that such an approach is largely impractical in terms of design actions. Those involved in the briefing, specifying, commissioning and design of health care environments are unlikely to find the time or have the expertise to read a thousand items of original research. For this reason an overall picture is needed, not in terms of causal factors and theories but couched largely in terms of the design considerations and direction needed to achieve the results suggested by the research. In simple terms, clients and architects want to know roughly what sort of things they should do, what features of buildings they should control or elaborate, and what sorts of qualities of environment they need to produce (Lawson 2005).

Taken together, then, this new evidence-based approach has the potential to improve the quality of patient experience and, in many cases, health outcomes, while simultaneously saving time and costs. However, the generic evidence suggests that to achieve these benefits, designs will need to improve quality. So far most design guidance has tended to concentrate on compliance with minimum standards. This approach therefore suggests a new departure in focusing on ways to drive up quality in relation to the evidence specifically for health care environments.

Ongoing development and keeping up to date the evidence base that underpins the indicators and tools is essential to ensure that these respond to changes in clinical practice, new technologies and the frequent organisational re-structuring or new NHS landscape structures, health and social policies and supply chain that serve the NHS.

In this book the complementary design tools have been categorised into four main headings according to their aims and primary objectives (Table 1.1). These are: Improving Compliance with Statutory and Other Requirements, Design Quality Improvement, Enhancing Efficiency and Effectiveness, and Achieving Sustainability in the Architectural Health Care Estate. Each tool is described, reviewed and assessed in a typical case study application to show its important characteristics and the benefits of using the tool.

Table 1.1 Four categories of Evidence-Based Design Tools

| Categories | Design Tools |
|---|---|
| Improving Compliance with Statutory and Other Requirements. | **P**remises **A**ssurance **M**odel (PAM): "A system-wide, nationally consistent approach to providing organisation board-level assurance of the quality and safety of premises in which NHS clinical services are delivered. The rigorous self-assessment methodology uses robust evidence, metrics and measurements to demonstrate that a health care provider's premises achieve the required statutory and nationally agreed standards on safety, efficiency, effectiveness and staff/patient (user) experience". <br> **A**ctivity **D**ata**B**ase (ADB): "Relates uniquely to health care and is well-regarded in the industry. Contractors in the health care sector point out that ADB data is used on 95% of all health care projects". |
| Design Quality Improvement. | **A**chieving **D**esign **E**xcellence **E**valuation **T**ool Kit (AEDET): "A sector-specific version of the industry standard Design Quality Indicator (DQI) widely adopted in the UK to establish a shared set of terms and concepts through which all those involved in the design process can map its quality". <br> **A S**taff & **P**atient **E**nvironment **C**alibration **T**ool (ASPECT): A plug-in for AEDET Evolution – "Can help communicate and allow sharing of values, clarify design strengths to build on, weaknesses to be overcome while identifying opportunities for improvement of the architectural health care environment". <br> **D**esign **Q**uality **I**ndicator (DQI): "A method of evaluating the design quality and construction of new buildings as well as the refurbishment of existing ones, including police stations, office buildings, college and university buildings, libraries, and many other civic and private building projects. The process involves a wide group of people responsible for the design and construction, those who will use the building or are affected by it". <br> DQI for Health: Launched in March 2013 in certain cases succeeding AEDET Evolution (above) which is no longer supported by the Department of Health. <br> **D**esign **A**nd **R**isk **T**ool (DART): "Estimates and manages the risks involved in a design under ProCure21 NHS Building Procurement, aids the client to make informed decisions when evaluating the inherent risks for specific design proposals". <br> **I**nspiring **D**esign **E**xcellence and **A**chievements (IDEAs): "Initiates the design of health care places through considerations of people (patients, staff and visitors), medical equipment and furniture to respond to emotional and functional requirements of health and social care delivery". |
| Enhancing Efficiency and Effectiveness. | **S**trategic **H**ealth **A**sset **P**lanning and **E**valuation (SHAPE): "A web-enabled evidence-based application which informs and supports the strategic planning of services across a whole health geographical economy in order to deliver health and social care more efficiently and effectively while enabling decisions to be made closer to the patients (and all those people) that will be affected by them". |
| Achieving Sustainability in the Architectural Health Care Estate. | **B**uilding **R**esearch **E**stablishment's **E**nvironmental **A**ssessment **M**ethod (BREEAM): "Sets the standard for best practice in sustainable building and construction design and has been widely acknowledged as the measure to describe a building's environmental performance. Credits are awarded in nine categories according to performance which are then aggregated or added together to produce a single overall score on a scale equivalent to 'Pass', 'Good', 'Very Good', 'Excellent' and 'Outstanding' rating". <br> **C**hartered **I**nstitution of **B**uilding **S**ervices **E**ngineers (CIBSE) TM22 (**E**nergy **A**ssessment & **R**eporting **M**ethodology (EARM™)): "A method for assessing a building's energy and services performance that can be handled by using a spreadsheet approach to consider feedback and operational performance and therefore allows building owners, facilities managers and designers to reconcile, for example, the total electrical use against various end uses". |

1  Improving Compliance with Statutory and Other Requirements (PAM and ADB).

A growing challenge for all health care providers worldwide is the need to comply with statutory demands and legislation on the quality and safety of hospitals and other health care facilities. As for any major infrastructure project, the holistic process of health care facility design requires considerable multi-disciplinary input due to the many elements to be considered which must also comply with the regimes and protocols of the health care provider or operator. Tools which improve compliance with all these requirements, such as fire safety, are important in managing risk and in achieving the necessary approvals, licensing and certification while supporting the rapid diffusion of information and innovation.

Suitable tools are essential to facilitate the deployment of new health care service models and patient pathways, utilise the latest technologies where appropriate, and deliver excellent outcomes at lower cost.

2  Design Quality Improvement (ASPECT/AEDET Evolution, DQI, DART and IDEAs).

Concerns and raising expectations for improved design quality can be largely associated with various hospital building programmes dating back to the 1960s 'Hospital Plan' and up to the 1990s PFI Hospital Building Programme. In all these cases, a response has been the development of tools to help the design process and ensure the delivery of quality buildings and environments able to support a stepped increase in the adoption of world class scientific endeavour, which includes diagnostics, imaging, experimental medicines, assistive technology and telehealth.

Design quality matters and its continuous improvement is essential and crucial in enhancing health care services, delivering efficiency, flexibility of use and control of comfort levels to improve the patient and staff experience, including contributing to the positive effects of health and well-being. It is also now widely accepted that the physical environment impacts on our productivity levels, capacity to relax, ability to easily navigate where we are, and our ability to interact with each other. Design quality is therefore an important factor in determining the success of the places where we live, work and are cared for.

A study by the University of Sheffield's School of Architecture Health Care Research Group into the NHS Estates Design Review System used 35 Design Review Panels and identified seven key design quality drivers: 1. Aspirations of the Trust; 2. Guidance and recommendations, 3. Championship (at board level), sponsorship and external reviewers (but not Design Champions); 4. Briefing; 5. Lifecycle costs; 6. Context (including the site), and 7.Practice.

3  Enhancing Efficiency and Effectiveness (SHAPE).

To deliver health care efficiently and effectively requires the identification of performance gaps, failures and successes along with actionable factors contributing to these. Historically key factors in hospital facility planning are time and efficiency, notably improving the staff's ability to treat patients quickly and safely as well as optimising clinical staff travel distance and adjacencies. One key issue facing developers and health care planners is reconciling the tools and standards for enhancing staff efficiency and cost effectiveness with those for design quality improvement and creating a healing, therapeutic environment that enhances patient's experience and ensures patients can easily and safely navigate throughout the hospital.

Reconciliation based on some sort of prioritisation, especially in times of resource scarcity, is an imperative to address consequences of the drive for time and efficiency in hospital facility planning through optimising staff travel distance and adjacencies, such as deep-plan hospitals with increased operational costs due to requirements for air-conditioning, mechanical ventilation, artificial lighting and lacking views and natural light or daylight. The focus on clinical staff's requirements often results in sterile health care settings and long-travel distances for patients and visitors, which contribute to poor patient experiences.

4  Achieving Sustainability in the Architectural Health Care Estate (BREEAM Healthcare and CIBSE TM22).

Hospitals are heavy users of energy, water and other resources. They also produce large amounts of waste. In 2007 20% of the UK's entire public-sector buildings output of annual $CO_2$ emissions were by the NHS estate. Tools which aid health care providers and their consultants to address sustainability are essential to meet targets such as those for delivering high quality care for diverse patient populations in carbon-neutral care settings by 2012.

## Conclusions

A major goal for this book is to raise awareness of the importance of tools underpinned by a robust evidence base and facilitate the adoption of best practice, eliminating waste and improving quality in health care. Emerging issues are identified from an approach that adopts a strategy of using design tools to aid the design process, the creation and delivery of health care facilities that lead to positive staff and patient outcomes. Notwithstanding all this, to achieve success, providers, commissioners and regulators of the delivery of health care, or more specifically the accommodation in which health and social care is provided, need to proactively embrace and implement such tools.

## References

Berry LL, Parker D, Coile RC Jr., Kirk-Hamilton D, O'Neill DD, and Sadler BL (2004) The Business Case for Better Buildings. *Frontiers of Health Services Management*, 21 (1), 3–24.

Lawson BR (2002) Healing Architecture. *The Architectural Review* CCXI (1261), 72–75.

Lawson BR (2005) Evidence-Based Design for Health care. In *Hospital Engineering and Facilities Management 2005*, W. Swaby, London, International Federation of Hospital Engineering, 25–27.

Lawson BR (2007) Design Indicators, in D. Stark, *UK Health care Design Review*. Keppie Design, Glasgow, 88–95.

Lawson BR, Bassanino M, Phiri M et al. (2003) Intentions, practices and aspirations: Understanding learning in design. *Design Studies*, 24 (4), 327–339.

Lawson BR and Phiri M (2000) Room for improvement. *Health Service Journal*, 110 (5688), 24–27.

Lawson BR and Phiri M (2003) The architectural health care environment and its effects on patient health outcomes. TSO, London ISBN 978 0113 224 807 (reprinted January 2004).

NHS Estates Design Brief Working Group (Chairman: Richard Burton) (2002) Advice to Trusts on the main components of the design brief for healthcare buildings. Leeds, UK.

NHS Estates (1994) *Better by Design: Pursuit of Excellence in Healthcare Buildings*. Leeds, UK.

O'Keeffe DJ (2008) Facilitating the design quality of hospitals by using AEDET (Achieving Excellence Design Evaluation Toolkit). Unpublished MBA Dissertation, College of Estate Management/University of Reading.

Phiri M (2006) Does the physical environment affect staff and patient health outcomes? A review of studies and articles 1965–2006. TSO, London.

Rubin HR, Owens AJ, and Golden G (1998) Status Report: An investigation to determine whether the built environment affects patients' medical outcomes. Concord CA: The Center for Health Design.

Sadler BL, Berry LL, Guenther R, Hamilton KD, Hessler FA, Merritt C, and Parker D (2011) Fable hospital 2.0: The business case for building better health care facilities. *Hastings Center Report* Vol. 41, No.1, January/February 2011: 13–23.

Sadler BL, Dubose J, and Zimring C (2008) The business case for building better hospitals through evidence-based design. *HERD: Health Environments Research & Design Journal*, 1 (3), 22–30.

Ulrich RS et al. (2004) The role of the physical environment in the hospital of the 21st century: A once-in-a-lifetime opportunity. Concord CA: The Center for Health Design.

Ulrich RS et al. (2008) A review of the research literature on evidence-based health care design. *HERD Journal*, 1 (3), 61–125.

Wotton H (1624/2011) *The Elements of Architecture*. John Bill, London. Architecture Revived, 28 September 2011.

# 2 Compliance tools

## Introduction

The NHS Premises Assurance Model (PAM) and Activity DataBase (ADB) are two important mechanisms to enhance compliance with UK statutory and other requirements. Specifically, PAM sets out a performance spectrum across a range of key deliverables in five domains: 1. Finance/value-for-money; 2. Safety; 3. Effectiveness; 4. Patient experience; and 5. Board capability as a mechanism that supports an organisation's ability to demonstrate baseline compliance for registration and regulation, while providing verifiable demonstration that premises are playing their part in supporting the objectives of the NHS Operating Framework and comply with the associated performance management system (the NHS Performance Regime).

Developed in the 1960s as a room-based programming and design system to aid the briefing, construction, asset management and alteration of health care facilities, Activity DataBase (ADB) was an essential component of the exhaustive 'databases' which detailed design requirements for each area of a hospital within an academically-based hospital information planning framework. Spaces designed using ADB data automatically comply with UK Department of Health Estates and Facilities guidance such as Health Building Notes (HBNs) and Health Technical Memoranda (HTMs), since ADB data generation forms an integral part of the publication process. Users can create their own project-specific briefs and designs using the extensive library of integrated graphics and text, which includes room data sheets, room layouts and departmental room schedules, based on Schedules of Accommodation produced as part of the Department of Health guidance programme.

## NHS Premises Assurance Model (PAM)

Developed as a universal, system-wide and nationally consistent approach to providing organisation board-level assurance of the premises in which NHS clinical services are delivered, the NHS Premises Assurance Model has a critical role to play in the design, construction and management of health care facilities. Released to support the NHS in enhancing the quality and safety of NHS premises while also increasing efficiency and effectiveness, PAM is an important component in the overall vision for quality in the NHS (*High Quality Care for All*, Darzi 2008). The methodology is a rigorous self-assessment that derives from evidence and measurements to demonstrate that a health care provider's premises achieve the required statutory and nationally agreed standards in terms of safety, effectiveness and patient (user) experience. Co-produced with the NHS, PAM relies on a 'bottom-up' rather than a 'top-down' approach to assurance regarding the premises in which NHS health care is delivered, driving premises-related performance improvements throughout the system and a greater understanding of the vital role that NHS premises play in the delivery of improved clinical and social outcomes (Figure 2.1).

Developed as metrics that support local NHS organisations to deliver improved NHS estate utilisation while reducing the need for new hospital space by up to £3 billion, and saving up to £100 million per annum of estate costs by 2013–14, PAM was conceived as a new framework for managing NHS health care property. The piloting of the model over 2009–10, involving four Strategic Healthcare Authorities and 13 NHS Trusts, first looked at the acute sector only during April 2009 to September 2009. During this period, requirements for Mental Health and Primary Care were also examined. This allowed for further development of the model from October 2009 onwards. The ultimate goal for the model is for a 'universal' version that

extends its application to provide assurance for all providers of NHS services after the national roll-out in 2010. This integrates with the Operating Framework for the NHS in England 2010/11, whose five priorities were to:

1    Improve cleanliness and reduce health care-associated infections.
2    Improve access through achievement of the eighteen-week referral to treatment pledge and improve access (including at evenings and weekends) to GP services.
3    Keep adults and children well, improve their health and reduce health inequalities.
4    Improve patient experience, staff satisfaction, and engagement.
5    Prepare to respond in a state of emergency such as an outbreak of pandemic flu, learning from our experience of swine flu.

Hence the reference to the need for NHS organisations to "develop robust plans to reduce their estate running costs and carbon emissions, drawing on available tools, including the new NHS Premises Assurance Model, which is currently being tested and will be launched in April 2010" (*The Operating Framework for the NHS in England 2010/11*, page 32).

The Universal NHS Premises Assurance Model provides a single, consistent, high-level but comprehensive reference point for applicable-premises regulation and best practice. PAM is implemented by health and social care service providers, supported by commissioners, to offer assurance on the efficiency, quality and capability of the provider's premises. In this way, PAM is used to inform the Board of a service provider on the performance of its premises. Commissioners can use PAM to manage the premises' performance of their service providers, while also allowing assessment of the overall premises' performance of a commissioner by the National Board or their equivalent and by other appropriate bodies.

Structured around the five domains (Finance/Value for Money, Safety, Effectiveness, Patient Experience and Board Capability), the Assurance Framework provides assurance on the efficiency, quality and capability of a provider organisation's premises. Each of the five domains is built

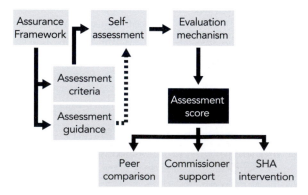

**2.1 Premises Assurance Model**

across three components: 1. information – what is collected on the performance of the premises?; 2. strategy and policy – how is information used to plan for the future?; and 3. delivery – how are the premises currently performing? Overall, the structure clarifies how well the health care premises support the delivery of effective and optimal patient care (Figure 2.2).

Health care premises are assessed against key criteria and evidence to define current performance as: 1. 'Not doing it'; 2. 'Not meeting the required standard'; 3. 'Meeting the required standard'; and 4. 'Best in class performance'. These assessments provide a set of scores which are then aggregated to give an overall assessment of performance. Using a combination of qualitative statements (National Inpatient Survey and Patient Environment Action Team – PEAT), quantitative metrics (Hospital Episode Statistics – HES and Estates Return Information Collection – ERIC data) and referring to Assessment-Level Guidance, PAM requires users to identify what evidence is held to justify the assessment. Outputs can then be presented to the Board and to commissioners, thereby providing assurance as well as identifying areas and targets for development or raising issues or the need for performance enhancements (Figure 2.3).

In each of these cases the Department of Health systems of guidance and toolkits have an important role to play in order to achieve performance and quality improvements. PAM is aspirational and has two main aims: to lift premises assurance from an operational perspective into a strategic objective, and to raise health care organisations' appreciation of the vital role that NHS premises play in the delivery of improved clinical and social outcomes. Valued at some £40 billion of real estate with an annual running cost of £7 billion, the NHS is the single largest property holder in the public sector and a key player in the delivery of government initiatives and legislation such as the Climate Change Act 2008, which calls for improvements in efficiency and a contribution to sustainability from the civil estate, and the Civil Contingencies Act 2004, which classifies the NHS as a Category 1 responder in the event of civil emergency.

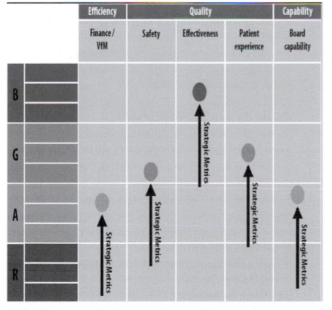

2.2 Premises Assurance Model – each of the five domains is built across three components

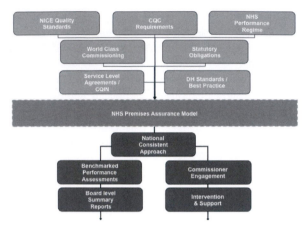

2.3 Darzi Report – a catalyst

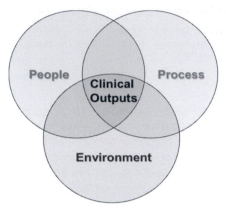

2.4 **Premises Assurance Model relates people, process and environment**

Key attributes which describe PAM relate to compliance, self-assurance, users, sources of data and different types of criteria. Under compliance PAM seeks to ensure that the quality and safety of premises used for NHS clinical services achieve the required statutory and nationally agreed standards in terms of safety, effectiveness and patient (user) experience. PAM is therefore a programme for the systematic monitoring and evaluation of these aspects.

Self-assurance refers to the management framework for achieving performance and quality improvements within the NHS linked to quality assurance (QA), a programme for the systematic monitoring and evaluation of various aspects of the service or facility to ensure that standards of quality are being met. Two key principles characterise QA: 'fit for purpose' (the product should be suitable for the intended purpose) and 'right first time' (mistakes should be eliminated). *Accreditation* is a process of ensuring that the organisation's quality assurance meets the relevant standards (Figure 2.4).

PAM was used by NHS acute and foundation trusts from April 2010 for self-assessment and internal reporting; the results can also be shared with commissioners (Schedule 5, Part 2, NHS Standard Contract) to demonstrate compliance (see *Guidance on the NHS Standard Contract for Acute Services 2010/11*, page 32, clauses 10.50 to 10.55 inclusive). However, there is a need to identify the individuals, whether experts or novices.

The different types of criteria include: 1. reports, registers and files; and 2. policies and procedures. The sources of data are: A. facilities management costs per m², deriving from ERIC (Estates Return Information Collection) data against a combined list of activity measures per m² (from HES [Hospital Episode Statistics] data); and B. PAM relies on 1. reports, registers and files; 2. policies and procedures; and 3. tools such as ASPECT/AEDET Evolution, PEAT, SHAPE and Drawings. However, there appears to be no mechanism to examine or challenge the details, contents or contribution of these documents. It may not be sufficient merely to possess them (Table 2.1).

## Activity DataBase (ADB)

As an individual activity space within a building, a room forms part of a schedule defining a department or particular speciality – for example, for maternity care, the elderly, mental health or outpatients. ADB holds data as a Master Project which contains information on some 30 hospital departments, 1500 clinical and non-clinical rooms and a library of 2500 components, assemblies or groupings of components and room layouts. This standard data held in the Main Project uses codes with numbers up to 900 for all items. Each room contains information on: activities such as handwashing, planning and adjacency relationships; spatial data such as recommended area, height and personnel; data on environmental conditions (temperature, lighting, air

Table 2.1 Comparison of ASPECT/AEDET Evolution 2005 and PAM

| | ASPECT/AEDET Evolution | Premises Assurance Model |
|---|---|---|
| | **A CHARACTER AND INNOVATION** | |
| 1 | There are clear ideas behind the design of the building | |
| | **B FORM AND MATERIALS** | |
| 4 | The external materials and detailing appear to be of high quality | 3B Effectiveness **E1** Providing premises in good physical condition |
| 5 | The external colours and textures seem appropriate and attractive | 3B Effectiveness **E1** Providing premises in good physical condition |
| | **C STAFF AND PATIENT ENVIRONMENT (ASPECT)** | |
| 1 | PRIVACY, COMPANY AND DIGNITY | |
| 1.1 | Patients can choose to have visual privacy | |
| 2 | VIEWS | |
| 2.1 | Spaces where staff and patients spend time have windows | |
| 2.5 | The view outside is interesting | |
| 3 | NATURE AND OUTDOORS | |
| 3.2 | Patients and staff have access to usable landscaped areas | |
| 4 | COMFORT AND CONTROL | |
| 4.6 | The design layout minimises unwanted noise in staff and patient areas | |
| 5 | LEGIBILITY OF PLACE | |
| 5.1 | When you arrive at the building, the entrance is obvious | |
| 6 | INTERIOR APPEARANCE | |
| 6.8 | Floors are covered with suitable material | |
| 7 | FACILITIES | |
| 7.1 | Bathrooms have seats, handrails, non-slip flooring, a shelf for toiletries and somewhere to hang clothes within easy reach | |
| 8 | STAFF | |
| 8.1 | Staff have a convenient place to change and securely store belongings and clothes | |
| | **D URBAN/SOCIAL INTEGRATION** | |
| 3 | The hard and soft landscape around the building contribute positively to the locality | |
| | **E PERFORMANCE** | |
| 1 | The building is easy to operate | |
| | **F ENGINEERING** | |
| 1 | The engineering systems are well designed, flexible and efficient in use | |
| | **G CONSTRUCTION** | |
| 1 | If phased planning and construction are necessary the various stages are well organised | |
| | **H USE** | |
| 1 | The prime functional requirements of the brief are satisfied | 3B Effectiveness **E2** Meeting Operational Policy requirements |
| 2 | The design facilitates the care model of the Trust | |
| 3 | Overall the building is capable of handling the projected throughput | 3B Effectiveness **E3** Handling capacity and throughput demands |
| 4 | Work flows and logistics are arranged optimally | 3B Effectiveness **E4** Supporting workflows and logistics |
| 5 | The building is sufficiently adaptable to respond to change and to enable expansion | 3B Effectiveness **E5** Anticipating future adaptability |

**Table 2.1 continued**

| | ASPECT/AEDET Evolution | Premises Assurance Model |
|---|---|---|
| 6 | Where possible spaces are standardised and flexible in use patterns | 3B Effectiveness **E6** Providing flexibility in use |
| 7 | The layout facilitates both security and supervision | 3B Effectiveness **E7** Facilitating security and supervision |
| | **I ACCESS** | |
| 1 | There is good access from available public transport including any on-site roads | 3B Effectiveness **E8** Meeting Transport Plan arrangements |
| 2 | There is adequate parking for visitors and staff cars with appropriate provision for disabled people | 3B Effectiveness **E9** Handling staff and public car parking arrangements |
| 3 | The approach and access for ambulances is appropriately provided | 3B Effectiveness **E10** Providing ambulance and fire access and egress |
| 4 | Overall the building is capable of handling the projected throughput | 3B Effectiveness **E3** Handling capacity and throughput demands |
| 5 | Pedestrian access routes are obvious, pleasant and suitable for wheelchair users and people with other disabilities / impaired sight | 3B Effectiveness **E12** Delivering pleasant landscapes and well-lit pedestrian, including disabled, access routes |
| 6 | Outdoor spaces are provided with appropriate and safe lighting indicating paths, ramps and steps | 3B Effectiveness **E12** Delivering pleasant landscapes and well-lit pedestrian, including disabled, access routes |
| 7 | The fire planning strategy allows for ready access and egress | 3B Effectiveness **E10** Providing ambulance and fire access and egress |
| | | 3B Effectiveness **E11** Achieving service segregation |
| | **J SPACE** | |
| 1 | The design achieves appropriate space standards | 3B Effectiveness **E13** Achieving space standards |
| 2 | The ratio of usable space to the total area is good | 3B Effectiveness **E16** Utilising space |
| 3 | The circulation distances travelled by staff, patients and visitors are minimised by the layout | 3B Effectiveness **E14** Minimising circulation distances |
| 5 | The design makes appropriate provision for gender segregation | 3B Effectiveness **E15** Accommodating gender segregation |
| 6 | There is adequate storage space | 3B Effectiveness **E17** Providing adequate storage |

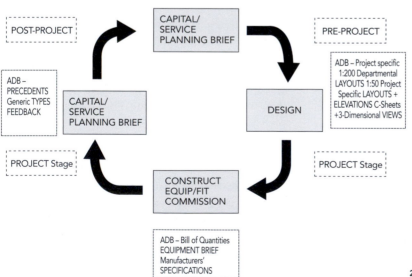

**2.5 ADB in the Design–Build–Occupy cycle**

filtration, noise levels and so on); a list of equipment; and a graphical room layout.

## Key features of ADB are:

- A computerised package to assist health care planners, architects, and teams involved in the briefing, design and equipping of health care environments. For example, ADB uploads equipment into rooms; ensures that rooms designed and uploaded using ADB conform to the necessary Department of Health requirements for health care facilities; schedules equipment/rooms/doors; and compares required equipment with the equipment placed in the design.

- The only data and software package that is sold on a commercial basis (unlike AEDET or NEAT – now BREEAM) and which is also endorsed by the UK Department of Health. Consequently, ADB represents the only source of Department of Health-approved best-practice briefing and design data.

- The only package that contains accurate and detailed data drawn directly from the Health Building Notes (HBNs), which support the Department of Health National Service Frameworks in identifying the way care will be delivered in the future, as well as Health Technical Memoranda (HTMs) publications. ADB data is therefore continuously updated by the Department of Health to align it with the latest standards and guidance in Health Building Notes and Health Technical Memoranda. These are similar to technical, process and quality standards developed and published by national or international bodies (e.g. BSI, ISO, and EN), typically defining measurable values in safety, design, engineering and manufacturing, building and construction, ICT, health care, business quality and many other industry sectors.

- Both ADB data and software are crown copyright. Where a licensed user makes a material change to the data, including any customisation, this crown copyright no longer applies and in turn the Department of Health endorsement ceases to apply. Also, the use of any element of the ADB data or software without a valid licence contravenes the crown copyright.

With ADB, the fact that it is a Department of Health-owned product in terms of both data generation and software means that the Department of Health is also entirely responsible for any investment or lack of investment towards its maintenance and continuous development, aspects which may be directly attributable to policy decisions regarding how, when and where ADB is implemented. ADB data reflects HBNs and HTMs and unless there is a rolling programme of commissioning new publications and/or data by the Department of Health, there are real risks that health care guidance and standards quickly become out of date and will not be aligned with changing legislative and policy requirements.

Activity Database and Room Layouts were developed for the rapid computation of briefing equipment schedules, department plans and whole hospital layouts in support of the hospital building programme for the 1962 'Hospital Plan'. The Bonham-Carter Report led to the 1962 'Hospital Plan', which intended over a ten-year period to build 90 new hospitals, remodel 134 others and provide 356 improvement schemes. The aim was not merely to modernise and rebuild many hospitals, but to change their pattern and content, while integrating them with health and social services provided in a community. There were some new hospitals built (e.g. Greenwich and Basingstoke) and there was more spent on hospital building between 1961 and 1963 than in the previous 13 years.

The Hospital Plan consolidated the concept of the 'district general hospital' (DGH) typically serving a population of 200,000 to 250,000. The Hospital Plan was based upon a bed norm of 3.3 acute beds per thousand, and although Nuffield Provincial Hospitals Trust studies showed that more efficient use of beds was possible, it was recognised that the norm might require revision downwards. However, the plan proved not to be financially viable, and within four years a major revision was required because of over-optimistic population projections and an under-estimate of costs.

The 1962 Hospital Plan led to the implementation of a system of design, procurement (Hospital Building Notes, Capricode, and Cost Guidance) and construction (Manufacturer's Data Base for building elements and components). The first Hospital Building Notes (subsequently Health Building Notes), published in 1961, comprised HBN1: Buildings for the Hospital Service; HBN2: The Cost of Hospital Buildings; and HBN3: The District General Hospital. By 2009 the entire set of Health Building Notes had grown to 136 publications, 87 of them being produced in the last twenty years.

With the Hospital Plan proving not financially viable, it was revised in 1966 into the 'Hospital Building Programme'. From the 1960s onwards Hospital Building Notes (HBNs), Hospital Equipment Notes (HENs), Hospital Technical Memoranda (HTMs) and Hospital Building Procedure Notes (Capricode) as well as other guidance were published and followed effectively. Based on good research and up-to-date clinical and nursing practice, they rapidly became respected and accepted standards for planning and procedure, not only in the UK but also in many other parts of the world (Moss et al. 2001).

Over the years the early NHS guidance system of three HBNs expanded to include the following tools and guides, some of which have not survived (*):

- CUBITH: Coordinated Use of Industrialised Building Technology for Hospitals*
- MDB: Manufacturer's Data Base – approved building components*
- ADB: Activity DataBase – all the data required to design a space for a specific activity
- DBS: Design Briefing System*
- HTMs: Hospital Technical Memoranda – Codes of Practice
- Capricode: the mandatory procedural framework for managing and processing NHS Capital Building Projects*
- CIM: Capital Investment Manual.

The design of new and revised guidance involved the parallel development of coordinated building components for the Manufacturers' Data Base for application during the design/production stage. The robust design data for elements such as ceilings, partitions, doorsets, storage units and worktops fitted within a central Purchasing Procedure which established the level of product quality as well as cost. This system underpinned the later development of the

Activity DataBase and Room Layouts, and justified the investment in developing and implementing it.

With the 'Blue Book' management structure that included ADB 'B sheets', the first full issue of the paper-based ADB system occurred in 1976 and the first PC-based product was released in 1989. Computerisation started to be considered in the early 1970s, with data based on the ideas generated from the Harness Hospital System.

The 1970s therefore coincided with the implementation of the 800-bed Greenwich Model Hospital Project serving a population of 165,000 (architect: WE Tatton Brown, Department of Health and Social Security with SE Metropolitan Regional Health Board), the Best Buy Hospitals, another model hospital providing for 550 beds on two storeys ("*indicative of the desire of central government to encourage semi-autonomous outlying executive authorities to adopt its suggestions*"; Cox & Groves 1990, page 61), the Harness Hospital System intended for hospitals of 500 to 1100 beds ("*conceived in terms of a more open-ended aggregation of units of accommodation along a linear spine of circulation*"; Cox & Groves 1990, page 61) and the Nucleus Planning tool (a neater and geometrically more lucid system developed from 'Harness' in 1975).

Harness is regarded as a system of hospital planning as well as an administrative method, embodying the results of research and experience in the formulation of standardised plans for various departments, and a method by which these may be fitted together in a variety of ways. For the Harness System, ADB was used to disseminate standard briefing and design data between the Regional Health Authorities and NHS Trust/specific project teams, resulting in standard department designs being produced that could be customised to suit specific projects and sites. This was beneficial to both the Regional Health Authorities and to individual projects in that the research, design and development work was centralised, saving the authorities from conducting their own research and therefore from the need to "reinvent the wheel".

The Harness programme of hospital building anticipated 70 new hospitals in the 1970s, but only two were built.

The Nucleus System consisted of standard departmental plans, based on standard operational policies and designed so that they can be assembled to form unique hospitals with differing functional content requirements and site constraints. Nucleus differed from Harness in that each preplanned unit was a star-shaped cluster or 'template' of identical overall dimensions. Nucleus was conceived so that it offered the opportunity of the construction of a hospital in stages, from a first phase of about 300 beds to a potential of expansion to about 900. The system enabled the completion of an efficient hospital in a single phase with the capability of growth and change in response to need and funding.

> The nucleus concept provides standard designs for units required in the first phase of a district general hospital and is based on a standard module, 2 storeys high, with variations in ward design kept to a minimum. The economic arguments for mass production are familiar and convincing, and to that extent the proposals will meet with a general welcome.
>
> (British Medical Journal Editorial 31 January 1976 p. 245)

Over 65 Nucleus hospitals were built including Maidstone General Hospital, Kent (Powell, Moya and Partners Architects), St Mary's Hospital, Isle of Wight, and additions to the North Staffordshire City General Hospital. During this period the 'Best-Buy hospitals' were built and ADB was the most common and effective application of standardising the production of room layouts and assemblies of furniture and equipment.

Overall, the different building programmes (notably Harness, Nucleus and Hospital Plan) set out different criteria against which HBNs/HTMs and therefore ADB data were drawn up. These have changed significantly over time, leading to variation in quality, level of content and details.

It is important to note that ADB developed in the context of a large, continuous and centrally financed national hospital building programme in which there has been development work, feedback and redevelopment, in parallel with an increasing need for achieving best value.

ADB relates uniquely to health care and is well regarded in the industry. Some major contractors point out that ADB data is used on 95% of all health care projects. ADB is used variously as a tool to:

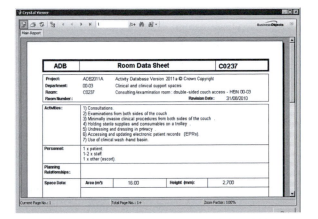

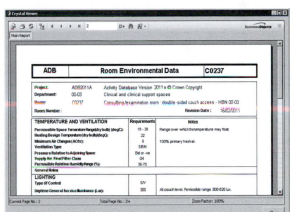

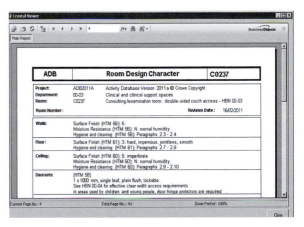

2.6 ADB examples of **room data sheets** indicating a list of activities, **room environmental data** showing environmental quality, and **room design character** sheets providing information on finishes

- produce Room Data Sheets indicating a list of activities, Room Environmental Data showing environmental quality and Room Design Character Sheets providing information on finishes; graphical representations of room layout drawings, room elevations and three-dimensional drawings to 1:50 scale (C-Sheets) (Figures 2.6 and 2.7).
- create and edit a BRIEF using a library of room or space types, schedules of equipment or components by room, department and project (Figure 2.8).
- benchmark health care facilities.
- export or upload data to Microsoft Word, Microsoft Excel, Adobe Acrobat Portable Document Format (PDF), Comma Separated Values (CSV), HTML, XML and software packages such as CodeBook.
- interface and integrate with Autodesk CAD products (AutoCAD 2004-6, 2006-9, ADT, and Revit) only. ADB 2013 software upgrade features support for 32- and 64-bit versions of AutoCAD 2013 and is compatible with 32- and 64-bit versions of Windows XP SP2/3 and Windows 7. The DXF facility allows export for AutoCAD LT, Microstation, Vector Works and others. An interface with Bentley's Microstation would probably pay back fairly quickly in terms of additional sales.
- as a source of reference and a checklist.
- produce a list, graphical locations of equipment as well as cost data for the equipment. Trusts, architects, quantity surveyors and others often use this data as a rough guide or 'starter' bill of quantities. Discontinuation of Departmental Cost Allowance Guides – DCAGs (groups 1 and 2 only) – has probably affected this. With DCAGs withdrawn because they no longer reflect the space requirements or cost of modern facilities, Health Care Premises Cost Guides (HPCGs) now provide a cost rate (a cost per $m^2$) for building works and engineering services for different hospital departments, and separate rates for public, clinical and staff spaces. HPCGs are based on ADB data, HTM standards and cost information from real schemes, reflecting modern construction forms, engineering, equipment technologies and the delivery of clinical services.
- create a list of, and track, assets.

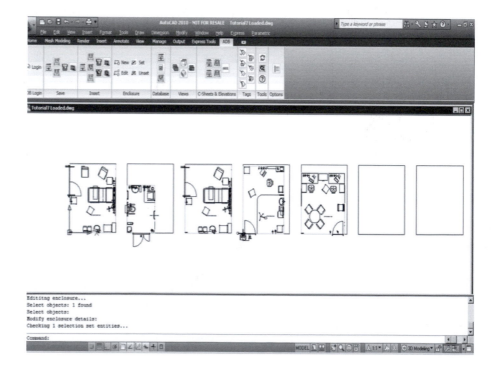

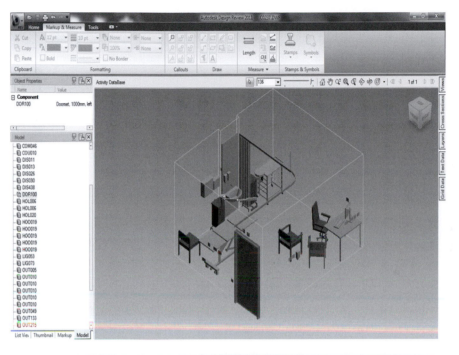

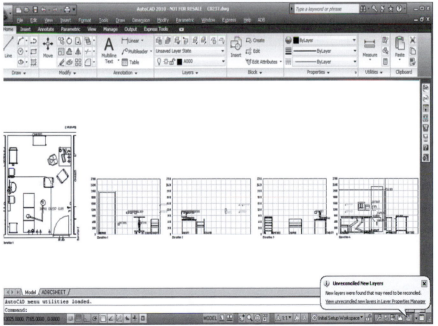

**2.7 ADB graphical representations** of room layout drawings, toom elevations and 3-dimensional drawings to 1:50 scale (C-sheets)

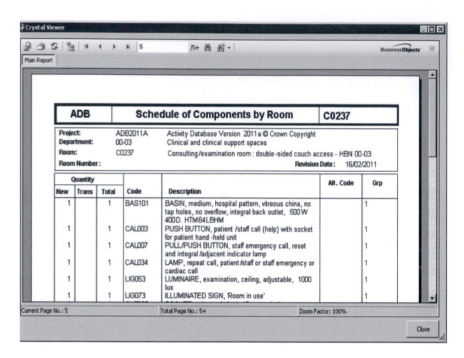

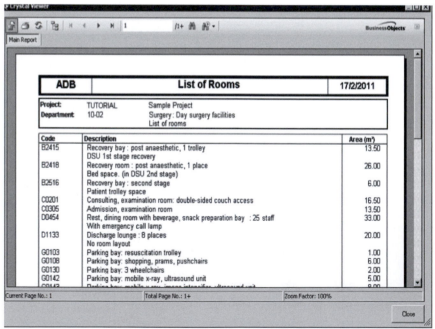

2.8 ADB examples of schedule of components by room and departmental level – Room schedule

Essentially, all this means that ADB has many stakeholders, audiences and users with different qualifications, capabilities and training, as well as varying interests and requirements as to what ADB should and ought to be doing. These include disseminating guidance and standards (Department of Health Estates and Facilities Division, project appraisal units, advisors to Strategic Health Authorities, NHS England, NHS London and so on), briefing (NHS and private sector capital planners, health care planners and others), aiding the designers (architects, engineers, health care planners, quantity surveyors, NHS Estates Departments), and helping to equip specialists in designing, manufacturing, supplying, placement and costing of equipment, as well as the ongoing management of accommodation/equipment (equity stakeholders and NHS Trust Estates and Facilities Managers). In 2007 there were 186 single-user ADB licenses and 44 multiple-user licenses (Table 2.2, Figure 2.9).

ADB has a code-driven hierarchical structure defined by Projects, Departments, Rooms, Assemblies and Components (Figures 2.10 and 2.11).

The database software used by ADB is Microsoft SQL Server, suitable for enterprise-wide solutions requiring simultaneous access for multiple users. With the introduction of the interface to Revit (BIM) the data sets are much larger and generally require a SQL server to operate efficiently. ADB has textual and graphical data in a single database, thereby ensuring synchronicity between text and graphics, an internal graphics facility called Graphical Editor, a Windows XP-style filter companion allowing simple and complex search criteria, Advanced SQL syntax searching, and a 'Google'-style search and preview facility allowing searching across projects. ADB is designed to work as a stand-alone or as a networked package for both MS Access and SQL Server versions. The ADB COM interface provides completely open access to the database allowing third party vendors to output to and from both ADB MS Access and SQL Server databases with crown copyright and licensing restrictions.

**Table 2.2 Total number of users of ADB 1973–2008**

|  | 1973 | 1978 | 1983 | 1988 | 1993 | 1998 | 2003 | 2008 |
|---|---|---|---|---|---|---|---|---|
| Total number of users | 85 | 100 | 77 | 99 | 110 | 140 | 170 | 232 |

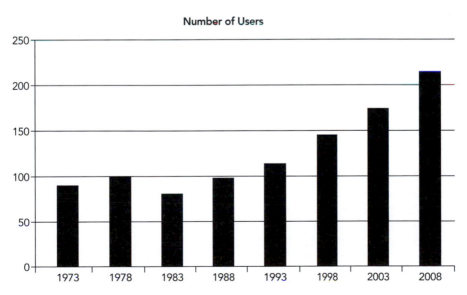

**Number of Users**

2.9 **Total numbers of users of ADB 1973–2008**

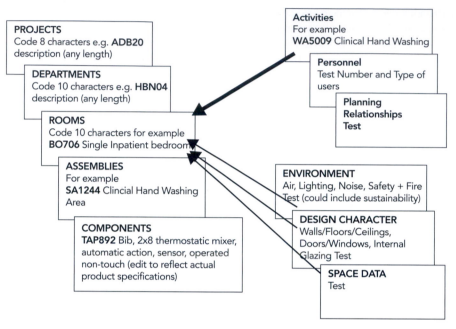

2.10 ADB coding system

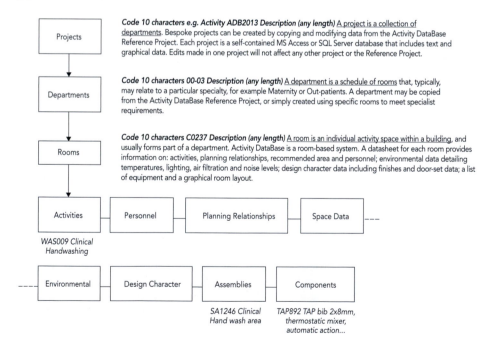

2.11 ADB coding system – the data is structured hierarchically with coded entities

In 2009 minimum system requirements for using ADB were a Pentium IV microprocessor or direct equivalent, 1Gb or more of available RAM, 5Gb or more of free space on the hard disk for the application, plus space for data and the Microsoft Windows XP or Microsoft Vista operating system to be installed. To interface with AutoCAD 2004–2009 or the equivalent of Architectural Desktop or Revit versions, the RAM and hard disk requirements listed above needed to be increased in accordance with the version of AutoCAD that was being used.

The ADB 2013 software upgrade features support for the 32- and 64-bit versions of AutoCAD2013, and is compatible with the 32- and 64-bit versions of Windows XP SP2/3 and Windows 7. The 64-bit version requires SQL Server projects. For Crystal Reports users with 32-bit Windows Vista and 32-bit Windows 7 need to upgrade to Crystal XI SP4. Scripts for configuring SQL for use with ADB and for the batch creation of projects are included in the SQL Server Scripts folder. ADB 2013 system requirements also reflect the increased needs of CAD and BIM software.

The relationship between HBNs, HTMs, MES and tools (AEDET, BREEAM) has had a varied history which has mirrored the NHS organisational restructuring and changes in government. At one extreme there was an interdependence of ADB and HBNs, and at the other there was an apparent and distinct separation between ADB and other health care guidance and tools. These relationships are the result of the historical and in some cases piecemeal development in which mandatory standards and compliance criteria have evolved separately from excellence, quality and safety factors. They may also be a reflection of different emphases by various sections within the Department of Health. However, it is clear that ADB's relationship to other guidance and tools is now intrinsically linked to its future development, which has yet to be clarified in order to build on possible synergies and overcome obstacles to continuous quality improvement in health care facilities (Figure 2.12).

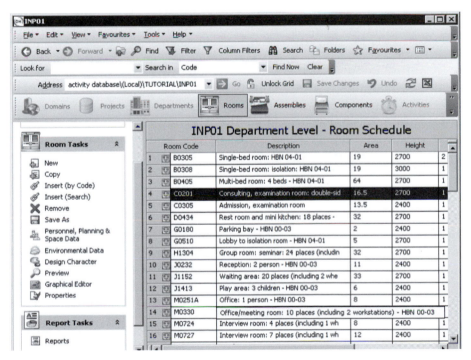

**2.12 ADB departmental level room schedule**

In the first instance this means addressing the problem of methodology, i.e. the evidence base, evidence experience or source of authority of the data, as well as the time taken to gather and analyse data and publish HBNs and supporting technical guidance (HTMs – Health Technical Memoranda or MES – Model Engineering Specifications) and then generate ADB data. This process can often be quite long, making the data almost irrelevant before its wide application on health care projects. HBNs (Health Building Notes) set the Department of Health's best practice standards in the planning and design of health care facilities, and are developed by working groups of specialists who gather and analyse data by evaluating specific clinical areas and associated clinical practices. The main drivers and timetable for the production of Department of Health guidance tools are therefore the requirements from National Service Frameworks (NSFs), and departmental policies in response to new and revised clinical practice and technological developments that relate to the environment for the delivery of health care. HTMs set health care-specific standards for building components, such as windows and sanitary ware, and the design and operation of engineering services, such as medical gas installations and fire safety requirements. HTMs are supported by other technical guidance, such as the MES.

The former range of NHS specifications, 'Model Engineering Specifications' (MES), have been archived and replaced. Embedded in the 'National Engineering Specification' (NES) and endorsed by CIBSE and the Department of Health Estates and Facilities, the specifications are obtainable from the Amtech Group (http://www.amtech.co.uk/nesplus). Written by specialist health care building services consultants, the content of the health care version of NES aims to ensure the information provided is accurate and up to date. This content is divided into sections containing a library of clauses and schedules that can be used to create health care compliant specification. One chooses and inserts relevant sections into a document to suit the exact requirements of a project.

- Each section provides references to standards and other legislation, creating a checklist that ensures nothing is missed in the specification.

- The specifications provide the basis of a QA system through the inclusion of audit trails and the standard formatting of sections.
- Updated regularly to ensure the service includes the latest changes to operating and maintenance manual clauses, legislation and standards, best practice and developments in technology.
- Contains additional data specifically tailored to replace the old NHS Model Engineering Specification, enabling the user to produce specifications that are health care compliant.

Clarifying the confusion between standards and compliance criteria on the one hand and excellence and quality on the other, including simplifying guidance on patient safety, would greatly benefit ADB.

*So much of what has been done in the past and to which extensive reference is made is about standards and compliance which our experience suggests drive quality down rather than up. Standards and compliance often get far too specific and thus compromise design innovation. An example is space standards, HBNs and the like, which often over-specify on a non-evidence based approach. So we get standards for minimum floor areas for an examination room and a consulting room that are minimally different. The result in design practice is that both become maxima not minima for cost reasons, and then cause inflexibility in design because they are different and inflexibility in use because experience shows neither room is actually likely to be used for the purpose specified after relatively short-use periods. This is an ignorant legacy of functionalism which believed we could actually specify functions accurately (which we cannot) and then compounded the error by neglecting qualitative measures of psychological rather than physical need. This is absolutely at the core of the failing of contemporary briefing and practice. Such documents also concentrated on what could easily be measured rather than what was desirable. So for example an HBN might specify the number of tiles needed for splash back over a washbasin or the number of coat hooks in* the bathroom, but say nothing about a view from a window.

ASPECT/AEDET Evolution, IDEAs tools were developed by the University of Sheffield Healthcare Research Group to foster excellence and quality in contrast to the mandatory standards and compliance criteria. However, AEDET Evolution is constrained by the need to relate to the DQI (Design Quality Indicator) which has many failings. DQIs contain statements that are not generally agreed to be valid and which are included without any justification or support. Many are inappropriate and are based on the value judgment of those who drew them up. The research group tried to remedy as many as they could. One example is the whole failure of DQI to deal with psychometrics. It uses such widely varying levels of specificity and subjectivity and terminology as to be highly suspect as a tool for eliciting psychometric responses. An important difference with ASPECT is the evidence-base, whereas AEDET 1st generation/DQI is prejudice-based. ASPECT is based on a survey and analysis of empirically based evidence. The IDEAs tool takes this set of notions even further by turning its back on the old constraints of the HBNs.

(ADB Workshop, Department of Health, London, 11 November 2011)

Further points have been made about HBNs which implicate ADB. The series of guide publications intended to assist managers in raising environmental standards "started off as a good idea but they became too prescriptive, presenting a limited and strictly utilitarian view of possibilities. We quote here from Health Building Note 51: 'Some spaces contribute to the well-being of patients, for example, a patients' library, but this is not essential to the smooth running of a hospital'. This series presents technical data well and on such issues as the legal and technical requirements of spacing, safety, public liability, fire precautions and so on they are very good and required reading and reference for anyone working in this field. Yet they purport to represent a high standard of advice and encourage Chief Executives and Chairs of Trusts to commission quality buildings without any guidance as to how do so. For example, it is suggested in these guides that

'art' is a good thing but it is not explained how to acquire it: that 'gardens' are peaceful, but not how to achieve them" (Hosking & Haggard 1999, page 18).

More recently there have been growing concerns about standards guidance, and this reflects on ADB. "The existing ensemble of systems and standards guidance is incomplete, out-of-date and not adapted to today's NHS and most importantly is not appropriate to guide well innovation in the future development of the service" (Moss et al. 2001). Particular reference to ADB, the use of out-of-date data, is often the result of the re-use of old data because data has not been updated or users do not have access to updated information or data. More curiously, this use of out-of-date data can also be attributed to the lengthy lead time for the production of HBNs/ADB data sheets.

UK health care also has a large amount of guidance with much uncoordinated regulation. The National Audit Office 2005 noticed that at least seven agencies and individual hospital policies were issuing guidance relating to patient safety: 1. Medicines and Healthcare Products Regulatory Agency; 2. Health Protection Agency; 3. NHS Litigation Agency; 4. NHS Estates (Department of Health Estates and Facilities Division); 5. National Patient Safety Agency; 6. Health & Safety Executive; and 7. Healthcare Commission. The level of guidance has produced duplication, fragmentation, non-standardisation and redundancy with, for example, the HBNs offering over 1240 different room specifications, including ten different pantry sizes, six different utility room sizes, and 88% of rooms less than 40m² (LaFratta 2006).

Hignett and Lu (2009) investigated the use of Health Building Notes by UK health care building designers and identified three main themes, which could affect the future of standards and guidance and perhaps impact on the development of ADB content. The first theme concerns the changes in the design culture over 20 years and the context of guidance use – for example, the conflict between consumerism (design for the patient) and efficiency (design for the service provider) reflecting complex social power relationships (Gesler et al. 2004); the use of the NHS Design Review Panels; the PFI, LIFT and ProCure21 procurement routes and processes; participatory design involving clinicians and other stakeholders; and so on.

The second theme concerns the quality of the evidence base to support the guidance – for example, understanding not only that the design is a good layout but also why it is a good layout, and therefore understanding Hamilton's (2003) four levels of evidence-based design. The first level describes the practitioner as a user of research making thoughtful interpretations of design implications, while the second to fourth levels plot the transition of the practitioner from a user of research to a generator of research by defining measures to evaluate outcomes of design interventions, publishing the results and writing in peer-reviewed academic journals.

The last theme is that future guidance needs to meet patient expectations from professional and personal experience (including privacy and dignity, choice, age preference, different cultural preferences based on geographic location, the role of the family as caregivers, etc.), new building techniques and generic room templates (with possible benefits such as modular construction with the option for off-site prefabrication).

The study found that the use of guidance was variable, with some participants seeing a clear role for new (more standardised) guidance in the future, while others were more concerned about the loss of design freedom. Two clear roles for ergonomics were identified as the ability or capacity to: a) facilitate the participation of patients and clinicians in the design process; and b) generate new research evidence with respect to spatial requirements for clinical activities to support standardisation.

Yet another important influence is the change in the role of the Department of Health as a result of the NHS structural reorganisation. This has seen the Department's NHS role greatly reduced, becoming more strategically focused *"on improving health, tackling health inequalities and reforming adult care. This shift in the direction of travel will have a direct impact on the Department's engineering and design guidance. Health Building Notes (HBNs) and Health Technical Memoranda (HTMs) will need reviewing in the light of the UK coalition government's priorities, to reflect the new focus on the regulatory framework for quality assurance. This, he stressed, would involve all stakeholders to consider new ways of working, and to embrace the spirit of quality, innovation, productivity and prevention. His advice to estates and facilities professionals: 'Tough it out and focus* on the job in hand. Raise your game to deal with the challenge'"* (NHS deputy chief executive at the Healthcare Estates Event, 2010).

Having looked at the relationship between ADB and HBNs/HTMs, it is worth considering the relationships between ADB and tools such as AEDET, DART and BREEAM. While HBNs/HTMs are not considered tools but components which form the foundation for the data to be generated for inclusion in ADB, ADB itself should not be regarded as a tool but an instrument, which allows or facilitates the Department of Health's policy requirements to be translated into physical environments, especially during the various hospital building programmes. This helps the Department of Health to discharge its responsibilities under the NHS Constitution to *"ensure that services are provided in a clean and safe environment that is fit for purpose, based on national best practice (pledge)"*. Even so, the use of ADB is not mandatory in England as is the case in Scotland, although its utility may have saved ADB from the same fate which befell NEAT/BREEAM and AEDET in not being supported by the Department of Health. Clearly, ADB's commercial status also makes a huge difference in how people view it, regard it and use it, as distinct from AEDET, DART and BREEAM. Another useful distinction between ADB and AEDET is that AEDET is often viewed more as an 'evidence-based' tool because of its direct underlying relationship with findings from scientific studies (in the architectural database), while ADB is largely 'experience-based' because of its use of data from practitioners which then informs best practice.

The role of the Department of Health Estates and Facilities in the development and sponsorship of ADB relates to the major functions of the Department of Health in relation to any hospital building programme. These functions include determining, in conjunction with the National Board, the pattern of provision of health care services throughout the country and allocating capital finance to Clinical Commissioning Groups, programming major building starts, approving costs and monitoring progress. Cost control is also by a series of cost limits for individual departments ('departmental costs') and percentage norms for all other works costs ('on-costs'). Departmental Cost Allowances initially derive from Health Building Notes etc. and are updated from time to time by a tender-linked index. Further functions concern determining policy (including planning/ building policy) and issuing guidance (including design guidance) by means of, for example, Health Building Notes, Health Technical Memoranda and Model Engineering Specifications, as well as Research and Development work into all aspects of hospital planning and building including the development of the Systems and Standards Programme.

In relation to ADB the role of the Department of Health concerns the strategic development linked to evidence-based clinical practice, facilitating key statements on health and social policy including compliance with the prevailing legislation of the day, complying with mandatory prescriptive requirements from the Secretary of State for Health and adhering with monitoring and reporting regimes or mechanisms, as well as endorsement of ADB to ensure that Trusts and other NHS organisations achieve minimum standards for their NHS estate which facilitate the delivery of appropriate and modern health care.

Between its inception and 2005, ADB was managed and administered by the Department of Health/NHS Estates, when administration and management was transferred to the Central Office of Information (COI), the Government's centre of excellence for marketing and communications, under a Memorandum of Understanding. The Department of Health oversaw policy regarding the development of standards and guidance, including ADB. From 2005 until 2011, the day-to-day administration of ADB was by the COI. Until its abolition the COI worked with government departments and the public sector to produce information campaigns on issues that affect the lives of every citizen – from health and education to benefits, rights and welfare. Since then the administration/ management of ADB has consisted of:

1 administration of the invoicing and payment functions handled by the Department of Health.
2 support provided by ADB software engineers Integra, and Talon Solutions (who also do ADB licence activations). However, there are no longer any training sessions on the use of ADB.

In summary, the role of the Department of Health as ADB's owner means that statements of health and social policy should not only be reflected in all the standards/guidance,

but also the Department of Health ought to be responsible for commissioning regular updates to mirror any changing health policy and other requirements.

## Case studies in implementing PAM and ADB to enhance compliance

Case studies for the Premises Assurance Model are usefully illustrated by referring to the piloting process, outcomes and analysis. Therefore, answers to the main question of how the NHS PAM can support the process of assurance demonstrate its practical application, with current considerations to make PAM mandatory. The results of piloting are that PAM appears to have:

- facilitated evidence-backed self-assessment for use by provider Trust Boards as strategic management inform-ation.
- allowed a dialogue with commissioners of service to demonstrate assurance of essential statutory under-takings and quality.
- agreed local needs and priorities, both internally and externally, for improving premises infrastructure efficiency and quality.
- demonstrated regard for the NHS constitution in the delivery of safe and effective environments that are utilised to deliver high quality health care services.
- derived a quality statement for the health care environment which can be utilised in providers' wider quality accounts should they so wish.
- provided evidence to any stakeholders requiring assurance regarding the safety and quality of the providers' estates and facilities – e.g. the Care Quality Commission (CQC).

Endorsements and testimonials have been provided for the NHS PAM.

*Monitor won't have any difficulties with – in fact would be supportive of – well thought through tools that support NHS organisations in the management of their estates and commissioners in commissioning quality services.*

(Monitor, Independent Regulator for NHS Foundation Trusts)

The NHS PAM enables the NHS Constitution to fulfil its two pledges on premises in which health care is delivered – i.e. health and social care are to be provided in a clean and safe environment that is 'fit for purpose' on national best practice, and continuous improvement in the quality of services (that users) receive, facilitated by identifying and sharing best practice in the quality of care and treatments.

> The NHS PAM supports NHS organisations to demonstrate how they are delivering the environmental components of the NHS Constitution. PAM provides a comprehensive reference point for organisations to compare the quality and efficiency of their premises with their peers.
>
> (Quality Accounts Toolkit 2010/11).

The NHS PAM is also described as a non-financial indicator for the Quality Innovation Productivity Prevention (QIPP) National Workstream: Back Office Efficiency and Management Optimisation, which aims to save the NHS £20 billion by 2016 without reducing quality and safety.

The NHS PAM supports local clinical leaders, Directors of Finance and Estates Managers who, in using the NHS PAM effectively, will have the right information to make informed decisions about the development of their estates and facilities. PAM provides important information on quality and safety to commissioners for use during the commissioning process, and to regulators in identifying risks which then require to be managed. As a key enabler, PAM allows the NHS to deliver its commitment to cross-government initiatives such as the Climate Change Act and the HM Treasury Operational Efficiency Programme.

# Great Ormond Street Children's Hospital, London

A case study of the Great Ormond Street Children's Hospital Phase 2A Morgan Stanley Building development shows how tools such as ADB help to enhance compliance with NHS requirements (Figures 2.13 to 2.17).

A Llewellyn Davies/WSP Group focus group used the redevelopment of Great Ormond Street Hospital for Children to examine issues surrounding the provision of carbon neutral environments for the treatment of sick children while integrating visual arts, acoustic requirements, poetry and kinetics in therapeutic settings for children, families and staff. The development is an exemplar that shows how lessons learnt from completed phases can feed forward into future phases based on a 2005 Development Control Plan strategy that seeks to unlock the site potential, to enable all clinical services to be provided in modern accommodation by the end of Phases 3 and 4. The wide ranging audience – children and young people from newborn to eighteen years of age, parents/carers, siblings, staff, visitors, donors, the general public and others – is a significant challenge.

The Phase 2A Morgan Stanley Building integrates the island site with horizontal connectivity, aspects that have increased pressure on building services due to restricted floor-to-floor levels, and achieves a modern environment containing three bed-pool ward floors, a cardiac intensive care unit, three operating theatres and a hybrid-angio theatre, and a restaurant which can be used for functions and events for the patients, families and staff. Phase 2B is to follow 2A once decants are complete. The layout separates public, clinical, staff and facilities management movements via separate vertical cores located at the north and south ends of the building, leaving the clinical floor plate clear, minimising disruption to the adjacent floors during any future reconfiguration/refurbishment and thus achieving a 'long-life loose fit' objective.

The Clinical Plan shows all the public activities located at the southern end of the building connecting into the existing hospital street (the main artery of the island site). The floor plan has a hierarchy which denotes movement from public to private, with the public areas featuring a large light and airy reception, waiting areas adjacent to parent sitting rooms on all ward floors, followed by a ward entrance and adjacent play/recreation/dining areas. The wards have over 60% single bedrooms and two four-bed high dependency bays, a practical response to the original strategy of providing 100% single rooms. Informed by evidence from both research and a mock-up of the site, the typical bedroom has a calm domestic feel with enhanced visual links to nursing staff and patient observation points (Principle 2). The bed-head unit design introduces a relaxing feature colour, and integrates lighting/medical services to minimise any institutional feel.

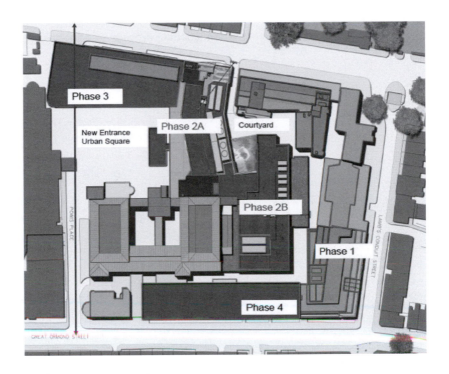

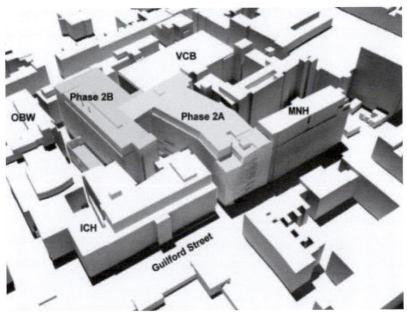

2.13 Great Ormond Street Hospital for Children: 2005 development control plan

# Room Loading Process – Codebook

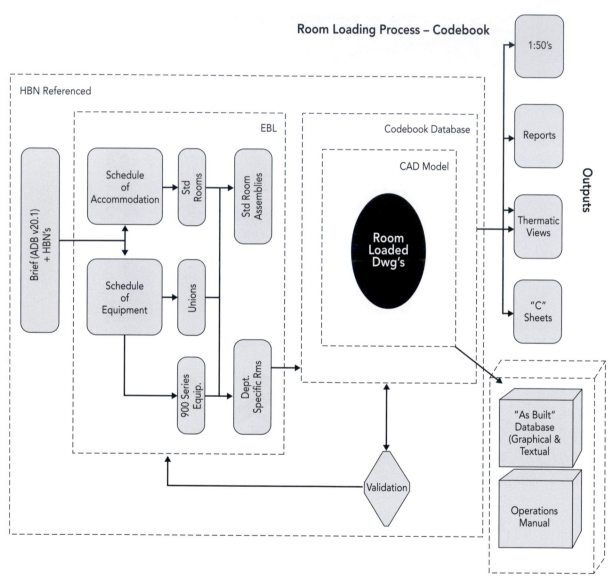

2.14  Great Ormond Street Hospital for Children: ADB interfaces

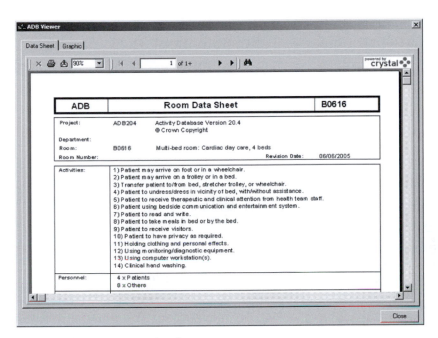

2.15  Great Ormond Street Hospital for Children: Room data sheets

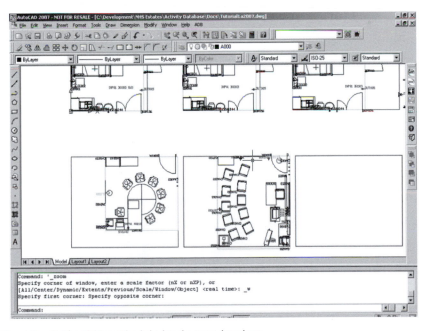

2.16  Great Ormond Street Hospital for Children: Plan linked to the room data sheet

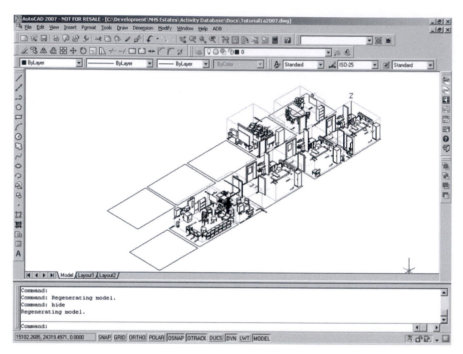

2.17 Great Ormond Street Hospital for Children: 3D images linked to the room data sheets

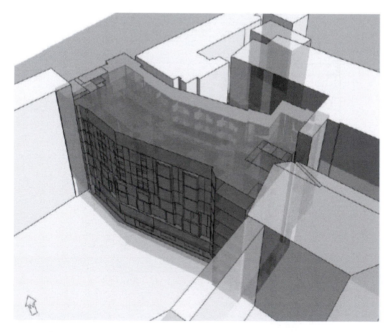

2.18 Great Ormond Street Hospital for Children: Phase 2A Morgan Stanley Building

Parents have a private area within the bedroom adjacent to an external window, and an integrated wardrobe provides storage space within the room for personal belongings. All bedrooms and intensive care units have openable windows (Figures 2.19 and 2.20, Tables 2.3 and 2.4).

The high acuity activity flow progresses around the floor, from the clinical entrance at the high dependency bays to the isolation rooms, and then on to single bedrooms and low dependency rooms before going home. All clinical support facilities are in the centre of the floor plate for easy access from both sides. At the most northern end of the building staff activities occur, with the staff rest area conveniently located with tranquil park views away from clinical and public areas. Theatres are internal with a clinical corridor on one side supported by a service corridor on the other, but with visual screens to the green roof bringing staff inside the

external environment via a live web link. An artist has been commissioned to create a distraction during the patient's journey to theatres, in the form of a nature trail as a sequence of abstract animal images in a woodland setting along which a patient travels to the anaesthetic room and theatre.

As at Evelina London Children's Hospital, wayfinding uses a natural world theme, with Phase 2 floors as a habitat and each ward named after an animal from that habitat. Graphics are strategically positioned throughout the building to aid wayfinding and provide informative and educationally positive distractions. The graphics also enhance legibility of place, providing visitors with familiarisation, orientation and a sense of identity. The hospital's active arts and humanities programme uses creative residences and workshops for patients and staff.

**2.19 Great Ormond Street Hospital for Children: Phase 2A Morgan Stanley Building**

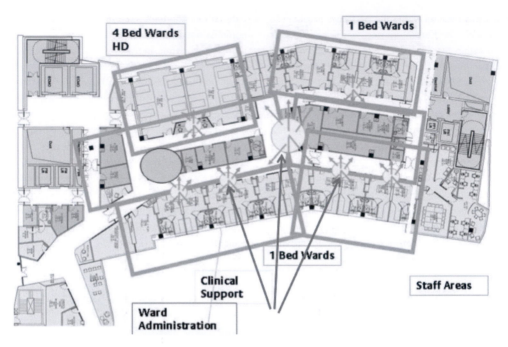

**2.20  Great Ormond Street Hospital for Children: Phase 2A Morgan Stanley Building – Application of the decentralised or dispersed clinical workstations**

Table 2.3 Great Ormond Street Hospital for Children: A long list of health care guidance for Phase 2A Morgan Stanley Building

| | List of Technical Health Care Guidance | |
|---|---|---|
| LEVEL 7 IP Bedpool | 4 Inpatient Accommodation 1997/4.1 Isolation Facilities 2005/18 Office Accommodation 1991/23 Accommodation for Children & Young People 2004/40.1 & 2 Common Activity Spaces 1995/53 – Renal 1996 | Design Guides |
| LEVEL 6 IP Bedpool | 4 Inpatient Accommodation 1997/4.1 Isolation Facilities 2005/18 Office Accommodation 1991/23 Accommodation for Children & Young People 2004/40.1 & 2 Common Activity Spaces 1995/53 – Renal 1996 | • The Art of Good Health 2002 – Design for Health 2004; |
| LEVEL 5 IP Bedpool | 4 Inpatient Accommodation 1997/4.1 Isolation Facilities 2005/18 Office Accommodation 1991/23 Accommodation for Children & Young People 2004/40.1 & 2 Common Activity Spaces 1995/53 – Renal 1996 | |
| LEVEL 4 Cardiac Critical Care | 57 – Clinical Care 2003/4 Inpatient Accommodation 1997/18 Office Accommodation 1991/23 Accommodation for Children & Young People 2004/40.1 & 2 Common Activity Spaces 1995/ | • Wayfinding: Guidance for Healthcare Facilities 1999 |
| LEVEL 3 Theatres and Interventional Procedures | 6-Diag. Imaging & Intervention Radiology Vol. 1 & 2 2001 & 3/18 Office Accommodation 1991/23 Accommodation for Children & Young People 2004/26 – Facilities for Surgical Procedures 2004/28 - Cardiac Services 2006/CAS 1, 2, 4 | • Friendly Healthcare Environments for Children & Young |
| LEVEL 2 Staff/Visitor Dining | 10 – Catering Department 1997/18 Office Accommodation 1991/40.1,2,3,4 Common Activity Spaces 1995 | People 2004 |
| LEVEL 1 Cardiac Day Care/Echo & ECG/Lung Function | 28 – Cardiac Services 2006/18 Office Accommodation 1991/23 Accommodation for Children & Young People 2004/40.1 & 2 Common Activity Spaces 1995/CAS 40, 4 1995/12 – OPD 1990 | • Ward Layouts for Single Rooms & Space for Flexibility |
| Level 0 Staff Change/Catering | 10 – Catering Department 1997/18 Office Accommodation 1991/40.3 Common Activity Spaces 1992/CAS 40.4 1995/41 – Staff Changing and Storage of Uniforms 1984 | |

Table 2.4 Great Ormond Street Hospital for Children: Legislative challenges for Phase 2A Morgan Stanley Building

**Health Technical Memorandum (HTM) Compliance**

| Clinical requirements | |
|---|---|
| Operational requirements | |
| Phase 2 | HTM 03–01 requires greater airflows |
| | HTM 04 – Inpatient Accommodation Great Ormond Street Hospital reduced temperature and copper silver ionisation |
| | HTM 07 series |
| | HTM 08–01 Acoustics |

**Part L Building Regulations Compliance**

| L2B 2010 reduces specific fan powers to 1.8 W/l/sec) |
|---|
| CCHP lower rating in calculation |

In general, the Great Ormond Street Children's Hospital development highlights several legislative challenges which involve satisfying both clinical demands and operational requirements while complying with Building Regulations, City of London targets on sustainability, and HTMs – for example HTM 03-01, 07, and 08-01, HBN23 Hospital Accommodation for Children and Young People (revised edition) 26th January 2005 (previously revised in 2004). In this case tools such as PAM and ADB have an important role to play in demonstrating the nature and extent of compliance with changing guidance standards and health policy demands.

# References

BMJ Editorial (1976) Nucleus Hospitals. *British Medical Journal*, 31 January 1976, 245–246.

Cox A and Groves P (1990) *Design for Health Care.* Butterworth-Heinemann Ltd, London, ISBN-10: 0408003898.

Darzi L (2008) Our NHS Our Future. http://www.ournhs.nhs.uk/ [Accessed May 2012].

Department of Health/NHS Finance, Performance & Operations (2009) *The Operating Framework in NHS in England 2010/11.*

Gesler W, Bell M, Curtis S, Hubbard P & Francis S (2004) Therapy by Design: Evaluating the UK hospital building program. *Health and Place*, 10, 117–128.

Great Britain, Ministry of Health, National Health Service (1962) *A Hospital Plan.* HMSO, London.

Great Britain, Ministry of Health, National Health Service (1966) *The Hospital Building Programme.* HMSO, London.

Hamilton KD (2003) The Four Levels of Evidence-Based Practice. *Healthcare Design*, 3(4), 18–26.

Hamilton KD (2008) Evidence is found in many domains. *HERD: Health Environments Research & Design Journal*, 1(3), 5–6.

Hignett S and Lu J (2009) An investigation of the use of Health Building Notes by UK healthcare building designers. *Applied Ergonomics*, 40 (4), 608–616 (http://www.sciencedirect.com/science/journal/00036870/40/4 [Accessed May 2012]).

Hosking S and Haggard L (1999) *Healing the Hospital Environment: Design, Maintenance and Management of Healthcare Premises.* E & FN Spon, London, ISBN 0419231706.

LaFratta A (2006) An investigation into multi-activity generic spaces in the design of healthcare facilities. Unpublished MSc Dissertation, Loughborough University.

Moss R et al (2001) *Rationalising Health Building Design: A Feasibility Study.* NHS Estates 2001.

NHS Premises Assurance Model Website: http://www.dh.gov.uk/en/Publicationsandstatistics/Publications/PublicationsPolicyAndGuidance/DH_128702 [Accessed May 2012].

Table 2.5  Room data sheet H1130

| | Room Data Sheet | H1130 |
|---|---|---|

| | | |
|---|---|---|
| Project: | ADB204 | Activity Database Version 20.4 ©<br>Crown Copyright |
| Department: | | |
| Room: | H1130 | Information centre with beverage bay: 5 persons |
| Room Number: | | Revision Date: 20/03/2006 |

| | |
|---|---|
| Activities: | 1) Patient may be ambulant, in a wheelchair or on a trolley.<br>2) Instructing with the aid of a television monitor for showing video tape recordings.<br>3) Using computer workstation(s).<br>4) Displaying periodicals, pamphlets and reports.<br>5) Holding books.<br>6) Preparing beverages. |
| Personnel: | 5 x Persons<br>Patients escort may be present. |
| Planning Relationships: | Close to waiting area.<br>Close to treatment area. |

| Space Data: | Area (m²): | 18.00 | Height (mm): | 2,700 |
|---|---|---|---|---|

| | |
|---|---|
| Notes: | Information should be provided in formats suitable for blind and visually impaired patients.<br>Any video material should be subtitled. |

| Activity DataBase | 01/10/2008 |
|---|---|

Table 2.6 Room environmental data H1130

| ADB | Room Environmental Data | H1130 |
|---|---|---|

| Project: | ADB204 | Activity Database Version 20.4 © Crown Copyright |
|---|---|---|
| Department: | | |
| Room: | H1130 | Information centre with beverage bay: 5 persons |
| Room Number: | | Revision Date: 20/03/2006 |

| AIR | Requirements | Notes |
|---|---|---|
| Winter Temperature (DegC): | 20 | |
| Summer Temperature (DegC): | | |
| Mechanical Ventilation (Supply ac/hr): | | |
| Mechanical Ventilation (Extract ac/hr): | | |
| Pressure Relative to Adjoining Space: | | |
| Filtration (%DSE and % Arrestance): | / | |
| Humidity (%RH): | | |

General Notes:

| LIGHTING | | |
|---|---|---|
| Service Illumination (Lux): | 300 | Desk/Table. Areas for VDT's: See CIBSE Lighting Guide LG3 "The Visual Environment for Display Screen Use" Addendum 2001. |
| Service Illumination Night (Lux): | | |
| Local Illumination (Lux): | | Dimmable |
| Colour Rendering Required: | N | |
| Standby Lighting Grade: | | Lighting of the level and quality one third to one half that provided by normal lighting |

General Notes:

| NOISE | | |
|---|---|---|
| Privacy Factor Required (dB): | 80 | |
| Mechanical Services (NR): | 30 | |
| Intrusive Noise (NR Leq): | 35 | |
| *Acceptable Sound Level [L10dB(A)]: | | |
| *Speech Privacy Required: | N | |
| *Quality Which Cannot Be Tolerated: | | |
| (* alternative format) | | |

General Notes:

| SAFETY | | |
|---|---|---|
| Hot Surface Max. Temp (DegC): | 43 | |
| Hot Water Max. Temp (DegC): | | |

General Notes:

| FIRE | | |
|---|---|---|
| Enclosure: | | |
| Automatic Detection: | | Smoke |

**Activity DataBase**  01/10/2008

Table 2.7 Room design character H1130

| ADB | Room Design Character | H1130 |
|---|---|---|

| Project:<br>Department: | ADB204 | Activity Database Version 20.4 © Crown Copyright | |
|---|---|---|---|
| Room: | H1130 | Information centre with beverage bay: 5 persons | |
| Room Number: | | Revision Date: | 20/03/2006 |

| Walls: | Surface Finish (HTM 56): 5:<br>Moisture Resistance (HTM 56): N:Normal humidity.<br>Cleaning Routine (HTM 56): To manufacturers recommendations |
|---|---|
| Floor: | Surface Finish (HTM 61): 6 i.e. Soft, impervious, jointless<br>Cleaning Routine (HTM 61): To manufacturers recommendations |
| Ceiling: | Surface Finish (HTM 60): 5 i.e. Imperforate<br>Moisture Resistance (HTM 60): N i.e. Normal Humidity<br>Cleaning Routine (HTM 60): To manufacturers recommendations |
| Doorsets: | (HTM 58) N/A, open to circulation |
| Windows: | (HTM 55) N/A, or Clear, solar control, privacy control |
| Internal Glazing: | N/A |
| Hatch: | |
| Notes: | |

**Activity DataBase**    01/10/2008

Table 2.8 Schedule of components by room H1130

| ADB | Schedule of Components by Room | H1130 |
|---|---|---|

| Project: | ADB204 | Activity Database Version 20.4 © Crown Copyright |
|---|---|---|
| Department: | | |
| Room: | H1130 | Information centre with beverage bay: 5 persons |
| Room Number: | | Revision Date: 20/03/2006 |

| Quantity | | | | | Alt. Code | Grp |
|---|---|---|---|---|---|---|
| New | Trans | Total | Code | Description | | |
| 1 | | 1 | SPA015 | Space for wheelchair | | |
| 1 | | 1 | MSW060 | WORKTOP, for 400mm facing inserts cabinets, 1000W 700D nominal, HTM71 | | 1 |
| 1 | | 1 | MSW074 | WORKTOP, for 400mm facing inserts cabinets, 2400W 700D nominal, HTM71 | | 1 |
| 4 | | 4 | OUT010 | SOCKET outlet switched 13amp twin, wall mounted | | 1 |
| 1 | | 1 | OUT052 | CONNECTION UNIT switched 13amp, wall/trunking mounted | | 1 |
| 3 | | 3 | OUT121 | SOCKET outlet computer data, wall/trunking mounted | | 1 |
| 1 | | 1 | OUT206 | SOCKET outlet television aerial, single, wall mounted | | 1 |
| 3 | | 3 | OUT215 | SOCKET outlet telephone, wall mounted | | 1 |
| 1 | | 1 | OUT315 | OUTLET drinking water for equipment | | 1 |
| 1 | | 1 | BOA013 | BOARD, display/notice, wall mounted, 900H 1200W | | 2 |
| 1 | | 1 | CLO001 | CLOCK battery, wall mounted | | 2 |
| 1 | | 1 | RAC089 | RACK, leaflet/pamphlet, 4 sections, with adjustable dividers, wall mounted, 300H 805W 215D | | 2 |
| 1 | | 1 | RAC090 | RACK, leaflet/pamphlet, single section, 5 dividers, wall mounted, 150H 1000W 100D | | 2 |
| 1 | | 1 | RAC091 | RACK, magazine, 3 shelves, floor standing, fixed to the wall, 1400H 900W 300D | | 2 |
| 1 | | 1 | CHA006 | CHAIR, easy, with open arms, low back, upholstered | | 3 |
| 2 | | 2 | CHA018 | CHAIR, upright, with arms, upholstered, stacking | | 3 |
| 2 | | 2 | CHA062 | CHAIR, height adjustable, with arms, medium back, swivel, 5 star base, on castors | | 3 |
| 2 | | 2 | COM031 | COMPUTER CPU | | 3 |
| 2 | | 2 | COM032 | COMPUTER VDT MONITOR | | 3 |
| 2 | | 2 | COM033 | COMPUTER KEYBOARD | | 3 |
| 1 | | 1 | COM038 | COMPUTER PRINTER, laser, A4, 250H 380W 385D | | 3 |
| 1 | | 1 | HOL006 | HOLDER, sack, with lid foot operated, medium, freestanding, 875H 430W 385D | | 3 |
| 1 | | 1 | REC030 | RECORDER/VIDEO, playback | | 3 |
| 1 | | 1 | SHE128 | SHELF BOOK UNIT, 3 shelves, double sided, open, island, 1370H 900W 500D | | 3 |
| 1 | | 1 | TAB056 | TABLE, occasional, round, 415H 610mm dia. | | 3 |
| 1 | | 1 | TRO372 | TROLLEY, television/video, with adjustable shelves, 1510H 457W 762D | | 3 |
| 1 | | 1 | TVM006 | TELEVISION monitor, colour, 585mm | | 3 |
| 1 | | 1 | VEN002 | VENDING MACHINE, hot/cold drinks | | 3 |

**Activity DataBase**   01/10/2008

# 3 Design quality improvement

## AEDET/ASPECT 2004

Two important evidence-based tools in the UK design quality improvement agenda are AEDET (**A**chieving **E**xcellence **D**esign **E**valuation **T**oolkit) and its plug-in ASPECT (**A Staff/Patient Environment Calibration Tool**).

### Milestones or key stages in the development of design quality tools are:

- September 1999: development starts on DQI (**D**esign **Q**uality **I**ndicator) based on a research project funded by the Department of Trade and Industry (DTI) and carried out at the Science Policy Research Unit (SPRU), University of Sussex to provide a generic tool for assessing the design quality of buildings and a toolkit for improving the design of buildings (Gann et al. 2003).
- March 2001: DQI version 1 complete and ready for testing.
- September 2001: alignment of related tools in order to create an industry-wide consensus on design evaluation, including: 1. DQI by Construction Industry Council; 2. AEDET by NHS Estates replaced by Department of Health Estates and Facilities Division, and Design Excellence Evaluation Process (DEEP) by Ministry of Defence's Defence Estates. This phase also saw an uptake of DQI by the Audit Commission in the analysis of PFI – a survey of 95 end-users in 18 PFI and non-PFI schools reported in 2002.
- November 2001: first publication of AEDET.
- 8 July 2002: trailblazing DQI scheme launched at the Design Council to carry out beta tests of the DQI and develop an interactive web-based interface. Each organisation signing up for the scheme would use the tool on six projects and attempt to elicit responses from 20 individuals per project.
- 2002: development of AEDET Evolution by the University of Sheffield School of Architecture Health Care Research Group under a commission from NHS Estates.

- February 2003: DQI uses represented about £900 million of UK construction output on projects ranging from £900,000 to £450 million.
- 1 October 2003: DQI launched.
- 4 February 2004: development of ASPECT by the University of Sheffield School of Architecture Health Care Research Group, co-funded by the Department of Health Estates and Facilities, BDP and Balfour Beatty Capital Projects.
- January 2005: DQI Facilitators Register launched in response to demands from users of DQI, who wanted a robust list of impartial professionals they could call upon to help them get the most from their use of the DQI tool.
- 2005: Development of Inspiring Design Excellence and Achievements (IDEAs) by the University of Sheffield School of Architecture Health Care Research Group, Parallel and Brandplace under a commission from the Department of Health Estates and Facilities.
- 2005: Imperial College London review the data collected to date by the DQI tool and evaluate the tool to "provide an appropriate source of knowledge and information for use in the investigation of design quality in the UK construction sector".
- July 2005: FAVE briefing tool launched.
- 8 December 2005: DQI for Schools launched.
- June 2008: DQI and DQI for Schools briefing tools launched.
- March 2013: DQI for Health launched.

## AEDET Evolution 2005

Although launched in 1994, AEDET was first published in November 2001 as a health care sector standard, a best practice guide for the evaluation of design quality. Developed to assist the NHS and Primary Care Trusts undertake design specifications for their health care facility schemes, AEDET is used on the majority of new health-related Private Finance Initiative (PFI) work in the United Kingdom (Department of Health 2009).

The AEDET tool allows a comprehensive overall assessment of buildings. It covers three main sections, Impact, Build Quality and Functionality, and is designed to cross-refer where possible to the pan-industry (construction) tool DQI (Design Quality Indicator) (http://www.dqi.org.uk/).

To better understand the AEDET tool it is both helpful and useful to consider not only its development but also the context within the Design Quality Improvement Agenda and its aspirations to support the successful delivery of the 2000s PFI hospital building programme.

## The development of AEDET Evolution by the University of Sheffield School of Architecture Health Care Research Group

This represents a refinement of the original AEDET tool developed alongside DQI. The improved version addressed major concerns about AEDET's source of authority, ease of use and issues of reliability. Before then there was a lack of clarity as to AEDET's source of authority for its knowledge, i.e. whether the tool was based on robust evidence, subjective judgement/criteria or personal taste assumptions. An architect remarked: "How do designers convince a sceptical consultant in a user-group meeting that aligning a bedroom to capture a view of nature will speed up recovery, even if that results in a slightly longer walk for the nurse from the staff base?" Although AEDET isolated sustainability and the NHS provided a separate tool for this called NHS Environmental Assessment Tool (NEAT), it did not localise or focus attention on the major core area of health care – the staff and patient architectural environment. It failed to link consistently either to research knowledge or to existing design guidance. It did not map entirely satisfactorily onto the DQI, and there was some variance with the ADVICE briefing guidance document produced for Trusts by the Design Brief Working Group 2002.

Prior to AEDET Evolution there were concerns that AEDET was not easy to use by the non-technically minded, especially medical or clinical staff and members of the general public, with some questions requiring detailed knowledge or expertise and back-up calculations. Many of the questions were worded in somewhat technical language. Some of the questions used language which suggested a world of design understanding only available to some. The tool did not help the design process but only the appraisal process, and in some instances it was too late to feed back into the project. Evaluating the design process, for example through continuous and developing ways of monitoring the designers' activity, would produce output to improve the design activity.

Concerns regarding AEDET's reliability were evident in how questions varied in their level of generality, to a point of further concern about the validity and consistency of responses they elicited. There was a need to recognise the various NHS sectors (such as primary care, mental health, maternity and children's facilities) or specialities. The tool was already somewhat cumbersome and complex. While there appeared to be some repetition, very similar issues cropped up under different headings in several places. Furthermore, the AEDET tool did not provide for local judgement to be used as a way to vary the relationships between factors. There was some evidence from its use that AEDET often produced middle scores. This was probably due to the combination of several factors under one heading, and more particularly due to different parts of the building scoring differently with the resultant averaging out of scores.

## Improvements to the original version of AEDET by the University of Sheffield School of Architecture Health Care Research Group to create AEDET Evolution

The research group opted for the landscape page set up or format of a typical A4 size because many across the construction industry were familiar with it. Also, this format gives the impression of the AEDET Evolution tool being relatively easy to respond to. The main heading of BUILD STANDARD was changed back to the more aspirational DQI main heading of BUILD QUALITY. The name of the existing heading 'Citizen satisfaction' was changed back to match the original DQI heading of 'External form and materials', since this was clearer and more accurate. Much more significantly, the title of the heading under IMPACT was changed from 'Internal Environment' to 'Staff and Patient Environment', thereby eliminating the confusion between the 'internal environment' heading under IMPACT with all the statements about heat, light, sound and air quality under the 'Performance' heading under BUILD QUALITY.

The heading titled 'Staff and Patient Environment' was restructured to contain eight sub-headings: 1. Privacy, company and dignity; 2. Views; 3. Nature and outdoors; 4. Comfort and control; 5. Architectural legibility of place; 6. Appearance; 7. Facilities; and 8. Staff. These headings were shown to be capable of representing the vast majority of all

the research in the Sheffield research database that covered the impact of the built environment on patients and staff. This therefore allowed for ASPECT to be used to obtain scores for this section, giving more detailed and reliable results.

A 'Layers/Sections/Headings/Statements' hierarchical structure was introduced to facilitate learning, and to enable both novice and expert use. Eventually this would enable linking electronically through hypermedia. The wording of the statements was substantially improved to make AEDET Evolution more user-friendly, unambiguous and to facilitate more consistent results. An issue of concern with both the DQIs and AEDET was complexity and the confusion that exists between responding to statements, reference to instructions for how to use such tools and guidance to help the user, as well as reference to the evidence and exemplars.

This confusion meant that these tools were not easy to use, whether by the expert or the novice, and were more likely to produce results which were inconsistent or unreliable. In addition, for AEDET, the need to customise the tool to suit the various NHS sectors, such as primary care, mental health, children's facilities and so on, tended to produce many versions of the tool, leading to even more confusion and practical difficulties in keeping various versions up to date.

The layered approach, initially consisting of the scoring, guidance and evidence layers, addresses all these concerns, facilitating ease of use by both the more experienced user and the novice. For example, the more experienced user may not need to refer to the guidance layer because he/she is already familiar with it, while users interested in the evidence may consult the evidence layer in order to direct them to the research evidence upon which each of the headings is based.

The scoring layer consists of five columns for identification, statements, confidence level, weighting and a scale. This layer is where users will arrive at their score for the building or design proposal under investigation. The second left-hand column consists of a series of carefully worded simple statements which a user responds to by agreeing or disagreeing on a scale of 1 to 6 (①②③④⑤⑥) in order to generate scores. Simpler or less general statements which are centred on human experience aim to make the tool more

| A | CHARACTER AND INNOVATION | ①②③④⑤⑥ | |
|---|---|---|---|
| | | **?** | **weight   score** |
| 1 | There are clear ideas behind the design of the building | | ⓪①②①②③④⑤⑥ |
| 2 | The building is interesting to look at and move around in | | ⓪①②①②③④⑤⑥ |
| 3 | The building projects a caring and reassuring atmosphere | | ⓪①②①②③④⑤⑥ |
| 4 | The building appropriately expresses the values of the NHS | | ⓪①②①②③④⑤⑥ |
| 5 | The building is likely to influence future designs | | ⓪①②①②③④⑤⑥ |

**3.1 Typical statements from AEDET Evolution 2005 'Character and innovation'**

user-friendly, especially to the less technically-minded, to make it unambiguous, and to give rise to more consistent results.

Experience of eliciting views about architecture and place from the public suggests that this approach of several smaller questions, each of which is related to real use of the building, is highly likely to be well understood or to generate similar ways of understanding in a lay audience, and therefore to yield far better results.

Guidance is given on instructions, sections, headings and statements. This explanatory or guidance layer gives additional notes to assist users in arriving at a reliable and appropriate score. This layer can also explain, where necessary, how to interpret the main scoring layer questions, in particular in relation to the types of building such as primary care, mental health, maternity, paediatrics and other specialities. This layer gives more clues as to what standards need to be achieved in order to get the various scores. Users can refer to it if and when they need to with the more experienced users hardly ever needing to look at it. Guidance is given on the main sections of AEDET Evolution, IMPACT, BUILD QUALITY and FUNCTIONALITY. Guidance is then given for the ten headings in AEDET Evolution. Finally, guidance is given for all statements under each of the headings.

Hence, for simplicity and ease of use, as well as to provide a less intimidating format, AEDET Evolution has three layers or documents: the scoring, the explanation or

guidance, and the evidence. In addition to these layers there are instructions for how to use AEDET Evolution and a score summary sheet incorporated into the first (scoring) layer.

Having identified key headings, we turned our attention to the issue of how best to represent them and how to elicit responses about the architectural experience of either existing buildings or proposed designs. Simply asking a respondent to evaluate the scheme under consideration against each heading would be too diffuse a task. Each heading therefore needed to be represented by a number of sub-issues which together cover the heading reasonably comprehensively in terms of the available research evidence. One possibility is to ask the respondent a series of questions. However, this may result in a confusing array of types of responses, and we have therefore adopted the Likert scale approach. A Likert scale consists of a clear statement about which the respondent is asked to express a level of agreement. An advantage of this approach is that the respondent is given the same range of possible responses for each statement and therefore quickly learns to make rapid assessments.

Although various lengths of scales can be used, research shows that respondents are consistent only up to seven points on the scale. In this case we were anxious to avoid a neutral central point since there was already evidence that AEDET scores tended to bunch around the centre. For these reasons we opted for a six-point scale, which is also in line with the DQI. For consistency and in order to obtain better

**Table 3.1 During the development of AEDET Evolution we investigated the different possible choices for the responses**

### Agreement

| # | | | | | | | | |
|---|---|---|---|---|---|---|---|---|
| 7 | | | | | | | | |
| 6 | Agree Very Strongly | Agree Strongly | **Virtually Total Agreement** | Completely Agree | | | | Disagree Strongly |
| 5 | Agree Strongly | Agree Moderately | **Strong Agreement** | Mostly Agree | | | | Disagree |
| 4 | Agree | Agree Slightly | **Fair Agreement** | Slightly Agree | Agree | | | Tend to Disagree |
| 3 | Disagree | Disagree Slightly | **Little Agreement** | Slightly Disagree | Undecided | | | Tend to Agree |
| 2 | Disagree Strongly | Disagree Moderately | **Hardly Any Agreement** | Mostly Disagree | Disagree | Yes | | Agree |
| 1 | Disagree Very Strongly | Disagree Strongly | **Virtually No Agreement** | Completely Disagree | | No | | Agree Strongly |

### Frequency

| # | | | (bold) | | | | |
|---|---|---|---|---|---|---|---|
| 7 | | | | | | | |
| 6 | A Great Deal | Very Frequently | **Always** | Always | | Always | Always |
| 5 | Much | Frequently | **Mostly** | Usually | Almost Always | Very Frequently | Always |
| 4 | To a considerable Degree | Occasionally | **More Often Than Not** | About Half the Time | Very Often | Occasionally | |
| 3 | Somewhat | Rarely | **Occasionally** | Seldom | Sometimes | Rarely | |
| 2 | Seldom | Very Rarely | **Seldom** | Seldom | Rarely | Very Rarely | |
| 1 | Never | Never | **Very Rarely** | Never | Never | Never | |

### Likelihood

| # | | | | (bold) | |
|---|---|---|---|---|---|
| 7 | | | Almost Always True | | |
| 6 | | Definitely | Usually True | True of Myself | |
| 5 | | Very Probably | Often True | Mostly True of Myself | |
| 4 | To a Great Extent | Probably | Occasionally True | About Halfway True of Myself | |
| 3 | Somewhat | Possibly | Sometimes But Infrequently True | Slightly True of Myself | True |
| 2 | Very Little | Probably Not | Usually not True | Not at All True of Myself | False |
| 1 | Not at All | Very Probably Not | Almost Never True | | |

### Quality

| # | | | |
|---|---|---|---|
| 7 | | | |
| 6 | Very Good | Excellent | |
| 5 | Good | Above average | Good |
| 4 | Barely Acceptable | Average | |
| 3 | Poor | Below Average | Fair |
| 2 | Very Poor | Extremely Poor | Poor |

### Importance

| # | | |
|---|---|---|
| 7 | | |
| 6 | Very Important | |
| 5 | Important | Very Important |
| 4 | | Important |
| 3 | Moderately Important | Moderately Important |
| 2 | Of Little Importance | |
| 1 | Unimportant | Unimportant |

results it is essential that all six points on the scale are used, not 'saving' 1 for an impossibly bad scheme or 6 for a perfect scheme. As part of this analytical process we investigated many choices denoting attitudes towards Agreement, Frequency, Importance, Quality, and Likelihood. For simplicity we adopted the six-point scale to be used in two ways. The first asks the respondent to express a level of agreement with a statement when appropriate. The second seeks to assess the extent to which the statement is accurate in all the relevant instances to be found in the design. The statements are worded so as to make it obvious which type of response is to be expected, and this is explained in the instructions.

① Virtually no agreement
② Hardly any agreement
③ Little agreement
④ Fair agreement
⑤ Strong agreement
⑥ Virtually total agreement

5.1 When you arrive at the building, the entrance is obvious     ①②③④⑤⑥

① Very rarely
② Seldom
③ Occasionally
④ More often than not
⑤ Mostly
⑥ Nearly always or always

2.1 There is a window in patients'
and staff rooms          ①②③④⑤⑥

**3.2 Two ways of using the six-point scoring scale in AEDET Evolution 2005**

Related to the issue of the level of confidence in a score is the problem of the weighting of considerations. Both the DQIs and AEDET provide some weighting, although this is less transparent. For example, the DQI operates a rather complex dual weighting system which first allows results to be visualised depending on how all the respondents judge the success of various aspects of the building, while the second level of weighting addresses fundamental factors –

the added value and the excellence to be achieved. With AEDET the analysis and feedback from its application revealed that the tool should both be simple to understand and allow local judgement to be used to vary the relationships between factors.

- **Has a simple weighting mechanism**
  - This
    - Enables users to tailor the tool to local circumstances and building types
      ⓪ **Zero weighting**
         this statement is not used in calculations
      ① **Normal weighting**
      ② **Double weighting**
         this factor is very important

- **Has a ? symbol signifying level of confidence**
  - This
    - Enables users to record when they use a weighting of ⓪ due to lack of information

**3.3 AEDET Evolution 2005 introduces a simple and transparent three-level weighting system 0, 1 and 2 (①②③)**

The weighting can be used to determine the effect of the statement in arriving at an overall score for that heading. The weighting is therefore attached to every question or statement under the eight headings, such that a weighting of 0 means 'not applicable' or 'do not know', a weighting of 1 is normal, and a weighting of 2 is double. Normally each statement is assumed to have a weighting of 1. However, if that statement is not applicable for some reason, or if it cannot be applied or answered due to a lack of information, a weighting of 0 can be used to remove it from the calculations. Alternatively, in some cases a statement may have a greater than usual importance and may be given a weighting of 2 to double its effect in arriving at the score for the section. The double and zero weightings can be used where the users wish to tailor or customise the tool to their own particular or specific need. Users decide for themselves when to use these weightings – for example, in order to reflect the care model applying to the building under examination. The guidance layer can suggest when these alternative weightings might be most applicable or give some hints as to particular circumstances or building types where the user might consider using double weightings. In the original DQI tool there is a weighting system of sorts, but it is less understandable, and the user cannot easily determine its effects.

An area of concern for both the DQI and AEDET was the level of confidence associated with a particular score. The point here is that the score could, for instance, be affected by the type and quality of information available, or by the stage of development of the design schemes. Often in the early stages of the design process little is known about the design or about the client's aspirations. Also, respondents do not know, or might simply have no knowledge or 'first hand' experience, of what is inferred by the statement. We need to reflect such concerns in the scores, both as a prompt to remind the user that different kinds of information would inevitably affect the score, or simply as a qualification for the set of results.

Consequently, a feature is included within the scoring layer to indicate the sort of confidence one has regarding the score. If the user feels that a score was allocated as a result of inadequate working information, this is recorded by placing a question mark against the statement under the '?' column. On the final score summary sheet a further question mark is entered in the '?' column against the heading to which the statement belongs. This column gives an indication of the user's confidence in arriving at the score for each heading. If at least half the statements under that heading have '?' against them, then the user automatically enters '???' in the final summary column to indicate low confidence in the score.

Yet another problem identified with the DQI and AEDET was that responding to statements results in a simple score. However, the reasons or explanations for this score were not recorded. The task of capturing and codifying attributes about perceptions of design qualities or the generation of categorical data reduces the richness of the information. For AEDET Evolution we were aware of the need to record this information for reference and to aid decision-making. We therefore introduced a feature to 'flag' these items using blank spaces for notes below the headings on each sheet. Without this feature there is a tendency to apply AEDET Evolution in a mechanistic way. This feature allows users to identify ('flag') strong and weak areas – that is, to record in more detail any exceptions to the overall score the user has

arrived at for a particular section. Effectively, flags might offer a further fine tuning of the design for people who wish to use them. Take, for example, a question of views. Virtually all rooms may have good views in a building, but one in particular is poor, and the users feel that this is an important deficiency in the design.

- **Has a flag system**
  - This
    - Enables users to record more detail should they wish to
      - Flagged as worse
        + Flagged as better

The Flags section on the score summary sheet can be used to record exceptions to the overall score you have arrived at for the section. This is particularly useful where a section generally achieves perhaps a very good score but where one or a few spaces are substantially poorer than this score suggests, or vice-versa.

3.4 AEDET Evolution 2005 introduces a 'Flag' system to name the deficient area or room under the heading in question

Table 3.2 AEDET Evolution 2005 introduces a 'Flag' system in which elements, features or spaces are recorded as significantly worse (–) or better (+) than the marked standard

| – Flagged as worse | + Flagged as Better |
| --- | --- |
| E.g. "The layout of the inpatient bed bays and single bedrooms does not take advantage of the views by the site…" | E.g. "The development of façades has been well handled paying particular attention to the selection of façade features and materials to ensure that these are complimentary to the physical elements of the site" |
| E.g. "Carry out daylight studies or light surveys to ensure natural light into buildings including the provision of natural light and ventilation for staff facilities…" | E.g. "the treatment of the main entrance and approach to the hospital creates a pleasant and coherent civic space…" |
| E.g. "Create a sketch study of the size of the new buildings imposed against the old buildings to evaluate the negative impact of the 4–6 storeys" | E.g. "Applaud and commend the removal of car parking from the square and creation of a car free zone, which will provide all users with an agreeable amenity and valuable urban social space" |

Without this technique the score will tend to a middle position because good and bad spaces will cancel each other out, but no record is kept of this. With the flag system users can score according to the normal or majority situation and then simply flag the deficient area or room under the heading as falling below the standard scored and needing special attention from the design team. This will simultaneously result in more variation in scores, removing the tendency to even out scores in large designs, and at the same time leave more specifically useful information about where a design was thought to be particularly good or bad. The positive and negative flags are carried forward to the score summary sheet at the end of the scoring.

Crucially for AEDET Evolution, we introduced an evidence layer to provide an authoritative basis to aid decision-making and underpin sound judgement. The evidence layer directs the user to the research evidence on which the headings are based, where it is available. The growing body of literature suggests that the health care environment can both positively and negatively affect the quality of life enjoyed by patients while in hospital. However, despite over 30 years of productive health care design research, relatively few health care facilities have become the therapeutic built environments that they could be if they are to improve medical outcomes and quality of life. Many environments could be better designed for well-being by applying research-based knowledge to design, or by taking account of available environment/behaviour research and knowledge.

The evidence base offers AEDET Evolution the necessary vehicle to provide an authoritative basis to aid decision-making and underpin sound judgement. We have amassed a great deal of information about the staff/patient architectural environment from the growing body of knowledge. This was achieved partly in this study on AEDET, partly in the development of the ASPECT tool, and partly in an earlier research project (Lawson and Phiri 2000). This accumulated published research evidence demonstrates links between the designed environment, the well-being of staff and patients and improved health outcomes for patients.

## Recommendations by the University of Sheffield School of Architecture Healthcare Research Group for the further development of AEDET Evolution

These recommendations involve a proposal for the development of compliance and exemplar layers as separate documents using the AEDET Evolution hierarchical structure. A compliance layer would address issues relating to compliance with specific legislation, Health Building Notes, Health Technical Memoranda and other NHS technical guidance. This will avoid AEDET Evolution looking cumbersome while allowing it to retain its streamlined structure.

An exemplar layer could point to designs in the NHS Estates design portfolio. These would be selected to show particularly good examples of resolving the issues dealt with by the heading. The material in the design portfolio represents projects that are thought to be exemplary in some way: they are nominated by Trusts and patients, which gives the portfolio a level of authority. However, the portfolio has many deficiencies as a design support tool and is not linked to the AEDET and ASPECT tools. It is also the case that people using AEDET and ASPECT are currently unable to look for detailed examples of good practice as they complete them. Both ASPECT and AEDET have guidance layers to assist, and ASPECT also has an 'evidence' layer that points to the research evidence. Creating an 'exemplar' layer by linking to appropriate images in the design portfolio would help to disseminate good design practice. A design practice could also customise the exemplar layer of AEDET Evolution to point to examples where designs and features were less successful and features which the practice wished to avoid in future.

## Analysis of the Results of Applying the AEDET Evolution tool and the introduction of a summary sheet

We introduced a linear graphical representation of the results to ensure that they are presented in a form that makes relevant information from the diagram easy to read, and makes it easy to discern differences between design schemes. Both the DQIs and AEDET confirm the importance of visualisation or the graphical representation of results, essentially because this facilitates a greater understanding of outcomes and enhances transparency. Jesinghaus' (2000) development of indicators of environmental sustainability argues that graphical indicators should represent and determine the perception of a given policy issue. Graphical representation not only aids the understanding of results but also enables and facilitates comparisons and benchmarking.

As with the DQI, we investigated the use of a spreadsheet format and different forms of visualisation or graphical representation of the results, including 3D bar charts, doughnut shapes and others. We evaluated the radar chart or spider diagram adopted by the DQI and AEDET especially because it was argued that this approach brought the appearance of DQI results in line with those used as key performance indicators in UK construction. The radar chart represents a summary of Likert-style responses to a series of statements describing design qualities. Feedback from

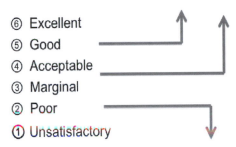

⑥ Excellent
⑤ Good
④ Acceptable
③ Marginal
② Poor
① Unsatisfactory

- **Pulled out into straight rather than spider web**
  - Gives much better perception of variations
  - Allows for flags to be alongside each heading
  - Allows for ? level of confidence alongside each heading
- **Brings the whole thing together on one easy to read sheet**

**3.5a and b  A six-point scoring scale is also used in the evaluation of AEDET Evolution results**

those who had used the DQI and AEDET indicated concern that excellence in design was not easily read from the spider diagram, and that conceptually the diagram is the wrong way round: the better building has a larger circle rather than hitting the bull's eye. Although the spider diagram is attractive, it is not easy to discern differences between design schemes. All this is inconsistent with the need to ensure that results are presented in a form that makes relevant inform-ation easy to read from the diagram (Tufte 1997). Also, DQI participants emphasised the need for the design tool to be more interactive in showing results graphically quite quickly as part of an ongoing discussion about design – i.e. "faster appearance of the spider diagrams".

When applying tools such as DQI and AEDET, one is aware that many bits of information are generated as users respond to 60 or more statements under various headings and sections. The problem is that it is difficult to remember this many bits of different information, and without some organisation or structuring mechanism this can ultimately affect the effectiveness of the tool and the associated

decision-making. With AEDET Evolution we were aware that scores and their visualisation are only part of the information generated. Notes, comments and flags are also recorded.

We therefore introduced a score summary sheet, to bring into one place disparate bits of information – all the scores, confidence levels, flags and graphical representations in order to facilitate information transfer and the application of results in a way which aids the generation of design solutions or the assessment of designs. The set of results is sufficiently rich to reflect the complexity of judging buildings.

A score summary sheet at the end of the scoring layer, pulled out into a straight format rather than presented as spider diagrams, gives a much better perception of variation, allows flags to be presented alongside each heading, allows the '?' level of confidence to be shown alongside each heading and brings the whole thing together on one easy-to-read sheet. The score summary sheet contains scores from each category in the form of a six-by-ten matrix and 'flags' a record of any exceptions to the overall scores that should be specifically noted. Both of these are presented side-by-side to provide a comprehensive summary of the results from AEDET Evolution. The chart allows a visual representation of the scores to indicate strong and weak areas.

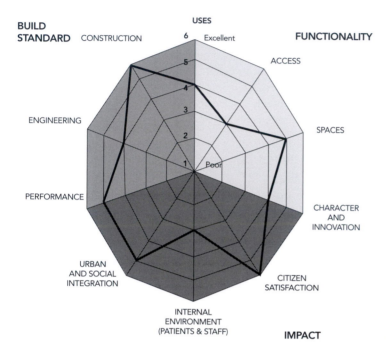

3.6 Graphical representation of the DQI and AEDET visualisation of results using a radar chart and a spider diagram

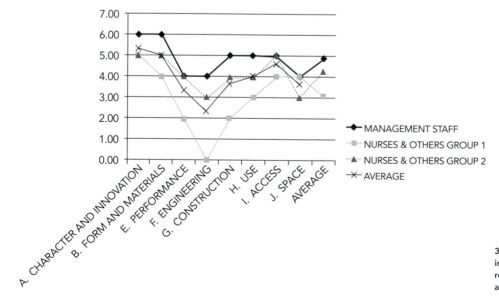

3.7 AEDET Evolution introduces a linear graphical representation of results or aggregate scores

AEDET
Achieving Excellence- Design Evaluation Toolkit

SCORE SUMMARY

FLAGS
List any elements, spaces or parts of the design that are
significantly worse (-) or better (+) than the marked standard.

Bring forward scores from each section in the scoring layer to the chart below.

This can be used to record any exceptions to the overall scores that you
specifically wish to have noted.

| | ? | ① | ② | ③ | ④ | ⑤ | ⑥ | - Flagged as worse | + Flagged as better |
|---|---|---|---|---|---|---|---|---|---|
| A CHARACTER AND INNOVATION | | + | + | + | + | + | + | | |
| B FORM AND MATERIALS | | + | + | + | + | + | + | | |
| C STAFF and PATIENT ENVIRONMENT | | + | + | + | + | + | + | | |
| D URBAN/SOCIAL INTEGRATION | | + | + | + | + | + | + | | |
| E PERFORMANCE | | + | + | + | + | + | + | | |
| F ENGINEERING | | + | + | + | + | + | + | | |
| G CONSTRUCTION | | + | + | + | + | + | + | | |
| H USE | | + | + | + | + | + | + | | |
| I ACCESS | | + | + | + | + | + | + | | |
| J SPACE | | + | + | + | + | + | + | | |

3.8 AEDET Evolution introduces a Summary Sheet which brings all the information together in one place for easy reading and reference

The side-by-side representation of scores, graphs, flags and records of information facilitates comparison and provides cues as to which headings require improvement or which areas must be protected from changes. It fosters discussion and acts as a catalyst for debate, aspects which are vital if there are to be harmonious 'joined up' aspirations for the built environment or settings.

**Table 3.3 Example of the scientific evidence for the ASPECT heading on 'Privacy, company and cignity'**

| Bibliographic Information | Findings | Authors' Conclusions |
| --- | --- | --- |
| Baldwin S, Effects of furniture rearrangement on the atmosphere of wards in a maximum-security hospital, *Hospital and Community Psychiatry*, Vol. 36, No. 5, May 1985, 525- 528 | A time-limited low-cost intervention, especially an intervention in the physical environment, often achieves favourable results in a facility treating patients with difficulties. In a study of the effects of a short-term environmental intervention alterations were made in furniture rearrangements in ward dayrooms in a maximum-security hospital in the UK. Over a 14-day period group seating patterns were introduced each day in conjunction with leisure-time resources such as cards and games to promote improvements in the wards' psychosocial atmosphere. The program was implemented through a system of behavioral contracting with ward staff. The findings suggest that the use of such simple low cost techniques can produce modest positive changes in different kinds of ward environments. | The data for intervention in wards showed that group furniture arrangements doubled in frequency during the intervention phases; this statistically highly significant increase then decreased during the reversal phase. Dependent variable was the number of group furniture arrangements; other variables were medication rates, seclusion rates, causality incidents, points earned, perception of the ward and nursing reports. The findings also show that rehospitalisation patterns differed between various sub-groups of the population. The study suggests that some individuals are more at risk than others which means administrators can use this to take precautions or implement programme changes to reduce the risk. |
| Barnhart SK, Perkins NH, and Fitzsimonds J, Behaviour and outdoor setting preferences at a psychiatric hospital, *Landscape and Urban Planning*, Vol. 42, 1998, 147–156 | This study investigated staff and patient preferences for outdoor behaviours and settings and the relationship between attributes of ideal settings and setting preferences at a 312-bed psychiatric hospital in Guelph, Ontario. Seventy-four subjects (50% staff and 50% patients) rated a number of preferred behaviours and ranked a range of environmental settings on the hospital's 48 acres of grounds. The study subjects responded to questions presented using a proprietary interactive computer survey located in one of the secure hospital wards. Data collection and analyses were conducted automatically without the investigators being present. Images of outdoor settings were ordered along two dimensions from built to natural and open to enclosed. Frequencies of first choice settings were analysed by preferred behaviour. | Both staff and patients selected natural open settings for passive behaviours such as sitting and viewing scenery, and natural enclosed settings for active behaviours such as walking and talking with others. Few statistically significant differences were found between staff and patients for preferred settings and/or behaviours. The study results demonstrated a consistent preference among participants for certain setting dimensions, particularly when combined with certain preferred behaviours. The results of the study are somewhat consistent with previous research findings that indicate a general preference for natural settings. Previous literature suggests that behaviour can affect setting preference (Purcell et al. 1994) although the degree of naturalness within stimuli plays an important role. |

| Bibliographic Information | Findings | Authors' Conclusions |
|---|---|---|
| Burlington M, Can Private Rooms Be Justified in Today's Health care Market? The Center for Innovation in Health Facilities, 1999 | The concept of the all private-room hospital is not a new one. The paper was initiated by a request from a Detroit area hospital to research and discuss the evidence that private rooms promote a higher level of quality health care while increasing efficiency and providing financial benefits to a hospital facility. Issues concerning infection control, demand for isolation rooms, environmental stress, privacy, flexibility of space, family-centred care, and patient preferences are examined. This report combines literature review and a study of current trends in hospital construction, with internal data and a patient preference survey conducted by William Beaumont Hospital, Royal Oak MI, in an attempt to illustrate that private rooms are an essential feature in today's competitive health care market. | Numerous benefits of private patient rooms have been realised for years. There is indication that less patient-to-patient contact decreases the incidence of costly nosocomial infections. All private rooms provide flexibility for more efficient use of beds promoting overall higher occupancy rates by as much as 10%. Larger single-care rooms also offer flexibility through a broader range of capabilities and being better able to accommodate technologically advanced medical equipment needed to treat patients of rising acuity levels. In addition, the potentially enormous cost of patient transfers due to double-occupancy problems is no longer a burden in an all private-room facility. |

The first six of these (1. Privacy, company and dignity; 2. Views; 3. Nature and outdoors; 4. Control and comfort; 5. Architectural legibility of place; 6. Appearance) are probably largely self-explanatory, but the last two are slightly different. Under facilities we find all the issues that evidence suggests are important, but which are not really so much characteristics of the buildings as of their contents – the presence of televisions, vending machines and so on. Since the consequences of these have different significance when designing, they are usefully located together. Finally, the staff category indicates that while most spaces in health care buildings are used both by patients and staff, some are reserved specifically for staff use. Evidence about the qualities and facilities of these spaces comes under this category.

Evidence is indicated by a study (Lawson & Phiri 2003) which examined the effects of the architectural environment on the lives of patients, and to some extent staff, in two NHS hospitals, one in the general medical sector and one in the mental health sector. Examining two wards, one in acute general medicine (Poole) and the other in mental health (Brighton), the study looked at cohorts of patients before and after the building of new accommodation. In both cases patients were referred in similar ways and underwent similar treatment regimes, often by the same staff, in both the new and the old wards. Findings indicate that patients are sensitive to and articulate about their architectural environment. They are able to discriminate between poor and good environments and say clearly what they like and dislike about them. Patients appeared to make significantly better progress in the new purpose-designed buildings than in their older counterparts. There is considerable evidence that an overall improved atmosphere and quality of life may be one of the benefits of better buildings. In the mental health sector patient treatment times were reduced by 14%, and in the general medical sector by about 21%. Patients rated both their treatment and the staff caring for them highly. Most of the architectural features apparently responsible for these benefits appeared to be generic place-making features rather than hospital-specific factors. Having a view of the outside world seemed to be very important, as was being comfortable and having personal control over their immediate environment.

Furthermore, the literature review from this project led to the development of a database containing a growing list of references – in excess of 300 citations for the 2002 version. The objectives of the *Sheffield Architectural Environment and Patient Health Outcomes Database* were to refer users to research evidence, sources of information or landmark studies for use by all those who commission, design, construct and operate health care facilities, especially practitioners who have to meet many deadlines and who have very limited time to research the many diverse types or sources of information. For researchers, the database allows them to build upon the works of others. It provides critical reference to primary sources or material written by person(s) who originated the ideas in the published literature.

The database was created using Microsoft Access 2002, commonly accessible database software chosen because NHS Estates uses the Microsoft Office suite of software. The database was loaded on a NHS Estates server within the Knowledge and Information Portal (KIP), allowing access via the NHS Estates website (www.knowledge.nhsestates.gov. uk) before the abolition of NHS Estates. KIP was a bespoke meta-database browser capable of searching multiple databases simultaneously. However, this database as implemented on KIP, was not in a designer-friendly form or an easily accessible format.

Also underlying the evidence base and relevant to the development of the ASPECT tool is the evidence-based approach as a dynamic four-step strategy about asking questions, searching relevant articles, evaluating in terms of validity and usefulness, and applying findings in practice. In the first step, it is always necessary to formulate clear and unambiguous questions. In the second step, tracking down the best evidence involves searching the right and relevant articles. The evaluation step entails interpreting the evidence and carrying out critical appraisals in terms of validity and usefulness. Applying the evidence is about implementing findings in practice, and managing on the basis of the best available research data.

## Microsoft Excel spreadsheet versions of the ASPECT tool and recommendations by the University of Sheffield School of Architecture Healthcare Research Group to utilise the internet and hypermedia

Following the precedent set by DQI Online, the automatic manipulation, reporting and generation of categorical data using a Microsoft Excel spreadsheet for the ASPECT tool (and subsequently for AEDET Evolution 2005) was implemented to facilitate the easy recording of information, the development of hypermedia links and navigation between the layers, thereby making the tool much more interactive, versatile and user-friendly. This was despite an initial resistance to putting things into electronic form because at the time many people preferred to use a paper design in some contexts.

**Table 3.4 Example of the Microsoft Excel spreadsheet for ASPECT heading 'Nature and outdoors': guidance shown as pull-down menu for item 3.01**

### C3: Nature and outdoors

*Section 3 deals with the extent to which patients, in particular, have contact with the natural world. It asks whether they can see and access nature both around and inside the building.*

| ID | Description | Weighting | Score | Notes |
|----|-------------|-----------|-------|-------|
| 3.01 | Patients can go outside | Normal (1) ▼ | Select... ▼ | |

*Consider using double weighting. This item is particularly important for places where patients may be for long periods especially if not in great pain or discomfort, and for mental health buildings. Much research shows the importance of contact with the outdoors and nature to most people. The ability to breathe fresh air is thought by many people to be therapeutic in itself. Part of the feeling of fresh air seems to be a degree of movement and breeze. This may be very important not only in itself but in giving patients a feeling of being in contact with a normal outside world. This is obviously most satisfactorily achieved by having direct access to outdoors. This could be in the open landscape, in a courtyard or even on a balcony.*

| ID | Description | Weighting | Score | Notes |
|----|-------------|-----------|-------|-------|
| 3.02 | Patients and staff have access to usable landscaped areas | Normal (1) ▼ | Select... ▼ | |
| 3.03 | Patients and staff can easily see plants, vegetation and nature | Normal (1) ▼ | Select... ▼ | |

◀ Views        ▶▶ Results summary        Comfort and control ▶

Once adopted, the ASPECT tool Excel spreadsheet allows easy recording of scores and notes in the scoring layer, incorporating comments, flags and levels of information available. There is now scope to develop the guidance layer as a set of drop-down menus for easier use and quick reference, and the provision of a help desk facility and explanatory features – e.g. the way an icon is explained in an item in the Microsoft Word or Excel menu. Access to the evidence layer and therefore to the research will be enhanced with an electronic interface. It is then straightforward to track changes and follow up-to-date developments. However, further work is needed to identify what tools can be downloaded for easy reference and use.

As with DQI Online, an interactive web-based version of the ASPECT tool could also evolve so as to provide an online interface. Advantages of web-based versions of such tools include the fact that they are straightforward to initiate, and they are easy to use. Results are not only generated automatically but can also be obtained graphically, thereby facilitating discussion about project aspirations and the extent to which these have been and could be met.

## Demonstrating the effectiveness of ASPECT over the application of AEDET Evolution's C Heading – Staff and Patient Environment

This demonstration involved a study of two sets of students, from schools of Architecture and Nursing. The commission in 2005 entitled 'Disseminating Good Practice' involved conducting separate sessions for groups of architects and nurses. During the sessions participants were shown six images corresponding to each of the statements in ASPECT and in AEDET Evolution. This study found that the ASPECT tool was more reliable, consistent and produced better results than the AEDET Evolution Heading C: Staff and Patient Environment.

## AEDET/ASPECT, DQI and IDEAs in the design quality improvement agenda

A study by the University of Sheffield School of Architecture Health Care Research Group into the NHS Estates Design Review System used 35 Design Review Panels to confirm that AEDET offers a useful framework, which provides:

- A 'useful checklist/benchmark' which ensures that all issues of a scheme are identified and dealt with.
- A very useful basis for carrying out comparisons of capital health care projects.
- A powerful toolkit for evaluation, which forms a very effective means for communication about design quality to all parties involved in design reviews, including bidding consortia.
- A useful framework for a high-level review of the scheme at various stages of development.
- A means to standardise the design review reports.

The Design Review Panels consisted of members of NHS Estates and largely independent professional practitioners and academics with particular knowledge of health care design. The analysis from the study also showed that the projects judged to have the highest design quality were normally those where the PFI public sector cost comparator design took in the views of the Design Review Panel. This research revealed that, at its final meeting, the Design Review Panel members often felt that the selection made by the Trust was not in line with their own views in design quality terms.

In 2010 the Commission for Architecture and the Built Environment (CABE) referred to AEDET as assisting health care trusts and the NHS to determine and manage their design requirements from initial proposals to post-project evaluation, concentrating on the product of their project. A design evaluation profile for project teams to use for benchmarking is created by discussing built environment factors through the three layers of scoring, guidance and evidence.

The AEDET Evolution toolkit has become a major influence, assisting trusts and the NHS in determining and managing their design requirements from initial proposals through to post-project evaluation. It supports key agenda items at NHS Design Reviews. It is a benchmarking tool, and forms part of the business case guidance for ProCure21, PFI, LIFT and conventionally funded schemes. AEDET evaluations remain requirements of the PFI process, but they inform rather than determine the outcome. In fact, design remains a small proportion (around 20%) of the overall judgements made between competing bids under the PFI process.

## DQI (Design Quality Indicator)

An important evidence-based tool in the UK design quality improvement agenda is the Design Quality Indicator (DQI). Developed by the UK's Construction Industry Council as an extension of Egan's Rethinking Construction agenda for targeting, mapping, measuring and managing performance improvement in construction, the DQI was developed explicitly to measure the quality of the design embodied in the product – the buildings themselves. The DQI tool is basically a questionnaire, in which respondents are asked to agree or disagree with a series of statements on a six-point scale, to which they later add a judgement of the relative importance (weighting) of the sets of statements. The final score is computed by applying the weightings from each respondent to that person's score on the statement.

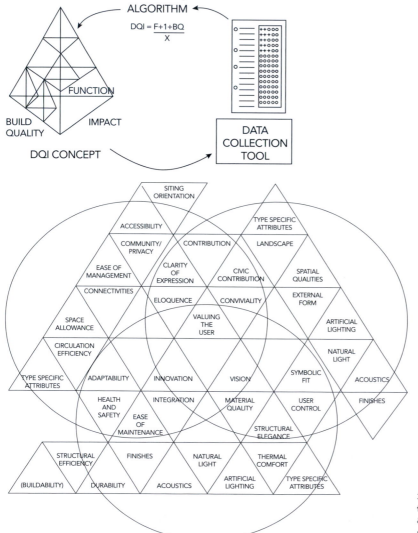

3.9 Representing the DQI conceptual framework (source: Gann et al. 2003) (Taylor & Francis Ltd www.tandfonline.com, reprinted by permission of the publisher)

## Development of DQI

The original aim of the DQI project was to develop a tool for benchmarking design quality. Since then benefits have been advocated for the DQI as 'a learning tool for thinking or learning' which covers all the stages of a capital project. At inception of a project, DQI allows clients to elicit their requirements and set out a framework for specific considerations of design quality. At the design stage of a project, DQI helps drive improvements in the focus of quality and value of design through discussion and evaluation of different schemes or options. During construction, DQI enhances understanding by the project team of its aims and aspirations. After completion and occupation of the building, DQI allows evaluation of the completed building (the product) to feed forward into the next project.

The three main elements of the DQI toolkit (conceptual framework, data gathering tool and weighting mechanism) map the value of buildings in relation to their design for different uses and their ability to meet a variety of physical, aspirational and emotional needs among the occupants and users. The conceptual framework leads back to Vitruvius (1999), who described design in terms of *firmitas, utilitas* and *venustas (De architectura*, Book 1, Ch. 3. §2); in Sir Henry Wotton's translation, firmness, commodity and delight (1624, p. 1). Through a proprietary algorithm DQI converts individual subjective perceptions into subjective measurable results. Clients, designers and building stakeholders rate the features and qualities of a project on a six-point scale by completing a questionnaire. The quantification of these 'design intangibles' is the unique feature of DQI, while the spider diagram is the system's signature output, whose missing 'chunks' from the pie represent deficiencies in the building or design.

Applied in a workshop setting mediated or led by a certified or accredited DQI facilitator, DQI is completed by a range of stakeholders during the briefing and design stages

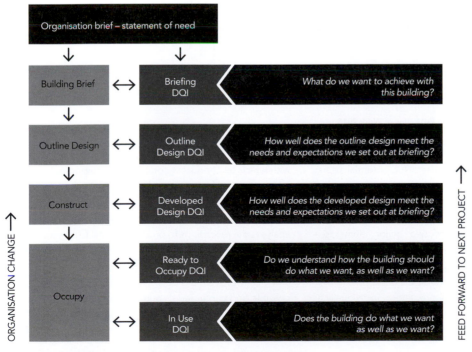

**3.10  Five stages of how DQI is used during a Design–Build–Occupy Cycle**

| RIBA | 0 Strategic Definition | 1 Preparation and Brief | 2 Strategic Definition | 3 Developed Design | 4 Technical Design | 5 | 6 Handover and Close Out | 7 |
|------|------------------------|-------------------------|------------------------|--------------------|--------------------|---|-------------------------|---|
| | | | | | | Construction | | In Use |

| Design Quality Indicator | 1. Briefing | 2. Concept | 3. Mid Design | 4. Ready for Occupation | 5. In-Use |
|---|---|---|---|---|---|
| Summary | The Project Team define and identify their priorities for the project.<br><br>A language will be developed which they will use throughout the project to communicate with stakeholders, the suppliers and review their designs.<br><br>The team will form a common understanding of what constitutes success by which they can assess all areas and stages of the project.<br><br>The team gain a more in-depth understanding of their client's brief and users' needs. | An effective dialogue continues between the members of the team.<br><br>The range of uses and needs of the building are made aware to all members.<br><br>Assessment group are able to review designs with the design team.<br><br>Design teams can expalin design decisions and uses of materials to the Assessment group.<br><br>Design teams gain valuable feedback on their designs and plans.<br><br>Project design teams remain critically informed of their clients' needs. | Assessment group can re-assess designs to ensure that any outstanding issues have been resolved.<br><br>Assessment group can be satisfied that the designs will deliver an exceptional proje t that satisfies the needs of its users and the community.<br><br>Project suppliers can affirm that the building they will deliver will succeed in reaching the expectations of the users.<br><br>Construction is ready to begin using designs that have been approved by the assessment group. | Assessment group recognise successes of the project.<br><br>Building suppliers understand the degree to which the delivered project fulfils the expectations of the Assessment group.<br><br>Building suppliers and the client gain an understanding of what people think of the building when it is new, which can be usefully compared to opinions once the building has been in use for a period of not less than 12 months. | The impact of the building on the local community and its users is captured and can be communicated to the client.<br><br>The successes, limitations and lessons of the building project are reviewed understood and recorded.<br><br>The importance of design quality is understood by all those included in, and effected by, the project. |

**3.11  Alignment of DQI stages with the RIBA Plan of Work 2013**

of a building project or on a completed building. Stakeholders comprise building users (or potential users), clients, designers (architects, structural and building services engineers, quantity surveyors), project managers, and facilities or resource managers.

DQI uses a combination of two major elements – structured workshops and online tools. At each workshop, presentations about the latest progress of the scheme are made to an assessment group made up of representatives from the stakeholders of the scheme, known individually as 'respondents'. DQI gives the group a structure or format with which to conduct a comprehensive appraisal of issues relating to the design. Questionnaires are used to generate discussions of key topics during the workshop. The DQI facilitator records the workshop sessions and subsequently analyses the recordings to produce results. DQI recommends that workshops take place at all stages of a building project, from briefing, through design and construction to occupancy, and ideally DQI should be implemented at the earliest stage possible and continued throughout the project.

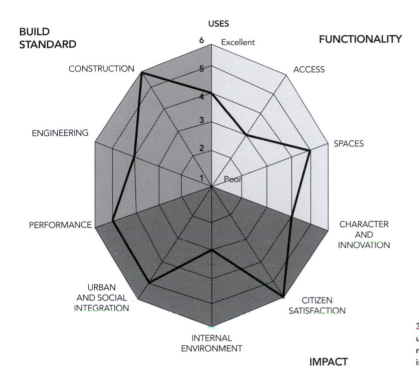

BUILD
STANDARD

USES

FUNCTIONALITY

6  Excellent
5
CONSTRUCTION
4
ACCESS
3
ENGINEERING
2
SPACES
1  Poor

PERFORMANCE

CHARACTER
AND
INNOVATION

URBAN
AND SOCIAL
INTEGRATION

CITIZEN
SATISFACTION

INTERNAL
ENVIRONMENT

IMPACT

**3.12 Visualisation of Results from the DQI using a spider diagram, adopted to bring the representation of results in line with those used in UK construction's key performance indicators**

## Relationship between DQI and AEDET Evolution

DQI (http://www.dqi.org.uk/) represents a pan-construction industry tool, while the AEDET Evolution toolkit evaluates a design by posing a series of 59 clear, non-technical statements encompassing the key areas of 'Impact', 'Build Quality' and 'Functionality' designed to cross refer to the design. By scoring statements in both DQI and AEDET Evolution it is possible to summarise how well a health care building complies with best practice. As with the DQI tool, AEDET Evolution also provides a common language that allows the clear identification of needs, and for a discussion to be initiated between the client, consultants and other parties to the health care project. The discussion can take place at any stage during the Design–Build–Occupy Cycle, thus ensuring a continuous response to changing client needs and expectations.

However, the major difference between DQI and AEDET Evolution is an emphasis on providing an appropriate evidence base for statements and the development of a

hierarchical organisational structure (in the form of scoring, guidance and evidence layers) for AEDET Evolution. The development of ASPECT as a plug-in to AEDET Evolution is also an important distinguishing feature when compared with DQI. Studies found that ASPECT produces better results than the same section heading in AEDET Evolution. ASPECT is also better supported by evidence from scientific studies.

However, a more important distinction between DQI and AEDET Evolution is that AEDET Evolution is a self-assurance tool similar to the NEAT tool, while DQI (DQI for Health) is a tool which relies on algorithms that are not shared with or revealed to participants, and is similar to BREEAM by BRE. The Construction Industry Council (CIC) manages and coordinates the operation of DQI, trains and registers independent facilities, provides a third party assured process that delivers a Quality Mark on completion, and maintains a centralised database for benchmarking derived from previous assessments by different stakeholder groups ('experience-based'). For this the CIC has a pricing structure

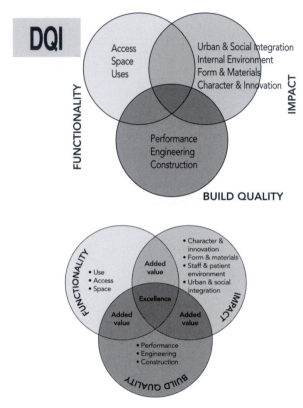

3.13 DQI and AEDET Evolution underlying framework

Table 3.5 Pricing structure for each of the 5 DQI stages as at February 2014 (http://www.dqi.org.uk/perch/resources/dqi-for-health-guidance-1.pdf)

| 5 DQI stages | Project Rating | | | |
| --- | --- | --- | --- | --- |
| | A | B | C | D |
| 1. Briefing | £2499 | £3499 | £3999 | £4999 |
| 2. Design 1 | £1999 | £2999 | £3499 | £4499 |
| 3. Design 2 | £1999 | £2999 | £3499 | £3499 |
| 4. Ready for occupation | £1999 | £2999 | £3499 | £3499 |
| 5. In use | £1999 | £2499 | £2999 | £3999 |
| Total | £10495 | £14995 | £17495 | £22495 |

## Further development of DQI

Since DQI's launch in 1999 and its availability as an online resource for the UK Construction Industry since 1 October 2003, three models of DQI have subsequently been developed: 1. DQI applicable to all building types; 2. DQI for schools and applicable to school buildings; and 3. DQI for health buildings, released in beta format in June 2012.

## DQI for health buildings 2014

This system was launched in February 2014 to provide an alternative evaluation tool to AEDET Evolution. It was originally developed from DQI but adopts a much more self-assessment-based approach in which both the professional and the lay person are able to take part in workshop sessions. The availability of both DQI and AEDET Evolution, supported by ASPECT, offers researchers an opportunity to investigate the impact of these tools on the Design Quality Improvement Agenda. However, with the Department of Health unable to support AEDET Evolution 2005, DQI for Health is seen and used by some organisations, notably NHS England and NHS London, as superseding AEDET Evolution.

**Quality criteria for a DQI accredited building** cover:

- Completion of all five DQI stages: 1. Briefing; 2. Concept design; 3. Mid design; 4. Ready for Occupation; and 5. In-use (for health projects > £3m).
- Participant numbers and profile.
- Format of the workshops.
- Briefing record (Table 3.6).
- Assessment reports.
- Satisfactory feedback from the participants and the client.
- CIC carries out spot checks.

to help offset the costs associated with administering the DQI process, including holding stakeholder events or meetings (Table 3.5).

In practice AEDET can employ either an internal or external facilitator, but it relies on the Department of Health or a similar central authority to continually fund and develop the tool, including coordinating the centralised database for benchmarking and collating assessments by different stakeholders.

# Functionality
## Access

| Access deals with the whole journey from home (or where you start) to the building, department or room you need to get to. This Section asks whether people will easily and efficiently get to and from the site using a variety of means of transport and whether they will logically, easily and safely get into and out of the building. | Strongly Disagree | Disagree | Tend to Disagree | Tend to Agree | Agree | Strongly Agree | Not Applicable | Don't know |
|---|---|---|---|---|---|---|---|---|
| 1 The location of the building will provide good access for everyone including people using public transport | | | △ | | | | | |
| Getting to and from the site should be straightforward and safe for all who need to go there. Access requirements for staff, patients and visitors arriving at the building using public transport should be well considered. Pedestrian routes from public transport points should be clear, safe and sensitively designed. Consideration should be given to bringing public transport into the site where possible and appropriate. Any on-site roads should be adequate and sensitively designed. | | | | | | | | |
| 2 The layout and landscape around the building will provide safe and convenient pedestrian access and will be suitable for use by wheelchair users and people with other disabilities | | | | | △ | | | |
| Getting to and from the building on foot should feel effortless with well-designed external routes and simple signage. Pedestrian routes should cross vehicular routes safely and should be well lit at night. Cars and other vehicles should not dominate the external public areas. See 8 below for internal circulation and signage | | | | | | | | |
| 3 Designated entrances will be obvious and are logically positioned in relation to access | | | | | | △ | | |
| Consider how easy it should be to find all ways into and out of the building for patients, visitors, staff, and goods. | | | | | | | | |

3.14 DQI for Health: Scoring the Questionnaire (statement and guidance)

Table 3.6 **Extract from DQI briefing record – four weighting considerations: Required** (compliance with standards + regulations); **Desired** (above plus setting targets beyond the minimum); **Inspired** (above plus setting exceptional targets); and **Not applicable** (where the question is not relevant to the project) (RDI tags)

| | Functionality | Default | Notes | Value |
|---|---|---|---|---|
| 16 | The ratio of usable space to total area should be good | Desired | | Desired |
| 17 | The building should provide a good balance of communal and private spaces | Desired | IMPORTANT ISSUE – Many different users will pass through the building during a day with different requirements, behaviours and expectations (see above); the layout and spaces should help to minimise conflict between different user groups | Desired |
| 18 | There should be adequate storage space | Desired | | Desired |
| | **Uses** | | | |
| 19 | The building should enhance the activity of people who use it regularly | Inspired | | Inspired |
| 20 | The building should contribute to the efficiency of the organisation | Required | The library will generally be staffed by only two people – it should be easy to supervise and manage | Required |
| 21 | The building should be able to accommodate the user's needs | Required | | Required |
| 22 | The building should provide good security | Required | IMPORTANT ISSUE – Physical security is a very important challenge. 'Secure by Design' standards should be applied. Protection of children in the nursery is paramount | Required |
| 23 | The building should be adequate to changing needs | Required | IMPORTANT ISSUE – Spaces need to be flexible to respond to needs change short term changing needs – during the day and the week – school groups, silver surfers, homework group, book club | Required |
| 24 | The lighting should allow for different user requirements | Desired | As above | Desired |
| 25 | The layout should allow for changes of use | Desired | As above | Desired |
| 26 | The heating, ventilation and IT installations should allow for changes of use | Desired | As above | Desired |
| 27 | The structure should allow for changes of use | Desired | Medical library use unlikely to change, although user requirements may do so. A framed structure with non-load bearing partitions is preferred | Desired |

Learning from AEDET Evolution, DQI for Health contains six areas of enhanced focus: 1. Patient safety; 2. Control of infection; 3. Privacy and dignity; 4. Sustainability; 5. Standardisation; and 6. Staff and patient environments. Also, DQI for Health expands the guidance notes for questions or statements in a different manner to the guidance layer in AEDET Evolution, which allowed customisation by individual organisations to recognise their own unique experiences or specialities.

## Build Quality, Engineering

| | | | | | | | | |
|---|---|---|---|---|---|---|---|---|
| 31 | The engineering systems will deliver benefits from standardisation and prefabrication where relevant | | | | | | | |
| | The benefits of standardisation and prefabrication are well understood and should be considered in appropriate schemes. Standardisation is not an end in itself but may offer efficiencies during construction and in operating and maintaining buildings. There are also effects on the design process requiring engineering services to be fully designed at an earlier stage than a more traditional approach. | | | | | | | |

| | | | | | | | | |
|---|---|---|---|---|---|---|---|---|
| 37 | The building will be efficient in its use of resources including energy and water | | | | | | | |
| | Respondents, assisted by design colleagues, should agree the basis of what should be considered "efficient". Consideration should be given to the inevitability of rising fuel prices over the lifetime of the building | | | | | | | |
| 38 | Engineering systems will adopt the principles of sustainable environmentally conscious design | | | | | | | |
| | This is a complex area and respondents should expect a good explanation of their proposals from engineering designers. Together with 42 below, many but not all issues in BREEAM will be addressed | | | | | | | |

3.15  DQI for Health: Scoring the Questionnaire (statement and guidance) Standardisation & Sustainability

## Impact, internal environment

| | | | | | | | | |
|---|---|---|---|---|---|---|---|---|
| 50 | The building will respect the needs of patients and allow for appropriate levels of privacy, dignity and confidentiality | | | | | | | |
| | Spaces where patients spend significant amounts of time, or where sensitive consultations, treatments or discussions take place should provide both visual and acoustic privacy. Company and privacy are highly valued by patients and staff and the building should facilitate both. Toilets and bathrooms should be nearby but located discretely | | | | | | | |

| | | | | | | | | |
|---|---|---|---|---|---|---|---|---|
| 59 | There will be high levels of both comfort and control of comfort | | | | | | | |
| | Comfort overall and the ability to control the various aspects of comfort. Control may be zoned, by department, by suite of rooms, in individual rooms and/or personal control | | | | | | | |
| 60 | Engineering systems will adopt the principles of sustainable | | | | | | | |

3.16  DQI for Health: Scoring the Questionnaire (statement and guidance) Privacy & Dignity – Staff & Patient Environment

## Funtionality; Use

| 24 | The layout will facilitate both security and supervision | | | | | | | | | |
|----|--------------------------------------------------------|--|--|--|--|--|--|--|--|--|
| | Security at entrances is commonplace. Within the building, security and supervision should be facilitated by the overall building design without being intrusive except where necessary as a deterrent | | | | | | | | | |

## Build Quality; Performance

| 27 | The building will be easy and safe to clean to required health standards | | | | | | | | | |
|----|--------------------------------------------------------------------------|--|--|--|--|--|--|--|--|--|
| | Defining and understanding the cleaning regime is often given low priority at early stages. Some health functions have rigorous cleaning requirements that will affect outcome activity. Selection of materials and finishes should consider cleaning from the outset. | | | | | | | | | |

## Impact; internal environment

| 58 | There will be a high air quality appropriate to use of spaces and the control of cross infection | | | | | | | | | |
|----|--------------------------------------------------------------------------------------------------|--|--|--|--|--|--|--|--|--|
| | Air quality is a key factor in personal comfort as well as control of infection | | | | | | | | | |

3.17 DQI for Health: Scoring the Questionnaire (statement and guidance) Patient Safety – Control of Infection

**Best practice – preparation of workshops** involves:

- Identifying a DQI client from the demand side, who is informed, engaged, energetic and with authority and with a good understanding of the process.
- Allocating adequate time before/during/after the workshop.
- Establishing adequate funding – budget for DQI included in project cost from the outset.
- Undertaking good preparation – good quality information on the project, clear objectives and outcomes.
- Ensuring that stakeholders and the design team are briefed and understand the process and its benefits.
- Confirming that everyone is aware of the importance of DQI engagement as integral to the project – not just 'a tick box exercise'.

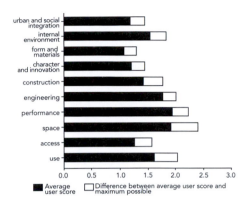

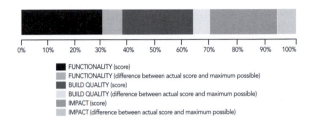

**All respondents**

FUNCTIONALITY (score)
FUNCTIONALITY (difference between actual score and maximum possible)
BUILD QUALITY (score)
BUILD QUALITY (difference between actual score and maximum possible)
IMPACT (score)
IMPACT (difference between actual score and maximum possible)

**Section Scores, weighted**
Respondents overall gave priority to sections Space, Use and Performance all these and the other sections were assessed 80% of maximum or better

**Quality Dimensions**
Overall respondents gave slightly more emphasis to Functionality (40%) than Build Quality or Impact (both 30%)

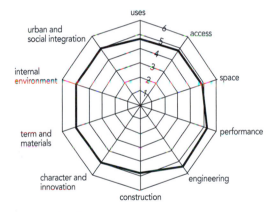

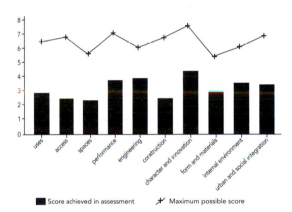

**Section Scores spider diagram**
The diagram shows a very good balanced assessment assessed at 5 for all sections

**Briefing record output**
This shows a good overall profile, well matched to the Briefing Stage priorities. The relatively poor score for Construction probably reflects the high proportion of Don't Know responses to this section

**3.18 Visualisation of the results from the DQI for Health: Section Scores – weighted; Quality Dimensions graph, Section Scores spider diagram and Briefing Record Output**

**Best practice – workshops** covers:

- Facilitation skills – presentation and reporting skills, group management, confident, supportive, sensitive to group signals, stimulating thinking and discussion.
- The right number and appropriate mix of stakeholders, with key stakeholders all present.
- Appropriate and high quality neutral venue with good facilities and catering; adaptable space with the right technology and pin up areas.

- Warm-up process – images exercises, building visits, KAC cards, pre-meeting with client to set goals.
- High quality bold design team presentation linked to DQI questions.

**Weighting scores targets**
Urban and Social Integration + Internal Environment + Form and Materials + Character and Innovation
= TOTAL 20

**Weighting Sections targets**

Functionality + Build Quality + Impact = TOTAL 15

**Visualisation of the results from the DQI for Health**

A **The Section Scores Weighted graph** is weighted using the data given by participants at the end of the main sections. This graph allows the team to see the most important sections (the overall length of the white bar) and how well the building/design is performing against each section (the dark bar). The project teams are therefore able to see which specific areas can be improved to deliver great design. The scale of this graph is not set and can vary due to the original weighting provided.

B **The Quality Dimensions graph** illustrates the overall DQI priorities and is scaled between 0% and 100%. The graph visualises two sets of results; first, it takes into account the overall weightings allocated to Functionality, Build Quality and Impact. The length of the segment shows the importance of that dimension compared to the other two. Second, the darker colour of the segment summarises how well the participants scored the building or design against the questions within that dimension.

C **The Section Scores graph** is a spider diagram scaled between 0 and 6. This graph displays the average of all the selected participants' answers to each section. The higher the score (the further out) the better the participants felt the design or building was achieving that characteristic. The graph provides an idea of how well a building or design is thought to have performed in each section. This graph can be set out to show two sets of data (a main group and a sub-group). It can also be used to see the different scoring of groups such as designers vs. users, and to highlight where there are significant differences in views.

D **The Target line graph** is generated by comparing the results achieved by the design or building in the DQI Assessment tool with the active Briefing Record tags – Required, Desired, Inspired, and Not Applicable. This is done using an algorithm which weights the results depending upon the tags; it will not weigh any statements that are tagged Not Applicable. The target line is the maximum the design or building can achieve. The green

bars display the results from the assessment and highlight where a building or a design is doing very well and meeting (or nearly meeting) the target line, so that participants can see that the building is not only achieving what is Required, but is also excelling in the Desired and Inspired categories to help deliver a building of distinction.

In summary, the DQI for Health may have replaced AEDET but without the vital essential link to the evidence base of health/clinical outcomes or scientific studies, aspects which give ASPECT/AEDET Evolution 2005 a source of authority, especially when challenged by clinicians. An important loss is also the rationale provided by ASPECT representing the core business of the NHS. Instead of self-assurance, DQI for Health transfers responsibility to the professionals for a fee. The introduction of the fees as a mechanism to fund the operation of the DQI process is a minimum cost which has to be met for the design quality improvement of the health care project. It is a minimum because there are other costs in terms of senior members of staff setting aside approximately five days of involvement in the stakeholder engagement events. As with BREEAM, with DQI for Health, research is needed to find out whether buildings labelled as exhibiting 'excellent' or 'good' design quality will also necessarily lead to better outcomes.

## IDEAs tool/Gallery

Yet another important evidence-based tool in the UK design quality improvement agenda is IDEAs (**I**nspiring **D**esign **E**xcellence and **A**chievements), a visually-based design tool that aids Trusts and all their architects and design consultants to develop their briefs and design ideas. Design Champions in NHS Trusts may find IDEAs useful and helpful in promoting design within their organisations. IDEAs is intended to help create aspirations towards good design from the beginning of the process, and direct attention towards qualities and features that might otherwise be lost in highly technical health care environments.

### IDEAs

The IDEAs tool treats both interior and exterior spaces as 'Places' where a number of activities commonly occur or take place. The tool works by understanding these activities and the functional and emotional needs or requirements of the people involved. IDEAs can either be used as a standalone tool within a workshop context or as a web-enabled integrated tool by individuals to generate a brief or programme. The IDEAs tool may also be used in conjunction with other design tools such as the evaluation tools AEDET Evolution and ASPECT.

To help us understand health care places, the IDEAs tool is displayed using two main windows on a screen: 1. Challenges and Considerations; and 2. Precedents. The Challenges and Considerations pane contains: a) Challenges – aspects about what people need to do, i.e. 'their activities'; and b) Considerations – which concern what the design should do to respond to these needs or demands (these are also mapped onto the ASPECT/AEDET Evolution evaluation tools). The Precedents pane is about what others have done, i.e. existing solutions to similar problems. Precedents are therefore represented by digital images (photographs, plans, sections, elevations, animations etc.) of existing design solutions.

The IDEAs tool therefore entails three basic types of information: pictograms, photographs and accompanying explanatory text. *Pictograms* are abstract and unrealistic illustrations, free of architectural style, which are not intended to be copied because they do not represent design solutions but act as a kind of visual index. *Accompanying explanatory text* details the range of activities and associated design considerations most commonly found or accommodated in each place. *Precedents* are digital images (photographs, plans, sections, elevations etc.) of both existing and proposed design solutions.

The Precedent pane links to the Gallery, previously referred to as the NHS Estates Design Portfolio of photographs of built health care schemes and not directly accessible to users of these tools. This link ensures that when photographs and images are uploaded to the Gallery they can be shown or indicated in the IDEAs tool as examples of better design practice. Similarly the images in IDEAs can be moved back to the Gallery and replaced by new ones.

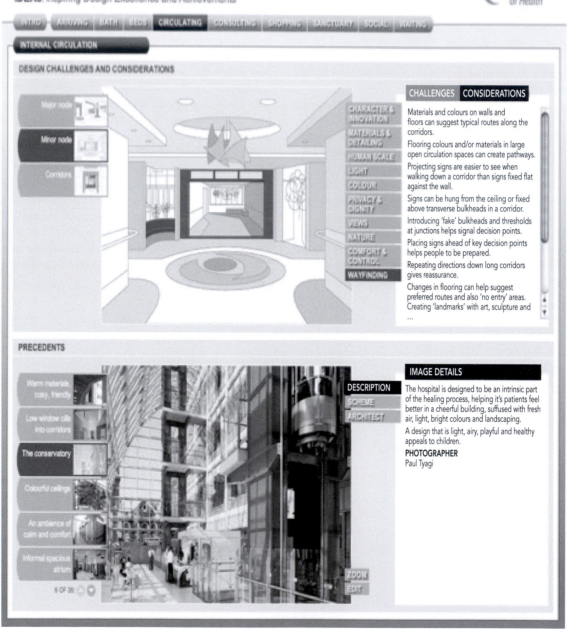

**IDEAs**: Inspiring Design Excellence and Achievements

INTRO | ARRIVING | BATH | BEDS | **CIRCULATING** | CONSULTING | SHOPPING | SANCTUARY | SOCIAL | WAITING

**INTERNAL CIRCULATION**

**DESIGN CHALLENGES AND CONSIDERATIONS**

CHARACTER & INNOVATION
MATERIALS & DETAILING
HUMAN SCALE
LIGHT
COLOUR
PRIVACY & DIGNITY
VIEWS
NATURE
COMFORT & CONTROL
WAYFINDING

Major node
Minor node
Corridors

**CHALLENGES  CONSIDERATIONS**

Materials and colours on walls and floors can suggest typical routes along the corridors.

Flooring colours and/or materials in large open circulation spaces can create pathways.

Projecting signs are easier to see when walking down a corridor than signs fixed flat against the wall.

Signs can be hung from the ceiling or fixed above transverse bulkheads in a corridor.

Introducing 'fake' bulkheads and thresholds at junctions helps signal decision points.

Placing signs ahead of key decision points helps people to be prepared.

Repeating directions down long corridors gives reassurance.

Changes in flooring can help suggest preferred routes and also 'no entry' areas. Creating 'landmarks' with art, sculpture and ...

**PRECEDENTS**

Warm materials, cosy, friendly
Low window cills into corridors
The conservatory
Colourful ceilings
An ambience of calm and comfort
Informal spacious atrium

6 OF 36

**DESCRIPTION**
SCHEME
ARCHITECT

**IMAGE DETAILS**

The hospital is designed to be an intrinsic part of the healing process, helping it's patients feel better in a cheerful building, suffused with fresh air, light, bright colours and landscaping.

A design that is light, airy, playful and healthy appeals to children.

**PHOTOGRAPHER**
Paul Tyagi

ZOOM
EDIT

**3.19** IDEAs uses two window panes on a screen, 1. CHALLENGES & CONSIDERATIONS and 2. PRECEDENTS, to help us understand the concept of a 'place' where human activities commonly occur or are accommodated

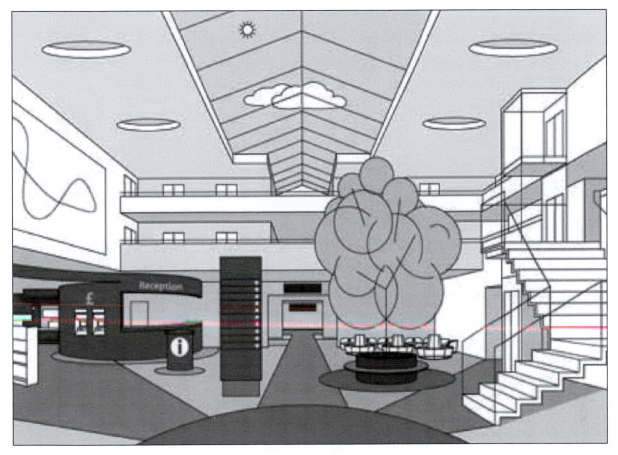

**3.20 Pictograms are abstract and not real illustrations, free of architectural style to indicate the design considerations of a place: example of 'Arrival Inside'**

The project-based NHS Estates Design Portfolio of images has several limitations, notably what has been called the 'Green Door' phenomenon, whereby a user remarks upon considering a particular image that they do not like the green-coloured door. The green door in the scene is of course irrelevant, and indeed it might even have gone unnoticed by others. The user may actually be looking at the wrong situation altogether. Therefore there is no indication or mechanism within the Design Portfolio to indicate which features of the image are being considered or referred to. The IDEAs tool/Gallery overcomes such limitations and inadequacies of the Design Portfolio by indicating the design features which users need to consider.

3.21 Precedents are digital images of existing completed designs uploaded from gallery, previously referred to as NHS design portfolio of photographs of built health care schemes (photo credit Gareth Gardner)

Table 3.7 Accompanying explanatory text details the range of activities and associated design considerations most commonly found or accommodated in a 'place'

---

**CHALLENGES – OVERVIEW: ARRIVING**

**These places signal the point of arrival outside and therefore point of entry into buildings.**

These kinds of places occur not only as you enter the site but also on reaching significant zones or buildings. They should be instantly recognisable and memorable and play a key role in enabling people to build their mental maps of the site as a whole.

**DESIGN CONSIDERATIONS – LIGHT**

Entrance ways should be well lit so as to be easily identified as a destination. Lighting the entrance creates a cheerful and welcoming impression. Well lit entrances feel safe and secure.

**DAYLIGHT:** Maintaining daylight is important to avoid a gloomy or dark approach to the building.

**ARTIFICIAL LIGHTING:** Illumination in darkness and winter months is crucial to helping people find their way to the entrance. Overhead (street) lighting is important but lower level lighting or lighting in the ground is also beneficial and less 'stark' than overhead lighting which causes deep shadows. 'Decorative' lighting in plants, trees, landscaping or sculpture further enhances feelings of confidence, security, safety, welcome and modernity. Any corners, nooks and crannies in and around the entrance should be lit to increase feelings of safety and security.

# The development of IDEAs tool/Gallery by University of Sheffield, School of Architecture Health Care Research Group in collaboration with Parallel and Brandplace

A review of architectural design and practice previously indicated a lack of appropriate tools to aid the process of generating and evaluating design solutions (Lawson and Phiri 2004). Whereas AEDET Evolution/ASPECT were developed to meet the need for evaluation design tools, especially during the NHS Design Reviews under PFI, ProCure21 and Lift programmes, the IDEAs tool/Gallery were developed as generative solution-based tools or mechanisms to complement these problem-based analytical tools, which have less to do with arriving at solutions and more to do with assessing or evaluating designs including completed hospital schemes.

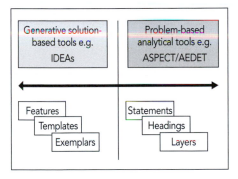

**3.22 Generative solution-based (e.g. IDEAs + Gallery) vs. problem-based analytical tools (e.g. ASPECT and AEDET Evolution)**

Whereas the problem-based analytical tools (AEDET Evolution and ASPECT) are characterised by a hierarchical structure comprising of layers (scoring, guidance and evidence), ten headings and constituent statements, which lends itself to consideration as a checklist, the generative solution-based tools (IDEAs tool/Gallery) have a hierarchical structure comprising of exemplars, templates and features, which cannot be seen as a checklist and neither can they be used as a basis to manage projects. The IDEAs tool/Gallery permits building up design solutions and their exploration.

Rather than referring to individual spaces or rooms, the IDEAs tool/Gallery identifies and defines a set of common

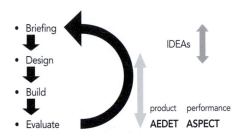

**3.23 Generative solution-based (e.g. IDEAs + Gallery) vs. problem-based analytical tools (e.g. ASPECT and AEDET Evolution) within the Briefing–Design–Build–Evaluate Cycle**

generic places indicating activities – i.e. arriving/entering, receiving, waiting, circulating, refreshment and relaxation, bed, consulting/examining, performing and bathing places, including special situations such as courtyards, communing places and others. The IDEAs tool/Gallery definitely does not address the specifics of, for example, a paediatric bedroom or a mental health bedroom and so on, but refers more to Alexander et al.'s (1977) 'Pattern Language'.

**Table 3.8 IDEAs identifies and defines a set of common generic 'places' graphically represented by icons**

| Generic Activities (usefully identified by Icons) |
|---|
| • Ablutions |
| • Eat & Drink |
| • Exam & Treatment |
| • Find |
| • Move |
| • Rest |
| • Shop |
| • Socialise |
| • Undress |
| • Wait |

Whereas AEDET Evolution has three main areas – impact, build quality and functionality – split into ten sections each of which yields a score, the IDEAs tool/Gallery has four elements which also relate to the same three main areas. The ten sections in AEDET Evolution summarise how well a health care facility complies with evidence from scientific studies and better practice. Each section has several statements which taken together build up a score for that

**3.24** IDEAs tool/Gallery identifies and defines a set of common generic 'places' graphically represented by icons

**Table 3.9 IDEAs identifies and defines a set of common generic 'places' graphically represented by icons (water marks)**

**ABLUTIONS**

PUBLIC FACILITIES & BATHROOM CHALLENGES

- A major challenge is not to allow the sanitary equipment to dominate and turn it into a purely functionalist place.
- Being able to choose between a bath and shower may be important to some people particularly after more than a couple of days.

**EAT & DRINK**

CAFE, VENDING ETC. CHALLENGES

- Patients and carers may want to have refreshment partly for reasons of comfort and partly to pass time. For staff there may be no convenient or affordable alternatives.

**EXAM & TREATMENT**

CONSULTING CHALLENGES

- At all times patients should feel they have both visual and acoustic privacy. Distraction may be needed in stressful situations but a simple calm and understandable place is highly desirable.
- Examination may range from discussion through to simple tests such as taking a pulse or listening to breathing on to more invasive procedures. Patients are more likely to find the transition less stressful if it can all be done in the same setting. Some procedures may require the patient to lie down.
- Patients may commonly be accompanied by a parent, partner or carer and want to discuss the situation with them.
- It is highly likely that the consultant will need to write and the patient may need to make a note, perhaps in a diary. The consultant is very likely to interact with a computer and may want to show the screen to the patient at times. It may feel discourteous to patients if the consultant has to turn away to work at a computer.

**FIND**

MAJOR & MINOR CIRCULATION NODES, CORRIDORS CHALLENGES

- People need to be able to find their way around by building their own mental map. They need understandable routes connected to internal landmarks with views out where possible. They need to feel each place has its own character. They need the way out to be obvious and to know whether they are in public or private places.
- Major nodes forming intersections of routes should be recognisably different from more minor nodes.

ARRIVING CHALLENGES

- Having arrived, the next need is to be able to see clearly any onward routes and points of information.

BATH CHALLENGES

- Toilet and washroom facilities should always be located so that it is clear where they are but the actual door should not be in full view of many other people.

BEDROOM CHALLENGES

- Patients and staff need to feel they are able to arrange for a range of lighting effects to avoid glare, offer bright light for reading, dim lights for night time rest and so on. Difficult though this may be, each patient needs to feel that they are able to control levels of comfort for themselves to be comfortable.

WAITING CHALLENGES

- Patients and visitors need to know automatically where to get information and where to find members of staff. Strangers need to see easily where there are onward routes and facilities.

section. Section C: Staff and Patient Environment within AEDET Evolution can also be handled in a more thorough way by another tool called ASPECT, in the same way that the NEAT tool or BREEAM Healthcare 2008 handles sustainability issues in particular, ensuring that a design meets all the NHS targets on energy conservation. ASPECT not only handles Section C in a thorough way but also allows more precision, thereby producing more reliable scores.

**Table 3.10 IDEAs identifies and defines a set of common generic 'places' described by explanatory accompanying text**

---

**MOVE**

ARRIVING CHALLENGES
- Entrances to buildings should be made obvious. The point of arrival should be distinct and memorable and easily recognised. It should suggest stopping and pausing rather than moving.
- People need time to pause, adjust themselves and gather their thoughts, without being in the way of others. They may need to use facilities either on the way in or out. Toilets in particular should be clearly and yet discretely located near to arrival points.

PUBLIC FACILITIES & BATHROOM CHALLENGES
- En-suite facilities in hospitals should provide short direct routes with something to hold onto all the way. (Automatic lighting of the route and arrival point linked to bed sensors can be a useful device in residential accommodation).

BEDROOM CHALLENGES
- Either patients are in shared accommodation or, if mobile, can easily find a place in which to socialise. If patients are with others they need to know that there is somewhere they can go to be alone.

CIRCULATING CHALLENGES
- A strong sense of direction is needed to ensure that strangers know which way they are going along a route. Patients and carers may move at different speeds to staff and take pauses during movement. A sense of hierarchy of routes is helpful as are views of landmarks. A sense of dignity is needed particularly for patients who are being moved and may not be feeling well or be fully clothed.

SHOPPING CHALLENGES
- A safe journey with a purpose is often a valuable asset to hospital in-patients. A destination where there may be some shops to look round, possible performances, people to meet, refreshment and art to look at.

SANCTUARY CHALLENGES
- A spiritual place does not have to be a single location. A walk could be therapeutic and diverting.

WAITING CHALLENGES
- People should be encouraged to pause and gather themselves without feeling they are in the way of others.

**REST**

BEDROOM CHALLENGES
- Patients in health care settings need to feel some sense of location and to feel private, and to be able to express their identity and to gain stimulation from both calming and interesting views.

CIRCULATING CHALLENGES
- Patients in particular may need to pause along a route and people often enjoy sitting just off a route watching others go by.

SHOPPING CHALLENGES
- People are likely to want small intimate places to sit that offer views of other activity and nature. Being able to choose to be outdoors when the weather permits or see outdoors is highly desirable. Anxiety however, may be increased if they feel cut off from sources of information about their appointment or progress of their case.
- Staff may want to feel less 'on duty' over meal breaks and to be able to share thoughts out of earshot.

**REST**

SANCTUARY CHALLENGES
- Patients and relatives/carers may need some sort of sanctuary. They may have had a shock or bad news and may want a place to be quiet and private before facing the world. Long stay patients may want a place to sit quietly away from their bed and yet in private contemplation.
- In large complex buildings, creating many simple small pausing places can be as important as one big purpose-made 'pastoral' place.

WAITING CHALLENGES
- Waiting is not a desirable activity. It should, as far as possible, be done in places that offer comfort, calmness away from noisy sources and distraction with easy access to facilities and information.

IDEAs: Inspiring Design Excellence and Achievements

DH Department of Health

INTRO | ARRIVING | BATH | BEDS | CIRCULATING | **CONSULTING** | SHOPPING | SANCTUARY | SOCIAL | WAITING

CONSULT, EXAMINE AND TREATMENT

FEEDBACK | PRINT

DESIGN CHALLENGES AND CONSIDERATIONS

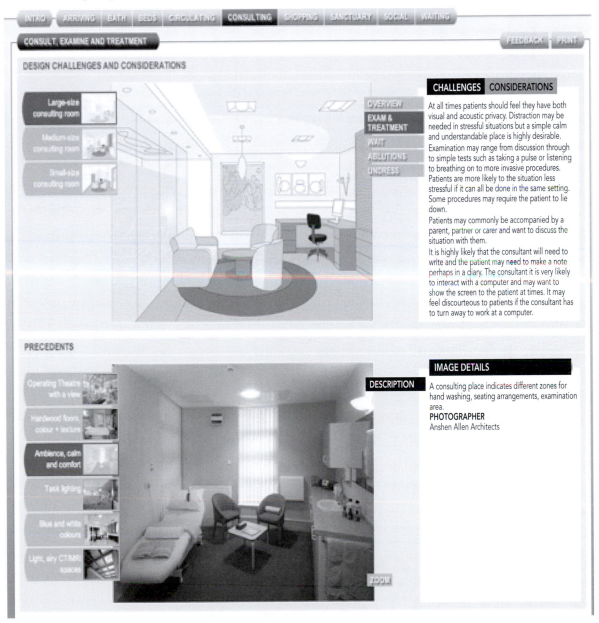

**CHALLENGES** CONSIDERATIONS

At all times patients should feel they have both visual and acoustic privacy. Distraction may be needed in stressful situations but a simple calm and understandable place is highly desirable. Examination may range from discussion through to simple tests such as taking a pulse or listening to breathing on to more invasive procedures. Patients are more likely to the situation less stressful if it can all be done in the same setting. Some procedures may require the patient to lie down.

Patients may commonly be accompanied by a parent, partner or carer and want to discuss the situation with them.

It is highly likely that the consultant will need to write and the patient may need to make a note perhaps in a diary. The consultant it is very likely to interact with a computer and may want to show the screen to the patient at times. It may feel discourteous to patients if the consultant has to turn away to work at a computer.

PRECEDENTS

**DESCRIPTION**

**IMAGE DETAILS**

A consulting place indicates different zones for hand washing, seating arrangements, examination area.

**PHOTOGRAPHER**
Anshen Allen Architects

3.25 IDEAs uses two window panes on a screen, 1. CHALLENGES & CONSIDERATIONS and 2. PRECEDENTS, to help us understand the concept of a 'place' where human activities commonly occur or are accommodated

**Table 3.11 IDEAs identifies and defines a set of common generic 'places' described by explanatory accompanying text**

**SHOP**

RETAIL, REFRESHMENT & BANKING CHALLENGES

• The location and the pattern of use of health care buildings means that daily essentials may be needed by staff and patients alike. Visitors may want to buy gifts. Out-patients may have time to kill and want to wander and browse. Retail can be practically essential but also offer positive distraction.

**SOCIALISE**

RETAIL, REFRESHMENT & BANKING CHALLENGES

• People may want to be 'private in public' more than normal here. The range of emotional states of people in a health care environment is likely to be far greater than in normal urban settings. For example, a group of staff joking about their social life are more likely to cause distress when right next to a patient waiting for an investigation about a serious illness.

SANCTUARY CHALLENGES

• Patients may feel the need to talk problems over with others. A suitable place near where skilled but informally arranged counselling can take place is desirable.

SOCIALISING & MEETING CHALLENGES

• For patients who are in hospital for long periods, a place to socialise is very valuable. Being able to go to a place where you are likely to meet others accidentally is helpful. Such places work best when they already have another reason for being there; this might be a view, something to watch or listen to, or some refreshment are all possibilities.

• Socialising is often done in an unselfconscious way so spaces that appear to provide for this in a very deliberate or functional way often fail miserably.

• Social places in long-term stay or residential environments may well become occupied territorially. People may come to feel that certain seats belong to them.

WAITING CHALLENGES

• People do not want to be forced into close proximity with strangers but may wish to share a small area with a friend or relative.

**UNDRESS**

BATHROOM CHALLENGES

• The dignity of dressing and undressing and adjusting clothing is vitally important to achieve here. Privacy is most important. Easy access to places to hang/store clothes is vital for those not moving freely. Having to call for assistance for basic activities is often distressing.

• When you are unwell and may not be 'functioning' normally, feeling that others may see or overhear you is an added stressor.

CONSULTING CHALLENGES

• Patients may need to remove some clothing. In order to retain dignity they need screening from view while dressing or undressing and have somewhere to put their clothes and belongings.

**WAIT**

ARRIVING CHALLENGES

• People may need to wait to meet up with others in an obvious location near, and yet aside from, the main point of arrival and departure.

BEDS CHALLENGES

• Patients in a health care building need to feel that they are able to control their privacy and their interaction with others. Patients need to feel private or that they can talk to a relative, doctor, nurse or therapist confident of not being overheard.

CONSULTING CHALLENGES

• Patients may need to wait for short periods depending on the pattern of the care model being used. In more demanding and specialised treatment situations a recovery period may be required.

WAITING CHALLENGES

• People need places to wait that enable them to be seen by others they are trying to meet. Where patients may be waiting for long periods, especially if not in great pain or discomfort, the patients need to feel they have the possibility of watching life going on or looking at nature.

# Evidence base for the IDEAs tool/ Gallery

The integrative nature of design shows how single features in design often solve many problems. So, for example, a feature such as a window offers a view, poses problems of visual privacy and dignity, creates problems of solar gain and heat loss and acoustic annoyance, and so on. This means that the headings under ASPECT and AEDET Evolution that have most to say about place are more likely to get pointed to. One problem is that some headings simply do not lend themselves to being helpful in this regard. Take, for example, 'Urban and Social Integration'. Since many of these issues deal with the building in context, we would have to stop dealing with generic places and start dealing with contextual design to

major on this, and that is really quite another area. Of course, it could be done, but it is not the main objective of IDEAs tool/Gallery at this moment. Similarly, the 'Engineering' heading is unlikely to be very helpful here, and so on.

It is also the case that some statements in AEDET Evolution simply do not offer the possibility of linking in a helpfully meaningful way to any single-place diagram. Take, for example, 'Character and Innovation 5: The building is likely to influence future healthcare designs'. This could be applied to every place, or to no places. Either way, it will not help a designer at an early stage as it is a purely analytical statement. We have not yet analysed the whole of AEDET Evolution to see how common this is. However, it is not a phenomenon that is linked exclusively with the headings structure itself.

3.26 IDEAs website introductory page during Phase 1 development (NB website address in the diagram is no longer active)

Take, for example, the AEDET Evolution heading 'Form and Materials 3: Entrances are obvious and logically positioned in relation to likely points of arrival on site'. This could well end up being pointed to in a diagram on arriving/entering places. However, 'Form and Materials 4: The external materials and detailing appear to be of high quality' is unlikely to be at all helpful in any place-based diagram. We still have to do more work to see how this actually turns out.

The IDEAs tool/Gallery is a briefing design tool to aid Trusts and all their consultants in determining and managing their design requirements, from inception and statement of need during the pre-project, project and post-project stages. It forms the primary tool at the pre-project stage to generate design solutions, enabling Trusts to be more aspirational and make tremendous advancements in their designs. Design champions in Trusts may find the IDEAs tool/Gallery are very useful, especially in promoting the role of design within the Trusts and leading the debate on design as an important component of hospital and health care planning.

In general, the main objectives for the IDEAs tool/Gallery are therefore to raise aspirations, increase understanding of the relationship between building design and service delivery, and allow clients to know what to ask for, what is being offered and when. Crucially, design champions will benefit by having a clearer set of visually-based materials explaining good design in terms of health care buildings and enabling them to become more aspirational within their Trusts.

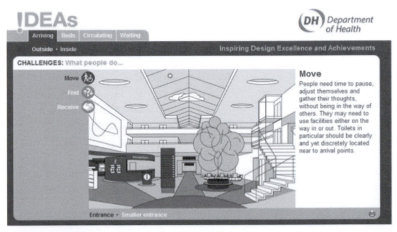

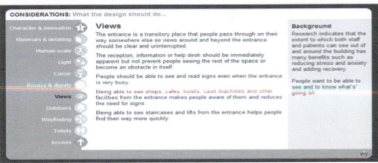

**3.27 IDEAs website content during Phase 1 development**

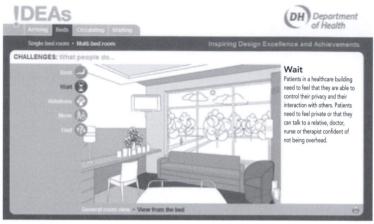

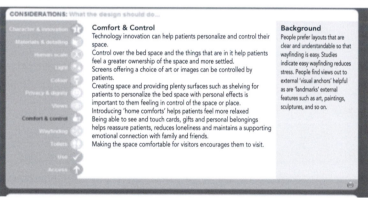

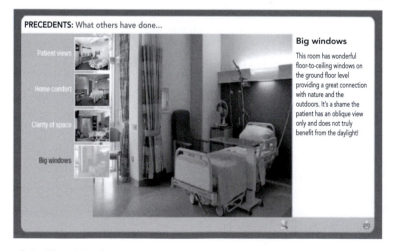

**3.28 IDEAs website content during Phase 1 development**

**3.29 IDEAs website content during Phase 1 development**

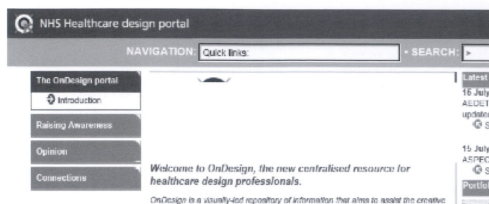

# NHS Healthcare design portal

NAVIGATION: Quick links:          • SEARCH:          GO

**NHS Estates**

The OnDesign portal
- Introduction

Raising Awareness

Opinion

Connections

*Welcome to OnDesign, the new centralised resource for healthcare design professionals.*

*OnDesign is a visually-led repository of information that aims to assist the creative and functional design process in healthcare design, and to encourage networking and the sharing of knowledge and best practice between healthcare design schemes.*

*OnDesign caters for all stages of a scheme from conception to post-project evaluation; it covers all building types from the smallest GP surgery to major acute hospitals; and includes all individuals associated with a scheme, from architects through to patient user group.*

King's Mill Hospital
Sherwood Forest Hospitals NHS Trust selects its preferred bidder for the £166m site reconfiguration.

 Bill Murray

 Jason Syers

The Chairman of NHS Estates gives his vision of future design for healthcare.

The head of regeneration at The Prince's Foundation gives an overview of the Enquiry by Design process.

Breast Care at Barts
New centre serving 80,000 London women opens its doors three weeks ahead of schedule.

Design competition brings in 'excellent' entries
Lewisham PCT's new centre for young people's health and social care services is due to open its doors in 2006. The PCT held a design competition, with the aid of CABE, to invite high-quality schemes

**Latest updates**
15 July '06:
AEDET Evolution toolkit updated
See details

15 July '06:
ASPECT toolkit updated
See details

**Portfolio gallery**

Bristol Children's Hospital
See larger image

**AEDET Evolution**
Latest version of the Design Evaluation toolkit now available for download.
See details

**ASPECT**
New version of the toolkit now available for download.
See details

**Opinion**
Susan Francis talks about the role good building design plays in healthcare design.
View interview

**The next ten years**

Design professionals talk about what the upcoming decade will bring in healthcare design.
View interviews

3.30 IDEAs + Gallery vs. ASPECT and AEDET Evolution within the NHS Estates OnDesign website, a centralised resource for health care design professionals

## Further future development of IDEAs tool/Gallery

The tool could benefit from updating of the evidence base and moving access from the Department of Health website http://www.ideas.dh.gov.uk/IDEAs, which is at risk of being discontinued, to the Space for Health website at http://www.spaceforhealth.nhs.uk/.[1] This will allow further dissemination and sharing of design information. Such a concept might well lead to major cultural changes in the approach to project investment decision-making in the industry. Overall, NHS Estates, Trusts and other health care providers, patients, academia and the construction industry will be the main beneficiaries of this further development. Specifically, the NHS will benefit from identifying good practice and facilitating lessons learnt from completed health care construction projects. This will improve the productivity and efficiency of material selection and maintenance decisions. Furthermore, it will help the NHS to influence the uncertain relationships between clinicians and designers, thereby increasing the transparency of the decision-making process. When they are challenged by clinicians, designers will have a credible source of authority to underpin their designs. The commissioner and regulator will have a rigorous basis for guidance.

Patients will benefit from positive health outcomes, e.g. a reduced risk of falls and reduced severity of injuries should falls occur, improved recovery rates, and so on. The proper choice of finishes will help to increase the resistance to the spread of infection through the use of antimicrobial agents, fungicides etc. Furthermore, research has shown that good design can have implications for psychological well-being and patient satisfaction. It is well-documented that hospital buildings are too often dangerous and stressful places for patients, families, and staff. The lesson for all health care organisations is clearly either to provide a physical environment that is welcoming to patients, which measurably improves their quality of life and which supports families and employees, or to suffer the financial consequences in an increasingly competitive and demanding economic environment.

Academia will benefit by having access to data on completed schemes of new builds, refurbishments and modernisations of NHS premises for analysis. Academics will become aware of recent technological innovations aligned to the latest research.

The health care sector will also benefit from further development of the IDEAs tool as a hierarchical structure comprising exemplars, templates and features, all of which permit the creation of better health care design solutions and allow for their exploration. Templates are useful because of the notion of developing standardised designs which avoid the need for designers and their clients to start from scratch each time. Standardised designs in turn lead to efficiencies in the delivery of health care facilities, while also facilitating speedy deployment and adaption where necessary to the exigencies of available sites.

In summary, the IDEAs tool/Gallery aids the generation of design briefs, proposals and schemes. Conceived and developed by the University of Sheffield, Parallel and Brandplace as a way of utilising the latest research evidence, the IDEAs tool/Gallery starts the design of health care places with people – patients, staff and visitors – and responds to the emotional and functional requirements of health care delivery. The IDEAs tool/Gallery deals with activities rather than individual spaces or rooms. Examples of activities that occur in health care places include: arrival, bathing, bed rest, circulating, consulting, shopping, sanctuary, socialising and waiting. The IDEAs tool/Gallery can be used either as a standalone tool within a workshop context, or as a web-enabled integrated tool by individuals.

The IDEAs tool/Gallery therefore not only closes the loop between the NHS Estates Design Portfolio, the DesignReview Panel and the ASPECT and AEDET Evolution tools, but may also increase the understanding between commissioning, operating and user clients and designers (architects, engineers and others), thereby facilitating knowledge transfer, lessons learnt from project-to-project and learning from the experience of others.

---

1 Space for Health – Information Healthcare Premises Professionals that draws together the official health care premises technical guidance published by the Department of Health; Northern Ireland's Department of Health, Social Services and Public Safety, Health Facilities Scotland and Welsh Estates.

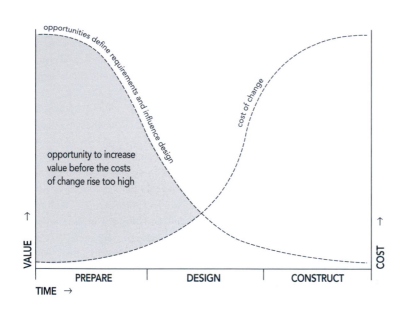

opportunities define requirements and influence design

cost of change

opportunity to increase
value before the costs
of change rise too high

VALUE ↑

COST ↑

PREPARE    DESIGN    CONSTRUCT

TIME →

3.31 Generative solution-based (e.g. IDEAs +
Gallery) vs. problem-based analytical tools (e.g.
ASPECT and AEDET Evolution) offer opportunities
to increase value before cost changes rise too high
during the Briefing–Design–Build–Evaluate Cycle

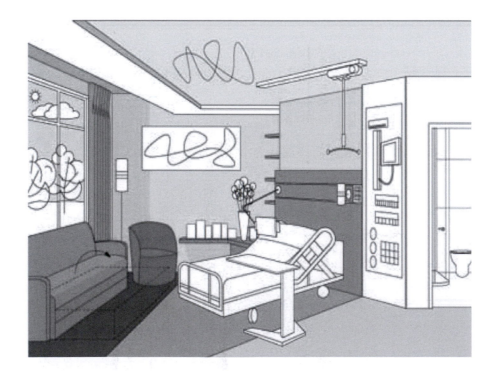

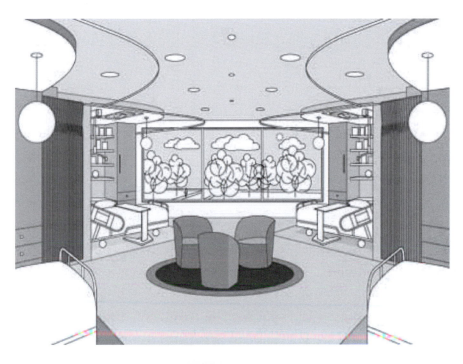

3.32 Examples of pictograms: 'single bed space, multi-bed place, staff area and waiting place'

3.33  Example of pictograms: 'consulting place'

3.34 Examples of precedents switched on from gallery

# NHS ProCure 21 DART (Design and Risk Tool)

Improving facilities is a priority for health care providers, but many have found that traditional procurement methods often result in delayed completions, over-spends and adversarial or confrontational relationships or arrangements which lead to major financial, operational and planning difficulties resulting in costly litigation. To overcome this, the UK Department of Health offers the ProCure 21 procurement route, involving a partnership between the public and private sectors, as an alternative to the traditional route of competitive tendering to aid the NHS to spend as efficiently as possible in terms of capital funding for new builds, refurbishments, repairs and reconfigurations. Developed in conjunction with Currie and Brown and launched in 2000, a key goal of ProCure21 is to reduce risk, and the DART tool is provided on all schemes to aid Trusts and principal supply chain partners in managing design and risk together. DART proactively manages risk by bringing the whole project team together in a focus group or workshop setting to identify, mitigate and cost both client and contractor risk.

## NHS ProCure 21 DART

NHS ProCure21 DART aids the identification of the client and contractor risks of a project and apportions them correctly while managing them out as much as possible. Where the NHS has largely disregarded risk or simply off-loaded or pushed it onto the contractor, thereby paying a high price through increased costs, a strategic approach to managing risk can lead to better outcomes such as lower prices. Designed specifically for the NHS, DART looks at both the Trust and construction risk and ensures a Trust is aware of its risks, helping it to make informed decisions with or without the help of a risk expert.

Risk management is seldom carried out in a methodical or structured way and very rarely at the beginning of projects, so that introducing a method of reviewing all aspects of risk when the multi-disciplinary team is initially assembled offers opportunities for health care projects to achieve true value for money, since they are better able to proactively manage for costly unquantified or unforeseen risk.

## Implementing DART within the project process

DART aligns with AEDET Evolution headings to produce a structured risk evaluation. Risks are identified and prioritised by all parties and allocated to those best able to manage them. These risks are costed and used to formulate the guaranteed maximum price as well as the client's own risk bucket.

To make DART work effectively, all the key people involved in the project – project leads from client and contractor, suppliers and clinicians – get together in a workshop to consider a scheme's design and the risks associated with it.

In practice, implementing the DART process involves adopting a three-dimensional strategy comprising of a first dimension (Value Management using the AEDET Evolution Toolkit), a second dimension (Risk Management using the QRA Toolkit) and a third dimension (using the DART Show Stopper Risk Toolkit). Superimposing the Dartboard show stopper risks onto AEDET Evolution's graphical representation indicates the potential effect of risks on maintaining an acceptable graphical output. Hence the overall design quality or risk profile of a building project is maintained at all stages during the project's life cycle.

## DART's evidence base and evidence-based process

The workshop setting ensures all parties are consulted and encourages project stakeholders to get on board and buy into the project or have their voices heard. DART follows a seven-step process, the first of which is building a 'rich picture', which illustrates how the various elements of the project fit and work together. By identifying the human elements of the scheme, such as communication between stakeholders, attitudes towards the scheme and potential areas of conflict, DART increases understanding of the scheme and how it might be delivered to the mutual benefit of the whole project team.

Identification of the objectives of the project and an evaluation of the design are made using AEDET Evolution. Statements on the performance of the design are produced, which participants in the workshop score by indicating the

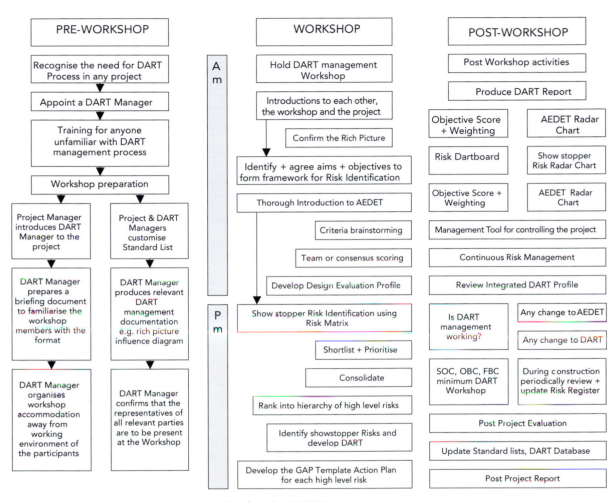

**PRE-WORKSHOP**

Recognise the need for DART Process in any project

Appoint a DART Manager

Training for anyone unfamiliar with DART management process

Workshop preparation

Project Manager introduces DART Manager to the project

Project & DART Managers customise Standard List

DART Manager prepares a briefing document to familiarise the workshop members with the format

DART Manager produces relevant DART management documentation e.g. rich picture influence diagram

DART Manager organises workshop accommodation away from working environment of the participants

DART Manager confirms that the representatives of all relevant parties are to be present at the Workshop

**WORKSHOP**

Am

Hold DART management Workshop

Introductions to each other, the workshop and the project

Confirm the Rich Picture

Identify + agree aims + objectives to form framework for Risk Identification

Thorough Introduction to AEDET

Criteria brainstorming

Team or consensus scoring

Develop Design Evaluation Profile

Pm

Show stopper Risk Identification using Risk Matrix

Shortlist + Prioritise

Consolidate

Rank into hierarchy of high level risks

Identify showstopper Risks and develop DART

Develop the GAP Template Action Plan for each high level risk

**POST-WORKSHOP**

Post Workshop activities

Produce DART Report

Objective Score + Weighting

AEDET Radar Chart

Risk Dartboard

Show stopper Risk Radar Chart

Objective Score + Weighting

AEDET Radar Chart

Management Tool for controlling the project

Continuous Risk Management

Review Integrated DART Profile

Is DART management working?

Any change to AEDET

Any change to DART

SOC, OBC, FBC minimum DART Workshop

During construction periodically review + update Risk Register

Post Project Evaluation

Update Standard lists, DART Database

Post Project Report

**3.35 DART workshop processes (source: Peter Woolliscroft ProCure21 2006)**

Table 3.12 DART – Extract from the risk register (Show stopper risks ≥ 10). Risk buckets are aligned with AEDET Evolution headings

| | Risk buckets | Risk ID | Risk description | Risk Assessment |
|---|---|---|---|---|
| AEDET Evolution Headings | Engineering | 9.6 | Failure by principal supply chain partners to co-ordinate M&E services with the building structure. | 12 |
| | Construction | 10.22 | The non-realisation of VAT reclaim and introduction of new statutory costs. | 11 |
| | Engineering | 9.5 | Failure by principal supply chain partner to co-ordinate M&E installations. | 11 |
| | Construction | 10.21 | The impact of changes in the rate of VAT. | 10 |
| | Construction | 10.71 | The compliance with any new Mandatory Standards. | 10 |
| | Engineering | 9.7 | Impact of any additional works in refurbished areas. | 10 |
| | Engineering | 9.3 | The continuing development of design by the principal supply chain partners. | 10 |
| | Character and innovation | 4.2 | The change in design required due to external influences specific to the NHS. | 10 |

extent to which they agree or disagree with each of the statements. The 100 statements in AEDET Evolution represent 100 risks in DART. The project workshop brainstorms those risks, adding and deleting any that may or may not be appropriate, and scores the likelihood of the risks occurring and their potential impacts to produce a risk register.

Major risks can be identified as show stoppers, which are plotted onto the AEDET profile comprising the score. The result in terms of the AEDET score is shown using specially developed diagrams. All the show stopper and other high-level risks are given a risk champion, who manages that risk throughout the life of the project. "DART is an evolving process" (cost consultant, Department of Health). "It requires constant review, but the results can be fantastic. If you can manage out your risks and reduce the cost of your scheme, any savings that you make can be put back in, increasing the quality of your building and your value for money."

The ProCure21 route offers advantages over the traditional route of competitive tendering. These include: faster procurement; access to the ProCure21 framework of principal supply chain partners; full support from the ProCure21 team at scheme and framework level; use of ProCure21 tools such as DART and mini-DART; free VAT recovery service; open-book accounting and audit process; and membership of the ProCure21 club.

DART aids NHS ProCure21 in addressing how contracts should lead to mutual benefit for all parties, and how they should be based on a target and whole life-cost approach by promoting the implementation of working collaboratively based on the adoption of a coherent cost management approach and informed by the principles of target costings. The National Audit Office (NAO) Report entitled 'Improving Public Services Through Better Construction' (14 March 2005) recommended the use of contracts that support collaborative working for the client and the entire integrated team. The Report added: "The Engineering and Construction Contract is one example of a contract written in plain English that embeds the principles of good project management in its procedures, and promotes role clarity. It encourages early issue resolution, and contains options as to the choice of procurement route. It is non-adversarial in its tone and spirit, and as such, many clients have adopted it for use in long-term collaborative working arrangements. The ProCure21 Minor Works method of procurement uses the Engineering and Construction Contract and the Trust's Estates Department has found it to be a very useful and effective project management tool whilst working on the delivery of the MRI, Operating Theatre, Endoscopy and HYMS schemes that were procured using the ProCure 21 major capital works system."

In 2006 NHS ProCure21 had more than 240 schemes registered, 60 of which were completed and another 65 were on site. Of the 130 trusts that had used ProCure21, 51 (39%) of these had more than one scheme under way, and 87% of further schemes used the same principal supply chain partners (PSCPs).

## Further development of DART

This is closely tied in with the development of AEDET Evolution and ASPECT. Another issue is that the collaborative working underpinning ProCure21 has not received a lot of attention in recent times, aspects which have affected DART's fortunes.

Overall, the benefits of implementing DART include: adopting a strategic approach to the incorporation of the inherent risks within a project prior to submission to a NHS Board for approval; establishing an acceptable design and risk footprint throughout the Strategic Outline Case, Outline Business Case, Full Business Case and Construction phases of a project; allowing the project team to use the dashboard analogy to diagrammatically assess the design and risk profiles and the mitigation actions being taken on the show stopper and high level project risks; developing an early warning process for the mitigation of the show stopper and the high level risks that may impact on the design, cost and time processes for the project; establishing realistic out-turn costs and programme durations, having taken into account all the design and risk issues that may impact upon the project; and calculating cost and time contingencies based upon quantitative computer assessments rather than relying on say +/–10% or a global allowance.

## Implementing DART

This section examines a project that used the NHS ProCure21 Design and Risk Tool (DART) – helping to identify the client and contractor risks, apportioning them correctly, and managing them out as much as possible. This provided further strength to the business case by demonstrating that risk was being managed proactively and that it had been considered in the Guaranteed Maximum Price.

The new £21.3 million Critical Care Unit at Northern General Hospital (NGH) in Sheffield is the largest of its kind in Europe. Designed with the help of Professor Roger Ulrich, an expert on critical care delivery, the unit will be the first ProCure21 scheme to get NHS Bank funding.

Northern General Hospital is part of the Sheffield Teaching Hospital NHS Foundation Trust (STH), the largest Foundation Trust in the country. The hospital takes about 70% of the adult emergency medical admissions in Sheffield and has speciality care for burns, spinal injuries and cardiac conditions. The existing 17-bed Critical Care Unit has provided an excellent level of care, but will be inadequate to cope with the future projected workload. Although an interim solution (a Post Operative Surgical Unit or POSU) opened in August 2005 to provide an extra seven beds, the lack of beds is leading to over-occupancy.

Sheffield, like elsewhere in the country, faces higher patient expectations and the prospect of caring for an ageing population – the number of patients aged over 75 who were admitted into the hospital's acute beds has trebled over six years. The Trust knew that they had to develop new facilities, and they started planning in October 2005. In December of that year the SHA approved an Outline Business Case for a new critical care unit, and HBG Construction, who were successfully working on five other schemes at the Trust, were appointed under the ProCure21 initiative. The construction of enabling works commenced in August 2006 and the critical care unit construction commenced in January 2007. Due to the amount of planning that went into the Full Business Case the new CCU had a relatively short construction phase and was delivered just 12 months later in January 2008.

The plan was for a 36-bed two-storey unit, with 20 of the 36 rooms being single occupancy. Each level has 18 beds; intensive care is on the ground floor, while high dependency beds and POSU beds are on the second floor. As the scheme was a new build on the site of the existing physiotherapy department, enabling works were necessary to move physiotherapy to the northwest of the NGH site.

**3.36  DART was used in the £21.3m Critical Care Unit, Northern General Hospital, Sheffield**

# Case Studies Applying AEDET, ASPECT and IDEAs/Gallery

To better understand the design quality improvement tools and assess their relevance and significance, it is helpful and convenient to consider their implementation in practice. The Vienna North Hospital project illustrates the application of ASPECT, AEDET Evolution and IDEAs in Europe during the design development stage, while the Children's Hospital, UK shows the application of ASPECT and AEDET Evolution as tools to aid and support the post-project evaluation of the hospital, one year after practical completion and occupancy. A commission by the Health Safety Executive, Ireland to the University of Sheffield School of Architecture Health Care Research Group to study wayfinding, navigation and accessibility at Hospital 1 and 2 provides scope for the further development of AEDET Evolution in the same way that Heading C Staff and Patient Environment produced ASPECT.

## Vienna North Hospital, Austria

The Vienna North Hospital is planned as an 800-bed main hospital in northeast Vienna. Launched in Spring 2006 with a European call for tender for cooperation partners and plans, this was followed in 2008 by an architectural competition, from which the Viennese architectural office Health team Albert Wimmer ZT GmbH emerged as the winner. The project team for Vienna North Hospital project also involves the client, the Vienna Hospital Association (consisting of all hospitals and geriatric centres of the City of Vienna and one of the biggest hospital operators in Europe, providing 8900 acute care beds and 4000 geriatric beds with annual expenditure of €3.2 billion on operating costs and €200 million on investments), with funding provided by the European Investment Bank.

The preliminary draft phase of the planning was completed, with construction beginning in 2012. The initial design competition for the appointment of the architect was organised in two stages and included an option for the Vienna Hospital Association to purchase the design directly from the architect. In this way, it was possible to apply relatively low entry thresholds for the design contest, thereby avoiding the exclusion of smaller practices that might otherwise lack the necessary capacity.

The assessment criteria for the design competition related to the urban, architectural and functional characteristics of the design, as well as the economy in construction, operation and maintenance. Drawing upon findings from a workshop held with experts and the project team, and from a number of established green building standards, a Sustainability Charter set out the detailed criteria to be included in each stage of the hospital's planning and building.

The four criteria consisted of: **Site**: protecting/restoring areas of unspoiled nature, building structures as part of the landscape, the use of potable water and rainwater, good transportation connections; **Interior**: thermal comfort, indoor air quality, flexibility of use, accessibility, user control (ventilation, shading, lighting); **Energy**: minimising overall energy demand, facilitating energy management (meters), ecological energy (district heating and cooling, photovoltaic and renewable sources); and **Construction**: environmental protection on site, reducing waste, dust, noise and vibrations, complying with the ÖkoKauf Wien standards, and using materials that are easy to clean and maintain.

The Sustainability Charter, which was extended to cover the operational phase of the hospital, also served as a checklist at the end of each planning step, to identify the extent and completeness of implementation for each of the identified criteria. By considering sustainability criteria early on in the process and applying life-cycle costing, it was possible to build these considerations into the economic aspect of the project from the outset. However, some elements, such as the proposed photovoltaic system, may still involve additional costs. For all elements incurring additional costs, decisions are made before the start of the procurement process on the basis of including variants provided by the planning team. The construction and use of buildings are responsible for a high percentage of the EU's $CO_2$ emissions and use of natural resources. Planning and implementing major new build projects, such as Vienna North Hospital, requires contracting authorities to take account of a wide range of potential impacts. Estimated reductions include energy demand for heating by 25% and energy for cooling by 20% below current minimum legal requirements.

**3.37 Vienna North Hospital, Austria: Contact with nature both indoors and outdoors**

The choice of the winning project from a two-stage open EU-wide competition with over 38 submissions from Switzerland, Germany and Austria, announced on 18 December 2008, acknowledged the atmosphere and quality of environment to be created in Vienna by the provision of a sizeable proportion of open outdoor space and a design solution that optimised workflow, logistics and health care organisational processes. Approximately two thirds of the site of 113,000m² in area is designed to be green, partly paved and landscaped outdoor areas.

The design concept combines the advantages of a pavilion-type hospital with those of a central general hospital, which maximises factors in order to promote health and well-being such as natural light and features of restorative natural settings (Nordh et al. 2009, Van den Berg et al. 2007; Sherman et al. 2005; Varni et al. 2004; Taylor et al. 2001; Taylor et al. 2002; Beauchemin and Hays 1996; Kaplan and Kaplan 1989; Ulrich 1984). A therapeutic park or gardens, a public urban plaza and a well-located vehicular drop-off and emergency service area enhance connection with nature by incorporating the planting of trees and shrubs, water bodies with riparian edges, citrus-filled or odiferous herb gardens as well as native Pannonian or flowering meadows to heighten one's sensory experience of the landscape.

During the early stages of the design the IDEAs tool is helpful in generating new ideas about the types of places to be created within the building and by the hospital, its siting or surroundings, which in turn aids the development of the briefing programme. Specific headings or sections of both the ASPECT tool and AEDET Evolution tool then allow evaluation of these design considerations. Specifically, key factors for evidence-based design interventions relate and correspond to ASPECT headings.

Also, the AEDET Evolution heading 'Form and Materials' deals with the nature of the building in terms of its overall form and materials, covering human scale, orientation on the site, and logical and obvious portioning of entrances in relation to arrival points on site. It is primarily concerned with how the building presents itself to the outside world in terms of its appearance and organisation. Although it deals with the materials from which the building is constructed it is not concerned with these in a technical sense, but rather in the way they will appear and feel throughout the life of the building. The ASPECT heading 'Views' deals with the extent to which both staff and patients can see out of and around the building, asking what they can see and relating this to their current activity and condition, while also considering the extent to which patients in particular have contact with the natural world, asking whether they can see and access nature both around and inside the building.

3.38a

3.38b

**3.38c Vienna North Hospital, Austria: Arrival**

Privacy Dignity and Company
  Allow people to control how and when they share space
View
  Give people a view of the outside world
Nature
  Enable contact both indoors and outdoors
Environment
  Provide both comfort and control (heat, light, sound, smell)
Spatial legibility
  Make places people understand and can navigate

**3.39 Vienna North Hospital, Austria: Key factors for Evidence-Based Design interventions correspond to the ASPECT headings**

<u>To aid navigation and wayfinding</u> the spatial organisational structure for the hospital is adopted as a landmark in Vienna, comprising three elements both horizontally and vertically: a horizontal order from north to south consisting of the Service Provision Wing, the Core Hospital, and a Park with therapeutic gardens, and a vertical order with Inpatient Wings on a promenade Deck above the Core Hospital. Travelling to Brünner Straße, northeast Vienna (21st district, Floridsdorf), visitors arrive in a new public urban square that invites them to linger. The two buildings 'Mars' and 'Venus', as well as the Service Provision Wing to the north, mark the boundary of the new square on Brünner Straße, which at 40x130 metres has dimensions similar to Vienna's Town Hall Square.

To further enhance navigation, a parallel decorative linear paving pattern seamlessly connects a variety of programme areas within the plaza, i.e. a main entry sub-plaza, outdoor cafes, a train station and associated sub-plaza, hotel and conference outdoor spill-out spaces and other circulation spaces. The pattern directs pedestrians along a route that bends and subdivides towards the hospital's main entrance, bringing them into the spacious light and airy hospital foyer. The spacious piazza connects the hospital with the public urban space to provide protection against noise on account of the building's position.

Both the IDEAs and ASPECT tools indicate how these design considerations for the Vienna North Hospital have been derived and can be evaluated or justified. The ASPECT heading 'Legibility of Place' deals with how understandable health care buildings are to the staff, patients and visitors who use them in terms of obvious entrances and ways out, easily understandable layouts, logical hierarchy of places, differentiated parts and obvious locations of members of

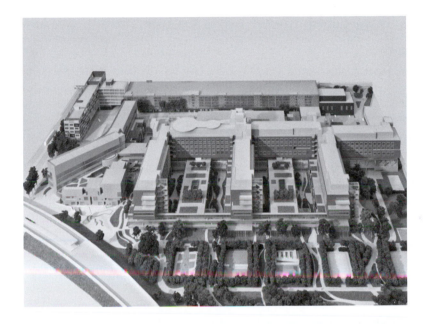

3.40 Vienna North Hospital, Austria: Environment

staff. Towns, areas, buildings, departments and rooms should have clear identities, be differentiated and have a hierarchy of structure. People generally like places that are not uniform and homogenous but have variety and variation of scale. Generally, layouts should therefore be clear and understandable so that wayfinding is easy and users depend only minimally on signage or maps.

Designed to a high standard reflecting the overall high specification of the wards, inpatient rooms are provided as either single or twin-bedded rooms, a feature that is consistent with the patient-centred approach to designing the hospital with regard to patients' needs for privacy, dignity and requirements for company or socialisation. To achieve privacy patients either have their own individual room or they can be screened off from others they share with, or, if they are mobile, they can easily find a private space. Privacy also means that activities can continue uninterrupted. For example, the opening of a door should not expose the occupants of the room to passers-by on the outside. Although curtains can achieve some degree of visual privacy they may not necessarily guarantee dignity, and will almost certainly not achieve acoustic privacy. Clearly individual rooms satisfy this feature, whereas multiple bed bays do not naturally do so. For example, in the case of twin-bedded rooms the arrangement of beds in space, the distances between beds and the provision of screens can all help to offset the natural loss of privacy and dignity to some extent. All patient rooms have large windows for unobstructed natural views and an abundance of sunlight (Baird and Bell 1995). A design that encourages connection with the outdoors creates a healing environment that promotes landscaped outdoor therapy.

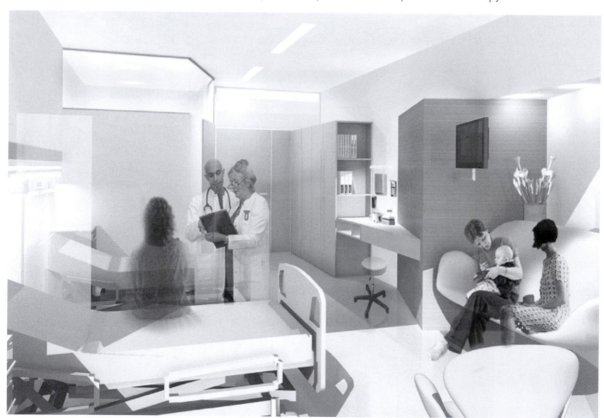

**3.41  Vienna North Hospital, Austria: Privacy, Company and Dignity**

3.42 Vienna North Hospital, Austria: Views

3.43 Vienna North Hospital, Austria: Contact with nature and outdoors

3.44a

3.44b

**3.44c Vienna North Hospital, Austria: Legibility of Place – understandable places**

Where the ASPECT heading 'Views' is about connection with the outside world, the ASPECT heading 'Privacy, Company and Dignity' allows the evaluation of the design in terms of the way people in the hospital are able to control their privacy and their interaction with others. It focuses on the way people can best maintain their dignity while under conditions that may not necessarily be found in ordinary life.

Supporting the Patient-Centred Health Care Approach, the Vienna North Hospital integrates landscape design principles that derive from a holistic concept of ideas of healing, recovery, well-being and growth to provide a therapeutic architecture with all the prerequisites for optimal healing processes. A patient-centred health care environment is configured so as to provide patients and families with fast access to reliable health advice, effective treatment by trusted professionals, clear information, assistance in self-care and emotional support and empathy. In other words, under a patient-centred approach, patients receive care in a therapeutic or healing environment that provides them with access to the information needed to enable them to become active participants in their own care and well-being.

Patient-centred health care has been interpreted in a variety of forms, from Planetree hospitals to the Picker Institute approach of patient surveys. On the one hand, originating as the result of disillusionment at the

3.45  Vienna North Hospital, Austria: Legibility of Place – inside

3.46  Vienna North Hospital, Austria: Legibility of Place – outside

(c) Health Team KHN - Albert Wimmer ZT GmbH

**3.47 Vienna North Hospital, Austria: Environment**

depersonalising treatment experienced in a conventional hospital by Angelica Thieriot, who was suffering from an acute viral infection, the Planetree philosophy of patient education and participation, family involvement and increased access to health and medical information for patients and their families is represented by an affiliation of hospitals and health care facilities of widely varying sizes, all of which are committed to patient-centred care. On the other hand, focusing not on changing the patients' immediate environment directly but rather on enhancing care by scrutinising feedback and ensuring it is acted on, the Picker Institute is a non-profit organisation dedicated to promoting patients' views on health care issues.

By focusing on patients, engaging them via non-technical language and allowing them to be involved in assessing or evaluating the hospital accommodation provided for them, ASPECT is basically a tool that supports and enhances the patient-centred approach. ASPECT results under the seven headings indicate what improve-

ments patients would like to see in their health and social care environments or settings.

Implementing an evidence-based design process by applying ASPECT, AEDET and IDEAs: To deliver a successful hospital project, proven design strategies and associated interventions alone are inadequate. They must be supported by an evidence-based process with clear project objectives and an adequate cost specification. In the Vienna North Hospital project the commitment by the client (Vienna Hospital Association) and the continuous and comprehensive involvement of users underlies a process that facilitated the development of design proposals for a hospital for the twenty-first century. Applying ASPECT and AEDET Evolution evaluated the overall design concept for the hospital and the extent to which it provides for clarity, optimised functional processes, a clear spatial organisational structure with a flexible module system, minimal travel distances for the nursing staff and streamlined networks creating a state-of-the art 800-bed hospital.

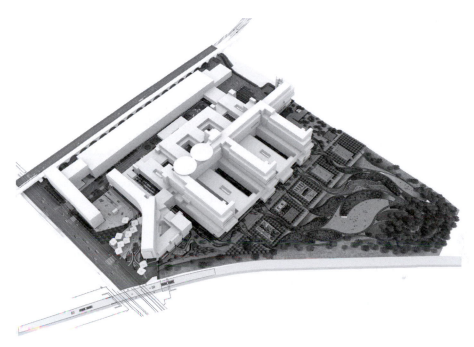

3.48  Vienna North Hospital, Austria: Models

# How to use ASPECT and AEDET Evolution

First decide at what scale you are going to use ASPECT and AEDET. ASPECT can be used to score a single space, ward or sets of spaces, while AEDET can be used to score at the scale of buildings, parts of buildings or complexes of buildings – for example, a department such as Accident and Emergency, a complete building, for instance a primary care centre, or a complex of buildings such as a hospital site. The scale at which you choose to work will probably depend on the level of detail in the information you have available. The minimum you need to use ASPECT or AEDET is the Scoring Layer. This guidance layer may be helpful, particularly if you are using ASPECT or AEDET Evolution for the first time. The Evidence Layer in ASPECT is only necessary either for interest or if you wish to see exactly why a particular heading and its constituent statements are included.

ASPECT and AEDET Evolution can either be used by individuals or in workshops by groups. In the latter case it is probably desirable that an experienced user of ASPECT/

AEDET should facilitate the group to avoid excessively lengthy debate. ASPECT and AEDET Evolution are helpful tools to enable a group to come to a common understanding. If you are using ASPECT and AEDET as a group it may be helpful to have a facilitator who can moderate the group discussions. There are two ways of doing this. You may try to arrive at a consensus for each statement score during discussions among the group as a whole. Alternatively, participants may prefer to score all the statements individually first, and then come together as a group to resolve differences. In either case it is important that the facilitator should ensure that any representatives of the public or patients who may lack experience of technical knowledge are able to express their views and have them listened to.

Always be sure about the scale at which you are using ASPECT 2004 and AEDET Evolution 2005 – for example, this could be at the building scale, the department scale or the complete site scale. It is particularly important to agree this before you begin if you are working as a group. To help decide on the scale you need to look first at the level of

**Table 3.13 Vienna North Hospital, Austria: Results of ASPECT focus group (scores). Headings: 6. Interior Appearance, 7. Facilities and 8. Staff were not facilitated**

| | 1. Privacy, Company and Dignity | 2. Views | 3. Nature and Outdoors | 4. Comfort and Control | 5. Legibility of Space | 6. Interior Appearance | 7. Facilities | 8. Staff | Total | AVERAGE |
|---|---|---|---|---|---|---|---|---|---|---|
| Participant 1 | 4.40 | 5.50 | 6.00 | 4.60 | 4.50 | 4.70 | 4.70 | 4.80 | 39.20 | 4.90 |
| Participant 2 | 4.40 | 5.50 | 6.00 | 4.60 | 4.50 | 4.90 | 4.60 | 5.10 | 39.60 | 4.95 |
| Participant 3 | 4.40 | 5.50 | 6.00 | 4.60 | 4.50 | 4.80 | 4.80 | 5.00 | 39.60 | 4.95 |
| Participant 4 | 4.40 | 5.50 | 6.00 | 4.60 | 4.50 | 2.20 | 4.80 | 5.60 | 37.60 | 4.70 |
| Participant 5 | 4.40 | 5.50 | 6.00 | 4.60 | 4.50 | 4.90 | 6.00 | 5.50 | 41.40 | 5.18 |
| Participant 6 | 4.40 | 5.50 | 6.00 | 4.60 | 4.50 | 5.10 | 4.90 | 5.60 | 40.60 | 5.08 |
| Participant 7 | 4.40 | 5.50 | 6.00 | 4.60 | 4.50 | 4.30 | 4.50 | 4.20 | 38.00 | 4.75 |
| Participant 8 | 4.40 | 5.50 | 6.00 | 4.60 | 4.50 | 4.10 | 4.20 | 4.60 | 37.90 | 4.74 |
| Participant 9 | 4.40 | 5.50 | 6.00 | 4.60 | 4.50 | 4.20 | 4.70 | 5.00 | 38.90 | 4.86 |
| Participant 10 | 4.40 | 5.50 | 6.00 | 4.60 | 4.50 | 4.40 | 4.40 | 4.90 | 38.70 | 4.84 |
| Participant 11 | 4.40 | 5.50 | 6.00 | 4.60 | 4.50 | 4.40 | 4.40 | 4.90 | 38.70 | 4.84 |
| Participant 12 | 4.40 | 5.50 | 6.00 | 4.60 | 4.50 | 4.30 | 4.50 | 4.20 | 38.00 | 4.75 |
| TOTAL | 52.80 | 66.00 | 72.00 | 55.20 | 54.00 | 52.30 | 56.50 | 59.40 | 468.20 | |
| AVERAGE | 4.40 | 5.50 | 6.00 | 4.60 | 4.50 | 4.36 | 4.71 | 4.95 | | |

detailed information available. If you decide to work at a smaller scale than a complete building then the NHS ADB (Activity DataBase) system may be helpful in deciding how to sub-divide the building. This database holds a master project which contains information on some 30 departments and 1500 rooms (as room data sheets).

In the Vienna North Hospital both approaches, using ASPECT and AEDET, were implemented via a facilitated ASPECT focus group consisting of over 11 participants from the project team, with these participants scoring the design proposals individually with their scores subsequently being consolidated. The results are indicated in Table 3.13 and also represented graphically. The ASPECT heading 'Nature and Outdoors' achieved a maximum score of 6 out of 6 while the heading 'Interior Appearance' scored 4.36 out of 6. One participant gave a below average score of 2.20 out of 6. Two participants scored an average of over 5 out of 6. These results confirm the focus by the designers on connection with nature, while the lower scores on the heading 'Interior Appearance' represent the stage of development of the design proposals. Overall, the results

indicate that the design is above average in all headings other than 'Nature and Outdoors', and therefore there is room for improvement.

## Children's Hospital, UK

The post-project evaluation which used ASPECT and AEDET Evolution tools was carried out by the University of Sheffield School of Architecture Healthcare Research Group under a commission won in competition with other evaluators. The post-project evaluation incorporates a post-occupancy evaluation with a focus on the satisfaction and behaviour of the users. The evaluation of the Children's Hospital was a condition of the Department of Health approval for the health care project, and covers stages 2 and 3 of the Department of Health Guidance on the Post-Project Evaluation: Stage 2 – monitor progress and evaluate the project outputs on completion of the facility; and Stage 3 – initial post-project evaluation of the service outcomes six totwelve months after the facility has been commissioned. Specifically, the objectives of the evaluation were also to:

**Figure 3.49 Vienna North Hospital, Austria: Linear graphical representation of results of ASPECT focus group (scores). Headings: 6. Interior Appearance, 7. Facilities and 8. Staff were not facilitated**

1  Learn any immediate and specific lessons.
2  Contribute to a database of such evaluations over a number of years.
3  Provide structured information on which to build more effective briefing tools for use by Trusts in their continuing building procurement programme.
4  Build up an illustrated structured database of best practice design and common faults under established headings that can be used in the briefing and design stages for future Trust projects.
5  Contribute to the growing body of international research into the links between the design of health care environments and patient/staff satisfaction, patient health outcomes and staff performance.

We conducted and facilitated three focus groups (held on 8, 15 and 11 July 2007) involving management staff, nurses and others. The management staff covered all the responsibilities at the Children's Hospital: General Manager Paediatrics, Head of Nursing Paediatrics, Clinical Director, Matron, Head of Financial Planning, Assistant Director Clinical Development, Commissioning Manager, IT Manager Paediatrics, Theatre Manager and Head of Capital Development. The two groups of nurses consisted of: Nursing (four in number), Environment Team, Metabolic Consultant, PICU Consultant, X-Ray Consultant (two in number), Physiotherapist, Occupational Therapist, Psychologist and a Speech and Language Therapist.

ASPECT 2004 and AEDET Evolution 2005 summary profiles were obtained from each of the focus groups while a six-point scoring scale (with a best score of 6 and poorest worst score of 1) was used in the subsequent final analysis of the evaluation of the building. Overall, we consider a score of 4 or over to represent a good acceptable standard. Analysis of the results confirms that both management staff and the nurses agree that the building is very good in terms of interior appearance and facilities and is good in terms of privacy, company and dignity.

3.50a

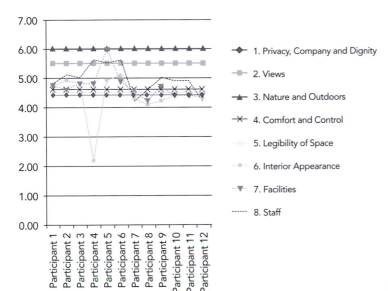

**3.50b Vienna North Hospital, Austria: Linear graphical representation of results of ASPECT focus group (scores). Headings: 6. Interior Appearance, 7. Facilities and 8. Staff were not facilitated**

A comparison of the ASPECT summary profiles obtained from the three focus groups carried out is indicated in Table 3.14. Across all three focus groups there was complete agreement that the factor Nature and Outdoors was excellent, receiving the maximum score of 6 out of 6. There was also complete agreement between groups 1 and 2 on five factors, namely: Privacy, Company and Dignity (a score of 4 out of 6), Views (a score of 5 out of 6), Nature and Outdoors (a score of 6 out of 6), Comfort and Control (a score of 2 out of 6) and Staff Amenities (a score of 3 out of 6).

**Table 3.14 Children's Hospital, UK: Results of ASPECT focus groups**

| ASPECT CATEGORIES | | MANAGEMENT STAFF | NURSES & OTHERS GROUP 1 | NURSES & OTHERS GROUP 2 | AVERAGE |
|---|---|---|---|---|---|
| C1. | PRIVACY, COMPANY AND DIGNITY | 5.00 | 4.00 | 4.00 | 4.33 |
| C2. | VIEWS | 6.00 | 5.00 | 5.00 | 5.33 |
| C3. | NATURE AND OUTDOORS | 6.00 | 6.00 | 6.00 | 6.00 |
| C4. | COMFORT AND CONTROL | 4.00 | 2.00 | 2.00 | 2.67 |
| C5. | LEGIBILITY OF PLACE | 4.00 | 2.00 | 4.00 | 3.33 |
| C6. | INTERIOR APPEARANCE | 5.00 | 3.00 | 4.00 | 4.00 |
| C7. | FACILITIES | 5.00 | 4.00 | 5.00 | 4.67 |
| C8. | STAFF | 5.00 | 3.00 | 3.00 | 3.67 |
| | AVERAGE | 5.00 | 3.63 | 4.13 | |

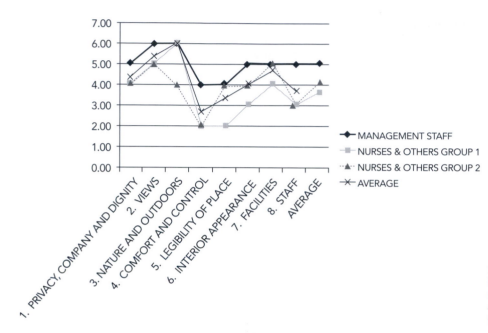

3.51 **Children's Hospital, UK: Linear graphical representation of results of AEDET Evolution 2005 focus groups**

Three factors that show disagreement (a point difference) between the focus groups are Privacy, Company and Dignity (scores of 4 and 5 out of 6), Views (scores of 5 and 6 out of 6) and Facilities (scores of 4 and 5 out of 6). There was a point difference for Interior Appearance as group 2 nurses and others scored 4 out of 6 and group 1 nurses and others scored 3 out of 6, compared with management staff's score of 5 out of 6. Factors that show the least agreement (a two point difference) between the three focus groups consisting of management staff and two groups of nurses and others were in terms of Comfort and Control, Legibility of Place, Interior Appearance, and Staff Amenities. Overall, the two groups of nurses and others are less satisfied than management staff.

A comparison of the AEDET Evolution summary profiles obtained from the three focus groups carried out is indicated in Table 3.15. The management staff gave two factors (A:

Character and Innovation; and B: Form and Materials) maximum scores of 6 out of 6, and group 2 nurses and others gave factor D (Urban/Social Integration) a maximum score of 6 out of 6. Factors that showed the least agreement (a two point or more difference) between the three focus groups of management staff and two groups of nurses and others were factor B (Form and Materials), C (Staff/Patient Environment), D (Urban/Social Integration), E (Performance) and H (Use). Factor G (Construction) shows a four-point difference between the first group of nurses and the management staff (scores of 2 out of 6 and 5 out of 6 respectively). Group 1 nurses and others were unable to score on factor F (Engineering). Reasons given include that the issues raised by the statements were not familiar to them, and the participants appeared to have no prior knowledge of the subject matter. Overall, the two groups of nurses and others were less satisfied than the management staff.

Table 3.15  Children's Hospital, UK: Results of AEDET Evolution focus groups

| AEDET Evolution CATEGORIES | | MANAGEMENT STAFF | NURSES & OTHERS GROUP 1 | NURSES & OTHERS GROUP 2 | AVERAGE |
|---|---|---|---|---|---|
| A. | CHARACTER AND INNOVATION | 6.00 | 5.00 | 5.00 | 5.33 |
| B. | FORM AND MATERIALS | 6.00 | 4.00 | 5.00 | 5.00 |
| C. | STAFF AND PATIENT ENVIRONMENT | 5.00 | 3.00 | 4.00 | 4.00 |
| D. | URBAN/SOCIAL INTEGRATION | 5.00 | 4.00 | 6.00 | 5.00 |
| E. | PERFORMANCE | 4.00 | 2.00 | 4.00 | 3.33 |
| F. | ENGINEERING | 4.00 | 0.00 | 3.00 | 2.33 |
| G. | CONSTRUCTION | 5.00 | 2.00 | 4.00 | 3.67 |
| H. | USE | 5.00 | 3.00 | 4.00 | 4.00 |
| I. | ACCESS | 5.00 | 4.00 | 5.00 | 4.67 |
| J. | SPACE | 4.00 | 4.00 | 3.00 | 3.67 |
| | AVERAGE | 4.90 | 3.10 | 4.30 | |

# Hospital 1 and 2 in the Republic of Ireland

A commission by the Health Safety Executive, Ireland to the University of Sheffield School of Architecture Health Care Research Group to study wayfinding, navigation and accessibility at Hospital 1 and 2 shows scope of further developing AEDET Evolution in the same way that Heading C: Staff and Patient Environment produced ASPECT. A starting point for the study was to establish the different headings under which statements could then be provided. This work produced the several categories which formed the basis for the design of questionnaire:

A   Approach, car parking and wayfinding
B   Routes and external level change, including ramps and steps
C   Entrances including reception
D   Horizontal movement and activities
E   Vertical movement and internal level change
F   Doors
G   WC facilities
H   Fixtures, fittings and equipment
I   Information and controls
J   Means of escape

The questionnaire was derived from headings and statements from both ASPECT and AEDET Evolution, combined with additional ones to produce 12 headings: Legibility of Place, Public Transport, Parking, Ambulances, Goods and Waste Disposal, Pedestrians, Outdoor Areas, Fire and Rescue, Travel Distances, Isolation Areas, Gender Segregation, and Storage. Using the self-administered questionnaire distributed to staff, patients and visitors over a three-month period, the Universal Access Audit of Hospital 1 yielded 12 priority considerations.

A   The Main Hospital Entrance and Reception area was a first priority consideration in order to address issues of lack of space, overcrowding, inadequate seating arrangements, restricted access/storage for wheelchairs, mothers with buggies and other users. A new reception desk needed to provide privacy, a low section for wheelchair users and to install hearing loops, minicom and text phones for users with impaired hearing. The variety of uncoordinated signage was to be addressed to improve the appearance of the entrance area and provide a welcoming atmosphere. A pronounced or projecting canopy would make it easier to identify the main entrance, rather than one set back from the face of the building.

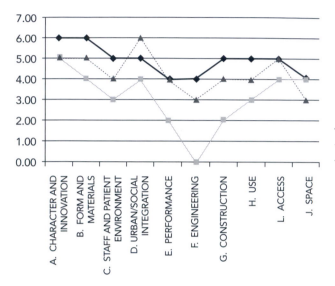

3.52 Children's Hospital, UK: Linear graphical representation of results of AEDET Evolution 2005 focus groups

Table 3.16 Hospital 1: Responses to questionnaires

|  | 1 | 2 | 3 | 4 | 5 | 6 |
|---|---|---|---|---|---|---|
| LEGIBILITY OF PLACE | 1 | 4 | 8 | 8 | 2 | 1 |
| PUBLIC TRANSPORT | 4 | 4 | 2 | 8 | 2 | 3 |
| PARKING | 9 | 7 | 4 | 3 | 0 | 0 |
| AMBULANCES | 2 | 8 | 2 | 4 | 4 | 3 |
| GOODS AND WASTE DISPOSAL | 3 | 10 | 3 | 4 | 3 | 0 |
| PEDESTRIANS | 3 | 9 | 4 | 1 | 3 | 1 |
| OUTDOOR AREAS | 1 | 2 | 6 | 5 | 6 | 4 |
| FIRE AND RESCUE | 0 | 2 | 4 | 5 | 6 | 5 |
| TRAVEL DISTANCES | 3 | 3 | 4 | 5 | 5 | 3 |
| ISOLATION OF AREAS | 1 | 3 | 10 | 5 | 3 | 1 |
| GENDER SEGREGATION | 1 | 3 | 6 | 3 | 1 | 3 |
| STORAGE | 1 | 5 | 5 | 7 | 3 | 2 |

Hospital 1 needed to work with the City Council to re-surface or repair pavements/kerbs to stop ponding when wet, remove the uneven surfaces and provide dropped kerb contrasts, especially at the main entrance, which may pose a risk of falls to patients and visitors.

B The Outpatients Department was a second priority consideration in order to address issues of a lack of space, overcrowding/congestion, restricted access/ storage for wheelchairs, mothers with buggies and other users. Of concern was the seating in the corridors and circulation routes, which raised questions about compliance with requirements to provide safe emergency exit or egress.

The building layout did not achieve appropriate standards, which require that all general spaces be suitable and sufficient to meet normal demand comfortably and peak demand at least adequately. In particular, entrance areas should be uncluttered and spacious, as should all circulation and social spaces. Provision for special areas for children should be considered. There is evidence to support a radical design solution such as the replacement of the entire Outpatient Department. This is important for Hospital 1 in the twenty-first century because the modern hospital is increasingly a centre for the treatment of day or out-patient care.

C ▣ Car Parking was a third priority consideration for the hospital. Hospital 1 did not have designated accessible parking for patients and visitors and needed to work with the City Council to provide the recommended number of disabled parking spaces, i.e. between 5% and 6% and within recommended travel distances from the entrances (less than 50 metres) and if possible under cover. Designated accessible car parking needed to be clearly marked, signed, easily found and kept free from misuse.

The idea of applying the principles of the well-known Shopmobility schemes to the hospital car parks is worth considering. For example, one such scheme would include the provision of wheelchairs and electric scooters for disabled patients and visitors, enabling them to park their cars, collect a scooter or a wheelchair in the car park and then make their way into the hospital for their appointments or visits.

A designated bicycle parking area for patients and visitors to the hospital should be provided near the main entrance to prevent bicycles being fixed to the railings.

D ◀ ♿ Access Routes, Disabled Access and the Use of Temporary Ramps constituted a fourth priority consideration for the hospital. Hospital 1 needed to work towards replacing all temporary ramps with well-designed permanent solutions. This helped compliance with: a) Manual Handling EU Directives and issues relating to moving the temporary ramps; b) the logistics of a 'managed solution' that entailed staff intervention to erect and remove the ramp as required; c) the inconvenience involved with patients and visitors having to make prior arrangements with Security in order to meet their needs as wheelchair, disabled and other users with special requirements; d) hazards posed by the temporary ramps because they do not have suitable

handrails or balustrades and may be an obstruction; and e) requirements for storage of the moveable ramps.

Crucially, the access route to Medical Units via the main entrance, turning left in the reception area and proceeding down a flight of stairs to the rear into the lane, posed the greatest hazard and risk of injury to users (especially patients and visitors seeking to use the smoking shelter, located across the rear lane). Although the stairs had been provided with a moveable ramp, this could not be made permanent because it obstructed the fire exit and did not provide adequate headroom.

The age and the listed nature of the main buildings was a challenge in terms of improving access, which limited the scope of providing suitable permanent ramps at a low cost.

E ▣ External signage: There was a variety of external signage throughout the site. An overhaul of all external signage was the fifth priority consideration. Upgrading the directional signage and rationalisation of all the signage together with the installation of 'You-are-here' maps, incorporating Braille or tactile features, would aid wayfinding. Exterior signage needed to identify each accessible entrance if this was not also the main entrance. Where necessary, it needed to indicate distances to key features or areas, the presence and grade of inclines, and how assistance may be obtained.

F Interior signage: An overhaul and rationalisation of all interior signage was the sixth priority consideration for Hospital 1. Interior signage should be considered for position, location, local clarity and visual contrast. Braille and embossed signage needed to be incorporated with sensitivity in most situations, but will always be most effective as part of an integrated communication scheme. Symbols and pictograms of a standard design should be used, accompanied by a language that focuses on the accommodation or service not who uses it (e.g. 'ramped entrance') and which fosters dignity (e.g. 'toilet for disabled'). Pictograms should be considered because they reinforce the written word and are helpful for people with learning difficulties or people who cannot read English or Irish.

The management of notices should be considered as part of an overall policy for Hospital 1 to discourage clutter of different type notices, signs and posters.

G Disabled Toilet provision was the seventh priority consideration for the hospital. An accessible toilet needed to be provided to replace the existing accessible toilet on the ground floor at the main entrance, which did not comply with the recommended space standards incorporating adequate manoeuvring space and the installation of hand and grab rails. Information about the location of accessible toilets relative to the entrances had to be provided as part of a patient and visitor guide.

H Patient and visitor facilities were the eighth priority consideration for Hospital 1. Although a shop was available on the ground floor at the main entrance, the hospital needed to consider providing an accessible coffee/tea shop/café/restaurant, a wheelchair accessible cash point and vending machines etc.

I An Access Guide giving information to users constituted the ninth priority consideration for Hospital 1. The guide could be sent out to allow people to plan their visit, giving details of how the building can be reached by public transport from the bus station, train/tram station or the airport, and what parking facilities are available and where they are located. Such a guide would also detail how the building can be accessed internally, highlighting any restrictions to independent and full access. An Access Guide forms part of an organisation's Communication Strategy.

Hospital 1 needed to formalise what appeared to be an informal **Communication Strategy** defining the hospital's policy relating to the provision of information in alternate formats for users, especially people with disabilities and different languages. A comprehensive set of access information needed to be provided in accessible formats in leaflets or via the internet.

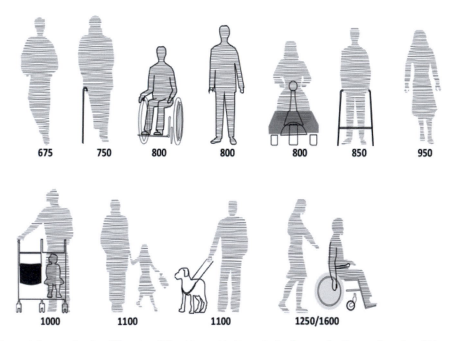

675    750    800    800    800    850    950

1000    1100    1100    1250/1600

**3.53 Space requirements for people using different mobility aids provided important references for the questionnaire which was an important part of the Access Audit for Hospitals in the Republic of Ireland**

J **Lift** installation was a tenth priority consideration for the School of Midwifery Building although it had five floors. Lifts would improve the use of the building by people in wheelchairs and others with impaired mobility while allowing easy and convenient use by everyone else, especially staff when delivering or collecting items such as furniture and equipment.

K **Other features** which formed the eleventh priority consideration included adopting a policy of preventative maintenance, especially towards the installation of lighting fixtures and fittings, repairs and making good the boundary fences around the hospital.

The same questionnaire was also distributed to staff, patients and visitors at Hospital 2. Analysis of the results indicated 12 main issues affecting accessibility at Hospital 2.

A **Car Parking**: The walking distance from the main car park to the entrance was approximately 128m. The recommended number of disabled parking spaces needed to be between 5% and 6%. There were ten designated spaces at the main entrance (i.e. 2.8%), four at the Renal Dialysis entrance, five near the Outpatients entrance and two at the Orthopaedic entrance.

The walking distances from other car parking facilities indicated in a previous audit were 10m, 32m, 59m, 68m, 122m, 148m and 206m across the different locations. Drop-off and pick-up points had been provided at the entrances for taxis, community transport, vehicles, cars and minibuses with varying degrees of compliance. The poor condition of the main car parking surface and the absence of pavements/kerbs deterred wheelchair users and other people with impaired physical mobility.

In the long term, a Development Control Plan needed to consider providing more car parking spaces. A strategy was required to address the location of the car parking relative to the entrances via a covered walkway. A designated bicycle parking area for patients and visitors to Hospital 2 needed to be provided near the main entrance to prevent bicycles being fixed to the railings. The idea of applying the principles of well-known Shopmobility schemes to the hospital car parks was worth considering. For example, one such scheme would include the provision of wheelchairs and electric scooters for disabled patients and visitors, enabling them to park their cars, pick up a scooter or wheelchair in the car park and then make their way into the hospital for their appointments or visits.

**Table 3.17 Hospital 2: Responses to questionnaires**

|  | 1 | 2 | 3 | 4 | 5 | 6 |
|---|---|---|---|---|---|---|
| LEGIBILITY OF PLACE | 0 | 5 | 19 | 14 | 4 | 0 |
| PUBLIC TRANSPORT | 10 | 17 | 8 | 5 | 2 | 0 |
| PARKING | 13 | 16 | 10 | 3 | 0 | 0 |
| AMBULANCES | 1 | 3 | 18 | 11 | 5 | 1 |
| GOODS+WASTE DISPOSAL | 1 | 8 | 18 | 8 | 2 | 0 |
| PEDESTRIANS | 6 | 13 | 10 | 8 | 3 | 0 |
| OUTDOOR AREAS | 3 | 17 | 11 | 8 | 3 | 0 |
| FIRE & RESCUE | 0 | 1 | 13 | 16 | 7 | 3 |
| TRAVEL DISTANCES | 3 | 8 | 18 | 11 | 2 | 0 |
| ISOLATION OF AREAS | 2 | 6 | 19 | 9 | 1 | 2 |
| GENDER SEGREGATION | 4 | 3 | 18 | 8 | 5 | 0 |
| STORAGE | 5 | 10 | 12 | 13 | 0 | 0 |

B  Accessible Car Parking: Although the main entrance of the 1990s building had ten designated accessible car parking spaces, only four complied with guidance. There were problems of the gradient of the access road, the length of the car parking bays, the surface of the road and the use of the bays. The condition of the surface was hazardous.

C  External signage: There was a variety of external signage throughout the site. The hospital appeared to be dominated by the Euro Parks signage. Upgrading the directional signage and rationalisation of all the signage, together with installation of 'You-are-here' maps incorporating Braille or tactile features, would aid wayfinding. There was an opportunity to install sculptural artworks at the entrances in order to provide suitable landmarks that signal arrival.

Exterior signage needed to identify each accessible entrance if this was not also the main entrance. Where necessary, there was a need to indicate distances to key features or areas, the presence and grade of inclines, and how assistance may be obtained. The hospital needed to work with the Council to provide directional signs in prominent locations in the city and to remove graffiti on signs around the hospital. The Council were also to be encouraged to provide a pedestrian crossing from the existing bus stop.

D  Disabled Access: The access route from the main car park to the main entrance was via an uncovered sloping walkway, crossing a service/access road and past parked cars to the entrance. The provision of handrails/balustrades would be helpful to all persons using the walkway.

E  Disabled Toilet: There were several accessible toilets in the hospital. The most conveniently located accessible toilet for wheelchair users was on Level 3, with 24-hour access. Manoeuvring space for wheelchair users within the toilet had been compromised by the installation of baby changing facilities and storage bins. The installation of a grab rail was not in accordance with the recommended

guidance. Hospital 2 needed to provide information about the location of accessible toilets relative to the entrances.

F  Reception Desk: The main reception and enquiries points were on Level 3. Hospital 2 needed to consider installing hearing loops, minicom and text phones.

G  Corridors and Passage Ways: Marked coloured lines on the floor aided navigation and wayfinding from the Emergency Department on Level 3 to the Radiology Department. However, it seemed that no one was using them or was familiar with how to use them.

H  Interior signage: Interior signage should be considered for position, location, local clarity and visual contrast. Braille and embossed signage may be incorporated with sensitivity in most situations, but will always be most effective as part of an integrated communication scheme.

I  Patient and Visitor Facilities: An accessible restaurant, a hospital shop, a wheelchair accessible cash point and a changing room with grab rails are situated on Level 3. The hospital shop sells a variety of snacks, drinks and confectionery as well as stationery and toiletry items. The pharmacy is also located on Level 3. Vending machines are available on designated stair landings, in the restaurant and café.

J  Lifts and Stairs: Four lifts and stairs provide access to all eight levels in the 1990s building. On Level 3 lifts and stairs are on the left past the reception desk. There are Braille signs and lift call buttons.

Colour contrasting has been used successfully to differentiate between levels in the 1990s Tower Block, and a similar technique should be used as a basis for upgrading and enhancing all interior signage throughout the hospital. Colour contrasting needs to recognise that many people have difficulty perceiving certain colour contrasts, especially red and green compared to black and white/yellow.

K 🔘 Other Features for Consideration: The hospital needed to work with the Council to repair damaged boundary balustrades/fencing. Hospital 2 needed to consider relocating the smoking shelter at the main entrance in order to improve its general appearance and to stop groups of people gathering at the entrance. Also, this would reduce litter from cigarette ends.

Hospital 1 and 2 case studies are helpful in showing how AEDET Evolution can be further developed along the lines of the ASPECT tool.

## Feedback from users of the IDEAs tool/Gallery

During the development of the IDEAs tool/Gallery we have sought to demonstrate the usefulness of applying the tool on actual hospitals or other health care projects. We have collected data about the type of requests for information using the IDEAs tool, looking at where this feedback is coming from as well as the typical comments made by people who have visited the website. Unlike ASPECT/AEDET Evolution and BREEAM Healthcare 2008, which have a mandatory status afforded them for capital projects to be signed off by the Department of Health, the IDEAs tool/Gallery is optional to Trusts, health care providers and their consultants. This, together with the absence of a dissemination strategy by the Department of Health, has meant that the potential of the IDEAs tool/Gallery to impact on the design quality improvement agenda is yet to be exploited.

**Table 3.18  Typical requests for information for IDEAs**

| |
|---|
| "I edit *Health Estate*, the *Journal of the Institute of Healthcare Engineering and Estate Management*, and would be keen to talk to someone involved with 'IDEAs' with a view to publishing an item in the journal" |
| "Would like information on the possibility of visiting new builds or seeing views of them on the web, also buildings for specific specialist client needs, such as older people's mental health" |
| "We are to design a children's waiting area at Norfolk & Norwich University Hospital with provision for adults' areas separate areas for children of different ages etc. – Do you have an information pamphlet that could be sent?...." |
| "How about some information on observation offices?" |
| "I am currently looking for guidance on designing buildings for people with challenging behaviour... Part of this project is helping with the design brief for a new build, which will be home for these individuals. I am finding it very hard to find anything that comments on or alludes to guidance for building functional homes for people with learning disability and challenging behaviour" |

**Table 3.19  Typical sources of feedback on the use of IDEAs or where the feedback came from**

| |
|---|
| I work in learning disability part of the Trust |
| Fair for All Disability Project which is a joint initiative between the Scottish Executive Health Departments and the Disability Rights Commission |
| Commission for Architecture and the Built Environment (CABE) a government's advisor on architecture, urban design and public space from 1999 to 2011 |
| Interior Designer, Working on Hospital Arts Project |
| Researcher: Arts and Environment, *MK Arts for Health* |
| Editor, *Health Estate Journal* |
| Clinical Project Coordinator, Northumberland, Tyne and Wear NHS Trust |
| Assistant Director Estate Development, Welsh Health Estates |
| Divisional Director, Stride Treglown |
| Senior Nurse Project Manager, Cardiff and Vale NHS Trust |

**Table 3.20  Favourable comments from users of IDEAs**

"Extremely useful, simple and masterly organised. Please keep up the good work!"

"Fantastic site: thank you!"

"I am interested in your design IDEAs and wondered if you could send me further details of same"

"A useful tool as part of the design process.

Concise information with appropriate pictograms and precedents"

"Very interesting website with invaluable information"

"Hello it's great to hear and see all of this information about improving healthcare!"

"Is the IDEAs toolkit a published item and could you tell me how I can obtain it please?"

"When can we have the rest of IDEAs please?"

"This idea could be used to create sort of benchmark. To show how we would like to see the qualitative aspects of our buildings realised and encourage clients to be aspirational".

"This is a good tool to get clients thinking about the important spaces within hospitals, but I am sure that most clients will want every suggestion made to be included within their design. I am unclear of the final purpose of this tool i.e.

Is it just to stimulate thought?

Can it be transformed into a design brief?

Although I cannot see any facility for this, is it to be used in a workshop session with the results being written into a design brief?"

Notwithstanding all the above issues, feedback from users of the IDEAs tool/Gallery is favourable, suggesting scope for further development.

# References

Alexander C, Ishikawa S, Silverstein M, with Jacobson M, Fiksdahl-King I, and Angel S (1977) *A Pattern Language: Towns, Buildings, Construction*. Oxford University Press, New York.

Baird CL, and Bell PA (1995) Place Attachment, Isolation and the Power of a Window in a Hospital Environment: A Case Study. *Psychological Reports*, 76, 847–850.

Beauchemin KM, and Hays P (1996) Sunny hospital rooms expedite recovery from severe and refractory depressions. *Journal of Affective Disorders*, 40, 49–51.

Department of Trade and Industry (DTI) (2001) *Better Public Buildings*. London, UK.

Donabedian A (1978) The Quality of Medical Care. *Science*, 200 (4344), 856–864.

Egan J (1998) *Rethinking Construction*. Department of the Environment, Transport and the Regions (DETR), London.

Gann DW, Slater AJ, and Whyte JK, (2003) Design Quality Indicators: Tools for thinking. *Building Research & Information*, 31 (5), 318–333.

Jesinghaus J (2000) On the Art of Aggregating Apples and Oranges. Working Paper, Fondazione Eni Enrico Mattei, Milan, Italy.

Kaplan S, and Kaplan R (1989) *The Experience of Nature: A Psychological Perspective*. New York: Cambridge University Press.

Lawson BR (2001) *A Language of Space*. The Architectural Press, Oxford, UK.

Lawson BR and Phiri M (2000) Room for improvement. *Health Service Journal*, 110 (5688), 24–27.

Lawson BR and Phiri M (2004) AEDET Evolution: Learning from the evidence base of NHS design. Report by the University of Sheffield School of Architecture, UK.

Lawson BR and Phiri M, in collaboration with Wells-Thorpe J (2003) The Architectural Healthcare Environment and its Effect on Patient Health Outcomes: A Report on a NHS Estates Funded Research Project. The Stationery Office, London, 2003, 1–22.

McCormick M and Shepley MM (2003) How can consumers benefit from therapeutic environments? *Journal of Architectural and Planning Research*, 20 (1), 4–15.

NHS Estates (1994) *Better by Design: Pursuit of Excellence in Healthcare Buildings*. Leeds, UK.

NHS Estates (2002) Achieving Excellence Design Evaluation Toolkit – AEDET. Leeds, UK.

NHS Estates (2002) *Improving the Patient Experience: The Art of Good Health: A Practical Handbook*. The Stationery Office, London, UK

NHS Estates Design Brief Working Group (Chairman: Richard Burton) (2002) Advice to Trusts on the main components of the design brief for healthcare buildings. Leeds, UK.

NHS Estates, Department of Trade and Industry (DTI), Department of Health (DH) (2002): NEAT (NHS Environmental Assessment Tool). London, UK.

Nordh H, Hartig T, Hagerhall CM, and Fry G (2009) Components of small urban parks that predict the possibility for restoration. *Urban Forestry & Urban Greening*, 8, 225–235.

Phiri M (2002) *Sheffield Architectural Environment and Patient Outcomes Database: Design and User Manual.* School of Architecture, University of Sheffield, UK.

Phiri M, in association with Worthington J and Leaman A (1998) Briefing a Continuous Building programme – Factors for success: 35 years of design and construction at the University of York. Institute of Advanced Architectural Studies, University of York, UK.

Royal College of Physicians (2003) *The Healing Environment: Without and Within.* London, UK.

Royal College of Psychiatrists (2000) *More than Bricks and Mortar.* London, UK.

Sherman SA, Varni JW, Ulrich RS, and Malcarne VL (2005) Post occupancy evaluation of healing gardens in a paediatric cancer centre. *Landscape and Urban Planning,* 73, 2–3, 167–183.

Taylor AF, Kuo FE, and Sullivan WC (2002) Views of nature and self-discipline: Evidence from inner-city children. *Journal of Environmental Psychology*, 22, 49–64.

Taylor AF, Kuo FE, and Sullivan WC (2001) Growing up in the inner city: Green places to grow. *Environment and Behavior*, 33, 54–77.

Tétreault M-H, and Passini R (2003) Architects' use of information in designing therapeutic environments. *Journal of Architectural and Planning Research*, 20 (1), 48–56.

Torbett R, Slater AJ, Gann DM, and Hobday M (2001) Design Performance Measurement in the Construction Sector: A Pilot Study. SPRU (Science and Technology Policy Research Unit) Submission to IEEE Transactions of Engineering Management, April 2001.

Tufte E (1997) *Visual Explanations: Images and Quantities, Evidence and Narrative.* Graphics Press, Cheshire, CT.

Ulrich RS (1984) View through a window may influence recovery from surgery. *Science*, 224, 420-421.

Van den Berg AE, Hartig T, and Staats H (2007) Preference for nature in urbanized societies: Stress, restoration, and the pursuit of sustainability. *Journal of Social Issues*, 63, 79–96 (doi:10.1111/j.1540-4560.2007.00497.x).

Varni JW, Burwinkle TM, Dickinson P, Sherman SA, Dixon P, Ervice JA, Leyden PA, and Sadler BL (2004) Evaluation of the built environment at a children's convalescent hospital: Development of the paediatric quality of life inventory™ parent and staff satisfaction measures for paediatric healthcare facilities. *Journal of Developmental & Behavioral Pediatrics*, 25, 1, 10–20.

Wotton H, (1624) *The Elements of Architecture.* John Bill, London.

# 4 Efficiency and effectiveness tools

The **S**trategic **H**ealth **A**sset **P**lanning and **E**valuation (SHAPE) tool represents an important tool to enhance efficiency and effectiveness in supporting the delivery of health and social care.

## Strategic Health Asset Planning and Evaluation (SHAPE)

Funded by the UK Department of Health, the Strategic Health Asset Planning and Evaluation (SHAPE) tool is a web-enabled evidence-based application which informs and supports the strategic planning of services across the entire health geographical economy. The SHAPE application is about delivering health care services more efficiently and effectively while enabling decisions to be made closer to the patients (and all those people) who will be affected by them. SHAPE was originally developed for NHS estates professionals by the UK Department of Health, to support several national policy priorities – namely the Joint Strategic Needs Assessment (JSNA), Quality Innovation Productivity and Prevention (QIPP) targets of the transformational programme for £20+ billion in savings by 2015, Transforming Community Services, and Clinically-Led Commissioning. Pilot work was undertaken in 2005–6.

From 2009–10, SHAPE was project-managed on a day-to-day basis by the NHS North East Public Health Observatory (NEPHO) at Durham University. During this period the SHAPE application was redeveloped with a range of flexibility capabilities to support Joint Strategic Needs Assessment (JSNA), Clinical Commissioning Groups (CCGs), and the drive for efficiency in strategic health care asset planning, decision-making, the identification of local priorities for health care improvement and the delivery of best practice care.

Since April 2013 SHAPE has been part of Public Health England, an executive agency of the Department of Health, whose mission is to protect and improve the nation's health and to address inequalities. SHAPE is free to NHS professionals and Local Authority professionals with a role in Public Health or Social Care facilitating interactive investigations by Local

Area Teams, Trust Providers, CCGs, GP practices and Local Authorities, in support of key policy initiatives such as QIPP, JSNA and Transforming Community Services.

SHAPE links the latest national datasets for clinical analysis, public health, primary care and demographic data with estates performance and facilities location. The locational information and site details are sourced from Organisation Data Services (part of Connecting for Health) who have responsibility for regularly checking, updating and validating the information (Figure 4.1).

All data handled in SHAPE can be described visually on a map. For example, SHAPE can present on a map clinical admissions for individual HRGs (Healthcare Resource Groups 4) by LSOA (Lower Super Output Area). This means that drive time and distance catchment options can be determined. Also, knowledge exchange in SHAPE allows users to find out how best to use a site, and how to seek instant help from the helpdesk if necessary.

4.1 **SHAPE terrain basemap: Showing the background mapping using Ordnance Survey OpenData that was awarded the OS OpenData Award 2013**

Table 4.1 SHAPE supports Joint Strategic Needs Assessment (JSNA)

| | Activity | SHAPE outputs |
|---|---|---|
| **Joint Strategic Needs Assessment (JSNA)** | Understanding the population characteristics (demography) in a geographical health area | • Population density by sex<br>• Age structure, for example percentage of population by broad age band and by quinary age bands<br>• Assessment of the population by ethnicity |
| | Analysing determinants of health in a geographical health economic area | • Index of multiple deprivation, including by assessment for disability, children and older people<br>• Childhood obesity levels<br>• Teenge pregnancy rates<br>• MMR immunisation uptake |
| | Investigating key epidemiology factors in a geographical health economic area | • Premature mortality figures for cancers and circulatory diseases as well as life expectancy for males and females<br>• Infant mortality rates<br>• QOF (Quality and Outcomes Framework) prevalence for CVD, COPD, CHD, atrial fibrillation, diabetes, epilepsy, heart failure, hypertension, hypothyroidism, stroke & TIA. |
| | Determining NHS service access, provision, utilisation and effectiveness in a geographical health economic area | • HRGs (Healthcare Resource Groups) representing the highest proportion of admissions and bed days by admission type.<br>• QOF (Quality and Outcomes Framework) prevalence indicators and also provides a link to actual QOF data at GP practice level.<br>• Analyses of emergency admissions, readmissions, excess bed days and length of stay by provider or comissioner.<br>• Estimate of savings that could be achieved by reducing emergency admissions, length of stay, excess bed days and multiple admissions if performance is improved to the level achieved by the top 25% of providers.<br>• Mapping of outpatient and A&E attendances available soon.<br>• Costs of care by programme budgeting categories. |

Table 4.2 SHAPE supports strategic commissioning by CCGs (Clinical Commissioning Groups)

|  | Activity | SHAPE outputs |
|---|---|---|
| Strategic Commissioning by CCGs (Clinical Commissioning Groups | **Understanding local needs. Assessing the health needs of the population being served, analysing economic and social inequalities** (e.g. demographic, lifestyle, inequality profile of the population being served). | • Age structure<br>• Ethnicity structure<br>• Population density<br>• A range of mortality figures<br>• Patterns of morbidity<br>• Deprivation measures<br>• Teenage pregnancies and child obesity<br>• A wide range of QOF (Quality and Outcomes Framework) prevalence indicators |
|  | **Evaluating available resources. Assessing existing service provision and performance in relation to the needs identified above, and the capital, financial and human resources required.** | • Clinical data provides analyses of emergency admissions, readmissions, excess bed days and length of stay by provider or commissioner: an overview of current performance and opportunities for improvement<br>• The financial opportunities of different scenarios e.g. if care was delivered differently by secondary care providers<br>• Cost of care by programme budgeting categories<br>• Map of the location of a number of health care facilities which can be directly compared to local needs<br>• Screening uptake rates and immunisation<br>• QOF (Quality and Outcomes Framework) prevalence indicators and also provides a link to actual QOF data at GP practice level<br>• Units of dental activity<br>• GP satisfaction survey |
|  | **Determining estate configuration** (site location information and map of the distribution of services to be built up for a defined area); travel time and distances, areas of poor access to services, opportunities for asset rationalisation, disposal, or investment. Comparing local data with the average, and range of values for England: | • Built 2005 to date and built pre-1948<br>• Percentage of unutilised space<br>• Percentage of functionally unsuitable space<br>• Percentage of building footprint/land area<br>• Risk adjusted backlog maintenance cost ($£/m^2$)<br>• Occupancy costs ($£/m^2$)<br>• Property maintenance costs ($£/m^2$) |

Table 4.3  SHAPE supports urgent and emergency care

|  | Activity | SHAPE outputs |
|---|---|---|
| "Urgent and emergency care is the range of healthcare services available to people who need medical advice, diagnosis and/ or treatment quickly and unexpectedly." (Department of Health) | **Understanding local needs Assessing the health needs of the population being served, analysing economic and social inequalities** (e.g. demographic, lifestyle, inequality profile of the population being served). | • Age structure<br>• Ethnicity structure<br>• Population density<br>• A range of mortality figures<br>• Patterns of morbidity<br>• Deprivation measures<br>• Teenage pregnancies and child obesity<br>• A wide range of QOF (Quality and Outcomes Framework) prevalence indicators |
|  | **Evaluating available resources. Assessing existing service provision and performance in relation to the needs identified above, and the capital, financial and human resources required.** | • Total emergency inpatient admissions of local populations<br>• Identification of admissions for most common emergency conditions<br>• Identification of admissions for less common emergency conditions<br>• Multiple emergency rates by condition (i.e. number of times a patient is admitted in a year)<br>• Examination of Length of Stay and excess bed days by particular conditions including an assessment of potential reduction in bed days if improvements were made<br>• Percentage of emergency re-admissions within 30 days, by particular conditions<br>• Map of location of a number of providers including A&E departments |

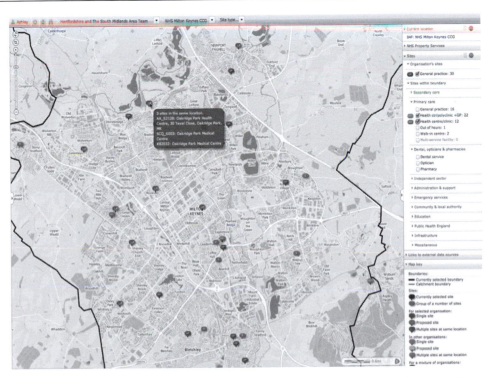

**4.2  SHAPE boundary and sites:** Location of primary care sites within a Clinical Commissioning Group boundary. Spatial distribution of primary and community facilities can establish whether there are any gaps in service delivery in relation to local needs

SHAPE outputs consist of downloadable reports, which summarise an organisation's performance on a range of indicators from hospital activity, public health and deprivation to estate performance. A set of predefined indicators allows easy identification and benchmarking of information of particular interest. Specifically, SHAPE provides benchmarked indicators for: SHMI (Summary Hospital-level Mortality Indicator) and contextual indicators; ERIC (Estates Return Information Collection) describing the NHS estate; and QOF (Quality and Outcomes Framework). Outliers (where a local situation differs significantly from the national average) can easily be identified and seen quickly as areas which may require consideration or where there are opportunities for improvement for an organisation.

Built around a mapping tool that supports Travel Time Analysis and configured to NHS England's Strategic Health Authorities (SHAs) and Primary Care Trust (PCT) boundaries,

SHAPE has been updated to recognise the abolition of SHAs and PCTs and to map out at local authority level general medical and dental practices, clinical networks and clinical commissioning units. This means the provision of locations and site details of surgeries, clinics and health care centres, other prescribing centres, pharmacies, dentists and optometric services, prisons, care homes, and private sector health and social care facilities. The data therefore recognises the fact that services can be commissioned from and delivered in non-NHS locations, and also that independent health care providers (e.g. care homes) do indeed play an important part in care pathways, while at the same time acknowledging that private health care sector providers may in future have a greater role in delivering NHS services. Key features for the SHAPE tool concern improving strategic health care service planning and delivery, as well as developing a robust evidence base.

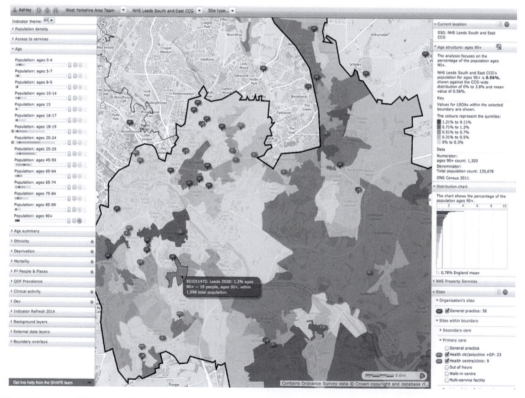

4.3 **SHAPE utilising census 2011 data:** Display of population ages 90+ by lower super output area from census 2011 data

Key features or characteristics for the SHAPE 2014 application are recognised by a number of notable objectives:

1 Improving Strategic Health care Service Planning and Delivery: SHAPE aims to meet the need for effective strategic health care planning which supports, informs and manages the future optimal and efficient design and delivery of health care services. It supports the shift of care from hospitals to primary and community settings, and has the potential to enhance the integration of health and social care and therefore ensure a seamless continuum of care for patients and staff alike.

SHAPE is about meeting the needs of many and diverse professional groups including managers for estates maintenance and development, estates and risk, capital plans, support services, commissioning and performance, service improvement, GP commissioning, public health, information analysis, medical and clinical planning and LIFT and other procurement routes.

Visualisation or graphical representation is an important feature of SHAPE that contributes to an increased understanding of the location of health care facilities and services delivered in them. Visualisation also allows for more effective public consultation to the introduction of new services and to any proposed changes to existing patterns of health care services delivery.

2 A Robust Evidence Base for SHAPE (ERIC, HES and ODS): SHAPE includes key performance indicators from NHS England ERIC (Estates Return Information Collection) data (www.hefs.ic.uk). ERIC is a method of recording numerical and geometric estates data. The Hospital Estates and Facilities Statistics is the national data warehouse for England, extracted from the ERIC returns and collected and published on behalf of the UK Department of Health. It is the main central data collection for estates and facilities services from the NHS, containing information dating back to 1999/2000. The data enables the analysis of Estates and Facilities information from NHS organisations in England; it is a compulsory requirement that NHS Trusts submit an Estates Return on a regular basis. However, the data is as provided by NHS organisations and has not been amended, and therefore its accuracy and completeness are the responsibility of the Trusts.

SHAPE uses ERIC data to enable users to benchmark their estate's performance against peers and other organisations, both internally within the geographical health economy and externally within NHS England. In mapping existing health care facilities SHAPE facilitates the identification of gaps in health and social care delivery, areas of under-provision and/or over-provision, as well as the identification of clusters of unsuitable accommodation that indicate the need for new build health care facilities.

SHAPE uses the Hospital Episode Statistics (HES) data managed by the NHS Information Centre for Health and Social Care (NHS IC) on behalf of the Secretary of State for Health. The HES data derives from all NHS Trusts in England including acute hospitals, primary care, ambulance and mental health. HES data dates back to 1987 and followed a report on the collection and use of hospital activity information published by a steering group chaired by Dame Edith Körner. HES data collects a detailed record for each 'episode' of admitted patient care delivered in England by NHS hospitals or delivered in the independent sector but commissioned by the NHS. In 2006–07 there were 13 million admissions, resulting in nearly 15 million episodes.

**Table 4.4** SHAPE supports transforming communities services to separate commissioning of services from provision

| | Activity | SHAPE outputs |
|---|---|---|
| **Transforming Communities Services** (The separation of commissioning of services from provision; empowering front-line staff to provide modern, personalised and effective care of a consistently high quality and to offer choice and control to patients over their community care and treatment) | **Understanding local needs. Assessing the health needs of the population being served, analysing economic and social inequalities** (e.g. demographic, lifestyle, inequality profile of the population being served) **relative to the natonal average.** | • Age structure<br>• Ethnicity structure<br>• Population density<br>• A range of mortality figures<br>• Patterns of morbidity<br>• Deprivation measures<br>• Teenage pregnancies and child obesity<br>• A wide range of QOF (Quality and Outcomes Framework) prevalence indicators |
| | **Assessing of available services:** Information on clinical activity which can be used to identify activity that may be more appropriately dealt with in primary and community care settings. | • Map of the distribution of patients with particular conditions to identify clusters of patients that require the support of neighbourhood teams that can help plan care and encourage self-help and self-management of long-term conditions in primary and community settings. |
| | **Evaluating Service performance and identifying opportunities for change** | • QOF prevalence indicators and a link to actual QOF data at GP practice level<br>• Clinical data provides analyses of emergency admissions, readmissions, excess bed days and length of stay by provider or commissioner for selected HRGs or diagnoses. This will help to provide an overview of current performance and opportunities for improvement<br>• Breast and cervical screening uptake<br>• Flu and MMR immunisation rates<br>• Benchmarking information on outpatient activity such as the ratio of first to follow-up appointments, the average number of days waiting for appointment, % of "Did Not Attends" by PCT, CCG and GP practice can help to identify opportunities for new referral guidelines and care pathways |
| | **Determining estate configuration** (site location information and map of the distribution of services to be built up for a defined area); travel time and distances, areas of poor access to services, opportunites for asset rationalisation, disposal, or investment. Comparing local data with the average, and range of values for England: | • Built 2005 to date and built pre-1948<br>• Percentage of unutilised space<br>• Percentage of functionally unsuitable space<br>• Percentage of building footprint/land area<br>• Risk adjusted backlog maintenance cost ($£/m^2$)<br>• Occupancy costs ($£/m^2$)<br>• Property maintenance costs ($£/m^2$) |

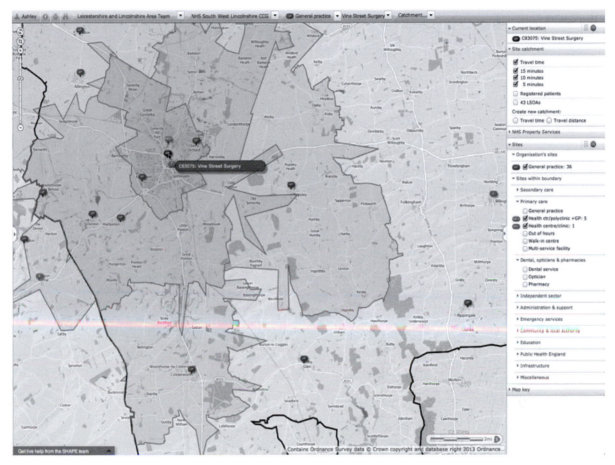

**4.4  SHAPE travel time catchments:** 5-, 10- and 15-minute peak-time travel catchments around a GP practice

**4.5 SHAPE GP registered patients:** Location of GP practice registered patients by lower super output area

Table 4.5 SHAPE supports the NHS programme Quality, Innovation, Productivity & Prevention (QIPP) safe care + right care

| | Activity | SHAPE outputs |
|---|---|---|
| The NHS programme for Quality, Innovation, Productivity and Prevention (QIPP) involving all NHS staff, clinicians, patients and the voluntary sector in improving the quality of care and making up to £20 bn of efficiency savings by 2015 for reinvestment in frontline care. | **Increasing understanding of RISK from Unsafe Care/Harm which** arises from:<br>• High volumes of elective + emergency clinical activity.<br>• Procedures that are carried out rarely.<br>• Inappropriate staffing deployments.<br>• Poor quality of the physical estate. | • Total inpatient admissions relative to national average<br>• Percentage of high volume admissions and number and length of stay of low volume admissions by condition<br>• An estate profile that is indicated by a number of buildings that were built pre-1948 and percentage of unutilised space. |
| | **Analysing Unsafe Clinical Performance indicated by:**<br>• High rates of conditions targeted by the Safety Express.<br>• Hospital and community-acquired pressure ulcers, blood clots (DVT and pulmonary embolism).<br>• High rates of urinary tract infections in patients with catheters.<br>• Increased incidents of falls in health and social care settings. | • Percentage of emergency readmissions within 30 days<br>• Screening uptake rates and immunisations.<br>• Hospital outpatient ratio of first to follow-up appointments and average waiting time for an appointment.<br>• Hospital-acquired infection, high rates of inpatient readmission, low rates of follow-up and screening rates, and in long waiting times for outpatient appointment.<br>• Unsafe workforce featuring low coverage of the population and poor levels of qualification.<br>• An unsafe estate profile featuring poor occupancy and high maintenance costs; risk-adjusted backlog maintenance; percentage of space considered 'not functionally suitable'.<br>• ERIC indicators |
| | **Investigating Costs for Safe Care+** implications of unsafe care e.g. those from readmissions and occupancy. | • Potential savings if multiple emergency admissions are reduced<br>• Evidence that 10% of patients are harmed during hospital care.<br>• Full impact of harm or its costs (estimated at £1 bn each year) to the NHS alone. |
| | **Increase understanding of local needs for Right Care:** as indicated by characteristics of the local population relative to the national average on a number of key factors | • Population density, age structure and ethnicity<br>• A range of mortality figures.<br>• Deprivation and lifestyle measures (e.g. teenage pregnancies and child obesity)<br>• A wide range of QOF (Quality and Outcomes Framework) prevalence indicators<br>• In many cases the information is available at lower super output area, allowing it to be aggregated and displayed for a variety of boundaries (Clinical Commissioning Groups, Local Authorities and organisational clusters). |
| | **Assessing the extent of available services for Right Care** by analysing existing local service provision, performance in relation to identified needs, and the capital, financial and human resources required to provide them. | • Total elective and emergency inpatient admissions of the local GP-registered population and by individual providers.<br>• Identification of elective and emergency admissions for less common conditions, for total population and by individual providers.<br>• A&E attendances.<br>• Outpatient attendances by specialty.<br>• Units of dental activity by general dental practice.<br>• QOF (Quality and Outcomes Framework) for palliative care. |

| Activity | SHAPE outputs |
|---|---|
| **Evaluating service performance and opportunities for change:** through analysing information on current performance of some relevant services and on opportunities/ savings resulting from performance changes. | • Hospital inpatients: savings potentially available by improving emergency and elective LOS and excess bed days by particular conditions, by commissioner and by individual providers<br>• Percentage of emergency re-admissions within 30 days.<br>• Day case rate.<br>• Breast and cervical screening uptake.<br>• Flu and MMR immunisation rates.<br>• Hospital outpatients: ratio of first to follow-up appointments, average number of days waiting for appointment, % of DNA by PCT and by GP practice/CCG.<br>• Hospital outpatient activity [referral or attendance] per 1000 patients by PCT and by GP practice/CCG.<br>• Percentage of uncoded activity. |
| **Estates configuration for the Right Care** Indicated by site location information and map presentation to build up a complete picture of the distribution of services to be built up for a defined area. Travel time and distance analyses, poor access to services and where service delivery may be rationalised without compromising access to services. Apply Estate (ERIC) key performance indicators to identify opportunities for asset rationalisation, disposal, or investment comparing local data with the average, and the range of values for England | • Built 2005 to date and built pre-1948<br>• Percentage of unutilised and functionally unsuitable space<br>• Percentage of building footprint/land area<br>• Risk adjusted backlog maintenance cost (£/m²)<br>• Occupancy and property maintenance costs (£/m²) |

HES information is stored as a large collection of separate records – one for each period of care – in a secure record level data warehouse (the NHS IC 2010). Each HES record contains a wide range of information about an individual patient admitted to a NHS hospital. For example:

- Clinical information about diagnoses/treatments and operations.

- Information about the patient, such as age group, gender and ethnic category.
- Administrative information, such as time waited, date of admission or date of discharge.
- Geographical information on where the patient was treated, e.g. the NHS Trust, Primary Care Trust or independent sector hospital (at home or abroad) and the area in which they lived.

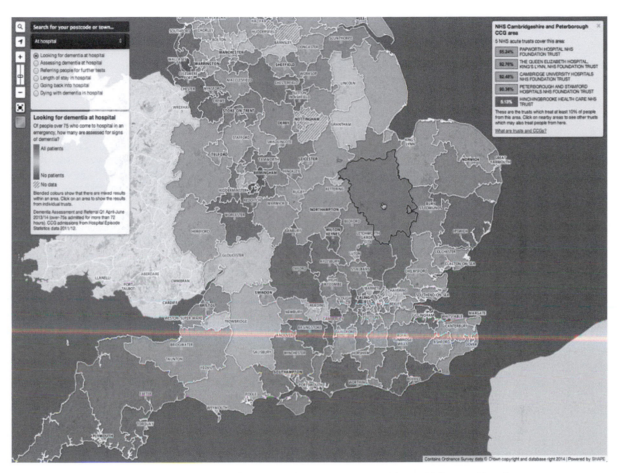

**4.6 SHAPE dementia atlas:** SHAPE mapping and data powering the dementia atlas – a standalone publicly accessible website

**Table 4.6 SHAPE supports long-term conditions**

| | Activity | SHAPE outputs |
|---|---|---|
| Around 15 m people living with a long-term condition in England: the main driver of cost and activity in the NHS accounting for around 70% of overall health and care spend; disproportionately higher users of health services – representing 50% of GP appointments, 60% of outpatient and A&E attendances and 70% of inpatient bed days. | **Understanding local needs. Assessing the health needs of the population being served, analysing economic and social inequalities** (e.g. demographic, lifestyle, inequality profile of the population being served). | • Age structure<br>• Ethnicity structure<br>• Population density<br>• A range of mortality figures<br>• Patterns of morbidity<br>• Deprivation measures<br>• Teenage pregnancies and child obesity<br>• A wide range of QOF (Quality and Outcomes Framework) prevalence indicators |
| | **Evaluating available resources. Assessing existing service provision and performance in relation to the needs identified above, and the capital, financial and human resources required** | • Clinical data highlight those HRGs representing the highest proportion of admissions and bed days by admission type<br>• Distribution of patients with particular long-term conditions is mapped to identify clusters of patients that require the support of neighbourhood teams that can help plan care and encourage self-help and self-management of long-term conditions. |
| | **Evaluating service performance and opportunities for change:** through analysing information on current performance of some relevant services and on opportunities/savings resulting from performance changes. | • QOF prevalence indicators and a link to actual QOF data at GP practice level. The map presentation shows values for individual practices in the form of colour coded quintiles.<br>• A proxy measure of the level of risk identification at practice level and help to identify where risk profiling could be improved.<br>• Clinical data analysis of emergency admissions, readmissions, excess bed days and length of stay by provider or commissioner for selected HRGs or diagnoses related to long-term conditions. This will help to develop a baseline assessment of long-term conditions in the locality.<br>• An estimate of savings that could be achieved by reducing emergency admissions, length of stay, excess bed days and multiple admissions if performance is improved to the level achieved by the top 25% of providers |

HES data uses the World Health Organization's International Classification of Diseases and Related Health Problems (ICD) to record diagnosis information, and the Office of Population Censuses and Surveys: Classification of Interventions and Procedures 4th Edition (OPCS-4) classification to record details of any procedures or interventions performed, e.g. hip replacements. Facts about individual patients are highly confidential and are not released. However, summary reports can be produced based on the contents of the records. For example, the total number of hip replacements can be found by searching the database for records that contain the appropriate procedure or intervention codes. In this case the resulting figure (many thousands per year) reveals nothing about the individuals concerned, and may be freely publicised. HES comprises three main datasets: 1. admitted patient, which includes inpatients and day cases; 2. outpatient, which was labelled as 'experimental data' until 2005–6; and 3. accident and emergency (A&E), which was labelled as 'experimental data' for 2007–8 until 2009–10.

Quarterly data is also to be included to meet user requirements for access to up-to-date information, allowing data to be examined from either a commissioner or provider perspective to support analysis of different admission types across Healthcare Resource Groups (HRGs) or ICD diagnostic codes. Clinical benchmarking data is provided in relation to a number of key indicators (Average Length of Stay, Excess Bed-Days, Day-Case Proportions, Pre-Operative Stay, Weekend Discharging and Multiple Emergency Admissions).

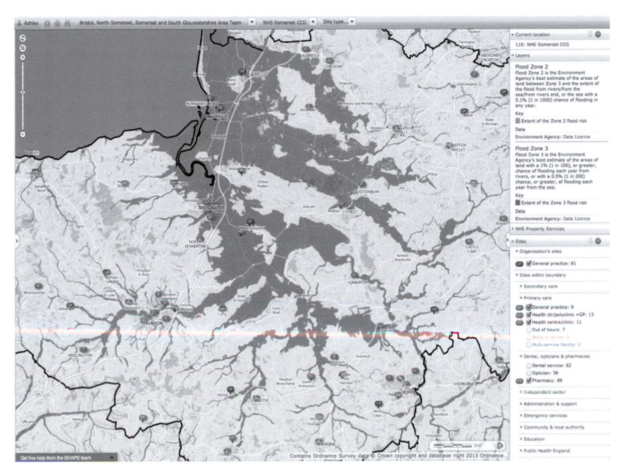

**4.7 SHAPE flood risk areas: Environment agency flood zone 2 and 3 data and the location of primary care and pharmacy sites**

SHAPE can therefore be used in the siting of new health and social care premises, the benchmarking of clinical services, mapping local populations by medical condition, age, socio-economic, and public health factors, investigating the performance of organisations on key estates indicators, or developing a repository of organisation and site estates information.

SHAPE's Estates Module utilises an Organisation Data Services-based database of over 86,000 geographically coded facilities of acute hospitals, health care centres, GP and dental practices and ambulance stations by a particular organisation, as well as by other organisations. The Organisation Data Service (ODS) is managed by NHS

Connecting for Health (NHS CFH), which is part of the Department of Health Informatics Directorate and has a role to maintain and develop the NHS national IT infrastructure.

ODS codes facilitate the process of identifying and communicating reliably, quickly, easily and efficiently the various locations involved in a patient's treatment. ODS does this by providing unique identification codes for the organisational entities of interest to the NHS, ensuring that only valid data and essential and correct information is exported to any NHS IT health care system. The ODS coding clarifies the NHS organisational hierarchical structure and the links between the various organisations at different levels – for instance the fact that a particular site is the responsibility of a certain Trust, the fact that the Trust reports to a particular NHS Geographical Health Economy or Regional Health Authority, and so on.

This data includes postcode information provided by the Office for National Statistics for use within the NHS and Department of Health. Data is archived and thus provides a detailed record of how NHS structure has changed over time, during Trust mergers and name changes or re-organisations.

SHAPE displays all operational sites used by an organisation to deliver health and social care services, as well as particular types of site or facility. Site data is validated at local level to ensure an accurate record of the NHS. Estates professionals can also input local data about site types and the range of services provided, adding site plans and photographs or images of buildings.

For a specific site location, SHAPE provides 'Catchment Area Analysis' based on either peak travel times or travel distances to enable the identification of opportunities for rationalisation of the health care estate and assessment of the relative accessibility of, for example, site options for new build developments, while also providing evidence for decision-making with regard to the best location for any additional community-based services transferred from hospital environments. 'Drive Time Analyses' are based on peak flow travel times with boundaries defined by whole lower super output areas (LSOAs).

Distance analyses can be used as a proxy for walking time. Additional drive time and distances can also be added locally. The Travel Time Tool also provides a demographic and deprivation profile of the population, thereby relating levels of service need to levels of access to services in particular locations.

Specialist indicators have been developed for SHAPE – for example, configuration to display eight-minute and nineteen-minute drive time catchments for ambulances. However, there is potential for the further development of more indicators for Mental Health, Outcomes Framework and Clinical Commissioning Groups infrastructure, as well as for more functionality provided by a mixing desk, 'Your area' profiles, export to Microsoft Excel, a dashboard component 'powered by SHAPE' and estate site profiles roll out.

## Case study in implementing SHAPE

Implementing the SHAPE application is usefully illustrated by referring to the piloting process, outcomes and analysis as well as looking at the Kent County Council implementation (Tables 4.7 and 4.8).

Table 4.7  SHAPE supports the planning and commissioning decisions in families and social care (Kent County Council)

| | Activity | SHAPE outcomes |
|---|---|---|
| Supports key health policy initiatives:<br><br>• Quality Innovation Productivity & Prevention (QIPP).<br>• Joint Strategic Needs Assessment (JSNA).<br>• Transforming Community Services.<br><br>Complements the range of tools we use to support planning and commissioning decisions in Families and Social Care. | • Linking to national datasets for clinical analysis, public health, primary care and demographic data with estates performance and location of facilities<br>• Enabling interactive investigations by NHS Commissioning Board Local Area Teams, Trusts Providers, Clinical Commissioning Groups, GP practices and Local Authorities;<br>• Providing a range of flexible application capabilities that facilitate scenario planning and testing | • Optimum efficiency in the design and delivery of services that is benchmarked to national indicators.<br>• Integration of health and social care services and settings.<br>• Strategic Needs Assessments, Risk Stratification and Predictive Modelling, and Service Planning.<br>• Strategic optimum location of services and premises that also meets targets for sustainability by reducing transport. |
| | • Improving access to services by different populations in different communities in the Kent County Council area.<br>• Reducing Hospital admissions.<br>• Shifting care closer to home.<br>• Aiding development of a Business Case for a new facility.<br>• Increasing understanding of clinical activity for a clinical network.<br>• Aiding the development of a Care Pathway Approach to service delivery.<br>• Helping with the identification of cost savings within a health and social care economy.<br>• Developing an appropriate Estate Strategy that aligns Strategic Services Plan.<br>• Evaluating the efficiency and effectiveness of an existing service model. | • Improved access to services to meet user expectations.<br>• Reduced hospital admissions and transfers to avoid user journeys to and from hospital.<br>• Care is provided closer to home to increase user satisfaction.<br>• Aids development of Business Case for a new facility, something which facilitates approvals by the Department of Health and other authorities<br>• Implementation of a Care Pathway Approach to service provision and delivery<br>• Produces an Estate Strategy that is aligned with the Strategic Services Plan<br>• Providing the evidence of the efficiency and effectiveness of an existing service model |
| | • Reducing inequalities in access to care by different groups in the community<br>• Supporting Clinical Commissioning by Clinical Commissioning Groups<br>• Supporting Joint Strategic Needs Assessment (JSNA)<br>• Supporting Quality Innovation Productivity & Prevention (QIPP) Right Care, Safe Care, Long-Term Conditions and Urgent & Emergency Care. | • Demographic data e.g. age structure, ethnicity and deprivation.<br>• Public health data e.g. mortality, screening, childhood obesity and lifestyle indicators.<br>• Clinical inpatient activity e.g. high volume case types, analysis of Length of Stay and readmission rates. |

**Table 4.8 Outcomes from the Implementation of SHAPE application by Kent County Council**

| |
|---|
| **Outcome 1  Workplace Planning and Evaluation** |
| • Mapping of physical social care asset interests and providers across Kent to enable a whole-system view for service design planning and evaluation. This was used to support Workplace planning, joint commissioning plans, and other intelligence for commissioning of servicess. In this case, Kent County Council mapped 280 asset and service delivery/access points, tested and geocoded, worked on categorising asset type and service descriptions to provide a common health and social care description. |
| • The Council identified next stage mapping to include key partner providers such as clinics from Age UK. SHAPE was used to support the development of workplace strategies as part of the Health and Social Care Integration Programme. |
| **Outcome 2 Integrated Emergency Planning** |
| • Asset and service mapping enables Kent County Council to plan a more holistic approach to business continuity and emergency preparedness for extreme events, resilience and climate change adaptation work. A pan-service and cross-sector approach is essential for the development and delivery of effective adaptation and resilience strategies across the health and social care system. |
| • Work is progressing as part of a multi-agency approach in resilience planning, including identifying vulnerable communities in flood planning and other high risk areas for Kent so that these are considered as part of core plans and organisational risk management and business continuity functions. |
| **Outcome 3 Strategic Commissioning** |
| • The application supported Commissioning Managers, Peformance Managers, and Service Improvement Managers. Strategic commissioners used SHAPE as a county level interactive mapping resource, allowing current and future planned services to be presented along with other relevant social care and health activities, and current and projected demographic profiling. This provides Kent County Council with the ability to select relevant data and match it with demographic trends for better strategic planning and market shaping. |
| • Modelling future planned housing developments and projected client numbers will inform joint service and asset planning with Health and other strategic partners across Adult and Children's Social Care. |
| • SHAPE was used to support the Good Day Programme, Kent's stragegy for improving days for people with learning disabilities. As part of Community Services, Kent County Council mapped specialist community facilities such as Changing Places and Gateway to support plans in meeting the needs of people with a range of disabilities and their carers. |
| • SHAPE application is to be developed further to include Voluntary Organisations Services, Catchment Areas and the Services Available, Local Population Needs, Demographic Profiling, Risk Stratification, and consideration of the impact of Adult and Children's Social Care transformation in Kent. |

Evidence of the usefulness of the SHAPE application has been provided by one Trust which reported achieving directly and indirectly a total of £3,802,000 of efficiency cost savings, as well as reducing the backlog maintenance (from £12m to £5.8m annually) as a result of rationalisation, intensive utilisation and addressing under-performance of the NHS estate. Infrastructure projects, although sometimes overlooked, do play a crucial role in the ongoing reconciliation of the Care Model, the Architectural Healthcare Environment and the Estates Strategy, which are essential requirements to deliver success. The selected case study example shows how SHAPE has been implemented in practice to achieve more efficiency and effectiveness in strategic health care asset planning or of land and property use. Evidence of what SHAPE is used for also comes from the many quotes provided by users:

> *SHAPE compares population needs and demographics for existing or proposed sites. It helps compare the clinical activity of sites or the number of patients registered at a GP.*
>
> Head of Estates, North Tees Cluster
> Primary Care Trusts.

*We have made regular use of SHAPE for mapping existing health services and how they would cope with increases in population.*

SW Essex Primary Care Trust

*We used SHAPE to inform our exploration of the efficiency and effectiveness of current service models and to help project future capacity requirements.*

Associate Director of Economic and Operational Research Directorate of Strategic Development North Tees and Hartlepool NHS Foundation Trust

*SHAPE is being used to support a strategic estates planning project across London. The aim is to capture high level estate and service details of every NHS site in London and to further develop a system that will assist the strategic estates planning process and link it to commissioner's service planning across London. The work will allow us to map the estate at organisation, sector and pan-London level and hence form the basis of the 'Where are we now?' element of a strategic estates plan. The SHAPE application is being used as the platform for this work, and has the potential to allow us to input locally collected data and then interrogate it at site level to generate additional performance indicators.*

Strategic Estates Advisor, NHS London

*We are using SHAPE to support the commissioning of primary dental care. SHAPE can help to compile reports of the population demographics within a ten-minute driving distance and a fifteen-minute walking distance of each NHS dental practice in County Durham and Darlington PCT, which will assist the commissioning of dental services.*

Senior House Officer in Dental Public Health

*The Cardio-Vascular Disease (CVD) network has used SHAPE, alongside NHS Comparators and a Programme Budgeting tool to present information to GPs and stimulate a debate about the efficiency and effectiveness of current CVD services in context of QIPP. Specifically, SHAPE was used to present CVD admissions as a percentage of total admissions; to highlight differences in admission patterns between PCTs for individual CVD Healthcare Resource Groups (HRGs), and to compare emergency re-admission rates for CVD HRGs.*

Gloucestershire, Wiltshire and Somerset CVD Network

The availability of a site-based database outside each individual organisation is helpful. The ERIC database is useful for an organisation-wide analysis, but it is limited by being based in aggregated data particularly in relation to the primary and community estate.

SHAPE combines clinical data, public health indicators, Quality and Outcomes Framework prevalence data and demographic information with a mapping capability to generate well graphically illustrated presentations for GP patient forums, local Health Watch bodies and local Health and Wellbeing Boards within local authorities. Collectively, Joint Strategic Needs Assessment will facilitate collaborative commissioning between clinical commissioning groups and authorities. This will enhance opportunities for partnership working in commissioning services and the rationalisation of delivery models and physical assets.

The Strategic Health Asset Planning and Evaluation (SHAPE) tool represents an important tool to enhance efficiency and effectiveness in supporting the delivery of health and social care. Two studies, on the development of the Sheffield Database of Architectural Health Care Environments and Staff and Patient Outcomes and on the evaluation of the ASPECT tool and AEDET Evolution Section C: Staff and Patient Environment, also provide mechanisms to enhance efficiency and effectiveness in evidence-based design.

## ASPECT vs. Heading C in AEDET Evolution

In Chapter 3, we showed that ASPECT can either be used as a standalone tool to evaluate the internal environment for staff and patients, or it can support AEDET Evolution to provide a more comprehensive evaluation of the design of health care environments. In the latter case, AEDET Evolution Section C: *The Staff and Patient Environment* can be supplemented by the much more detailed ASPECT tool.

When used to support AEDET Evolution, ASPECT enables the user to score the Staff and Patient Environment heading in AEDET Evolution in a more detailed, accurate way. This is entirely based on the empirical research. ASPECT therefore effectively takes charge of what was referred to as Performance factors. In other words, the better the scores for a design in ASPECT, the more likely it is that the building will achieve the performance savings indicated by the research.

A study by the Sheffield Health Care Research Group was conducted to test the effectiveness of the more detailed ASPECT tool over AEDET Evolution Section C: The Staff and Patient Environment. In the study, images of health care projects were shown to groups of graduate nurses (without design training or expertise) and graduate architects (with design training or education). These students were asked to assess the images against the relevant AEDET Evolution and ASPECT scales. A selection of images was found for each relevant scale. Among this selection were several that were expected by the research team to be highly rated. The results of the exercise were expected to show the extent of fit with the appropriate metrics for measuring mental capacities/processes. Other interesting results were expected to show the extent to which the scales produced homogeneity, and the extent to which architects and nurses could operate the scales and how far they agreed or disagreed about them. However, a very important outcome would also be a selection of images that were highly rated and which can form the basis for the development of an exemplar layer for the AEDET Evolution/ASPECT tools.

The study methodology covered the following steps.

- A selection of 15 to 18 suitable UK NHS projects were initially identified by the University of Sheffield Health Care Research Group, and these schemes were then agreed with Jonathan Millman and Sue Taylor at the Department of Health.
- The selected schemes were appropriately professionally photographed to the standards required. This was conducted under a separate contract or commission between the Department of Health Estates and Facilities Division and an approved photographer. However, the photographer worked closely with the University of Sheffield as follows:

  - The University of Sheffield assisted and trained the photographer in the use of the AEDET Evolution and ASPECT scales.
  - In each case the photographer was shown the kinds of image content required for each scale under investigation.
  - The University of Sheffield accompanied the photographer on four site visits to further reinforce what was expected from the images.

- The University of Sheffield then analysed, collated and structured all the images and prepared PowerPoint slide presentations for the student nurses and student architects.
- Presentations took place following dummy-run versions of the PowerPoint materials in November and December 2005 to test and validate the study methodology. For both groups of nurses and architects the conditions, including venues, needed to be identical.
- Data from evaluations, collected from the matching samples of approximately 12 student nurses and 12 architectural students for all scales, were analysed, evaluated and documented.
- Conclusions and recommendations were drawn from the analytical focus group exercises.
- A final report and files of the typical exemplar layer images and scores were prepared to provide an appropriate basis for the development of an Exemplar Layer for ASPECT, and where possible for AEDET Evolution as well.

This study uses photographs as a tool to clarify the participants' understanding of what a particular statement or question refers to in both tools, ASPECT and AEDET Evolution Section C: Staff and Patient Environment. This use of photographs in design studies is not new. Previous studies have often used photographs as a tool for examining preferences for landscape and clarifying the understanding of what is aesthetically pleasing.

Much of the landscape preference literature has focused on identifying features or qualities included in a photograph which seem to correlate with either preference decisions or high scenic beauty scores (for example, Herzog 1985, 1989; Gimblett 1990; Patsfall et al. 1984; Bernaldez et al. 1987;

Ruddell et al. 1989). These studies have produced some consistent results. For instance, when people categorise various landscapes, the division between what is rural and what is urban is strong (Ulrich 1977; Uzzell & Lewand 1990), with rural places being preferred to urban places (Zube 1973; Hodgson & Thayer 1980; Zube et al. 1983; Hull & Revell 1989). The presence or absence of water is also a clear division (Zube 1973; Zube et al. 1983; Blankson & Green 1991). Its presence seems to increase scenic value. A study by Scott and Canter (1997) also demonstrates that there is a theoretical and empirical distinction between evaluations of pictures and evaluations of the places they represent.

The selection of participants for the study was based on the following criteria:

- Participants needed to represent a sample of typical occupants or users of health care facilities or settings
- Participants with some training or background in design education and therefore representing an expert viewpoint
- Participants without any formal design education or training and therefore representing a non-expert viewpoint
- Participants without the baggage of too much experience of the design and operation of health care facilities

The selection of the health care schemes/projects was based on the following criteria:

- NHS schemes (i.e. PFI, non-PFI, LIFT, ProCure21 and others) in order to be able to disseminate good design practice nationally throughout the UK
- UK health care projects to provide users of AEDET Evolution and the ASPECT tool the opportunity to be able to visit them as necessary and see for themselves what is deemed good design
- European schemes to facilitate learning or lessons learnt from non-UK capital projects
- USA or other international examples to encourage design considerations from further afield

Seven schemes provided the initial selection of recently completed hospital or health care projects, which were seen as examples of good or better architectural design practice.

1 Bristol Royal Hospital for Children, Bristol
2 James Cook University Hospital, Middlesbrough
3 Kidderminster Minor Injuries Treatment Centre
4 Leicester City West Braunson Integrated Health and Social Care Centre (Primary Care)
5 Norfolk and Norwich Hospital
6 Nottingham Breast Institute
7 Woodhaven Mental Health Unit, Loperwood, Calmore

A lack of suitable images for most of the seven selected projects soon led to a change of strategy, to one which allowed pertinent issues below to be addressed.

The selection of ASPECT and AEDET Evolution statements was also based on several criteria. Early on during the project when we were considering the nature of statements or questions in both ASPECT and AEDET Evolution, we realised that not all statements can easily be matched with images or photographs. In some cases this was not necessary because the statements were already clear and unambiguous, and in others it was simply not sensible to do so. We therefore employed some basic rules for selection of statements, as follows:

1 Statements which could easily be matched with images. In this case, a statement could be matched with a single image or several images.
2 Statements which, if matched with images/photographs, would lead without confusion to exemplars whose content would highlight good design features and thereby help to promote or disseminate good design practice.
3 Statements which did not involve mathematical calculations.
4 Statements which were not about compliance with guidance or recommendations.

All this meant that during the exercise we were able to use 40 out of a total of 45 statements in ASPECT (that is, 85%) and 32 out of a total of 58 statements in AEDET Evolution (that is, 55%).

The seven ASPECT statements which were excluded from the test are:

C4 Comfort and control
    C4.2 Patients and staff can easily control the artificial lighting
    C4.4 Patients and staff can easily control the temperature
    C4.6 The design layout minimises unwanted noise in staff and patient areas
C7 Facilities
    C7.2 Patients can have a choice of bath/shower and assisted/unassisted bathrooms
    C7.5 There are easy chairs, tables and desks in the patients' spaces
    C7.7 There are easily accessible vending machines for snacks
    C7.8 There are facilities for patients' relatives/friends to stay overnight

**Table 4.9 Forty out of forty-seven (85%) of the ASPECT statements were tested in the exercise**

| C STAFF AND PATIENT ENVIRONMENT | | |
|---|---|---|
| C1 PRIVACY, COMPANY AND DIGNITY | 5 | 5 |
| C2 VIEWS | 5 | 5 |
| C3 NATURE AND OUTDOORS | 3 | 3 |
| C4 COMFORT AND CONTROL | 6 | 3 |
| C5 LEGIBILITY OF PLACE | 6 | 6 |
| C6 APPEARANCE | 8 | 8 |
| C7 FACILITIES | 8 | 4 |
| C8 STAFF | 6 | 6 |
| Total | 47 | 40 |

**Table 4.10 Thirty-two out of fifty-eight (55%) of the AEDET Evolution statements were tested in the exercise**

| IMPACT | | |
|---|---|---|
| A CHARACTER AND INNOVATION | 5 | 5 |
| B FORM AND MATERIALS | 5 | 5 |
| C STAFF AND PATIENT ENVIRONMENT | 8 | 8 |
| D URBAN/SOCIAL INTEGRATION | 4 | 4 |
| **BUILD QUALITY** | | |
| E PERFORMANCE | 4 | 4 |
| F ENGINEERING | 5 | 0 |
| G CONSTRUCTION | 7 | 0 |
| **FUNCTIONALITY** | | |
| H USE | 7 | 1 |
| I ACCESS | 7 | 5 |
| J SPACE | 6 | 0 |
| Total | 58 | 32 |

The 26 AEDET Evolution statements which were excluded from the test are:

F   Engineering
    F1 The engineering systems are well designed, flexible and efficient in use
    F2 The engineering systems exploit any benefits from standardisation and prefabrication where relevant
    F3 The engineering systems are energy-efficient
    F4 There are emergency backup systems that are designed to minimise disruption
    F5 During construction, disruption to essential services is minimised

G  Construction

G1  If phased planning and construction are necessary, the various stages are well organised

G2  Temporary construction work is minimised

G3  The impact of the building process on continuing health care provision is minimised

G4  The building can be readily maintained

G5  The construction is robust

G6  The construction allows easy access to engineering systems for maintenance, replacement and expansion

G7  The construction exploits any benefits from standardisation and prefabrication where relevant

H  Use

H1  The prime functional requirements of the brief are satisfied

H2  The design facilitates the care model of the Trust

H3  Overall the building is capable of handling the projected throughput

H4  Work flows and logistics are arranged optimally

H5  The building is sufficiently adaptable to respond to change and to enable expansion

H6  Where possible, spaces are standardised and flexible in use patterns

I  Access

I2  There is adequate parking for visitors and staff cars, with appropriate provision for disabled people

I7  The fire planning strategy allows for ready access and egress

J  Space

J1  The design achieves appropriate space standards

J2  The ratio of usable space to the total area is good

J3  The circulation distances travelled by staff, patients and visitors are minimised by the layout

J4  Any necessary isolation and segregation of spaces is achieved

J5  The design makes appropriate provision for gender segregation

J6  There is adequate storage space

**Table 4.11 Examples of the type of photographs/images requested from the photographer**

**PATIENT BEDROOMS**

1  View from patient bed to and through the external window looking at good natural scenes (gardens, water, sculptures, woodlands and so on) for example, view of Poole Harbour from patients' bedrooms, i.e. picture postcard views.

2  View from patient bed looking towards and through the external window showing human activities and recreation.

3  View of single patient room from patient bed showing the door or way out.

4  View from patient bed looking towards the bathroom and shower area.

5  View from patient bed looking towards the ceiling noting interesting patterns and artwork.

6  View from patient bed looking towards other bed spaces.

7  View from visitors' easy chair looking towards the patient bed.

8  View of patient bed and chair close together.

9  View of patient bed and lifting hoists (mobile or ceiling-mounted).

10  View from visitors' overnight fold-up bed/couch looking towards the patient bed (made up) showing bed linen, fabrics and furnishings.

11  Views of multi-bed areas from the patient bed.

12  View from a patient bedhead control console looking towards blinds/curtains.

13  View from the patient bed towards the television (ceiling-mounted, wall-mounted or mounted on an extendable arm).

14  View from the patient bed looking towards display shelving showing 'get well' cards, flowers, ornaments etc.

15  View from the patient bed to writing desk/chair or dressing table/chair.

16  View from the patient bed towards the cupboard and personal storage area.

**WAITING, RECEPTION, SEATING, MILLING AND WORKING AREAS**

1  View out of large windows with low cill heights and high window heads (evoking 'a room with a view').

2  View of two people sitting and talking quietly.

3  View of several people sitting around a coffee table and side tables with magazines, flowers, ornaments, table lamps etc.

4  View of a sofa arrangement with cushions, throws, rugs etc. creating a comfortable and sleek 'homely' look and feel.

5  View of stylish corner seating arrangement with cushions, throws, rugs etc.

6  Views of groups of people in waiting areas (compare with the BA lounge at the airport).

7 View looking towards the reception desk from patients and visitors' waiting areas.

8 View from waiting areas showing TV and plasma screens for information.

9 View from waiting area showing the way in and way out of the building.

10 View of shops, coffee areas from waiting areas.

11 View of minimalist designs indicating simple shapes, clean lines and contemporary features.

## Issues

- Standards and content of photographs/images
- Quality of the photographs/images – for example, the quality of the photographs may not easily indicate the design features we would like to see
- Copyright and permissions to publish the photographs/images

In the end we settled for a combination of the following to address all the above issues and ensure that an adequate number of images would be obtained for AEDET Evolution and ASPECT statements:

- Images by a photographer commissioned by the Department of Health
- Images provided by the Department of Health from their photographic library
- Images provided by NHS Trusts
- Images obtained from architects/designers
- Images obtained from product manufacturers and other trade literature

Two one-day focus group sessions were held for the graduate architects on Wednesday 6 December 2006 and for the graduate nurses on Wednesday 13 December 2006. These followed dummy runs of the one-day sessions held earlier in the year.

Below is what happened on each of the one-day sessions, both held in meeting room 15.3 on the fifteenth floor of the Arts Tower, School of Architecture:

A Objectives of the day: Participants/subjects were presented with photographs (six images corresponding to each statement in AEDET Evolution and ASPECT) and then asked to score these on a scale of 1 to 6, providing their responses on a form (see Appendix for the response forms). Participants were continually reminded not to base their score on the quality of the photographs/images. The completed response forms were collected at the end of each session. These were then coded and analysed, forming the main output of this event.

B Participants: A sample of 12 to 15 students of nursing in their later years of study were invited to take part in the study to match a sample of architectural students in order to facilitate comparison.

C Venue: The sessions took place in meeting room 15.3, Arts Tower, Sheffield University S10 2TN. Two projectors were used simultaneously to show the six photographs and the individual photographs alongside the guidance associated with each statement or heading from AEDET Evolution and ASPECT. Participants were therefore continuously reminded of the guidance material and could refer to it when making their assessments.

D Times: Each session commenced at 9.30am on the respective Wednesday, with the final session of the day involving a discussion and allowing participants to provide feedback and reactions to the whole exercise. Each of the exercises ended at 4.00pm.

E Refreshments: Lunch was provided. Coffee, tea and light refreshments were also provided throughout the day, starting at 9.00am, to ensure that participants were alert and their concentration was maintained for the duration of the exercise.

F Payment: To encourage recruitment participants were paid for taking part in the event. University of Sheffield expenses claim forms were issued at the end of the day to allow participants to provide bank details and enable their remuneration to be paid directly into their bank. Overall the inducements were intended to obtain the right sort of participation and interested participants.

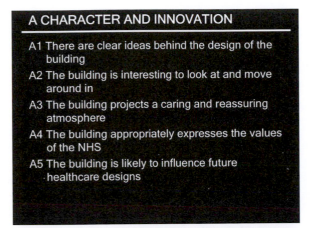

## A CHARACTER AND INNOVATION

A1 There are clear ideas behind the design of the building

A2 The building is interesting to look at and move around in

A3 The building projects a caring and reassuring atmosphere

A4 The building appropriately expresses the values of the NHS

A5 The building is likely to influence future healthcare designs

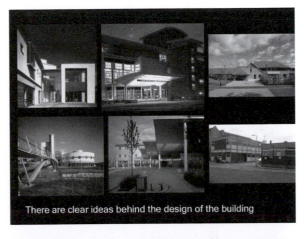

There are clear ideas behind the design of the building

### Guidance

A1 There are clear ideas behind the design of the building

The design should embody a clear and coherent vision confidently communicating its function and aspirations through its physical elements.

There are clear ideas behind the design of the building

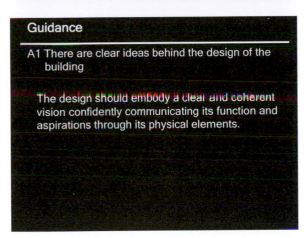

4.8  Examples of simultaneous projector 1 and 2 AEDET Evolution presentations to both graduate nurses and architects

## C1 PRIVACY, COMPANY AND DIGNITY

C1.1 Patients can choose to have visual privacy.

C1.2 Patients can have a private conversation.

C1.3 Patients can be alone.

C1.4 Patients have places where they can be with others

C1.5 Toilets/bathrooms are located logically, conveniently and discretely

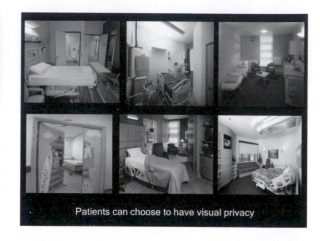

Patients can choose to have visual privacy

### Guidance

C1.1 Patients can choose to have visual privacy.

Either patients have their own individual room or can be screened off from others they share with or, if mobile, can easily find a private space. Privacy also means that activities can continue uninterrupted. For example the opening of a door should not expose the occupants of the room to passers-by outside. Although curtains can achieve some degree of visual privacy they may not necessarily guarantee dignity and almost certainly will not achieve acoustic privacy. Clearly individual rooms satisfy this feature whereas multiple bed bays do not naturally do so. In the case of for example four bed bays the arrangement of beds in space, distances between beds and the provision of screens can all help to offset to some extent the natural loss of privacy and dignity.

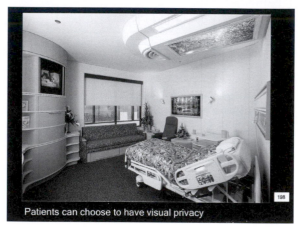

Patients can choose to have visual privacy

**4.9 Examples of simultaneous projector 1 and 2 ASPECT presentations to both graduate nurses and architects**

The scores from the response forms were coded and analysed (see extract below, or the appendix for the entire set of response forms).

Table 4.12 Extract of the AEDET Evolution response form and of the ASPECT response form for use by both graduate nurses and graduate architects (see Appendix for the entire set)

**AEDET Evolution**

A1  There are clear ideas behind the design of the building

| No | Image(s) | Scale | | | | | |
|----|----------|-------|---|---|---|---|---|
|    |          | 1 | 2 | 3 | 4 | 5 | 6 |
| 1  |          |   |   |   |   |   |   |
| 2  |          |   |   |   |   |   |   |
| 3  |          |   |   |   |   |   |   |
| 4  |          |   |   |   |   |   |   |
| 5  |          |   |   |   |   |   |   |
| 6  |          |   |   |   |   |   |   |

**ASPECT**

C1.1  Patients can choose to have visual privacy

| No | Image(s) | Scale | | | | | |
|----|----------|-------|---|---|---|---|---|
|    |          | 1 | 2 | 3 | 4 | 5 | 6 |
| 193 |         |   |   |   |   |   |   |
| 194 |         |   |   |   |   |   |   |
| 195 |         |   |   |   |   |   |   |
| 196 |         |   |   |   |   |   |   |
| 197 |         |   |   |   |   |   |   |
| 198 |         |   |   |   |   |   |   |

## Summary of feedback

The feedback sessions at the end of each PowerPoint slide presentation yielded several comments along key themes. Specifically:

- Participants found the one-day focus group session hard work and mentally challenging, but overall very worthwhile and enjoyable.

  *"We feel we have learnt something about design quality in health care buildings."*

  (Graduate architect)

  *"We will definitely be involved in capital schemes within our NHS Trust."*

  (Graduate nurse)

- There was general agreement among all participants in the two study groups that ASPECT statements were far easier to understand than those in AEDET Evolution. They could easily relate to the ASPECT statements about the patient and staff environment. Some participants suggested than AEDET Evolution be reformulated or redefined. Other participants were of the opinion that they had little or no knowledge of the issues raised by AEDET Evolution. Overall, the AEDET Evolution statements or questions seemed to take longer to complete or to respond to than the ASPECT statements.

- Participants in the two study groups confirmed that they seemed to have greater prior knowledge and experience of issues addressed by ASPECT statements than those raised by AEDET Evolution.

## Results and discussion

The data from the response forms was coded and then analysed. What follows is an analysis of the results and a discussion with reference to the validation of AEDET Evolution and ASPECT as evaluation tools.

### Significance of response

We first tested the scores given for each image against each statement with each group for significance using the Chi-Square test. This test shows whether or not there were significant differences in the numbers of people giving each rating. If there were no differences and the results were purely random we would expect to find equal numbers voting for rating 1, rating 2 and so on up to rating 6. We used the usual $p < 0.05$ criterion to decide whether the results were significant. The majority of images in both AEDET Evolution and ASPECT showed significant differences. In other words, the groups of respondents showed significant tendencies to rate the images in a particular way. Overall, this is an encouraging result.

Where an image did not attract significantly skewed ratings, this indicates that the group as a whole could not collectively make up their mind about what rating to give it. This could occur for three main reasons.

First, the image did not give the respondents enough information of the kind they needed to make the assessment against the statement. Second, the statement itself might be unclear. Finally, the pattern might simply be due to personal variations in response. If the second or third reasons were responsible we would expect to see a similar pattern for all or most of the six images tested against the statement.

Of the 32 statements tested in AEDET Evolution, only two showed more than three images, with no significant results for the architects and six for the nurses. Of the 40 statements tested in ASPECT, only two for the architects and seven for the nurses had more than three images showing a lack of significance. We shall return to the possible problems with this relatively small number of statements in a later section. However, at this point it is worth noting that in all cases the nurses showed slightly less ability to arrive at consensus than the architects. This theme will be taken up again in the next section using different statistics.

### Consistency of response

A key question that we want to try to answer with this data is the extent to which both AEDET Evolution and ASPECT elicit consistent responses. For each group of respondents (architects and nurses) we calculated the mean and standard deviation response to each image (usually six) shown against each statement in both AEDET Evolution and ASPECT. For each statement we averaged the means and standard deviations, arriving at an overall mean and standard deviation for that statement.

Remembering that these responses were all given under identical conditions but entirely independently, we can now test our question. If the responses were random we would expect to see equal numbers of responses in each of the six possible response score slots. Such an event is of course highly unlikely, but it is the theoretical extreme position of random inconsistency. If we imagine a sample size of N = 18 (very near to our sample), this would result in three people voting for each of the six categories on the six-point scale. Such a situation would lead to a standard deviation of 1.7. However, the ultimate in extreme inconsistency would be a result in which nine people voted for scale point 1 and nine voted for scale point 6, with none in between. Such a distribution would lead to a standard deviation of 2.5. The other extreme would be all 18 participants voting for the two central points on the scale equally, which would lead to a standard deviation of 0.5.

In general, the standard deviations in our data tended to be around 1 or just below. This indicates a high degree of consistency. In general, we can conclude that within each group the scores are very consistent. The usual assumption for a normal distribution is that just less than 70% of the population is found to be within the range plus or minus one standard deviation from the mean. In simple terms, for our data this is very encouraging.

Effectively, we can say that on average, between two-thirds and three-quarters of the scores are either the mean score or the score below or above the mean. Thus, if an image gets an average score of 3, most of the scores will have been 2, 3 or 4.

Given that some individuals inevitably tend to score highly while others habitually score lower, this seems to suggest that there is a high degree of overall consensus in the scoring. In general, then, within their two groups our respondents seem to be largely agreeing about the scores that should be given. The architects and nurses showed no significant difference in their degree of consensus.

This in turn enables us to look in detail at the relatively small number of images where there was less than the usual level of agreement. We shall discuss the images and statements where this might be the case in a later section.

## Agreement between the groups

Next we correlated the average scores of the architects and nurses within each statement across the six images presented. What this shows is not the degree of consensus within each group as above, but whether architects and nurses agree about which images should get high or low scores against each statement. We produced correlations for every statement and then averaged these for both AEDET Evolution and ASPECT. The overall grand correlation for AEDET Evolution statements was 0.3, while that for the ASPECT statements was much higher at 0.7. In fact, in AEDET Evolution some 37.5% of the statements yielded a strong correlation (0.7 or greater) whereas in ASPECT this was almost double at 70%. It clearly looks as if ASPECT achieves much higher levels of agreement between architects and nurses than AEDET Evolution.

Overall, the AEDET Evolution score raised some concerns, which we address below.

## Variation in AEDET Evolution correlations

We investigated these correlations further by producing average correlations for each section of the AEDET Evolution statements. These are shown in Table 4.13.

**Table 4.13 Variations in AEDET Evolution correlations**

| Section | Correlation |
| --- | --- |
| A CHARACTER & INNOVATION | 0.5 |
| B FORM & MATERIALS | −0.2 |
| C STAFF & PATIENT ENVIRONMENT | 0.5 |
| D URBAN/SOCIAL INTEGRATION | 0.0 |
| E PERFORMANCE | 0.3 |
| H USE | 0.1 |
| I ACCESS | 0.6 |

What this indicates is that while there is overall a small correlation, here it is:

- Almost non-existent in the following sections:
  B FORM AND MATERIALS
  D URBAN/SOCIAL INTEGRATION
  H USE
- Moderate in the following sections:
  A CHARACTER AND INNOVATION
  C STAFF AND PATIENT ENVIRONMENT
  E PERFORMANCE
- And reasonable in the following section:
  I ACCESS

Therefore, it would appear that for a substantial part of AEDET Evolution we should provisionally not expect groups as different as architects and nurses to be seeing the same things.

We can investigate this further by comparing these correlations with those found in ASPECT. Remember that each section in ASPECT expands one of the statements in AEDET Evolution Section C. We can therefore compare the correlation found for the single statement in AEDET Evolution Section C with the average for its corresponding whole section in ASPECT. These results are shown in Table 4.14.

**Table 4.14 Comparison of AEDET Evolution and ASPECT correlations**

| AEDET Evolution statement | Correlation | ASPECT section | Correlation |
|---|---|---|---|
| C1 The building respects the dignity of patients and allows for appropriate levels of privacy and dignity. | 0.5 | C1 | 0.9 |
| C2 There are good views inside and out of the building. | 1.0 | C2 | 0.7 |
| C3 Patients and staff have access to outdoors. | 0.5 | C3 | 0.9 |
| C4 There are high levels of both comfort and control of comfort. | 0.9 | C4 | 0.8 |
| C5 The building is clearly understandable. | –0.2 | C5 | 0.6 |
| C6 The interior of the building is attractive in appearance. | 0.2 | C6 | 0.5 |
| C7 There are good bath/toilet and other facilities for patients. | 0.7 | C7 | 0.7 |
| C8 There are good facilities for staff, including convenient places to work and relax without being on demand. | 0.9 | C8 | 0.8 |
| Overall | 0.5 | | 0.7 |

Thus, while the ASPECT sections all show consistently high correlations, the AEDET Evolution statements are extremely variable. In particular, statements C5 (The building is clearly understandable) and C6 (The interior of the building is attractive in appearance) in AEDET Evolution show virtually no correlation between architects and nurses. Statement C6 (The interior of the building is attractive in appearance) might be said to offer too much opportunity for individual interpretation and personal taste. The corresponding statements in ASPECT, however, manage on average a respectable correlation of 0.5.

Statement C5 (The building is clearly understandable) could be difficult for the non-expert to interpret correctly. This also requires considerable ability to look around and imagine the building as a whole. The corresponding statements in ASPECT unpack this into six statements, which on average get a correlation of 0.6.

### Possible future actions with regard to AEDET Evolution

We suggest that, taken together, all these results indicate the benefit of the finer-grain nature of the ASPECT statements. These appear to be able to generate more shared understanding by different user groups. Of course, ASPECT was not primarily written for this purpose, but because there was so much empirical evidence to support all the statements. However, this new data suggests that it may be worth investigating similar expansions of the sections in AEDET Evolution that give poor correlations.

We strongly recommend that this should be investigated. Clearly, when AEDET Evolution was under development there was pressure to minimise the number of statements involved in order to be able to reduce the amount of time an assessment would take. At face value this seems a sensible strategy. However, our data here questions the utility of the strategy. First, it is simply no good reducing the tool beyond the point where the results are valid. Second, our data suggests that such reductions may actually be a false economy to some extent. The table of correlations above strongly suggests that decision making and discussion for ASPECT statements would both be far quicker than for AEDET statements. Thus, some appropriate expansion of AEDET Evolution may not necessarily result in a longer process.

### Differences between architects and nurses

In general, the level of agreement overall is remarkably strong in ASPECT and gives considerable confidence in the tool. It is less strong in AEDET Evolution, but this is both understandable and remediable. However, it does suggest that using AEDET Evolution in a mediated group trying to arrive at consensus is a far more valid method than aggregating ratings given by individuals independently.

It was noticeable that the nurses are slightly more generous overall in their assessments than the architects. On average this difference was 0.6 of a scale point in AEDET Evolution and 0.7 in ASPECT. Finally, the nurses showed less consistency in their marking than the architects, who were a slightly more coherent group.

Taken together, all these differences are not particularly surprising. We were almost always looking at health care facilities, so this factor might appear to favour the nurses. However, the task was always to assess a building, and that must inevitably favour the architects. The task required was much more like ones normally performed by architects than by nurses.

## Selection of exemplars

One of the added value benefits of this piece of research was the ability to find images that represent good scores as exemplars for the statements in both AEDET Evolution and ASPECT. This will enable the AEDET and ASPECT tools to have a further (Exemplar) layer added, which will allow users working on a statement in the scoring layer to see examples of high scoring images for that statement.

We have used a number of rules to identify potential candidates for this exemplar role. First, the overall mean rating must be above 4. Second, this must be true for both the architect and nurse groups.

## AEDET Evolution statements needing investigation

- A1 There are clear ideas behind the design of the building.
  - Four images showing no clear result from the nurses. Moderate correlation (0.5) between architects and nurses. Probably too much of an architectural concept for non-experts to understand. The question is: expand or elaborate guidance?
- A3 The building projects a caring and reassuring atmosphere.
  - No correlation between architects and nurses and four images showing no clear result from nurses. Expand, expand guidance or consider scrapping this statement. It may not be needed, given that statement A4 seemed to work better and could be seen to incorporate this idea.
- A5 The building is likely to influence future health care designs.
  - Although there is a strong correlation between architects and nurses, the nurses have a weak internal view of this. Consider expanding or elaborating guidance.

- B1 The building has a human scale and feels welcoming.
  - Actually shows a negative correlation. Consider expanding or elaborating guidance to assist non-experts.
- B2 The building is well oriented on the site.
  - Similar to B1.
- B4 The external materials and detailing appear to be of high quality.
  - Only one image showed a clear result for the nurses. This may be too technical a statement for non-experts to make a judgement.
- B5 The external colours and texture seem appropriate and attractive.
  - No correlation between architects and nurses. Consider elaborating guidance for non-experts?
- D1 The height, volume and skyline of the building relate well to the surrounding environment.
  - The nurses gave uniformly high scores to all the images for this question, resulting in means ranging only from 4.3 to 4.8. This strongly suggests they were unable to discriminate on this dimension. Consider elaborating guidance.
- D2 The building contributes positively to its locality.
  - No correlation between architects and nurses. Possibly difficult for non-experts to answer this question without seeing the real place. Consider expanding or removing.
- D4 The building is sensitive to neighbours and passers-by.
  - Very similar to D2, and in retrospect probably possible to double these two questions together or expand into new section.
- E2 The building is easy to clean.
  - No single image produced a significant result for the nurses. This may be the result of too many issues being considered.
- H7 The layout facilitates both security and supervision.
  - No correlation between architects and nurses. Neither group appears to be able to discriminate here. Could be an artefact of the images presented?

*ASPECT statements needing investigation*

- C6.3 The interior has a variety of colours, textures and views.
  - Little correlation between architects and nurses, and nurses have little discrimination. Probably due to the method of presentation of images here. In order to establish this, probably far more information is needed.
- C6.5 The interior has provision for art, plants and flowers.
  - Little correlation between architects and nurses, and the nurses showed few significant results. Not clear why nurses were unable to read these images in this case.
- C6.8 Floors are covered with suitable material.
  - Little correlation, and neither group seemed sure how to answer this statement. Perhaps this statement may be too technical for this type of exercise.

## Conclusions and future development

There are several conclusions from this study. Results from the study indicate a fine grain of ASPECT statements indicating consistently high correlations. This reflects reference to empirical evidence. Participants/subjects from the two study groups (graduate nurses and architects) indicated that the 40 ASPECT statements were easier to understand than the 32 AEDET Evolution statements.

Results from the study confirm that the strategy of expanding sections of AEDET Evolution has been shown to be a good thing and worth doing. When AEDET Evolution was under development there was pressure to minimise the total number of statements involved in order to reduce the amount of time an assessment would take. This study suggests that expanding sections of AEDET Evolution may lead to statements that were easier to understand and which might be more quickly responded to. There is a strong indication that this would yield more reliable data, which would be useful during briefings by NHS Trusts, designers and other members of the project team. The strategy could probably be applied to other sections in AEDET Evolution, especially D URBAN/SOCIAL INTEGRATION; B FORM & MATERIALS and H USE, where there was little or no agreement between our two study groups.

Overall, 16 statements have been shown to need investigation – notably, 80% (13) of the statements in AEDET Evolution compared to 20% (three) of the statements in ASPECT. The investigation should investigate the nature of the statements, the type of matching photographs and how they are presented.

The exemplars have been selected because we expect groups as different as architects and nurses to be seeing the same things about design quality in these images. The results of the study confirm that the next stage of getting copyright permissions can proceed to allow the selected exemplars to be published. The exemplars can be used to provide the basis for a photographic gallery as a useful reference for the IDEAs generative design tool. Architects/designers can now be invited to provide comments about their design intentions with regard to the selected exemplars.

AEDET Evolution assessment focus groups, in our experience, currently take four to six hours (105 statements, 58 in AEDET Evolution and 47 in ASPECT, at two to three minutes a statement). We need to investigate the impact on this timing of expanding AEDET sections. It may be that expanded sections will provide the ability to target specific user groups, as when using ASPECT where ordinary occupants of health care premises are often invited to take part in exercises.

A replication of the study should be conducted with different user groups, such as doctors and other health care workers versus interior designers or engineers, to expand the number of exemplars.

This study also confirms that ASPECT/AEDET Evolution could be developed further to provide a cohesive framework for NHS Trust project teams to refer back to statutes and NHS guidance through the provision of another layer (a Compliance Layer). Our view is that this Compliance Layer could be provided as a separate document, in order to avoid AEDET Evolution itself looking cumbersome due to the burgeoning legislation but nevertheless while following the same structure.

ASPECT/AEDET Evolution is a tool specifically directed towards achieving excellence in design rather than ensuring compliance with specific legislation, regulation or guidance. Accurate predictive and performance measures exist and can be used on models and drawings to assess things like amount of storage, size of space, lighting, air quality, temperature, smell, acoustics, energy consumption, environmental conditions, health and safety, access to wheelchair users and so on.

# Recommended exemplar images

The following images are those recommended for use in the development of the Exemplar Layer against the AEDET Evolution and ASPECT statements.

## Recommended exemplars – AEDET Evolution

A1   There are clear ideas behind the design of the building.
Image 5

A2   The building is interesting to look at and move around in.
Images 7.1, 7.2, 9.1 and 9.2

A4   The building appropriately expresses the values of the NHS.
Image 22

A5   The building is likely to influence future health care designs.
Images 28.1 and 28.2

B1   The building has a human scale and feels welcoming.
Images 36.1 and 36.2

B3   Entrances are obvious and logically positioned in relation to likely points of arrival on site.
Images 43, 45 and 46

B4   The external materials and detailing appear to be of high quality.
Images 50.1 and 50.2

B5   The external colours and texture seem appropriate and attractive.
Images 58.1 and 58.2

C1   The building respects the dignity of patients and allows for appropriate levels of privacy and dignity.
Image 61

C2   There are good views inside and out of the building.
Images 67.1, 67.2, 69.1 and 69.2

C3   Patients and staff have access to outdoors.
Images 73.1, 73.2, 78.1, 78.2 and 78.3

C4   There are high levels of both comfort and control of comfort.
Images 81.1 and 81.2

C5   The building is clearly understandable.
Image 85

C6   The interior of the building is attractive in appearance.
Images 95.1, 95.2, 96.1 and 96.2

C7   There are good bath/toilet and other facilities for patients.
Images 97.1, 97.2, 97.3, 99.2, 102.1 and 102.2

C8   There are good facilities for staff, including convenient places to work and relax without being on demand.
Images 103.1 and 103.2

D1   The height, volume and skyline of the building relate well to the surrounding environment.
Images 111.1 and 111.2

D2   The building contributes positively to its locality.
Images 115.1, 115.2 and 115.3

D3   The hard and soft landscape around the building contributes positively to the locality.
Image 125

E1   The building is easy to operate.
Images 138.1 and 138.2

E3   The building has appropriately durable finishes.
Image 150

H7   The layout facilitates both security and supervision.
Image 160

I4   The building will weather and age well.
Image 175

I6   Outdoor spaces are provided with appropriate and safe lighting indicating paths, ramps and steps.
Images 190, 192.1, 192.2 and 192.3

## Recommended exemplars – ASPECT

C1.1   Patients can choose to have visual privacy.
Images 195, 197 and 198

C1.2   Patients can have a private conversation.
Image 204

C1.3   Patients can be alone.
Images 206, 208.1, 208.2 and 210

C1.4   Patients have places where they can be with others.
Images 211, 212, 213 and 216

C1.5   Toilets/bathrooms are located logically, conveniently and discreetly.
Images 217.1 and 217.2

C2.1   Spaces where staff and patients spend time have windows.
Images 223, 224, 225 and 227

C2.2   Patients and staff can easily see the sky.
Images 230.1, 230.2 and 231

C2.3  Patients and staff can easily see the ground.
Images 235.1, 235.2, 237, 239.1 and 239.2

C2.4  The view is calming.
Images 249.1 and 249.2

C2.5  The view is interesting.
Images 247, 248, 249.1 and 249.2

C3.1  Patients can go outside.
Images 253, 254.1, 254.2, 254.3, 258.1, 258.2 and 258.3

C3.2  Patients and staff have access to usable landscaped areas.
Images 259, 262.1 and 262.2

C3.3  Patients and staff can easily see plants, vegetation and nature.
Images 265.1, 265.2 and 265.3

C4.1  There is a variety of artificial lighting patterns appropriate for day and night and for summer and winter.
Images 273.1 and 273.2

C4.3  Patients and staff can easily exclude sunlight and daylight.
Images 277 and 281

C4.5  Patients and staff can easily open windows/doors.
Images 283.1 and 283.2

C5.1  When you arrive at the building, the entrance is obvious.
Images 289, 290, 291 and 292

C5.2  It's easy to understand the way the building is laid out.
Image 296

C5.3  There is a logical hierarchy of places in the building.
Images 301.1, 301.2, 301.3, 301.4, 306.1 and 306.2

C5.4  When you leave the building, the way out is obvious.
Images 307.1, 307.2, 312.1, 312.2 and 312.3

C5.5  It is obvious where to go to find a member of staff.
Images 315.1, 315.2, 316.1, 316.2, 317, 318.1 and 318.2

C6.1  Patients' spaces feel homely.
Images 328 and 330

C6.2  The interior feels light and airy.
Images 331, 332.1, 332.2, 333, 334 and 335

C6.3  The interior has a variety of colours, textures and views.
Image 339

C6.4  The interior looks clean, tidy and cared for.
Images 343, 346.1, 346.2, 347.1, 347.2, 348.1 and 348.2

C6.5  The interior has provision for art, plants and flowers.
Images 349.1, 349.2 and 353

C6.6  Ceilings are designed to look interesting.
Images 355 and 357

C6.7  Patients can have and display personal items in their own space.
Image 363

C6.8  Floors are covered with suitable material.
Images 368, 370.1 and 370.2

C7.1  Bathrooms/toilets are provided with appropriate seats, handrails, non-slip flooring, a shelf for toiletries and somewhere to hang clothes within easy reach.
Images 374.1 and 374.2

C7.3  There is a space where religious observances can take place.
Images 380, 382.1, 382.2, 383.1, 383.2 and 384

C7.4  There is a place where live performances can take place.
Images 385, 388.1 and 388.2

C7.6  Patients have facilities to make drinks.
Images 391, 393.1, 393.2, 394.1, 394.2 and 394.3

C8.1  Staff have a convenient place to change and securely store belongings and clothes.
Images 398 and 399

C8.2  Staff have convenient places to concentrate on work without being on demand.
Images 407.1, 407.2 and 408

C8.3  There are convenient places where staff can speedily get snacks and meals.
Images 409, 412, 413.1, 413.2 and 414

C8.4  Staff can rest and relax in places segregated from patient and visitor areas.
Images 415.1, 415.2, 417.1, 417.2, 419.1, 419.2 and 420

C8.5  All staff have easy and convenient access to IT.
Images 422 and 424

C8.6  Staff have convenient access to basic banking facilities and can shop for essentials.
Images 430.1, 430.2, 431.1 and 431.2

# Sheffield database of architectural health care environments and staff and patient outcomes

Evidence-based design has become a popular strategy in health and social care as a useful vehicle for improving patient and staff well-being, patient healing processes, stress reduction and safety. The development of a dynamic and responsive architectural evidence base has always underpinned the goal of enhancing efficiency and effectiveness in evidence-based design.

Emphasising the importance of using robust evidence or credible data deriving from rigorous methods and studies, evidence-based design aims to influence both the design process and its outcomes. In referring to the four levels of evidence-based architectural design practice, Hamilton (2003, pp. 18–26) provides the defining principles of evidence-based design: "The deliberate attempt to base design decisions on the best available research evidence… Evidence-based healthcare designs are used to create environments that are therapeutic, supportive of family involvement, efficient for staff performance, and restorative for workers under stress. An evidence-based designer, together with an informed client, makes decisions based on the best information available from research and project evaluations."

It is obvious that evidence comes in a variety of forms, which is the source of a lot of confusion, especially in terms of the easy application of evidence-based approaches and acknowledging that definitive scientific evidence is not always available. The grading of evidence according to the source or the way it is generated offers a way out of this.

Grade A: Evidence based on systematic reviews, i.e. where there are diverse primary studies to draw from (not primarily modelling), well-designed studies or especially experimental studies (randomised controlled trials and the gold standard of research). The challenge in this case is that there are many settings or situations in which RCTs are impossible because of ethical and logistical issues.

Grade B: Evidence that derives from well-designed studies, substantial observational studies or experimental studies typically with five to fifty subjects, or experimental studies with other limitations.

Grade C: Evidence based on case or practice reports, small poorly controlled observational studies, poorly substantiated larger studies, application of knowledge of mode of transmission and infectiousness period.

The HaCIRIC[1]/EPSRC[2]-funded project Nurturing an Evidence-Based Learning Environment which supports the Innovative Design of Healthcare Facilities (EBLE), and Loughborough University's commission from the European Investment Bank on the nature of evidence that demonstrates health gain from health care infrastructure investment on new hospitals, have both found that measures of hospital efficiency, volume-outcome, care-closer-to-home, 'Care-in-the-Community', access, adaptability and flexibility, and the reduction of waste or carbon emissions are vital considerations of significant relevance.

The Center for Health Design highlights the challenges in reaching an optimal understanding of the complex and interacting factors that characterise the care environment. Myriad factors from multiple domains – for example, treatment, workflow, processes, cultures, policies, physical environments, sociological and psychological processes at both the individual and group levels – interact in complex ways in care delivery and healing (Quan et al. 2011, p. 65).

A lack of common definitions, tools, measures and metrics associated with the physical environment is a major obstacle to further research and the development of theoretical frameworks that are based on meaningful study outcomes and which facilitate the translation of study findings to aid design decision-making and the production of guidance and tools. Gathering baseline data on the factors is particularly complex because of the intersection of many specific application areas and themes other than sustainability and evidence-based design. The nature of the

---

1 HaCIRIC – Health and Care Infrastructure Research and Innovation Centre, UK.
2 EPSRC – Engineering Physical Sciences Research Council, UK.

data collection on these factors and evaluation using a hard science methodology poses a challenge for the development of the evidence base. Also, the drive for efficiency in health care needs to be reconciled with the goal of therapeutic environments.

To help address all these concerns, the Center for Health Design has produced a standard glossary of terms, definitions, metrics, and measurement tools that are commonly accepted by interdisciplinary design team members, including researchers, designers, administrators, clinicians, and other stakeholders (Quan et al. 2011).

Fable Hospital 2.0 in 2011 (Sadler et al. 2011, based on Sadler et al. 2008) has distinguished evidence-based innovations supported by evidence from experience, but these warrant further study. The evidence-based innovations supported by research evidence include large single inpatient rooms, acuity-adaptable larger windows, larger patient bathrooms with double-door access, ceiling-mounted patients' lifts, enhanced indoor air quality, decentralised nursing substations (alcoves), hand-hygiene facilities, medication area task lighting, noise-reducing measures, energy and water demand reduction, e-ICU comprehensive remote ICU monitoring capability, healing art, positive distraction measures and healing gardens. Design innovations supported by experience but warranting further study include family/social spaces, improved wayfinding, a Health Information Resource Centre, respite areas, a staff gym, decentralised nursing logistics, and environmentally responsible materials.

## Relevance of the evidence base

An evidence database essentially makes a link between structural and process measures of the estate and patient and staff outcomes. It is thus an essential tool in a system for measuring quality and safety in the health care estate. It indicates how the designed health care estate can impact on such things as length of stay, reduction of falls, rates of cross-infection, risks of clinical error and consumption of medication. It also shows very detailed results such as heart rates; sleep patterns, staff absenteeism and the like, and it links to more qualitative measures such as patient satisfaction and staff recruitment and retention. The research in this field is international and extensive.

## Benefits of the Sheffield database to the NHS

The beneficiaries include NHS Estates, NHS Trusts and other health care providers, patients, academia and the construction industry (Table 4.15).

- The NHS benefits from testing, implementing and the development of an 'intelligent or smart' database, which enables the quality of the scientific evidence to be monitored, measured and controlled. This will improve the productivity and efficiency of material selection and maintenance decisions. Furthermore, it will help the NHS to influence the uncertain relationships between clinicians and designers, thereby increasing the transparency of the decision-making process. When challenged by clinicians, designers will have a credible source of authority to underpin their designs. The Commissioner and Regulator will have a rigorous basis for guidance.

- Patients benefit from positive health outcomes, e.g. reduced risk of falls and reduced severity of injuries should falls occur, improved recovery rates and so on. The proper choice of finishes will help to increase resistance to the spread of infection through the use of antimicrobial agents, fungicides etc. Furthermore, research has shown that good design can have implications for psychological well-being and patient satisfaction. It is well documented that hospital buildings are too often dangerous and stressful places for patients, families and staff. The lesson for all health care organisations is clearly either to provide a physical environment that is welcoming to patients, which measurably improves their quality of life and supports families and employees, or to suffer the financial consequences in an increasingly competitive and demanding economic environment.

- Academia benefits from the development of an evidence base to use in new builds and the refurbishment and modernisation of NHS premises. Academics will become aware of recent technological advances aligned to the latest research.

- The industry benefits by sharing the information available on the database. There is also a recognition that this concept will lead to major cultural changes in the approach to project investment decision-making in the industry.

Table 4.15 Benefits and beneficiaries from a rigorous and robust 'smart' evidence base

| Beneficiaries | Benefits arising |
|---|---|
| Health and social care providers | • Better tools to assess the fit of health care infrastructure with patient needs.<br>• Better management of changes required realising improvements.<br>• Greater flexibility in use of health care infrastructure. |
| Central government | • Better modelling and decision support tools for capacity planning and investment policy decisions.<br>• Lower risks related to implementation of innovation.<br>• Better knowledge to support policy development and implementation. |
| Infrastructure supply chains | • Improved specifications and communication with better-informed customers.<br>• Rigorous support for novel approaches to provision of physical infrastructure. |
| Service users | • Improved care pathways and better patient care outcomes. |
| Medical technology supply chains | • More effective integration of innovative technologies within the care system infrastructure. |

## Sheffield database of architectural health care environments and staff & patient health outcomes

A database of research for the evidence base for the Department of Health was started some years ago with funding from the old NHS Estates (Lawson & Phiri 2000). The database was updated annually until 2004, when NHS Estates was reorganised in the Department of Health (Lawson & Phiri 2003). The need for an electronic database and resource directory emerged during the comprehensive literature review for the NHS Estates-funded research project (Reference Code: B (99) 54) entitled "Architectural Environment and its effect on Patient Health Outcomes" (1999), carried out by University of Sheffield School of Architecture and others.

An important conclusion from the literature survey and critical analysis was that the volume and diffuse nature of existing material and literature evidence deters use by those who plan, design and operate health care buildings, particularly those involved in the development of briefs and designs for NHS buildings. The evidence is not only difficult to access or retrieve from the many diverse or esoteric sources, but is often in a form or format, or of a type, quality, relevance, usefulness, extent or completeness, which is not appropriate to aid decision-making.

## Development of the Sheffield database

The objective of the *Sheffield Architectural Environment Staff and Patient Outcomes Database* is to refer users to research evidence, sources of information or landmark studies for use by all those who commission, design, construct and operate health care facilities. This is especially relevant for practitioners who have to meet many deadlines and who have very limited time to research the many diverse types and sources of information. For example, at the most basic level the database provides bibliographic information in standard format: Ulrich RS, "*View through a window may influence recovery from surgery*" **Science**, Vol. 224, 27 April 1984, 420–466; or Beauchemin KM & Hays P, "*Sunny hospital rooms expedite recovery from severe and refractory depressions*" **Journal of Affective Disorders** 40: 49–51, 1996. Even for researchers, it is essential that their work should be built upon the works of others (Kaplan 1964). In all cases it is critical to have access to primary sources or material written by the person(s) who originated the ideas in the published literature.

The electronic database sought to overcome the tendency by existing databases to provide limited bibliographic details and profiles, leaving the users to review and distil the main message or establish the relevance of the research findings. Copyright law prevents the reproduction of full texts or detailed research material. The view is also taken that fully comprehending a source can only be achieved by reading all of it carefully.

The database also aims to provide reference to evidence which links environmental factors to the outcome measures that are used to assess treatment efficacy. Two types of information are relevant: first, to act as a catalyst for design solutions and ideas; and second, to provide a body of knowledge for testing design options and ideas (Zeisel 1981). Provision of this sort of information is directed at fuelling innovative developments in health care design.

Furthermore, the database aims to refer users to information sources on scientific collaboration or research (if any) that are undertaken primarily to inform design. This is necessary in order to fulfil the need for evidence-based architectural design (Martin 2000) (the importance of which was reiterated by Kenneth Schwartz, a London-based architect specialising in the planning and design of health care facilities, at the second International Conference on Health and Design). Evidence-based design would promote and foster

environmental quality in health care buildings and settings. Inspiration comes from evidence-based medicine, a concept first developed in Canada in the 1980s as an invaluable tool to aid decision-making and sound judgement and ensure the effective and efficient management of patients.

## Characteristics and design of the Sheffield architectural environment staff and patient outcomes database

The database was originally created using Microsoft Access 2002, a commonly accessible database program. This was chosen because NHS Estates routinely used the Microsoft Office suite of software.

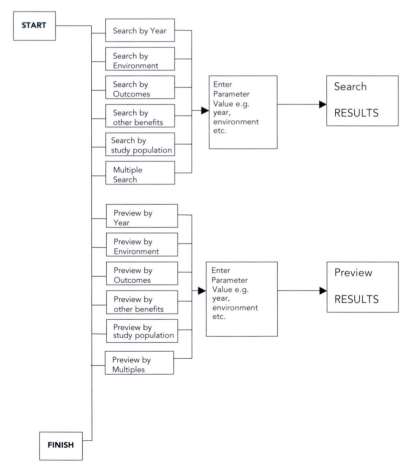

**4.10 Flow chart of activities involved in accessing the database**

The database was loaded on a NHS Estates server within the Knowledge and Information Portal (KIP). It was accessible through the NHS Estates website and also directly via www.knowledge.nhsestates.gov.uk. The KIP was a bespoke metadatabase browser, which was capable of searching multiple databases simultaneously. It was written in C#, using Microsoft.net technology. The indirect access to the database was a source of frustration for users who complained about these difficulties which deterred its use.

As a standalone database (i.e. not accessed via KIP) the user could search following step-by-step procedures prompted by any of the following:

> *Year of publication, Environmental Variables, Specific categories of outcomes, Other benefits, Study population, Multiple 'AND' search, and Alternative 'OR' search*

Records data was provided according to:

> *ID (identification) number, Year of publication, Bibliographic Information, Environmental Variables, Specific categories, Other benefits, Study population, Authors' findings, Authors' Conclusions, and Links*

## Searching the database using command buttons

This involves double-clicking on the relevant icon indicated in Figure 4.11 and typing in the required words or numbers in the appropriate box and then clicking 'OK'. There are seven command buttons and therefore seven options – 'Search by Year', 'Search by Environment', 'Search by Outcome', 'Search by Other benefits', 'Search by study population', 'OR keywords Search' and 'Multi-Search'. Below the Command buttons are associated 'Preview Report' buttons to allow the user to look at the results from the search.

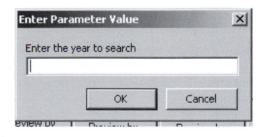

**4.11 Search Command buttons**

### Search by year

This search strategy retrieves relevant literature references using the year of publication, e.g. 1984, 1998, 2000, 2002 etc. Clicking on the button 'Search by Year' yields the prompt 'Enter Parameter Value' or 'Enter the year to search' – i.e. asking the operator to type in the year of publication of the article or citation. After typing the year, click 'OK' to proceed. The outcome of typing in the year brings up information sources indicated in Figure 4.12. There are ten citations shown at the bottom.

**4.12 Enter Parameter Value**

**4.13 Outcome of year search '1984'**

### Search using environmental variables

This search strategy retrieves relevant literature references using environmental variables or keywords, e.g. *light*, *colour*, *noise level*, *space*, *ICU (Intensive Care Unit)*, *environment* etc. Keywords are major concepts in the area of study. The database also allows retrieval of information using synonymous terms and sub-headings, or variant spellings or truncated words – for example, *light*, *lighting*, *orthopedic*, *orthopaedic*, *anesthetic*, *anaesthetic*, *color*, *colour* etc.

A wild card symbol * allows the user to enter parts of words as the search phrase so that the search locates all the occurrences of that part of the word or phrase, which in some cases may have additional letters attached, for example *light* displays *sunlight*, *daylight*, *moon light*, *lighting*, *natural light*, *artificial lighting* and so on.

### Search by specific category variables

The search retrieves sources of literature and references using the specific outcome categories, e.g. *length of hospital stay*, *patient satisfaction*, *stress*, *anxiety*, *pain*, *postoperative recovery*, etc.

### Search by Other benefits

The search retrieves relevant literature references using Other benefits or outcomes such as *staff turnover*, *productivity*, *costs*, etc.

### Search by Study population

The search process involves retrieving sources of literature and references using the study population by age, for example *neonates*, *infants*, *children*, *adults* and *elderly*.

*Alternative 'OR' search*

The three most common ways of performing complex searches in order to define relationships or groupings are by using: 1) Boolean operators – AND, OR, and NOT; 2) locational operators – ab, rf and tx; and 3) positional operators – NEAR, WITH and ADJ. In this database the Boolean operators AND and OR are used to perform complex searches. The NOT operator was not used because it narrows the number of citations and therefore it would be easy to lose some good references.

The first of the two complex searches used in this database retrieves relevant literature references using the *Author OR Title*. OR was therefore used when searching for the presence of any of a group of terms. Most electronic databases, especially bibliographic databases or compilations of citations, are searched using either Author or Title.

*Multiple 'AND' search*

AND was the second of the complex search strategies combining two or more concepts or terms in the citation. The search strategy was to retrieve relevant literature and references using the *Author AND Title*.

Although only the searches using Command buttons have been described here, the database was also designed to allow searches using drop-down menus. It was hoped that narrowing the options for users would be helpful in making the database simpler to use.

## Data types

Examples of environmental variables are natural and artificial lighting, noise levels, intensive care unit, incubators, etc. Examples of Specific category variables by outcomes are length of hospital stay, stress, anxiety, patient satisfaction, etc. Examples of study population are foetus, neonates, children, adults and elderly. The following are examples of other authors' findings and conclusions.

- A research study was conducted to compare the performance of patients assigned to a room with a view of natural setting versus a window facing a brick wall. Twenty-three surgical patients assigned to the natural view windows had shorter postoperative hospital stays, received fewer negative evaluations in the nurses' notes, and took fewer potent analgesics than the control group. The authors conclude that decisions concerning hospital design and siting should take into account the quality of window views for the patients (Ulrich, 1984).

- A study of noise levels in the recovery room found that the number of patients and conversation among staff were principal sources. Noise levels could have adverse effects on patients taking antibiotics, could be disruptive of sleep and could enhance perception of pain. Recommendations include staff limiting unnecessary conversation, positioning patients at intervals or in cubicles, and increasing distance between patients and noise-producing devices (Falk & Woods, 1973).

- *"Once a particular room has been adopted, it is extremely difficult to change. The principal reason for the room layout remaining fixed is the relationship of the head end of the bed to the medical wall (oxygen, medical gas, suction, power, lighting, nurse call) and the difficulties and expense of relocating this service panel. Further, the minimal size and shape of most patient rooms does not allow for many alternative bed arrangements. Consequently, a poorly resolved room plan must be accommodated by a lot of people for many, many years given the long life span of most hospitals. Without question, the development of the patient room's basic plan or configuration is the most fundamental design issue related to this environment"* (Campbell, 1984, p. 100).

Table 4.16 Initial database report outputs

| Author | Title | Source/ Location | Date/Pages | Findings: Conclusions: Design Principles |
|---|---|---|---|---|
| Ackerman B, Sherwonit, Williams J | Reduced incidental light exposure: Effect on the development of retinopathy of prematurity in low birth weight infants | **Pediatrics 83** | 1989, 958-962 | Findings: There was no difference in the incidence and severity of retinopathy of prematurity between groups exposed to different intensities of light. |
| Anderson RL, Mackel DC, Stoler BS, Mallison GF | Carpeting in Hospitals: an epidemiological evaluation | **Journal of Clinical Microbiology** | March 1982, 408-415 | Findings: Typable organisms (incl. *Pseudomonas aeruginosa*, *Klebsiella pneumniae* and *Staphyloccus*) were isolated more frequently from patients in carpeted rooms than those in rooms with bare floors. However, patients in both type of room had similar rates of colonisation with all organisms (whether Typable or non-typable) found on the floor and similar rates of hospital-acquired infection. Hospital-acquired infections were not associated with organisms found as contaminants of the carpet or floor |
| Baker CF, Carvin BJ, Kennedy CW et al | The effect of environmental sound and communication on CCU patients' heart rate and blood pressure | **Res. Nurs. Health 16** | 1993, 415-421 | Findings: Subjects had higher maximum heart rate during room conversation than during background sound. The effect was independent of the decibel level. |
| Baker CF | Discomfort to environmental noise: heart rate response to SICU patients | **Crit. Care Nurs. Q.** | 1992, 75-90 | Findings: Mean heart rate was higher during talking in the room and non talking noise compared with talking inside the room and ambient noise only. |
| Baldwin S | Effects of furniture rearrangement on the atmosphere of wards in a maximum-security hospital | **Hospital & Community Psychiatry 36(5)** | May 1985 525-528 | Findings: During the study the intervention wards had lower rates of patients requiring seclusion, a lower rate of casualty incidents and nurses' reports showed favourable attitudes and improved noise only. |
| Baumgart S, Engle W, Fox W et al | Effect of heat shielding on convective and evaporative heat losses and on radiant heat transfer in the premature infant | **Journal Pediatr.** | 1991, 948-956 | Findings: Water losses were lower in the shielded conditions. Radiant power demand was the same for control and walled environments but lower when infants were covered with plastic blankets. Thin plastic blankets were the most effective heat shields. |

Great care was taken in checking accuracy, selecting and assessing the articles, and locating key studies, seminal or landmark research papers for inclusion in the database. These elements draw from many reports, reviews, commonly cited authors' names and references, and utilise as many published comments and as much material as possible – for example, the report by Rubin and her associates (Rubin et al. 1998) and reviews by authors such as Ulrich (1991, 2000), the Color Research Center (**http://www.acrccolors.com**) and the Taste and Smell Research Centre (**http://www.med. upenn.edu/stc/index.html**). Also, they are largely based on primary sources or material written by person(s) who originated the ideas in the literature, as opposed to secondary sources, summaries or quotes from primary sources. Secondary sources are interpretations of works by others and are therefore prone to the interpreter's perception and bias. Authors using secondary sources have promulgated errors and misinterpretations.

Other than the annual maintenance review and periodic update until 2005, and in order to exploit the Internet, the database initiated three main direct links:

1   E-journals and related publishers' websites, e.g. the Health Service Journal **www.hsj.co.uk**, the British Medical Journal **www.bmj.com**, the British Journal of Psychiatry **www.rcpsch.org.uk**, the Journal of Bone and Joint Surgery **www.jbjs.org.uk**, the Journal of Affective Disorders **www.jad.com**, and so on. This gave users access to full texts or papers/articles and the entire contents of the article, paper or document by the publishers.
2   Bookshop websites, e.g. HMSO, Amazon.com etc., who may be able and are authorised to distribute or sell hard copies or full texts of the reference.
3   Library websites such as the British Library, in order for the users to request hard copies of the desired article or document, especially those that are out of print.

## Citations in the database

We are now aware of around a thousand relevant items of research. The EBLE study has steadily been increasing this number (Phiri et al. 2011a and 2011b). The evidence suggests that factors that the architect/designer has control over can make significant differences to patient satisfaction, quality of life, treatment times, levels of medication, displayed aggression, sleep patterns and compliance with regimes, among many other similar factors.

The database was cross-referenced to a similar literature search conducted in the USA by Prof. Roger Ulrich's team (Ulrich et al. 2004, 2008). Ulrich's team looked for studies that were:

- Rigorous, in that they used appropriate research methods that allowed reasonable comparisons, and discarded alternative hypotheses. The research studies were assessed on their rigour, quality of research design, sample sizes and degree of control (e.g. Ulrich 1984).
- High impact, in that the outcomes they explored were of importance to health care decision-makers, patients, clinicians and society.

Previously, Rubin, Owens and Golden (1998) identified 84 studies (out of 78,761 papers) since 1968 that met similar criteria and rigorous standards of hard science. Reviewing the research literature in 2004, they estimated that they would find around 125 rigorous studies. Ulrich's team and Lawson's team found more than 600 studies. We have therefore good reason to have high confidence in the Sheffield database, and believe we have identified the overwhelming majority of work in the field internationally. The database was published annually on the Department of Health Knowledge Portal (KIP) until 2004. Users of the KIP regularly consulted the database, and there were lots of requests to make the database widely available to NHS Trusts, their consultants and others such as researchers in health care facility design and operation. The database was also summarised in a Department of Health publication (Phiri 2006).

Overall, however, there is now little doubt that all this adds up to a significant body of knowledge that can no longer be ignored in the design of new health care facilities and the management and upgrading of existing ones (Lawson 2002). Studies suggest that in general, designs complying with this evidence may be capable of repaying any small additional capital costs on an annual basis (Berry, Parker et al. 2004). Other analysis suggests that total operating costs of secondary care buildings may normally be expected to exceed the capital construction costs in less than two years (Lawson & Phiri 2003).

It is entirely appropriate that summaries of all the original research, together with very basic analysis, should be made available to those people who wish to check or question its validity. This is in line with normal practice that allows others to judge the value of research for themselves and to go back to primary sources.

However, it is recognised that such an approach is largely impractical in terms of design actions. Those involved in the briefing, specifying, commissioning and design of health care environments are unlikely to find time or have the expertise to read a thousand items of original research. For this reason an overall picture is needed – not in terms of the causal factors and theories, but couched largely in terms of the design considerations and direction needed to achieve the results suggested by the research. In simple terms, clients and architects want to know roughly what sort of things they should do, what features of buildings they should control or elaborate, and what sorts of qualities of environment they need to produce (Lawson 2005).

Taken together, then, this new evidence-based approach has the potential simultaneously to improve the quality of patient experience and, in many cases, health outcomes, while also saving time and costs. However, the generic evidence suggests that to achieve these benefits, designs will need to improve in quality. So far most design guidance has tended to concentrate on compliance with minimum standards. This approach therefore suggests a new departure in focusing on ways to drive up quality in relation to the evidence specifically for health care environments.

## Development of HEAR

For a while after the discontinuation of the KIP portal, the database was accessed via the website **www.spaceforhealth**, which itself has now been succeeded by the all.gov website. Since then the database has been under development at **http://hear.group.shef.ac.uk** as a facility planning, design and management resource[3] that makes available summaries of all the original research, together with very basic analysis to those people who wish to check or question its validity. Studies referred to in this case range in size and scope, with some small and little more than anecdotal, while others are major longitudinal controlled investigations. Some are multi-factorial and some are much more parametric.

The evidence database essentially makes a link between structural and process measures of the health care estate and patient and staff outcomes. It is thus an essential tool in a system for measuring quality and safety in the health care estate. It indicates how the designed health care estate can impact on such things as length of stay, reduction of falls, rates of cross-infection, risks of clinical error and consumption of medication. It indicates very detailed results such as heart rates, sleep patterns, staff absenteeism and the like. It also shows links to more qualitative measures such as patient satisfaction and staff recruitment and retention. The research in this field is international and extensive.

The web-based database (HEAR) aims to disseminate evidence published in over a thousand pieces of research. This includes providing the findings about each piece of research and links to where the original research publications may be found. The records in the database contain bibliographic information on each piece of research, and

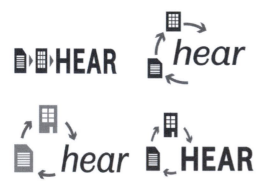

**4.14** Development of HEAR logo options

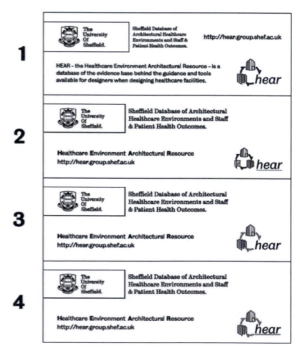

**4.15** Development of HEAR bookmarks

3 'Healthcare Environment Architectural Resource' (acronym **HEAR**)

summarise and analyse the literature to provide insights on how the information might be used during the design process.

## Search methods in developing HEAR

A literature review, a critical comparative analysis and exploration have been carried out to discover primary research studies which indicate the impact of the hospital physical environment on health care outcomes. The activities performed involve accessing, retrieving, consulting and collating original research papers via e-journals (e.g. www.sciencedirect.com [Elsevier Science Direct], http://joe.sagepub.com [Sage Online Journals], http://ovidsp.tx.ovid.com, www.ideallibrary.com, www.swetswise.com,

http://proquest.umi.com [ProQuest Nursing Journals] and other publishers' journals) and various other electronic databases (e.g. Cochrane, ENB Healthcare, Current Research in Britain, MEDLINE, and others).

In previous comparable studies, some key words have been identified. For instance, in Ulrich et al.'s (2004) study 32 words were used, referring to patient and staff outcomes (such as infection, medical error, pain, sleep, depression, stress and privacy), and other health care related issues (such as patient- and family-centred care). In this study, search terms or criteria consisted of words, phrases, subject headings such as 'hospital', 'built environment', 'healing', 'design', 'noise', 'lighting', and others.

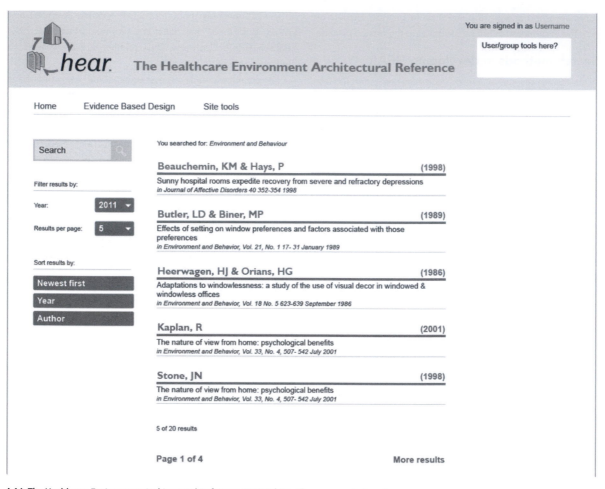

**4.16** The Healthcare Environment Architectural Reference (HEAR) **http://hear.group.shef.ac.uk**

**hear.** The Healthcare Environment Architectural Reference

Home     Evidence Based Design     Site tools

Search

**Beauchemin, K M  & Hays, P** (1998)

**Sunny hospital rooms expedite recovery from severe and refractory depressions**
*in Journal of Affective Disorders 40 352-354 1998*

Back to results

Link to article

**Tags**

sunny and dull rooms

well-being    health status

cost per bed    adults

### Findings

Bright light therapy is an effective treatment for seasonal affective disorder, an uncommon condition marked by mild winter depression. Bright lights have been used as adjuncts in the pharmacological treatment of other types of depressive illness. The rooms in a psychiatric inpatient unit are so placed that half are bright and sunny and the rest are not. Reasoning that some patients were getting light therapy inadvertently, comparisons were made of the length of stay of depressed patients in sunny rooms with those of patients in dull rooms. The length of stay for depressed patients in sunny rooms averaged 16.9days whereas those in dull rooms required 19.5 days of care a difference of 2.6 day a (15%) : $P < 0.05$.

### Authors Conclusions

Access to nature and natural daylight is critical to treatment. Sunshine can be incorporated into interior with skylights, solariums, atriums and courtyards. Light must also minimize shadows, exaggerated images and sensory distortion. The findings of this study have obvious practical implications for reduction in suffering, the confounding of inpatient drug trials, the optimal sitting and orientation of dwellings, new hospital design, the lighting of hospital rooms and the utilisation of existing units.

**Comments**

**Author's name**  Posted on April 05 2011 at 14:53 | Reply ↴

Nullam posuere odio ac mauris iaculis vel dictum diam tristique. Integer a convallis dolor. Nam ut nisi odio, vel lacinia orci. Maecenas ultricies sodales mollis. Duis vitae nunc et erat elementum pulvin orci dui, eget malesuada.

**Author's name**  Posted on April 04 2011 at 11:05 | Reply ↴

Nullam posuere odio ac mauris iaculis vel dictum diam tristique. Integer a convallis dolor. Maecenas ultricies sodales mollis. Duis vitae nunc et erat elementum pulvinar. Ut at orci dui, eget malesuada.

**Author's name**  Posted on April 05 2011 at 14:53 | Reply ↴

Nullam posuere odio ac mauris iaculis vel dictum diam tristique. Integer a convallis dolor. Nam ut nisi odio, vel lacinia orci. Maecenas ultricies sodales mollis. Duis vitae nunc et erat elementum pulvin orci dui, eget malesuada.

**Author's name**  Posted on April 05 2011 at 14:53 | Reply ↴

Nullam posuere odio ac mauris iaculis vel dictum diam tristique. Integer a convallis dolor. Nam ut nisi odio, vel lacinia orci. Maecenas ultricies sodales mollis. Duis vitae nunc et erat elementum pulvin orci dui, eget malesuada.

**Leave comment**

Name

Email

Comment

Submit

4.17  **The Healthcare Environment Architectural Reference (HEAR) http://hear.group.shef.ac.uk**

## Inclusion and exclusion criteria, data extraction

Studies are included if they are concerned with interventions involving the health effects of environmental stimuli and variables in health care settings on patients, and if they aspire to have a basis in 'controlled clinical trials' published in peer-reviewed journals. Both clinical and psychological outcome measures will be included. The search will continue for the duration of the EBLE project. For all the studies, the methodological quality will be evaluated under: study design/method; baseline measurements and data sources; participants/subjects – age, gender, type of disease and health care settings – type and size; and intervention and outcome measures.

## Aims and objectives of HEAR

1  Make available summaries of all the original research, together with very basic analysis, to those people who

wish to check or question its validity. This is in line with normal practice that allows others to judge the value of research for themselves and to go back to primary sources.

The evidence database essentially makes a link between structural and process measures of the health care estate and patient and staff outcomes. It is thus an essential tool in a system for measuring quality and safety in the health care estate. It indicates how the designed health care estate can impact on such things as length of stay, reduction of falls, rates of cross-infection, risks of clinical error and consumption of medication. It indicates very detailed results such as heart rates, sleep patterns, staff absenteeism and the like. It also shows links to more qualitative measures such as patient satisfaction and staff recruitment and retention. The research in this field is international and extensive.

2   Link or interface with existing web-enabled design tools and key websites in the health care sector – IDEAs, AEDET Evolution/ASPECT, BREEAM Healthcare, Activity Database, Design Quality Indicator (DQI), DQI for Health, and others.
   –   http://www.ideas.dh.gov.uk/IDEAs
   –   http://www.dh.gov.uk/en/Publicationsandstatistics/Publications/PublicationsPolicyAndGuidance/DH_082089 Department of Health website
   –   http://design.dh.gov.uk/content/introduction/home.asp OnDesign website
   –   http://www.spaceforhealth.nhs.uk/ Space for Health – Information Healthcare Premises. Professional website that draws together the official health care premises technical guidance published by the Department of Health, Northern Ireland's Department of Health, Social Services and Public Safety, Health Facilities Scotland, and Welsh Estates
   –   http://www.communityhealthpartnerships.co.uk/ Community Health Partnerships
   –   http://www.breeam.org/ BREEAM Healthcare
   –   http://adb.dh.gov.uk/ Activity DataBase
   –   http://www.dqi.org.uk/website/default.aspa Design Quality Indicator
   –   www.cabe.org.uk The Commission for Architecture and the Built Environment
   –   http://www.designcouncil.org.uk/ The Design Council

   –   http://www.hse.gov.uk/ Health and Safety Executive
   –   http://www.shef.ac.uk/library/elecjnls/introejs.html The University of Sheffield Library for e-journals
3   Update and refresh the database previously developed with funding from the old NHS Estates (Lawson & Phiri 2000).

## How the HEAR website is anticipated to meet the aims

1   Identify all the relevant literature with regard to whether physical environments can have a positive effect on the therapeutic experience and other patient and staff outcomes.
2   Draw out summaries and authors' conclusions to facilitate detailed analysis and ease reference by those involved in the design, construction, operation and occupation of health care facilities.
3   Develop web-enabled capability: i.e. recognise the contribution the internet can provide to dissemination. This includes providing links to where:
   –   The original research publications may be found, as well as allowing users to provide comments or indicate where similar research studies have been conducted. The users may also highlight areas where research is needed.
   –   The original research has been evaluated or reviewed.
   –   The findings from the original research have been applied, e.g. to underpin the development of specific building guidance/standards/codes/norms or design tools.

## Status of the HEAR website

At 1 February 2011, the website consisted of a preliminary online version of the earlier 2004 Microsoft Access-based database. All the data from that original database had been uploaded onto the online database and was in the process of being adjusted to separate the bibliographic information out into individual fields (previously held in one field as all the bibliographical information for each paper). Separating this data out and creating individual fields, for example into a field for date, a field for title, a field for authors, will make sorting and organising by bibliographic information possible, and allowing for more targeted searching.

A major aim is to extend website functionality beyond:

- Listing all research papers and separating them into pages of ten each.
- Searching all fields within the database for a match with an exact phrase entered in the search box and displaying the number of papers or articles found.
- Listing items in a condensed format comprising authors, date and paper title (and other bibliographic information for records that have yet to be refined).
- Snapping on an item to expand its entry to show the Findings (text area shown will ultimately allow selection of Findings, Authors' Conclusions, Comments, Bibliographic Information).

Initially hosted at the development address or holding page, which was used to indicate information about the database project in the short term (rather than the database itself) for interested parties to read, the website has been moved to its permanent address. However, there is still a link to the temporary address from here.

## Outline of development of HEAR

1   V0.5 – read-only version of the database with extensive search tools and embedded information for download by Zotero. Adding records requires direct administrator access to the database (not through the website).
2   V1.0 – add user accounts and the means to modify records (based on user rights) and add comments.
3   V2.0 – team and user tools focused on needs of different audiences.

## Features aimed at specific members of the target audience

### Researchers

- Generate pre-formed URLs to search Google, Google Scholar, Google Books and similar sites to facilitate searching for relevant articles.
- Ability to add references and comments from a Zotero account.

### Designers

- Ability to customise the database, i.e. set up a team account for the practice to build up a dedicated bespoke library of papers which the practice regularly refers to.
- Add projects to the team account for reference in practice.
- Ability to record Post-Project or Post-Occupancy Evaluations for completed health care projects or schemes, along with AEDET/ASPECT scores, thereby facilitating benchmarking or comparisons between them. This is critical for the handover/commissioning stage of projects, to ensure that the as-designed performance is achieved as soon as possible and that the ongoing operation continues to conform to as-designed parameters. Crucially, this area is also being supported by the implementation of the UK Government Soft Landings (GSL) policy.
- Ability to link up with Building Information Modelling (BIM) models for schemes, including non-geometric data from COBie.

### Health care professionals, estates and facilities or resource managers

- Ability to customise the database, i.e. set up a team account for the practice, to build up a dedicated bespoke library of papers the practice regularly refers to.
- Add projects to the team account for reference in practice.
- Ability to record Post-Project or Post-Occupancy Evaluations for completed health care projects, along with AEDET/ASPECT scores, thereby facilitating benchmarking or comparisons between them.
- Ability to link up with Building Information Modelling (BIM) models for schemes including non-geometric data from COBie.

### Guidance, standards and tools authors

Search for past guidance and feedback on previous projects based on that guidance, norm or code of practice.

## Full list of features for HEAR

- Search methods.
- Inclusion and exclusion criteria: studies that are:
  - Rigorous, in that the research used appropriate research methods that allowed reasonable comparisons, and discarded alternative hypotheses. The research studies are assessed on their rigour, quality of research design, sample sizes and degree of control.
  - High impact, in that the outcomes they explored are of importance to health care decision-makers, patients, clinicians and society.
- Search for specific terms or any item in the list, possibly also including wildcards.
- Data extraction.
- Search results: specific and related studies.
- Sort-by options to list search results in different orders.
- Drop-down lists of authors and tags to filter results by and filter by date options.
- Methodological characteristics.
- Studies of the impact of the physical environment of health outcomes.
- Post-Project and Post-Occupancy Evaluations.
- Literature reviews and comparative analysis of published studies.
- Updating the database: with a variety of layers of user control.
  - Administrators able to make any changes.
  - Contributors (either researchers or architects) able to propose references (papers, projects and any developments) for inclusion in the database following review. Ability to make comments without requiring review.
  - Anyone with a user account can contribute to a team's library (for example, adding a research paper that is not present in the publicly available database) and adding a comment/starting a comment thread only visible to their team, but only submitted for review and comments to the database that is publicly available.
- Integration with Zotero and other bibliographical managers.
  - Include RDFs or unAPI data in a page to present content in a semantic form which Zotero will recognise.
  - Include link to download data import for Bibtex, Endnote and similar.
  - Include API for updating Zotero groups online. This means that the HEAR website can be set up to automatically update a companion Zotero group account which researchers can subscribe to and list in their Zotero plugin if they so wish. Likewise, groups registering a team account on the database could link it to a companion Zotero group account.
  - Database user accounts could be associated with personal Zotero accounts to make the import of data about research papers easier.
- Integration with IDEAs, AEDET Evolution/ASPECT, DQI for Health, Activity Database and other tools or mechanisms.
  - IDEAs integration could take the form of linking entries on the IDEAs site with the articles on the database that the recommendations are drawn from. There could be corresponding links from the database showing what IDEAs recommendations particular research papers have had an influence on. The 'influence' of a paper (i.e. the number of recommendations the paper has influenced) could be used to refine searches of the database due to the perceived relevance of a paper.
  - AEDET Evolution and ASPECT integration could be similar, once the online versions of these tools are available, with the relevant research papers in the database linked from the AEDET Evolution/ASPECT statements or questions.
  - Link to the database homepage from the NHS AEDET Evolution and ASPECT web pages instead of (or supplementing) the current Evidence Layer document.
- Technical – database tables.
  - Users and teams.
  - Research papers and source documents: base database fields on those available in Zotero to ease data exchange between the two. Bear in mind the requirements of Dublin Core, which describes data saved for research papers.
  - Comments: where information does not fit the Zotero data structure it can be saved as a 'special comment' (for example, Findings or Authors' Conclusions).

These will then be listed separately to regular comments.

- – Projects.
- – Guidance and Tools.
- Appearance and Usability.
  - – Clean fresh modern design.
  - – Collapsible entries in search results list (more user-friendly text display – menu within each item display to choose from bibliographical information/data, abstract, comments).
  - – Registered users can set up list of bookmarked articles frequently referenced (personal equivalent to the lists available within a team).
  - – Option of registering with a variety of username options – for example, allowing the use of OpenID.
  - – List of changes since the last visit (cookie in the case of unregistered users, linked to user account for registered users).
  - – Tags and tag weighting: ability to tag anything with any keyword (and any number of keywords), but also to give the tag a weighting based on the relevance of the tag to that document. This should assist with the searching, such that a paper with a tagged search term but with a low rating on that tag will appear further down the list than a paper with the same tagged search term with a higher rating.
  - – Homepage: link to/search library, about the project, links to other EBLE resources, contacts and information.

# References

Alexander C, Ishikawa S and Silverstein M, with Jacobson M, Fiksdahl-King I, and Angel S (1977) *A Pattern of Language – Towns, Buildings, Construction*. Oxford University Press, New York.

Beauchemin KM, and Hays P (1996) Sunny hospital rooms expedite recovery from severe and refractory depressions. *Journal of Affective Disorders*, 40, 49–51.

Bernaldez FG, Gallardo D, and Abello RP (1987) Children's landscape preferences: From rejection to attraction. *Journal of Environmental Psychology*, 7, 169–176.

Berry L, Parker D, Coile R, Hamilton DK, O'Neill D, and Sadler BL (2004) The business case for better buildings. *Frontiers in Health Services Management*, 21 (1), 3–21.

Blankson EJ and Green BH (1991) Use of landscape classification as an essential prerequisite to landscape evaluation. *Landscape and Planning*, 21, 149–176.

Campbell MI (1984) Hospital patient room: A design and planning study. Unpublished graduate research project at Syracuse University, US, p. 100.

Darzi L (2008) Our NHS Our Future. http://www.ournhs.nhs.uk/) [Accessed May 2012]

Falk SA, and Woods, NF (1973) Hospital noise-levels and potential health hazards. *New England Journal of Medicine*, 289 (15), 774–781.

Gann DW, Slater AJ, and Whyte JK (2003) Design Quality Indicators: Tools for thinking. *Building Research & Information*, 31 (5), 318–333.

Gimblett HR (1990) Environmental cognition: The prediction of preference in rural Indiana. *Journal of Architectural and Planning Research*, 7 (3), 222–234.

Hamilton KD (2003) The Four Levels of Evidence-Based Practice. *Healthcare Design*, 3 (4), 18–26.

Herzog TR (1985) A cognitive analysis of preference for waterscapes. *Journal of Environmental Psychology*, 5, 225–241.

Herzog TR (1989) A cognitive analysis of preference for urban nature. *Journal of Environmental Psychology*, 9, 27–43.

Hodgson RW, and Thayer RL (1980) Implied human influence reduces landscape beauty. *Landscape Planning*, 7, 171–179.

Hull RB, and Revell GR (1989) Cross-cultural comparison of landscape scenic beauty evaluations: A study in Bali. *Journal of Environmental Psychology*, 9, 177–191.

InformeDesign, http://www.informedesign.org/ developed at The University of Minnesota, USA with a difference that they provide an analysis of the research studies [Accessed 20 August 2013].

Kaplan A (1964) *The Conduct of Inquiry: Methodology for behavioral science*. Chandler, New York.

Lawson BR (2002) Healing Architecture. *The Architectural Review* CCXI (1261), 72–75.

Lawson BR (2005) Evidence-Based Design for Healthcare. In *Hospital Engineering and Facilities Management 2005*, W. Swaby, London, International Federation of Hospital Engineering, 25–27.

Lawson BR (2007) Design indicators: UK Healthcare Design Review. In Stark D, *UK Healthcare Design Review*. Keppie Design, Glasgow, 88–95.

Lawson BR, Bassanino M, Phiri M. et al. (2003) Intentions, practices and aspirations: Understanding learning in design. *Design Studies*, 24 (4), 327–339.

Lawson BR and Phiri M (2000) Room for improvement. *Health Service Journal*, 110 (5688), 24–27.

Lawson BR and Phiri M (2003) *The Architectural Healthcare Environment and its Effects on Patient Health Outcomes*. London, TSO, ISBN 0-11-322480-X.

Lawson BR and Phiri M (2005) *AEDET Evolution: Learning from the Evidence Base of NHS Design*. A report by the University of Sheffield, School of Architecture, UK.

Lawson BR, Phiri M, and Wells-Thorpe J (2004) *The Architectural Healthcare Environment and its Effects on Patient Health Outcomes: A Report on an NHS Estates funded Research Project*. London: The Stationery Office (TSO).

Martin C (2000) Putting patients first: Integrating hospital design and care. *The Lancet*, 356, 518.

McCormick M, and Shepley MM (2003) How can consumers benefit from therapeutic environments? *Journal of Architectural and Planning Research*, 20 (1), 4–15.

NHS Estates (1994) *Better by Design: Pursuit of Excellence in Healthcare Buildings*. Leeds, UK.

NHS Estates (2002) Achieving Excellence Design Evaluation Toolkit – AEDET. Leeds, UK.

NHS Estates (2002) Department of Trade and Industry (DTI), Department of Health (DH): NEAT (NHS Environmental Assessment Tool). London, UK.

NHS Information Centre for Health and Social Care (2010) Hospital Episode Statistics: HES User Guide http://www.hesonline.nhs.uk [Accessed August 2012]

Patsfall MR, Feimer NR, Buyhoff GJ, and Wellman JD (1984) The prediction of scenic beauty from landscape content and composition. *Journal of Environmental Psychology*, 4, 7–26.

Phiri M (2006) *Does the Physical Environment Affect Staff and Patient Health Outcomes? A Review of Studies and Articles 1965–2006*. London, UK: TSO.

Phiri M, Mills GR, Chang C-L, and Price ADF (2011a) *Evidence-Based Design: Refurbishment & Reconfiguration of the Healthcare Estate to Enhance Compliance with Standards and Tools to Optimise Innovation*. IBEA Innovation and the Built Environment Academy 1st Annual Conference – Innovation & Integration: Science, Technology and Policy in the Built Environment: *7, 8 & 9 October 2011*, London South Bank University, UK, pp 341–360. IBSN 978-1-898523-02-4

(available online at www.lsbu.ac.uk/w2/ibeaconference) [Accessed 10 August 2014].

Phiri M, Mills GR, Chang C-L, Price ADF, and Austin SA (2011b) *Evidence-Based Design at a Time of Austerity: Do Building Standards and Tools Reflect the Reality of Designing for Dementia, the Elderly, Children and Refurbishment or Reconfiguration?* 4th Annual Conference of the Health and Care Infrastructure Research and Innovation Centre (HaCIRIC11): Global health infrastructure – challenges for the next decade: Delivering innovation, demonstrating the benefits, 26–28 September 2011, Manchester, UK, 2011: pp. 190-208 (available online at http://www.haciric.org/static/doc/events/HaCIRIC_11_conference_proceedings.pdf) [Accessed 10 August 2014].

Quan X, Joseph A, Malone E, and Pati D (November 2011) Healthcare Environmental Terms and Outcome Measures: An Evidence-based Design Glossary Phase 1 Report, Concord CA, USA: The Center for Health Design.

Rubin HR, Owens AJ, and Golden G (1998) *Status Report: An Investigation to Determine Whether the Built Environment Affects Patients' Medical Outcomes*. Martinez CA: The Center for Health Design.

Ruddell EJ, Gramann JH, Rudis VA, and Westphal JM (1989) The psychological utility of visual penetration in near view forest scenic beauty models. *Environment and Behavior*, 21 (4), 393–412.

Sadler BL, Berry LL, Guenther R, Hamilton KD, Hessler FA, Merritt C, and Parker D (2011) Fable hospital 2.0: The business case for building better health care facilities. *Hastings Center Report* Vol. 41, 1 (January/February), 13–23.

Sadler BL, Dubose J, and Zimring C (2008) The business case for building better hospitals through evidence-based design. *HERD: Health Environments Research & Design Journal*, 1 (3), 22–30.

Scott MJ, and Canter DV (1997) Picture or place? A multiple sorting study of landscape. *Journal of Environmental Psychology*, 17, 263–281.

Tétreault M-H, and Passini R (2003) Architects' use of information in designing therapeutic environments. *Journal of Architectural and Planning Research*, 20, 48–56.

Tufte E (1997) *Visual Explanations: Images and Quantities, Evidence and Narrative*. Graphics Press, Cheshire, CT, 1997.

Ulrich RS (1977) Visual landscape preference: a model and application. *Man-Environment Systems*, 7, 279–293.

Ulrich RS (1984) View through a window may influence recovery from surgery. *Science*, 224, 420–421.

Ulrich RS (1991) Effects of interior design on wellness: Theory and recent scientific research. *Journal of Health Care Interior Design*, 3, 97–109. [Reprinted in Marberry SO (Ed.) (1995) *Innovations in Healthcare Design*. New York: Van Nostrand Reinhold, 88–104.]

Ulrich RS (2000) Environmental research and critical care. In Hamilton DK (Ed.) *ICU 2010: Design for the Future*. Houston: Center for Innovation in Health Facilities, 195–207.

Ulrich RS, Quan X, Zimring C et al. (2004) *The Role of the Physical Environment in the Hospital of the 21st Century: A Once-in-a-Lifetime Opportunity*. The Center for Health Design: Concord, CA.

Ulrich RS, Zimring CM, Zhu X, DuBose J, Seo H, Choi Y-S, Quan X, and Joseph A (2008) A review of the research literature on evidence-based healthcare design. *Health Environments Research and Design Journal*, 1 (3), 61–125.

Uzzell DL, and Lewand K (1990) The psychology of landscape. *Landscape Design*, 1990, 34–35.

Zeisel J (1981) *Inquiry by Design: Tools for Environment-behavior Research*. Brooks/Cole, Monterrey, California.

Zube EH (1973) Rating everyday rural landscapes of the Northeastern US. *Landscape Architecture*, 1973, 370–375.

Zube EH (1984) Themes in landscape assessment theory. *Landscape Journal*, 3, 104–110.

Zube EH, Pitt DG, and Evans GW (1983) A lifespan development study of landscape assessment. *Journal of Environmental Psychology*, 3, 115–128.

Zube EH, Simcox DE, and Law CS (1987) Perceptual landscape simulations: History and prospect. *Landscape Journal*, 6, 62–81.

## Websites

http://shape.dh.gov.uk – A website to access SHAPE (free of charge to NHS professionals) by formal registration and licence agreement with the SHAPE help desk (shape@nepho.org.uk), which also offers a number of regionally-based training events for all new and existing SHAPE users and includes organisation-based bespoke training sessions on a cost recovery basis.

The SHAPE 2014 application requires a modern, standards-compliant browser to run. The latest versions of Google Chrome, Firefox, Safari and Opera on a PC or Mac, or Internet Explorer 8 and 9 on a PC, are recommended. The application will run in a basic mode in Internet Explorer 7, but it has not been possible to ensure compatibility with Internet Explorer v6.

## Appendix

Table 4.17 List of schemes for the photograph shoots

| | Source | Scheme and Location | Architects | Comments |
|---|---|---|---|---|
| 1 | NHS Acute | Evelina Children's Hospital, St Thomas' Hospital, Lambeth Place Road; Client: Guy's and St Thomas' NHS Foundation Trust; The landmark feature is its huge glass roof, which creates a 4-storey conservatory, 140 inpatient beds including 20 intensive care beds for the most seriously ill children. £41.8m Design and Build Contract | Hopkins Architects | Open in late Autumn 2005 "A hospital that doesn't feel like a hospital" |
| 2 | NHS | Great Ormond Street Hospital (GOSH) A new Orangery restaurant built on the roof of a boiler house received the 2005 award. Client: Great Ormond Street Hospital £390k value funded by the Friends of Great Ormond Street charity "The Orangery is a place of serenity dropped into the heart of the hospital, this is architecture as therapy and both architect and client deserve equal credit for it" | SpacelabUK architects | Completed 2004 |
| 3 | | Dublin Dental School and Hospital, Republic of Ireland | ABK | Completed 1998 |

| | Source | Scheme and Location | Architects | Comments |
|---|---|---|---|---|
| 4 | | Mater Hospital, Belfast (£14m Contract value) "As well as providing a new entrance to all buildings, old and new, the new facilities accommodate wards, a day surgery unit, other ancillary medical accommodation and a modern coffee dock." | Todd Architects | |
| 5 | NHS Primary Care | Lisburn Road Community Treatment and Care Centre, Lisburn Road, Belfast Client: South & East Belfast Trust; Procurement: NIHE performance-based partnering (£3.8m Contract value) "A landmark centre for health and social services serving a diverse population of 70,000" | Penoyre & Prasad Architects | Started on site 2003 |
| 6 | NHS Maternity | Wansbeck Hospital Phase 2; The winner of Best Designed Hospital, 2003 relocates maternity services, plus providing day surgery, outpatients, rehab facilities and a child health clinic, in a two-storey building with ample natural light. (A PFI scheme) | Reiach & Hall Architects | |
| 7 | NHS Acute | Hexham General Hospital; Client: The Northumbria Healthcare NHS Trust (£28m PFI scheme) "The hospital has 98 beds (as 27-bed medical wards, 28-bed surgical wards, 10-bed maternity unit, 6-bed CCU), four operating rooms and four radiology rooms". | Jonathan Bailey Associates | |
| 8 | NHS Acute | John Radcliffe emergency department, Client: Oxford Radcliffe Hospital NHS Trust | YRM Architects | Best Designed Hospital at Building Better Healthcare Awards 2004 |
| 9 | NHS | Small Heath Health Centre, Client: East Birmingham Health Authority (£1.8m Contract value) "It represents an opportunistic piece of joint commissioning, bringing together a health centre, GP practice and a community mental health centre with 14 acute beds in the same facility within an inner city location" | MAAP Architects | Completed 1994 |
| 10 | NHS Primary Care | Greenwich Millennium Health Centre, A sustainable approach to community care; Client: Greenwich Teaching Primary Care Trust (£2.75m Contract value) | Edward Cullinan Architects | Opened June 2001 |
| 11 | NHS Acute | Romford Hospital, Oldchurch Park; Client: Barking Havering and Redbridge Hospitals NHS Trust (£200m PFI scheme) | Jonathan Bailey/ BDP | Topped out March 2005 |
| 12 | NHS Mental Health | Chase Farm Hospital, The Oaks Ward, Client: Barnet, Enfield and Haringey Mental Health NHS Trust (£4.02m Contract value) | Devereux Architects | Completed 2005 |
| 13 | NHS Acute | Golden Jubilee Wing, Client: Kings College Hospital NHS Trust; A large ambulatory care centre (£75m PFI scheme) | Nightingale Associates | Completed 2002 |
| 14 | NHS | Sir Michael Sobell House Hospice, Oxford; Client: Sobell Hospice Charity (Cost: £3.3m) Floor area: 1,500m² | Nightingale Associates | Completed 2003 |
| 15 | NHS Mental Health | Woodhaven Mental Health Unit, Southampton Woodhaven is an innovative £7m state-of-the-art adult mental health unit located at Calmore, in the New Forest. Designed in close collaboration with West Hampshire NHS Trust, the unit has been designed to incorporate the views of mental health carers, service users and staff. The 36-bed unit creates a therapeutic setting for patients suffering from a wide range of mental illnesses. | Broadway Malyan | Best Mental Health Building award at the NHS Building Better Healthcare Awards 2004 |
| 16 | NHS | Glasgow Homeopathic Hospital, Part of Gartnavel General Hospital site, Client: NHS Greater Glasgow; "This purpose-built, fifteen bed hospital, which incorporates a therapy garden and art installations is a place of calm, light and healing. A superb project incorporating creativity within tight controls and a fine example for future healthcare buildings to emulate." | MacLachlan & Monaghan | |
| 17 | | St Joseph's Hospital, Mount Desert, Cork Ireland; Client: The Sisters of Ben Secours "Domestic scale has been achieved, with all patient areas on one level and splendid views from the lounges at the end of each wing" | BDP | RIBA Award 2003 |
| 18 | NHS Acute | Hammersmith Hospital Renal Unit, Client: Hammersmith Hospitals NHS Trust | Ansell & Bailey | Completed 2005 |

**Table 4.18  List of six images for each of the AEDET Evolution statements used in the workshops**

AEDET Evolution

A1 There are clear ideas behind the design of the building.

| No | Image(s) | Scale | | | | | |
|---|---|---|---|---|---|---|---|
| | | 1 | 2 | 3 | 4 | 5 | 6 |
| 1 | | | | | | | |
| 2 | | | | | | | |
| 3 | | | | | | | |
| 4 | | | | | | | |
| 5 | | | | | | | |
| 6 | | | | | | | |

A2 The building is interesting to look at and move around in.

| No | Image(s) | Scale | | | | | |
|---|---|---|---|---|---|---|---|
| | | 1 | 2 | 3 | 4 | 5 | 6 |
| 7 | | | | | | | |
| 8 | | | | | | | |
| 9 | | | | | | | |
| 10 | | | | | | | |
| 11 | | | | | | | |
| 12 | | | | | | | |

A3 The building projects a caring and reassuring atmosphere.

| No | Image(s) | Scale | | | | | |
|---|---|---|---|---|---|---|---|
| | | 1 | 2 | 3 | 4 | 5 | 6 |
| 13 | | | | | | | |
| 14 | | | | | | | |
| 15 | | | | | | | |
| 16 | | | | | | | |
| 17 | | | | | | | |
| 18 | | | | | | | |

A4 The building appropriately expresses the values of the NHS.

| No | Image(s) | Scale | | | | | |
|---|---|---|---|---|---|---|---|
| | | 1 | 2 | 3 | 4 | 5 | 6 |
| 19 | | | | | | | |
| 20 | | | | | | | |
| 21 | | | | | | | |
| 22 | | | | | | | |
| 23 | | | | | | | |
| 24 | | | | | | | |

A5 The building is likely to influence future healthcare designs.

| No | Image(s) | Scale | | | | | |
|---|---|---|---|---|---|---|---|
| | | 1 | 2 | 3 | 4 | 5 | 6 |
| 25 | | | | | | | |
| 26 | | | | | | | |
| 27 | | | | | | | |
| 28 | | | | | | | |
| 29 | | | | | | | |
| 30 | | | | | | | |

A3 The building projects a caring and reassuring atmosphere.

| No | Image(s) | Scale | | | | | |
|---|---|---|---|---|---|---|---|
| | | 1 | 2 | 3 | 4 | 5 | 6 |
| 31 | | | | | | | |
| 32 | | | | | | | |
| 33 | | | | | | | |
| 34 | | | | | | | |
| 35 | | | | | | | |
| 36 | | | | | | | |

B1 The building has a human scale and feels welcoming.

| No | Image(s) | Scale | | | | | |
|---|---|---|---|---|---|---|---|
| | | 1 | 2 | 3 | 4 | 5 | 6 |
| 37 | | | | | | | |
| 38 | | | | | | | |
| 39 | | | | | | | |
| 40 | | | | | | | |
| 41 | | | | | | | |
| 42 | | | | | | | |

B2 The building is well oriented on the site.

| No | Image(s) | Scale | | | | | |
|---|---|---|---|---|---|---|---|
| | | 1 | 2 | 3 | 4 | 5 | 6 |
| 43 | | | | | | | |
| 44 | | | | | | | |
| 45 | | | | | | | |
| 46 | | | | | | | |
| 47 | | | | | | | |
| 48 | | | | | | | |

**B3 Entrances are obvious and logically positioned in relation to likely points of arrival on site.**

| No | Image(s) | Scale | | | | | |
|----|----------|---|---|---|---|---|---|
| | | 1 | 2 | 3 | 4 | 5 | 6 |
| 49 | | | | | | | |
| 50 | | | | | | | |
| 51 | | | | | | | |
| 52 | | | | | | | |
| 53 | | | | | | | |
| 54 | | | | | | | |

**B4 The external materials and detailing appear to be of high quality.**

| No | Image(s) | Scale | | | | | |
|----|----------|---|---|---|---|---|---|
| | | 1 | 2 | 3 | 4 | 5 | 6 |
| 55 | | | | | | | |
| 56 | | | | | | | |
| 57 | | | | | | | |
| 58 | | | | | | | |
| 59 | | | | | | | |
| 60 | | | | | | | |

**B5 The external colours and texture seem appropriate and attractive.**

| No | Image(s) | Scale | | | | | |
|----|----------|---|---|---|---|---|---|
| | | 1 | 2 | 3 | 4 | 5 | 6 |
| 61 | | | | | | | |
| 62 | | | | | | | |
| 63 | | | | | | | |
| 64 | | | | | | | |
| 65 | | | | | | | |
| 66 | | | | | | | |

**C1 The building respects the dignity of patients and allows for appropriate levels of privacy and dignity.**

| No | Image(s) | Scale | | | | | |
|----|----------|---|---|---|---|---|---|
| | | 1 | 2 | 3 | 4 | 5 | 6 |
| 67 | | | | | | | |
| 68 | | | | | | | |
| 69 | | | | | | | |
| 70 | | | | | | | |
| 71 | | | | | | | |
| 72 | | | | | | | |

**C2 There are good views inside and out of the building.**

| No | Image(s) | Scale | | | | | |
|----|----------|---|---|---|---|---|---|
| | | 1 | 2 | 3 | 4 | 5 | 6 |
| 73 | | | | | | | |
| 74 | | | | | | | |
| 75 | | | | | | | |
| 76 | | | | | | | |
| 77 | | | | | | | |
| 78 | | | | | | | |

**C3 Patients and staff have access to outdoors.**

| No | Image(s) | Scale | | | | | |
|----|----------|---|---|---|---|---|---|
| | | 1 | 2 | 3 | 4 | 5 | 6 |
| 79 | | | | | | | |
| 80 | | | | | | | |
| 81 | | | | | | | |
| 82 | | | | | | | |
| 83 | | | | | | | |
| 84 | | | | | | | |

**C4 There are high levels of both comfort and control of comfort.**

| No | Image(s) | Scale | | | | | |
|----|----------|---|---|---|---|---|---|
| | | 1 | 2 | 3 | 4 | 5 | 6 |
| 85 | | | | | | | |
| 86 | | | | | | | |
| 87 | | | | | | | |
| 88 | | | | | | | |
| 89 | | | | | | | |
| 90 | | | | | | | |

**C5 The building is clearly understandable.**

| No | Image(s) | Scale | | | | | |
|----|----------|---|---|---|---|---|---|
| | | 1 | 2 | 3 | 4 | 5 | 6 |
| 91 | | | | | | | |
| 92 | | | | | | | |
| 93 | | | | | | | |
| 94 | | | | | | | |
| 95 | | | | | | | |
| 96 | | | | | | | |

| C6 The interior of the building is attractive in appearance. | | | | | | | |
|---|---|---|---|---|---|---|---|
| No | Image(s) | Scale | | | | | |
| | | 1 | 2 | 3 | 4 | 5 | 6 |
| 97 | | | | | | | |
| 98 | | | | | | | |
| 99 | | | | | | | |
| 100 | | | | | | | |
| 101 | | | | | | | |
| 102 | | | | | | | |

| C7 There are good bath/toilet and other facilities for patients. | | | | | | | |
|---|---|---|---|---|---|---|---|
| No | Image(s) | Scale | | | | | |
| | | 1 | 2 | 3 | 4 | 5 | 6 |
| 103 | | | | | | | |
| 104 | | | | | | | |
| 105 | | | | | | | |
| 106 | | | | | | | |
| 107 | | | | | | | |
| 108 | | | | | | | |

| C8 There are good facilities for staff, including convenient places to work and relax without being on demand. | | | | | | | |
|---|---|---|---|---|---|---|---|
| No | Image(s) | Scale | | | | | |
| | | 1 | 2 | 3 | 4 | 5 | 6 |
| 109 | | | | | | | |
| 110 | | | | | | | |
| 111 | | | | | | | |
| 112 | | | | | | | |
| 113 | | | | | | | |
| 114 | | | | | | | |

| D1 The height, volume and skyline of the building relate well to the surrounding environment. | | | | | | | |
|---|---|---|---|---|---|---|---|
| No | Image(s) | Scale | | | | | |
| | | 1 | 2 | 3 | 4 | 5 | 6 |
| 115 | | | | | | | |
| 116 | | | | | | | |
| 117 | | | | | | | |
| 118 | | | | | | | |
| 119 | | | | | | | |
| 120 | | | | | | | |

| D2 The building contributes positively to its locality. | | | | | | | |
|---|---|---|---|---|---|---|---|
| No | Image(s) | Scale | | | | | |
| | | 1 | 2 | 3 | 4 | 5 | 6 |
| 121 | | | | | | | |
| 122 | | | | | | | |
| 123 | | | | | | | |
| 124 | | | | | | | |
| 125 | | | | | | | |
| 126 | | | | | | | |

| D3 The hard and soft landscape around the building contribute positively to the locality. | | | | | | | |
|---|---|---|---|---|---|---|---|
| No | Image(s) | Scale | | | | | |
| | | 1 | 2 | 3 | 4 | 5 | 6 |
| 127 | | | | | | | |
| 128 | | | | | | | |
| 129 | | | | | | | |
| 130 | | | | | | | |
| 131 | | | | | | | |
| 132 | | | | | | | |

| D4 The building is sensitive to neighbours and passers-by. | | | | | | | |
|---|---|---|---|---|---|---|---|
| No | Image(s) | Scale | | | | | |
| | | 1 | 2 | 3 | 4 | 5 | 6 |
| 133 | | | | | | | |
| 134 | | | | | | | |
| 135 | | | | | | | |
| 136 | | | | | | | |
| 137 | | | | | | | |
| 138 | | | | | | | |

| E1 The building is easy to operate. | | | | | | | |
|---|---|---|---|---|---|---|---|
| No | Image(s) | Scale | | | | | |
| | | 1 | 2 | 3 | 4 | 5 | 6 |
| 139 | | | | | | | |
| 140 | | | | | | | |
| 141 | | | | | | | |
| 142 | | | | | | | |
| 143 | | | | | | | |
| 144 | | | | | | | |

E2 The building is easy to clean.

| No | Image(s) | Scale | | | | | |
|----|----------|---|---|---|---|---|---|
| | | 1 | 2 | 3 | 4 | 5 | 6 |
| 145 | | | | | | | |
| 146 | | | | | | | |
| 147 | | | | | | | |
| 148 | | | | | | | |
| 149 | | | | | | | |
| 150 | | | | | | | |

E3 The building has appropriately durable finishes.

| No | Image(s) | Scale | | | | | |
|----|----------|---|---|---|---|---|---|
| | | 1 | 2 | 3 | 4 | 5 | 6 |
| 151 | | | | | | | |
| 152 | | | | | | | |
| 153 | | | | | | | |
| 154 | | | | | | | |
| 155 | | | | | | | |
| 156 | | | | | | | |

E4 The building will weather and age well.

| No | Image(s) | Scale | | | | | |
|----|----------|---|---|---|---|---|---|
| | | 1 | 2 | 3 | 4 | 5 | 6 |
| 157 | | | | | | | |
| 158 | | | | | | | |
| 159 | | | | | | | |
| 160 | | | | | | | |
| 161 | | | | | | | |
| 162 | | | | | | | |

H7 The layout facilitates both security and supervision.

| No | Image(s) | Scale | | | | | |
|----|----------|---|---|---|---|---|---|
| | | 1 | 2 | 3 | 4 | 5 | 6 |
| 163 | | | | | | | |
| 164 | | | | | | | |
| 165 | | | | | | | |
| 166 | | | | | | | |
| 167 | | | | | | | |
| 168 | | | | | | | |

I1 There is good access from available public transport including any onsite roads.

| No | Image(s) | Scale | | | | | |
|----|----------|---|---|---|---|---|---|
| | | 1 | 2 | 3 | 4 | 5 | 6 |
| 169 | | | | | | | |
| 170 | | | | | | | |
| 171 | | | | | | | |
| 172 | | | | | | | |
| 173 | | | | | | | |
| 174 | | | | | | | |

I3 The approach and access for ambulances is appropriately provided.

| No | Image(s) | Scale | | | | | |
|----|----------|---|---|---|---|---|---|
| | | 1 | 2 | 3 | 4 | 5 | 6 |
| 175 | | | | | | | |
| 176 | | | | | | | |
| 177 | | | | | | | |
| 178 | | | | | | | |
| 179 | | | | | | | |
| 180 | | | | | | | |

I4 Goods and waste disposal vehicle circulation is good and segregated from public and staff access where appropriate.

| No | Image(s) | Scale | | | | | |
|----|----------|---|---|---|---|---|---|
| | | 1 | 2 | 3 | 4 | 5 | 6 |
| 181 | | | | | | | |
| 182 | | | | | | | |
| 183 | | | | | | | |
| 184 | | | | | | | |
| 185 | | | | | | | |
| 186 | | | | | | | |

I5 Pedestrian access routes are obvious, pleasant and suitable for wheelchair users and people with other disabilities/impaired sight.

| No | Image(s) | Scale | | | | | |
|----|----------|---|---|---|---|---|---|
| | | 1 | 2 | 3 | 4 | 5 | 6 |
| 187 | | | | | | | |
| 188 | | | | | | | |
| 189 | | | | | | | |
| 190 | | | | | | | |
| 191 | | | | | | | |
| 192 | | | | | | | |

I6 Outdoor spaces are provided with appropriate and safe lighting indicating paths, ramps and steps.

| No | Image(s) | Scale | | | | | |
|---|---|---|---|---|---|---|---|
| | | 1 | 2 | 3 | 4 | 5 | 6 |
| 193 | | | | | | | |
| 194 | | | | | | | |
| 195 | | | | | | | |
| 196 | | | | | | | |
| 197 | | | | | | | |
| 198 | | | | | | | |

| ASPECT |
|---|

C1.1 Patients can choose to have visual privacy.

| No | Image(s) | Scale | | | | | |
|---|---|---|---|---|---|---|---|
| | | 1 | 2 | 3 | 4 | 5 | 6 |
| 199 | | | | | | | |
| 200 | | | | | | | |
| 201 | | | | | | | |
| 202 | | | | | | | |
| 203 | | | | | | | |
| 204 | | | | | | | |

C1.2 Patients can have a private conversation.

| No | Image(s) | Scale | | | | | |
|---|---|---|---|---|---|---|---|
| | | 1 | 2 | 3 | 4 | 5 | 6 |
| 205 | | | | | | | |
| 206 | | | | | | | |
| 207 | | | | | | | |
| 208 | | | | | | | |
| 209 | | | | | | | |
| 210 | | | | | | | |

C1.3 Patients can be alone.

| No | Image(s) | Scale | | | | | |
|---|---|---|---|---|---|---|---|
| | | 1 | 2 | 3 | 4 | 5 | 6 |
| 211 | | | | | | | |
| 212 | | | | | | | |
| 213 | | | | | | | |
| 214 | | | | | | | |
| 215 | | | | | | | |
| 216 | | | | | | | |

C1.5 Toilets/bathrooms are located logically, conveniently & discretely.

| No | Image(s) | Scale | | | | | |
|---|---|---|---|---|---|---|---|
| | | 1 | 2 | 3 | 4 | 5 | 6 |
| 217 | | | | | | | |
| 218 | | | | | | | |
| 219 | | | | | | | |
| 220 | | | | | | | |
| 221 | | | | | | | |
| 222 | | | | | | | |

C2.1 Spaces where staff and patients spend time have windows.

| No | Image(s) | Scale | | | | | |
|---|---|---|---|---|---|---|---|
| | | 1 | 2 | 3 | 4 | 5 | 6 |
| 223 | | | | | | | |
| 224 | | | | | | | |
| 225 | | | | | | | |
| 226 | | | | | | | |
| 227 | | | | | | | |
| 228 | | | | | | | |

C2.2 Patients and staff can easily see the sky.

| No | Image(s) | Scale | | | | | |
|---|---|---|---|---|---|---|---|
| | | 1 | 2 | 3 | 4 | 5 | 6 |
| 229 | | | | | | | |
| 230 | | | | | | | |
| 231 | | | | | | | |
| 232 | | | | | | | |
| 233 | | | | | | | |
| 234 | | | | | | | |

C2.3 Patients and staff can easily see the ground.

| No | Image(s) | Scale | | | | | |
|---|---|---|---|---|---|---|---|
| | | 1 | 2 | 3 | 4 | 5 | 6 |
| 235 | | | | | | | |
| 236 | | | | | | | |
| 237 | | | | | | | |
| 238 | | | | | | | |
| 239 | | | | | | | |
| 240 | | | | | | | |

### C2.4 The view is calming.

| No | Image(s) | Scale | | | | | |
|----|----------|-------|---|---|---|---|---|
| | | 1 | 2 | 3 | 4 | 5 | 6 |
| 241 | | | | | | | |
| 242 | | | | | | | |
| 243 | | | | | | | |
| 244 | | | | | | | |
| 245 | | | | | | | |
| 246 | | | | | | | |

### C2.5 The view is interesting.

| No | Image(s) | Scale | | | | | |
|----|----------|-------|---|---|---|---|---|
| | | 1 | 2 | 3 | 4 | 5 | 6 |
| 247 | | | | | | | |
| 248 | | | | | | | |
| 249 | | | | | | | |
| 250 | | | | | | | |
| 251 | | | | | | | |
| 252 | | | | | | | |

### C3.1 Patients can go outside.

| No | Image(s) | Scale | | | | | |
|----|----------|-------|---|---|---|---|---|
| | | 1 | 2 | 3 | 4 | 5 | 6 |
| 253 | | | | | | | |
| 254 | | | | | | | |
| 255 | | | | | | | |
| 256 | | | | | | | |
| 257 | | | | | | | |
| 258 | | | | | | | |

### C3.2 Patients and staff have access to usable landscaped areas.

| No | Image(s) | Scale | | | | | |
|----|----------|-------|---|---|---|---|---|
| | | 1 | 2 | 3 | 4 | 5 | 6 |
| 259 | | | | | | | |
| 260 | | | | | | | |
| 261 | | | | | | | |
| 262 | | | | | | | |
| 263 | | | | | | | |
| 264 | | | | | | | |

### C3.3 Patients and staff can easily see plants, vegetation and nature.

| No | Image(s) | Scale | | | | | |
|----|----------|-------|---|---|---|---|---|
| | | 1 | 2 | 3 | 4 | 5 | 6 |
| 265 | | | | | | | |
| 266 | | | | | | | |
| 267 | | | | | | | |
| 268 | | | | | | | |
| 269 | | | | | | | |
| 270 | | | | | | | |

### C4.1 There is a variety of artificial lighting patterns appropriate for day and night and for summer and winter.

| No | Image(s) | Scale | | | | | |
|----|----------|-------|---|---|---|---|---|
| | | 1 | 2 | 3 | 4 | 5 | 6 |
| 271 | | | | | | | |
| 272 | | | | | | | |
| 273 | | | | | | | |
| 274 | | | | | | | |
| 275 | | | | | | | |
| 276 | | | | | | | |

### C4.3 Patients and staff can easily exclude sunlight and daylight.

| No | Image(s) | Scale | | | | | |
|----|----------|-------|---|---|---|---|---|
| | | 1 | 2 | 3 | 4 | 5 | 6 |
| 277 | | | | | | | |
| 278 | | | | | | | |
| 279 | | | | | | | |
| 280 | | | | | | | |
| 281 | | | | | | | |
| 282 | | | | | | | |

### C4.5 Patients and staff can easily open windows/doors.

| No | Image(s) | Scale | | | | | |
|----|----------|-------|---|---|---|---|---|
| | | 1 | 2 | 3 | 4 | 5 | 6 |
| 283 | | | | | | | |
| 284 | | | | | | | |
| 285 | | | | | | | |
| 286 | | | | | | | |
| 287 | | | | | | | |
| 288 | | | | | | | |

| C5.1 When you arrive at the building, the entrance is obvious. | | | | | | | |
|---|---|---|---|---|---|---|---|
| No | Image(s) | Scale | | | | | |
| | | 1 | 2 | 3 | 4 | 5 | 6 |
| 289 | | | | | | | |
| 290 | | | | | | | |
| 291 | | | | | | | |
| 292 | | | | | | | |
| 293 | | | | | | | |
| 294 | | | | | | | |

| C5.2 It's easy to understand the way the building is laid out. | | | | | | | |
|---|---|---|---|---|---|---|---|
| No | Image(s) | Scale | | | | | |
| | | 1 | 2 | 3 | 4 | 5 | 6 |
| 295 | | | | | | | |
| 296 | | | | | | | |
| 297 | | | | | | | |
| 298 | | | | | | | |
| 299 | | | | | | | |
| 300 | | | | | | | |

| C5.3 There is a logical hierarchy of places in the building. | | | | | | | |
|---|---|---|---|---|---|---|---|
| No | Image(s) | Scale | | | | | |
| | | 1 | 2 | 3 | 4 | 5 | 6 |
| 301 | | | | | | | |
| 302 | | | | | | | |
| 303 | | | | | | | |
| 304 | | | | | | | |
| 305 | | | | | | | |
| 306 | | | | | | | |

| C5.4 When you leave the building, the way out is obvious. | | | | | | | |
|---|---|---|---|---|---|---|---|
| No | Image(s) | Scale | | | | | |
| | | 1 | 2 | 3 | 4 | 5 | 6 |
| 307 | | | | | | | |
| 308 | | | | | | | |
| 309 | | | | | | | |
| 310 | | | | | | | |
| 311 | | | | | | | |
| 312 | | | | | | | |

| C5.5 It is obvious where to go to find a member of staff. | | | | | | | |
|---|---|---|---|---|---|---|---|
| No | Image(s) | Scale | | | | | |
| | | 1 | 2 | 3 | 4 | 5 | 6 |
| 313 | | | | | | | |
| 314 | | | | | | | |
| 315 | | | | | | | |
| 316 | | | | | | | |
| 317 | | | | | | | |
| 318 | | | | | | | |

| C5.6 Different parts of the building have different characters. | | | | | | | |
|---|---|---|---|---|---|---|---|
| No | Image(s) | Scale | | | | | |
| | | 1 | 2 | 3 | 4 | 5 | 6 |
| 319 | | | | | | | |
| 320 | | | | | | | |
| 321 | | | | | | | |
| 322 | | | | | | | |
| 323 | | | | | | | |
| 324 | | | | | | | |

| C6.1 Patients' spaces feel homely. | | | | | | | |
|---|---|---|---|---|---|---|---|
| No | Image(s) | Scale | | | | | |
| | | 1 | 2 | 3 | 4 | 5 | 6 |
| 325 | | | | | | | |
| 326 | | | | | | | |
| 327 | | | | | | | |
| 328 | | | | | | | |
| 329 | | | | | | | |
| 330 | | | | | | | |

| C6.2 The interior feels light and airy. | | | | | | | |
|---|---|---|---|---|---|---|---|
| No | Image(s) | Scale | | | | | |
| | | 1 | 2 | 3 | 4 | 5 | 6 |
| 331 | | | | | | | |
| 332 | | | | | | | |
| 333 | | | | | | | |
| 334 | | | | | | | |
| 335 | | | | | | | |
| 336 | | | | | | | |

C6.3 The interior has a variety of colours, textures and views.

| No | Image(s) | Scale | | | | | |
|---|---|---|---|---|---|---|---|
| | | 1 | 2 | 3 | 4 | 5 | 6 |
| 337 | | | | | | | |
| 338 | | | | | | | |
| 339 | | | | | | | |
| 340 | | | | | | | |
| 341 | | | | | | | |
| 342 | | | | | | | |

C6.4 The interior looks clean, tidy and cared for.

| No | Image(s) | Scale | | | | | |
|---|---|---|---|---|---|---|---|
| | | 1 | 2 | 3 | 4 | 5 | 6 |
| 343 | | | | | | | |
| 344 | | | | | | | |
| 345 | | | | | | | |
| 346 | | | | | | | |
| 347 | | | | | | | |
| 348 | | | | | | | |

C6.5 The interior has provision for art, plants and flowers.

| No | Image(s) | Scale | | | | | |
|---|---|---|---|---|---|---|---|
| | | 1 | 2 | 3 | 4 | 5 | 6 |
| 349 | | | | | | | |
| 350 | | | | | | | |
| 351 | | | | | | | |
| 352 | | | | | | | |
| 353 | | | | | | | |
| 354 | | | | | | | |

C6.6 Ceilings are designed to look interesting.

| No | Image(s) | Scale | | | | | |
|---|---|---|---|---|---|---|---|
| | | 1 | 2 | 3 | 4 | 5 | 6 |
| 355 | | | | | | | |
| 356 | | | | | | | |
| 357 | | | | | | | |
| 358 | | | | | | | |
| 359 | | | | | | | |
| 360 | | | | | | | |

C6.7 Patients can have and display personal items in their own space.

| No | Image(s) | Scale | | | | | |
|---|---|---|---|---|---|---|---|
| | | 1 | 2 | 3 | 4 | 5 | 6 |
| 361 | | | | | | | |
| 362 | | | | | | | |
| 363 | | | | | | | |
| 364 | | | | | | | |
| 365 | | | | | | | |
| 366 | | | | | | | |

C6.8 Floors are covered with suitable material.

| No | Image(s) | Scale | | | | | |
|---|---|---|---|---|---|---|---|
| | | 1 | 2 | 3 | 4 | 5 | 6 |
| 367 | | | | | | | |
| 368 | | | | | | | |
| 369 | | | | | | | |
| 370 | | | | | | | |
| 371 | | | | | | | |
| 372 | | | | | | | |

C7.1 Bathrooms/Toilets are provided with appropriate seats, handrails, non-slip flooring, a shelf for toiletries and somewhere to hang clothes within easy reach.

| No | Image(s) | Scale | | | | | |
|---|---|---|---|---|---|---|---|
| | | 1 | 2 | 3 | 4 | 5 | 6 |
| 373 | | | | | | | |
| 374 | | | | | | | |
| 375 | | | | | | | |
| 376 | | | | | | | |
| 377 | | | | | | | |
| 378 | | | | | | | |

C7.3 There is a space where religious observances can take place.

| No | Image(s) | Scale | | | | | |
|---|---|---|---|---|---|---|---|
| | | 1 | 2 | 3 | 4 | 5 | 6 |
| 379 | | | | | | | |
| 380 | | | | | | | |
| 381 | | | | | | | |
| 382 | | | | | | | |
| 383 | | | | | | | |
| 384 | | | | | | | |

C7.4 There is a place where live performances can take place.

| No | Image(s) | Scale | | | | | |
|---|---|---|---|---|---|---|---|
| | | 1 | 2 | 3 | 4 | 5 | 6 |
| 385 | | | | | | | |
| 386 | | | | | | | |
| 387 | | | | | | | |
| 388 | | | | | | | |
| 389 | | | | | | | |
| 390 | | | | | | | |

C7.6 Patients have facilities to make drinks.

| No | Image(s) | Scale | | | | | |
|---|---|---|---|---|---|---|---|
| | | 1 | 2 | 3 | 4 | 5 | 6 |
| 391 | | | | | | | |
| 392 | | | | | | | |
| 393 | | | | | | | |
| 394 | | | | | | | |
| 395 | | | | | | | |
| 396 | | | | | | | |

C8.1 Staff have a convenient place to change and securely store belongings and clothes.

| No | Image(s) | Scale | | | | | |
|---|---|---|---|---|---|---|---|
| | | 1 | 2 | 3 | 4 | 5 | 6 |
| 397 | | | | | | | |
| 398 | | | | | | | |
| 399 | | | | | | | |
| 400 | | | | | | | |
| 401 | | | | | | | |
| 402 | | | | | | | |

C8.2 Staff have convenient places to concentrate on work without being on demand.

| No | Image(s) | Scale | | | | | |
|---|---|---|---|---|---|---|---|
| | | 1 | 2 | 3 | 4 | 5 | 6 |
| 403 | | | | | | | |
| 404 | | | | | | | |
| 405 | | | | | | | |
| 406 | | | | | | | |
| 407 | | | | | | | |
| 408 | | | | | | | |

C8.3 There are convenient places where staff can speedily get snacks and meals.

| No | Image(s) | Scale | | | | | |
|---|---|---|---|---|---|---|---|
| | | 1 | 2 | 3 | 4 | 5 | 6 |
| 409 | | | | | | | |
| 410 | | | | | | | |
| 411 | | | | | | | |
| 412 | | | | | | | |
| 413 | | | | | | | |
| 414 | | | | | | | |

C8.4 Staff can rest and relax in places segregated from patient and visitor areas.

| No | Image(s) | Scale | | | | | |
|---|---|---|---|---|---|---|---|
| | | 1 | 2 | 3 | 4 | 5 | 6 |
| 415 | | | | | | | |
| 416 | | | | | | | |
| 417 | | | | | | | |
| 418 | | | | | | | |
| 419 | | | | | | | |
| 420 | | | | | | | |

C8.5 All staff have easy and convenient access to IT.

| No | Image(s) | Scale | | | | | |
|---|---|---|---|---|---|---|---|
| | | 1 | 2 | 3 | 4 | 5 | 6 |
| 421 | | | | | | | |
| 422 | | | | | | | |
| 423 | | | | | | | |
| 424 | | | | | | | |
| 425 | | | | | | | |
| 426 | | | | | | | |

C8.6 Staff have convenient access to basic banking facilities and can shop for essentials.

| No | Image(s) | Scale | | | | | |
|---|---|---|---|---|---|---|---|
| | | 1 | 2 | 3 | 4 | 5 | 6 |
| 427 | | | | | | | |
| 428 | | | | | | | |
| 429 | | | | | | | |
| 430 | | | | | | | |
| 431 | | | | | | | |
| 432 | | | | | | | |

# 5 Design for sustainability tools in healthcare

BREEAM and CIBSE TM22 represent some of the most important tools that can be implemented in health care to enhance sustainability in the design, construction and operation of accommodation to support efficient and effective delivery of health and social care. A key challenge for health care providers is to ensure that buildings perform as predicted and expected, and that targets for sustainability are continuously being met. As with medical outcomes underpinning evidence-based medicine, the results of hospitals-in-use studies are crucial in yielding better design practice to provide a foundation for evidence-based architectural design. Several metrics underpin the Sustainability Reporting Framework for mandatory annual sustainability reporting in the UK NHS from 2011/12 onwards (Table 5.1).

## BREEAM

Worldwide, a variety of assessment programmes have been developed around the environmental and energy impacts of buildings. The first environmental certification system, BREEAM (**B**ritish **R**esearch **E**stablishment **E**nvironmental **A**ssessment **M**ethod) was created by the British Research Establishment (BRE) in 1990 in the UK. The LEED® (**L**eadership in **E**nergy and **E**nvironmental **D**esign) Green Building Rating System, which is based quite substantially on BREEAM, was introduced in 1998 in the USA. The Green Building Initiative (GBI) launched Green Globes in 2005 by adapting the Canadian version of BREEAM and distributing it in the USA market.

## Development from NHS Environmental Assessment Tool (NEAT) to BREEAM Healthcare (B4H):

BREEAM Healthcare represents an important strategy in the UK for meeting the challenges posed by the sustainability agenda and the environmental performance of NHS buildings. From its historical development and origins as the self-assessment NEAT, BREEAM

Table 5.1 Key metrics within the sustainability Reporting Framework in the UK NHS for mandatory sustainability reporting

| | Activity | SHAPE outcomes |
|---|---|---|
| Supports key health policy initiatives:<br><br>• Quality Innovation Productivity & Prevention (QIPP).<br><br>• Joint Strategic Needs Assessment (JSNA).<br><br>• Transforming Community Services.<br><br>Complements the range of tools we use to support planning and commissioning decisions in Families and Social Care. | • Linking to national datasets for clinical analysis, public health, primary care and demographic data with estates performance and location of facilities.<br>• Enabling interactive investigations by NHS Commissioning Board Local Area Teams, Trusts Providers, Clinical Commissioning Groups, GP practices and Local Authorities.<br>• Providing a range of flexible application capabilities that facilitate scenario planning and testing. | • Optimum efficiency in the design and delivery of services that is benchmarked to national indicators.<br>• Integration of health and social care services and settings.<br>• Strategic Needs Assessments, Risk Stratification and Predictive Modelling, and Service Planning.<br>• Strategic optimum location of services and premises that also meets targets for sustainability by reducing transport. |
| | • Improving access to services by different populations in different communities in the Kent County Council area.<br>• Reducing Hospital admissions.<br>• Shifting care closer to home.<br>• Aiding development of a Business Case for a new facility.<br>• Increasing understanding of clinical activity for a clinical network.<br>• Aiding the development of a Care Pathway Approach to service delivery.<br>• Helping with the identification of cost savings within a health and social care economy.<br>• Developing an appropriate Estate Strategy that aligns Strategic Services Plan.<br>• Evaluating the efficiency and effectiveness of an existing service model. | • Improved access to services to meet user expectations.<br>• Reduced hospital admissions and transfers to avoid user journeys to and from hospital.<br>• Care is provided closer to home to increase user satisfaction.<br>• Aids development of Business Case for a new facility, something which facilitates approvals by the Department of Health and other authorities.<br>• Implementation of a Care Pathway Approach to service provision and delivery.<br>• Produces an Estate Strategy that is aligned with the Strategic Services Plan.<br>• Providing the evidence of the efficiency and effectiveness of an existing service model. |
| | • Reducing inequalities in access to care by different groups in the community.<br>• Supporting Clinical Commissioning by Clinical Commissioning Groups.<br>• Support Joint Strategic Needs Assessment (JSNA).<br>• Supporting Quality Innovation Productivity & Prevention (QIPP) Right Care, Safe Care, Long-Term Conditions and Urgent & Emergency Care. | • Demographic data e.g. age structure, ethnicity and deprivation.<br>• Public health data eg. mortality, screening, childhood obesity and lifestyle indicators.<br>• Clinical inpatient activity e.g. high volume case types, analysis of Length of Stay and readmission rates. |

**Variations in AEDET Evolution correlations**

| Section | Correlation |
|---|---|
| A CHARACTER & INNOVATION | 0.5 |
| B FORM & MATERIALS | −0.2 |
| C STAFF & PATIENT ENVIRONMENT | 0.5 |
| D URBAN/SOCIAL INTEGRATION | 0.0 |
| E PERFORMANCE | 0.3 |
| H USE | 0.1 |
| I ACCESS | 0.6 |

| Measurement and targets | Indicator | Measure | Target |
|---|---|---|---|
| Building energy use | Metered energy use | Tonnes $CO_2$e | Reduction of 10% |
| | Metered energy use | Kg $CO_2$e/m² | Reduction of 10% |
| | Energy from renewables | % | Increase to over 10% |
| DEC Report | Reviewed DEC Advisory Report | Yes/No | Yes/No |
| BREEAM Standard | Excellent for New Build, Very Good for Refurbishments | Yes/No | Yes/No |
| Facilities – GCC | Progress | Score | |
| | Quality | Score | |

Healthcare has been developed as a measurement tool and not as a design tool, distinguished by the scope of environmental issues addressed, metrics and performance standards. However, key considerations are application in practice of the credits-based tool, the certification process, reasons for the tool's development, and benefits and comparisons with other environmental assessment systems. Case studies illustrate some of these aspects within a context which indicates that despite 300 health care schemes being registered in 2008, in 2012 only one scheme had completed the entire certification process.

The BREEAM family of assessment methods and tools was designed to help construction professionals understand and mitigate the environmental impacts of the developments they design and build. A leading and very widely used environmental assessment method for buildings in the UK, BREEAM (or an equivalent) is advocated at UK Government level as a robust means of setting standards and assessing the sustainability of the Government estate, including the estate of the public sector bodies. The operation of BREEAM is overseen by an independent Sustainability Board (the UK Green Building Council), representing a wide cross-section of construction industry representatives.

BREEAM's major goal is to set the standard for best practice in sustainable design by mitigating the impacts of buildings on the environment, enabling buildings to be recognised according to their environmental benefits, while providing a credible, environmental label for buildings as well as stimulating demand for sustainable buildings. In developing BREEAM, the BRE's objectives seek to: provide market recognition of low environmental impact buildings; ensure best environmental practice is incorporated in buildings; set criteria and standards surpassing those

required by regulations and challenge the market to provide innovative solutions that minimise the environmental impact of buildings; raise the awareness of owners, occupants, designers and operators of the benefits of buildings with a reduced impact on the environment; and allow organisations to demonstrate progress towards corporate environmental objectives (Figure 5.1).

Since its introduction in 1990 BREEAM has become widely accepted by designers, developers and building occupiers as an important means to measure a building's environmental performance. Credits are awarded in nine categories according to performance. These credits are then added together to produce a single overall score on a five-point scale: pass; good; very good; excellent; and outstanding. A certificate is awarded on successful conclusion.

BREEAM for Health Care was developed by the BRE following a commission by the Department of Health and the Welsh Health Estates to replace NEAT, a self-assessment tool developed in 2002 by the BRE on behalf of NHS Estates (later abolished with some responsibilities assumed by the Department of Health Estates and Facilities Division). NEAT was the result of a joint research and development project between NHS Estates and the Department for Trade and Industry, produced by the Building Research Establishment to ensure a consistency with BRE Environmental Assessment Methodology (BREEAM). NEAT was a part of a package of measures to enable the NHS to understand, identify and, importantly, take action to reduce and limit negative impacts on the environment. NEAT's aims were to: raise environmental awareness within NHS facilities and services; estimate the environmental impact of NHS facilities and services; and seek to establish an environmental improvement programme (Tables 5.2 and 5.3).

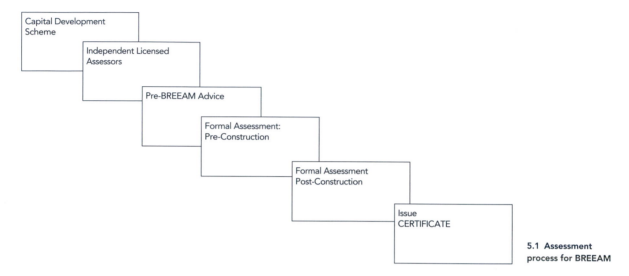

**5.1 Assessment process for BREEAM**

A study by Capper et al. (2005) found out that although NEAT could provide a measure of environmental performance, the tool could not on its own establish an environmental improvement programme. NEAT was also essentially designed for two different user groups with varying levels of knowledge and understanding – on the one hand the professional design team involved in the construction of new multi-million pound health care facilities, and on the other the administrative staff required to provide environmental returns by government. For the latter group who had minimal knowledge of construction and/or building services, NEAT had to work at a relatively unsophisticated level.

**Table 5.2 Characteristics of NEAT 2002**

**Factors covered**

| Environment | Social | Economic | Governance |
|---|---|---|---|
| 1 | 1 | 0 | 0 |

**Sectors of use**

| Waste | Energy | Water | Transport | Green/Blue | Building & Land Use |
|---|---|---|---|---|---|
| 1 | 1 | 1 | 1 | 0 | 1 |

Key: M – main sector, 1 – sub sector and 0 – n/a

**Scale of applications**

| Component | Building | Neighbourhood | City | Region |
|---|---|---|---|---|
| 0 | 1 | 0 | 0 | 0 |

**Project stage when tool is usually used**

| Inception | Design | Design assessment | Construction | Operation | Demolition |
|---|---|---|---|---|---|
| 1 | 1 | 1 | 1 | 1 | 0 |

**NEAT Credits by Project Stage**

| Strategic | Planning | Design | Construction | Operation | Disposal | Whole-life |
|---|---|---|---|---|---|---|
| 7 | 15 | 52 | 6 | 20 | 0 | 100 |

Other tools or mechanisms produced by NHS Estates that were designed to complement NEAT were 'Sustainable development: environmental strategy for the NHS'; 'Sustainable development in the NHS'; the Estates Returns Information Collection performance management system (ERIC); the Achieving Excellence Design Evaluation Tool (AEDET); the ProCure21 capital development procurement process; and Estatecode.

**Table 5.3 Characteristics of NEAT 2002 (strengths vs. weaknesses)**

| NEAT's strengths: | NEAT's weaknesses: |
|---|---|
| • Sought to increase recognition by all Government departments that new-builds and refurbishments should be sustainably constructed. <br> • Developed as a Microsoft Excel-based assessment tool to allow NHS staff to carry out assessments without calling in an independent, specialist assessor from outside the NHS. <br> • Aimed to increase awareness of environmental agenda <br> • Involved a holistic approach to environmental assessment of: <br> 1) Existing Sites, and 2) New Build/Refurbishment Projects. <br> • Aimed to improve NHS building stock via <br>   – Resource efficiency <br>   – Cost effectiveness <br>   – Development of more pleasant healthcare environments <br> • Drives change | • Out of date with <br>   – Changes in Building Regulations being based in Part L of the Building Regulations <br>   – BREEAM developments <br>   – Improving standards – Department of Health and industry <br>   – Best practice <br> • No third party verification <br> • Lack of guidance for users/specifiers |

All NHS trusts had to be assessed for environmental performance using the NHS Environmental Assessment Tool (NEAT). NEAT was to be used to provide criteria for the design process and to set design parameters for energy use. NEAT was produced as a result of the Sustainable Construction Action Plan, which required all new buildings to achieve a NEAT rating of Excellent and refurbished buildings to achieve a Very Good rating. NEAT was also produced as a result of the Government Construction Client Panel requirements detailed in the Sustainable Construction Action Plan (copy available on the NHS Estates website at http://www.nhsestates.gov.uk under Sustainable Development/Construction). This places a requirement on all Government departments according to which new builds and refurbishments should be sustainably constructed. As part of this process, new builds were required to achieve a NEAT score of Excellent and refurbishments a score of Very Good (Tables 5.4 to 5.6).

For the purposes of NEAT, health care facilities fell into two categories. Existing Sites covered all NHS health care facilities irrespective of their size or the type of services provided. The aim was to identify the extent and type of impacts of NHS services and facilities created during the performance of its day-to-day operational activities. New Build and Refurbishment Projects covered all capital development projects irrespective of whether they were publicly or privately funded. New Build consisted of all capital development projects to provide new health care facilities of any size, large or small, from acute multi-bed hospital sites to small health clinics or walk-in centres, while Refurbishment concerned the complete renewal of the exterior and/or interior of a building, or part of a building, and its fixtures and fittings. The description does not include capital replacement programmes such as windows, doors or plant renewal.

**Table 5.4 Typical NEAT scores achieved for hospital projects**

| Year | Project | Designer/Developer | Total NEAT score |
|---|---|---|---|
| 2002 | John Radcliffe Hospital, Oxford | Carillion | 75% |
| 2003 | Queen Alexandra Hospital, Portsmouth | Carillion | 82% |
| 2007 | Greater Peterborough NHS | Nightingale Associates | 72.94 |

Table 5.5 From NEAT to BREEAM Healthcare 2008

| From NEAT to BREEAM Healthcare | Overview of BREEAM Healthcare |
|---|---|
| • Update to<br>  – Current best practice standards<br>  – Building Regulations 2006 from Part L of the Building Regulations<br>  – New Health Technical Memoranda (HTMs) etc<br>• Develop in line with BREEAM family of tools.<br>• Ensure reporting will be as per BREEAM methods.<br>• Credit filtering system to meet the scale of primary, intermediate and acute developments.<br>• More links to sustainable development such as Good Corporate Citizen Tool www.corporatecitizen.nhs.uk.<br>• Provide guidance early on in the procurement process.<br>• Training and technical support.<br>• Certification.<br>• New self-assessment tool for Existing Buildings in Operation. | • Building Research Establishment's Environmental Assessment Method for buildings.<br>• Nationally and internationally recognised.<br>• Updated annually in line with best practice and legislation<br>• Independent.<br>• Certification scheme<br>  – Accreditation vs. Self-assessment<br>    • Validation check<br>    • Improvement of standards<br>    • Independent advice for the trust/contractor<br>    • Costs vs. benefits<br>• ISO 9001/UKAS accreditation<br>• Covers any type of building (offices, homes – industrial, retail)<br>• Developed for UK Government Departments<br>  – NEAT (NHS)<br>  – BREEAM for Schools<br>  – BREEAM for Prisons<br>  – MoD (Ministry of Defence)/Defence Estates<br>  – DWP (Department of Work & Pensions) (JobCentrePlus; Pensions)<br>• Bespoke Schemes (mixed use/special buildings) |

Table 5.6 Comparison of NEAT and BREEAM Healthcare 2008

| NEAT (NHS Environmental Assessment Tool) | BREEAM Healthcare |
|---|---|
| • Self assessment tool | • Can only be carried out by independent licensed BREEAM assessors who charge a fee |
| • No quality control process | • Two stage quality controlled assessment process (design and post construction). Quality Assurance managed by BRE |
| • No mandatory requirements | • Mandatory credit scores and weightings for different environmental impact categories e.g. energy and transport |
| • Mandatory for new build at Outline of Business Case approval stage | • Mandatory for new build at Outline of Business Case (OBC) approval stage of a project – rating of EXCELLENT must be achieved |
| • Voluntary for existing buildings | • Mandatory for existing buildings at Outline of Business Case approval stage of a project – rating of GOOD must be achieved |
| • No update since 2002 on Building Regulations, Health Technical standards or best practice | • Regulation and Health Technical standards to 2008 requirements and the scheme will be regularly updated to follow Building Regulations, Health Technical Memorandum and best practice |

NEAT was the first stage and a stepping stone to a more intensive Environmental Management System (EMS) approach to environmental improvement. Once NEAT had been embraced, the next progressive step was to consider the benefits of introducing an EMS. EMS aims to help organisations to:

• Reduce their negative impact on the environment;
• Reduce the possibility of unforeseen environmental risks;
• Ensure compliance with environmental legislation and regulations (non-compliance can mean costly fines and cause adverse publicity);
• Reduce costs by helping to identify waste areas, thereby reducing waste and using resources more efficiently;

- Improve the effectiveness of existing management systems – management control is enhanced by improved business planning as it includes objective setting and performance monitoring;
- Reduce use of energy and resources while minimising waste, thereby saving money;
- Introduce a consistent, systematic approach to environmental management;
- Continually improve environmental and overall performance and quality;
- Involve people, raise their awareness, realise their potential, harness motivation, and help them develop new skills.

For a time NEAT was a necessary competent benchmark of sustainable design and a credible standard from which to demonstrate that the NHS continued to be a leading public sector body in setting the carbon reduction and sustainability agenda. However, NEAT was soon to become out-of-date with new legislation and standards, and as such it was no longer fit for purpose. Since its launch in 2002 NEAT had not evolved to keep up with other environmental assessment tools such as BREEAM for offices, which was modified annually. Capper et al. (2005) found that in practice the application of NEAT was haphazard, and the government requirement that all new health care facilities must achieve a NEAT Excellent rating had not been incorporated into the bid documents for new build PFI schemes. In some specifications the requirement for sustainable building was absent or couched in general terms which were difficult to evaluate. Another difficulty was that of attaining collective responsibility for achieving credits when project teams could only undertake to achieve an excellent rating for their elements of the work, with some issues determined prior to the appointment of the design team. A further issue was that although the government had set out ambitious targets for $CO_2$ reduction and other sustainability measures, they had not ensured that these targets were integrated into the set of Trusts' performance indicators for effective budget administration. The study also found that NEAT needed to evolve to develop measurable outcomes alongside those for health and wellbeing, and to take account of social issues such as community consultations.

The BREEAM Healthcare scheme developed as an update and improvement on the existing self assessment NEAT, going beyond the remit of the NEAT methodology and including major step changes in the underlying business model (Table 5.7).

**Table 5.7 Comparison of BREEAM and LEED**

|  | BREEAM | LEED |
| --- | --- | --- |
| Green Building Organisation | United Kingdom Green Building Council | US Green Building Council (USGBC) |
| Certification | BRE | Green Building Certification Institute |
| Quality Assurance | BRE & UKAS | US Green Building Council |
| Country of Origin | United Kingdom | USA |
| Year started | 1990 | 1998 |
| Certified buildings | 100,000 | >2150 |
| Countries using the method | UK, Ireland, Netherlands | USA and 69 countries worldwide |
| Types of Buildings | New Construction (Offices, Industrial, Retail, Data Centres, Education, Healthcare, Prisons, Law Courts, Multi-residential Institutions, Non-residential Institutions, Assembly & Leisure + Other); Refurbishment; Code for Sustainable Homes; Communities; and In-Use. | New Construction + Major Renovations; Existing Buildings: Operations + Maintenance; Commercial Interiors; Core + Shell; Schools; Retail: Healthcare; Homes; and Neighbourhood Development. |
| Degrees of performance | >25% Pass, >40% Good, >55% Very good, >70% Excellent, and >85% Outstanding | Certified, Silver, Gold and Platinum |
| Minimum Standards | Minimum standards are tiered based on the target rating, e.g. relating to 4 specific credits or criteria for a Pass rating, 6 for Good, 8 for Very Good, 18 for Excellent and 26 for Outstanding | Eight Prerequisites in addition to the credits below, plus seven primary Minimum Program Requirements for eligibility which apply across all rating systems (except those adopted pre-2009) |

**Table 5.7 continued**

| | BREEAM | LEED |
|---|---|---|
| Number of Credits | Up to c.150 credits depending on building type | 49 Credits |
| Credit Weighting | Based on relative environmental impact, reviewed periodically | Based on relative environmental impact and human benefit, reviewed periodically. |
| Evidence Collation | BREEAM Assessor, Design, Construction & Management Teams + Accredited Professional (AP) | Design, Construction & Management Teams and Accredited Professional (AP) |
| Assessment/Review | Design Stage & Post-Construction Assessment by trained and Licensed BREEAM Assessors | Design & Construction Review by Green Building Certification Institute through network of third party certification bodies. |
| Assessment/Review Fees | Design Stage & Post-Construction Assessments: c. £5000–£15000 (not fixed, varies by project size/ complexity and market competition between BREEAM Assessors) | Design & Construction Reviews <50000 sq ft $2250 (Members), $2750 (Non members) 50000–500000 sq ft: $0.045/sq ft (Members), $0.055/sq ft (Non members) >500000 sq ft: $22500 (Members), $27500 (Non members) |
| Registration & Certification Fees | Registration £120.00 Certification £1170.00 | Registration $900 (USGBC members), $1200 (Non-members) Certification including in Review Fee |
| Accredited Professional Fee | c. £5000–£10000. Varies by project size, complexity and market competition between Accredited Professionals. | $10000–$30000 (Inbuilt 2010) Varies by project size, complexity and market competition between Accredited Professionals. Higher on average partly because of the Accredited Professional's greater involvement in collating evidence as there is no "assessor" role. |
| Credit Appeal Fee | Free of charge | Complex credits $800 per credit, all other credits $500 per credit. |
| Credit Interpretation Fee | Free of charge | $220 per credit |
| Availability of Information | Pre-Assessment Tool and Scheme Manual available free of charge. Technical Guidance only available by Attending BREEAM Assessor and/or Accredited Professional training courses run by the BRE. | Tools and Public Guide can be downloaded free of charge. Reference Guides cost $195 (hard copy) or $180 (E-book) for each Rating System. Further Technical Guidance available through LEED Green Associate and Accredited Professional training courses. |
| Other comments | As "Green Building" label focused on ecological aspects | As classical "Green Building" Label/ focused on ecological aspects (energy) |

The development of BREEAM Healthcare 2008 by the BRE, working in partnership with the Department of Health, sought to ensure that standards are raised, credibility is increased, and the changing needs of the NHS are met. Importantly, the tool will be regularly updated in line with the latest legislation and best practice standards. BREEAM Healthcare 2008 was developed as a points-based system for rating the environmental performance of buildings with 'Credits' grouped under ten headings.

1 **Management** (weighting 12.5%) – Encouraging the sustainable commissioning of the building, environmental management systems, staff education and training and purchasing.

2 **Health and Well-being** (weighting 15.0%) – Linking and consulting the community, sharing of facilities, staff and patient empowerment, access for the disabled, provision of views out of the building, budget for green plants, high frequency ballasts on lighting, signage and artwork.

3 **Energy** (weighting 19.0%) – Reducing carbon emissions, providing heating and lighting controls, energy monitoring and usage reduction facilities, use of daylight and alternative electricity tariffs.

4 **Transport** (weighting 8.0%) – Reducing carbon emissions via provision of car parking, cyclist facilities, proximity to public transport facilities, distance to local amenities, green transport plan and compliance with controls assurance.

5 **Water** (weighting 6.0%) – Minimising water consumption through leak detection, water use monitoring, low flush toilets and grey water recycling.

6 **Materials** (weighting 12.5%) – Using materials from sustainable sources, prohibition of hazardous substances.

7 **Waste** (weighting 7.5%) – Reducing waste by providing recycling facilities and waste stream analysis, staff waste interviews, storage for recycling.

8 **Land Use and Ecology** (weighting 10.0%) – Protecting ecological features and introducing natural habitats, re-use of sites and ecological enhancement.

9 **Pollution** (weighting 10.0%) – Monitoring and addressing pollution, $NO_x$ emissions, ozone depleting substances, noise pollution and incineration practices.

10 **Innovation** (weighting 9.0%) – Providing additional recognition for a procurement strategy, design feature, management process or technological development that innovates sustainability, above and beyond the level that is currently recognised and rewarded within standard BREEAM issues.

Since its origins BREEAM has expanded massively, going from a 19-page BRE Report with 27 credits to a massive 350-page Technical Guide (for the Office Version) with some 105 credits. Reviewed periodically, the BREEAM weighting is based on relative environmental impact. The maximum weighted percentage points equals (12.5 + 15.0 + 19.0 + 8.0 + 6.0 + 12.5 + 7.5 + 10.0 + 10.0 + 9.0) = 109.5%. The detailed definition of BREEAM's weighting system is set out in the BRE Global Core Process Standard (BES 5301) (Tables 5.8, 5.11 to 5.13).

The Department of Health aims to assist and enable the health care sector to lead by example in producing a sustainable health care estate. BREEAM Healthcare 2008

(the B4H tool) aims to assist Trusts in their dealings (whether contractual or otherwise) to ensure that sustainability is embraced within all capital health care schemes. Because this is an accredited process, it enables a Trust to ensure that the requirements of briefs and specifications are delivered, and that a Trust is well placed to benefit from the efficiency savings, both carbon and cost, that should potentially result. The Department of Health requires all capital development schemes to achieve scores of Excellent for new builds and Very Good for refurbishments.

Once a health care building is commissioned and operational its environmental impact is assessed using B4H for existing buildings. This tool is a voluntary commitment and its use is based on membership. Membership offers a number of benefits in terms of: access to a robust accredited tool that is updated annually; guidance manuals; training; helpdesk and IT support; user networks; and an opportunity to display a Certificate of Achievement by applying for accreditation as a method of demonstrating commitment and corporate social responsibility through environmental improvement for the benefit of the community and stakeholders.

BREEAM Healthcare 2008 for new builds/refurbishments was launched on 1 July 2008. As of 1 July 2008, the Department of Health and other UK Health Authorities required, as part of the Outline of Business Case approval, that all new build health care projects achieve an Excellent rating and all refurbishments achieve a Very Good rating under BREEAM Healthcare. Additionally, all projects needed to achieve BREEAM credit indicated under 'Tra 5 Travel Plan'. Trusts who wish to announce successful achievement may seek to undertake the Certification process. Use of this tool is on a membership basis. BREEAM Healthcare 2008 can thus be used to assess all health care buildings containing medical facilities, and at different stages of their lifecycle: whole new buildings; major refurbishments of existing buildings; new build extensions of existing buildings; a combination of new build and existing building refurbishment; and new builds or refurbishments which are part of a larger mixed use building. B4H has a credit filtering mechanism which makes it appropriate across the entire range of health care facilities, from GP surgeries and clinics to acute teaching/specialist units.

**Table 5.8** Minimum levels set for all the five BREEAM classified ratings from a 'pass' to 'outstanding' show the onus increasing as the rating rises

| | | |
|---|---|---|
| <25% | **Unclassified** | |
| >25% | **Pass** | To gain a **Pass** (30%) Rating Compulsory credits: |
| | | • Management:        Man 1 – Commissioning. |
| | | • Health & Wellbeing:    Hea 4 – High Frequency Lighting. |
| | | • Health & Wellbeing:    Hea 12 – Microbial Contamination. |
| >40% | **Good** | To gain a **Good** (45%) Add Compulsory credits: |
| | | • Water:        Wat 1 – Water Consumption. |
| | | • Water:        Wat 2 – Water Meter. |
| | | In NHS healthcare facilities achieving a 'Good' rating is mandatory for existing buildings at Outline of Business Case approval stage of a project. |
| >55% | **Very Good** | To gain a **Very Good** (55%) Rating Add Compulsory credits: |
| | | • Energy:        Ene 2 – Sub-metering of Substantial Energy Uses. |
| | | • Land Use & Ecology:    LE 4 – Mitigating Ecological Impact. |
| >70% | **Excellent** | To gain an **Excellent** (55%) Rating Add Compulsory credits: |
| | | • Management:        Man 2 – Considerate Constructors. |
| | | • Management:        Man 4 – Building User Guide. |
| | | • Energy:        Ene 5 – Low or Zero Carbon Technologies. |
| | | • Waste:        Wst 3 – Storage of Recyclable Waste. |
| | | • Plus in Energy:    Ene 1 – Reduction of $CO_2$ Emissions (i.e. an EPC (Energy Performance Certificate) of 40 or less for new build office) a minimum of 6 points must be awarded. |
| | | In NHS healthcare facilities achieving an 'Excellent' rating is mandatory for new build at Outline of Business Case approval stage of a project. |
| >85% | **Outstanding** | To gain an **Outstanding** (>85%) rating in addition to all of the above (plus scoring 85% or more) Add Compulsory credits: |
| | | • Management:        Man 2 – Commissioning needs 2 points. |
| | | • Management:        Man 2 – Considerate Constructors. |
| | | • Water:        Wat 1 – Water Consumption (Total available in Wat is 3). |
| | | • Energy:        Ene 1 – Reduction of $CO_2$ Emissions – a minimum of 10 points must be awarded (i.e. an EPC or 25 or less for a new build office). |
| | | Also the building has to be published as a case study (written by BRE Global). |

Note: In addition, the building has to have a Post-Construction Review (before then this was not mandatory unless the client required them. It is not possible to value engineer out the BREEAM features between the design and completion stages without getting penalised (or put another way, being caught).

BREEAM Healthcare 2008 was superseded by BREEAM 2011. BREEAM 2011 is deliberately a single, consolidated scheme document covering all building types. The BRE pointed out that although separate scheme documents would cease, generic BREEAM *"continues to maintain assessment criteria specific to the range of building functions, sector stakeholders and end-users covered by its scope"*. The particular changes to the health care credits in BREEAM 2011 are:

• Man 13 – Good Corporate Citizenship is now included in the 2011 credit 'Man 04 Stakeholder Participation' (there are additional criteria but no additional credits).

• Ene 16 – Community CHP is effectively dropped in 2011 and is now considered part of a Low and Zero Carbon Assessment.

• Hea 19 – Art is now in 'Hea 01 – Visual comfort' – as Visual Arts (1 credit).

An important consequence of this change is that BREEAM 2011 also requires ongoing assessments after project completion in order to maintain currency of the certification. However, this is an issue for the NHS, which does not encourage the production of BREEAM assessments beyond the initial Business Case. The NAO report in 2007 highlighted this situation, indicating that there is little enforcement of policies and procedures, and if a BREEAM assessment is not done then nothing happens. Therefore, in order to ensure assessments at post-construction or post-occupancy phases, the Department of Health needs to consider a system that involves the retention of capital support monies against certification.

Sustainable development is on the UK Government's agenda for the long term. Although climate change is the most serious global environmental threat, promoting new, modern, sustainable ways of living, working, producing and travelling also stand to achieve wider benefits to human health and well-being (taken from 'Securing the Future – delivering UK sustainable development strategy'). This is in accordance with the Department of Health's commitment to sustainable development and in line with the principles of the White Paper 'Our health, our care, our say'. The key is to embrace the concept and take this forward with renewed vigour to realise the benefits from social reform, improved environmental performance and realise the economic rewards necessary to maintain the impetus.

Sustainability and the environmental performance of NHS buildings are increasingly a priority not only for new developments but also for existing buildings in operation. BREEAM Healthcare XB was therefore developed as a tool to complement BREEAM Healthcare which can be used for new and major refurbishment projects. BREEAM Healthcare XB offers a solution for existing buildings in operation. Developed by BRE Global on behalf of the Department of Health, BREEAM Healthcare XB helps NHS Trusts and other health care organisations to improve the efficiency of their existing building portfolio and the indoor environment of their occupied buildings, thereby increasing staff and patients' well-being, and reduce energy waste and consequently reduce utility bills while demonstrating commitment to sustainable development. BREEAM Healthcare XB is also a credit-based self-assessment tool that substitutes and improves on the NHS Environmental Assessment Tool (NEAT) for existing sites. Although this is a self-assessment tool, certification can be sought only when a licensed BREEAM Healthcare assessor has been appointed to carry out a formal assessment and produce a BRE Global-compliant report.

Annual membership to the BREEAM programme offers NHS Trusts and other health care organisations the opportunity to use the tool with a choice of different packages of additional support services, including comprehensive supporting guidance, BREEAM customer service for troubleshooting and technical enquiries, ad hoc training aimed specifically at BREEAM Healthcare XB users, and exclusive access to newsletters and updates. The 2008 BREEAM Healthcare Assessor Manual and Pre-Assessment Estimator were available for download from BRE's website.

The context for NEAT or BREEAM Healthcare tools is in green hospitals and health care facilities. Several authors have set out to demonstrate the net benefits of green buildings. Yates (2001) sees many economic advantages. Capital costs are not higher for many green construction elements, and even where upfront costs are more elevated, they can often be offset by decreased operational costs. The author also mentions green construction as a way of risk and liability management; it may well help protect owners against future regulation changes and lawsuits. Indeed, ecological construction is being recognised increasingly as a means to manage risks. Improved construction practices associated with green design have been linked to some insurance companies providing lower premiums to owners of green buildings. Roodman and Lenssen (1995) discuss evidence that real estate values for green buildings appreciate faster than those of conventional buildings. They also point to shorter resale and release times, combined with longer tenant occupancy terms. Nevertheless, green building is not seen as being inevitably profitable. Matthiessen and Morris (2004) find that while overall cost savings are possible in green building, they depend on factors such as climate, topography, timing, credit synergies and local building standards.

Less visible benefits of green building are also garnering interest. For instance, Fisk (2000) seeks to establish a link between indoor environmental quality on the one hand and higher productivity and better health on the other. He estimates that in the United States, increased worker performance alone could amount to up to $160 billion in efficiency gains. Another $48 billion could be saved thanks to fewer occurrences of asthma, allergies and sick building syndrome. Daylighting is also a major focus of authors studying the effects of environmental design. Like indoor air quality, it has been linked to performance gains and health improvements (New Buildings Institute 2003; Nicklas and Bailey 1996).

*Issues*

1   Do current methods address the key issues concerning clients and the environmental agenda?

2   Can schemes do more to help create and support markets and commercial benefits for sustainable products/buildings/solutions?

3   Should methods cover fewer issues and be more focused?

4   Do assessment methods improve building operational performance and what evidence of this is there?

5   Which existing assessment issues are standard practice and should possibly be removed, replaced or updated?

6   Which issues are too costly to meet and prevent uptake, considering the cost of solution and cost/effort of demonstrating compliance vs. supporting driver for change/innovation?

7   What new environmental issues should future versions include, and what new or alternative ways of assessing existing issues should be considered?

A number of key drivers which indicate the way BREEAM Healthcare 2008 is implemented in the construction industry and in the health care sector include:

1   Legislation and Planning: for example, some local planning authorities require BREEAM pre-assessments and, increasingly, accreditation, including Section 106 Agreements. Other than being relevant to UK policies, climatic environment and CIBSE (Chartered Institution of Building Services Engineers) guidance, the judging criteria for BREEAM Healthcare 2008 also keep pace with legislative developments and current best practice.

2   Public Sector Organisations: for example, a minimum BREEAM rating for all new buildings and refurbishments has been in place since 2006 (UK Department of Health, Office of Government Commerce, Homes and Communities Agency and Department of Education). Specifically, the Department of Health requires the achievement of a BREEAM Healthcare 'Good' rating (> 45%) as mandatory for existing buildings at the Outline

of Business Case approval stage of a project, while a BREEAM 'Excellent' rating (> 70%) is mandatory for new builds at the Outline of Business Case approval stage of a project. All this has helped to embed BREEAM Healthcare into UK planning and building system.

3   Private Sector Organisations: for example, some developers have set voluntary minimum BREEAM ratings for all new buildings (e.g. British Land and Land Securities). A must for organisations in our new sustainably-aware society, multi-national companies are keen to publicly display their green credentials and to show that every part of their business is green, including their buildings.

4   Quantitative thresholds rather than percentages: for example, BREEAM's minimum standards (relating to specific credits or specific criteria for credits) are tiered based on the target rating, ranging from 4 to 26 credits.

5   Assessor involvement rather than team involvement, but involves design, construction and management teams and an Accredited Professional (AP): BREEAM has trained licensed assessors who assess the evidence against the set credit criteria and report to the BRE, who validate the assessment and then issue a Certificate. Since its origins BREEAM has expanded massively, going from a 19-page BRE Report with 27 credits to a massive 350-page Technical Guide (for the Office Version) with some 105 credits. Assessor involvement is an advantage for BREEAM in that an assessor can work with BRE to develop assessment criteria specially tailored to a building where it does not fit neatly into one of the existing schemes.

6   Based on Carbon Dioxide: for example, BREEAM encourages reduction in $CO_2$ to zero net emissions in relation to English Building Regulations Part L 2010, to achieve maximum points worth 10.56% of the total score.

This situation, together with a lack of objective evidence that any more energy efficient buildings are a result of the use of BREEAM, has been largely behind the move by some in the construction industry to consider alternative assessments, such as using CIBSE TM22. The NAO Report 2007 noted that departments were struggling to reconcile sustainability and value for money and that the benefits of sustainable buildings were generally not measured or quantified:

*If departments are to make progress towards achieving the targets for Sustainable Operations on the Government Estate, they will need to focus increasingly on incorporating specific output-oriented specifications in new construction or major refurbishment projects, rather than simply specifying a requirement for BREEAM 'Excellent'. These should include specifications for water consumption per person per year and for energy consumption and carbon emissions per square metre. Such an approach would also match the trend towards more specific assessments of building performance, such as the forthcoming requirement under the Energy Performance of Buildings Directive for all public buildings to display energy efficiency ratings.*

The BREEAM Healthcare 2008 figures from the BRE also indicated that in the period up to 9 February 2012 there were some 737 NHS buildings registered across the UK, but only 15% (110) of these were certified. One issue is to do with the fact that the numbers simply represent a time lag between the implementation of the mandatory requirement to do a BREEAM assessment and/or the lag between project inception and completion. Another reason is that BREEAM projects can 'wither on the vine' for a variety of reasons, including design teams 'moving on' to more pressing matters, a consequent lack of forthcoming information from design team members, exacerbated by a situation where there is no perceived pressure from the client.

## CIBSE TM22

Developed in the early 1990s, CIBSE (**C**hartered **I**nstitution of **B**uilding **S**ervices **E**ngineers) TM22 describes a method for assessing a building's energy and building services performance that can be handled by using a spreadsheet approach to consider feedback and operational performance. The detailed analysis of energy use from applying CIBSE TM22 allows building owners, facilities managers and designers to reconcile, for example, the total electrical use against various end uses (Tse 2012). John Field (Target Energy Services) was the lead author of the CIBSE group responsible for the development of the method. Initial research was carried out for BRE by William Bordass Associates, Target Energy Services, Building Energy Solutions and ARUP.

Trialled on various buildings in the late 1990s including those in the PROBE Post-Occupancy studies (1995–2002), the software was published by CIBSE in 1999 primarily as an assessment method for offices, using benchmarks in the *Energy Consumption Guide 19: Energy Use in Offices*. The systematic framework for undertaking an energy survey, reporting and benchmarking results was extended in 2006, anticipating Display Energy Certificates (DECs), to cover bank and agency branches, hotels and mixed-use factory-office and industrial buildings. The approach can also be used for schools and residential homes with appropriate benchmark data. CIBSE TM22 users can choose one of three reference benchmarks, i.e.: 1. A Display Energy Certificate; 2. CIBSE TM46: Energy Benchmarks; and 3. A user specification.

CIBSE TM22's 2011 version was developed by Camco on behalf of CIBSE and was trialled under the Technology Strategy Board's Building Performance Evaluation Programme. TM22's 2011 version, released in 2012, allows for a building's energy use to be calculated in greater detail, with more scope for using sub-meter data and different benchmarks.

This method for assessing the energy performance of an occupied building based on metered energy use also comprises a software implementation of the method. Recent UK and European initiatives mean that the benefits of performance assessment are being backed by legislation. CIBSE TM22 provides software support for these assessment needs. While primarily directed at assessing energy performance, the procedure has a wide range of uses for building managers, design professionals, and energy management specialists contributing to the 'virtuous circle' of good building management and satisfied occupants.

The sheets within the Excel workbook implement a method for assessing a building's energy and building services performance. While primarily directed at finding out about energy performance, the information produced has a wide range of uses for building management and design professionals – for example, benchmarking operational procedures such as hours of use and levels of service provision, e.g. lighting levels and system efficiencies.

The method can be used to identify poorly performing buildings and systems and indicate the cause(s) of poor performance, as well as benchmark operating procedures, including hours of use, and levels of service provision including lighting levels and system efficiencies. The procedure has proved highly effective in use, forming a key part of work for the PROBE investigations and the DETR's Energy Consumption Guide 19 *Energy use in offices*.

The Energy Assessment and Reporting Methodology Office Assessment Method assesses a building's actual energy consumption per unit floor area, and other aspects of performance, against established benchmarks from Energy Consumption Guide 19, in three stages. Stage 1 provides a quick assessment in terms of energy use per unit floor area, something which can be carried out using in-house resources. Stage 2 provides a deeper assessment for a building that has special energy uses or occupancy. A Stage 2 assessment can also, in most cases, be carried out in-house. Stage 3 allows for a full understanding of the performance of the building and its systems. A Stage 3 assessment requires specialist capabilities, but the results are of direct interest to building owners and managers.

The approach improves the level of understanding of building and system performance and reduces the time taken to complete an assessment. It provides a highly effective way of introducing feedback into the design/construct/evaluate process as recommended in the CIBSE Guide: *Energy efficiency in buildings*. This assessment approach can be used in combination with other approaches such as the CIBSE Application Manual: AM5 *Energy audits and surveys*.

The method assesses a building's actual energy consumption per unit floor area and other aspects against benchmarks, at three levels of detail denoted by three stages of assessment. Often only the initial level (Stage 1) is required, but all levels may, in different circumstances, be of interest to building managers and designers who may not be energy specialists.

1  Description of the TM22 Method and the Energy Tree Diagram Assessment: Main procedure options cover: quality assurance; selection of building types, energy supplies and services features; allowing for systems not included in the benchmarks; and allowing for different use and occupancy.

A hierarchical tree diagram assessment (Levels A to H) is at the heart of the TM22 Method. In this case data is gathered for an existing building or projected for a proposed new building. The $m^2$ denominator measures building size, such as gross floor area depending on the benchmarks used, or as a sector-specific measure such as sales floor area for retail buildings. At the top level, box A is calculated from a building's annual energy consumption, deriving from actual energy bills to provide an overall energy consumption index for comparison with benchmarks. Box A represents the sum of all the boxes of type B. If more than one fuel is used, each fuel is assessed separately, or they may be combined in terms of a meaningful measure such as total cost or $CO_2$ emissions. Multiplying the contents of boxes C and D and dividing by 1000 to scale for kilowatt hours, box B represents an energy consumption index for each system that allows comparisons with benchmarks (Figures 5.3 and 5.4, Table 5.9).

Used directly or combined to form a whole building index, box C indicates installed power per $m^2$ – a simple but powerful check on the energy efficiency of installed plant and equipment. Multiplying the contents of boxes E and F (and, in the case of lighting, dividing by the scaling factor of 100 due to the units used for lighting efficiency) yields box C. Multiplying the contents of boxes G and H yields box D, the effective hours at nominal full load for each system which allows comparisons with typical values.

Boxes E to H provide more details for boxes C and D and notably box E, the level of service provided (e.g. the amount of light or ventilation), and they can be compared with published guidelines such as CIBSE Guides. Box F is a measure of the efficiency of the equipment for which benchmarks are available. Box G is the number of hours per year that the service is required for each system, and box H is a management factor which indicates the fraction of the time-enabled systems that are working (for part load operation the hours are effectively reduced pro-rata) (Table 5.10).

Overall, data for new building designs can be generated from experience or from published benchmarks yielding the installed power densities (box

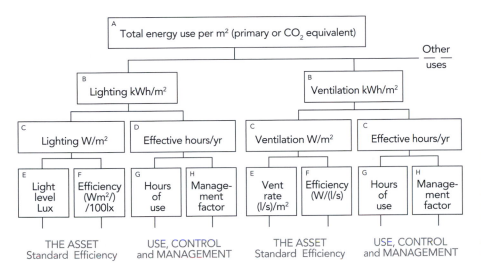

5.2 Tree diagram analysis of building energy consumption and service provision – capturing information from electrical sub-metering, gas sub-meters (such as for catering for kitchens) and other systems (source: CIBSE TM22 et al. 1997)

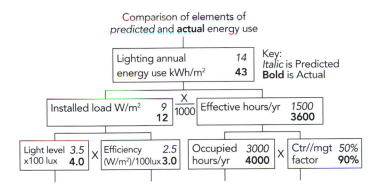

5.3 Tree diagram analysis of building energy consumption and service provision: Comparison of predicted and actual energy use

Table 5.9 Tree diagram analysis of building energy consumption and service provision: Comparison of predicted and actual energy use

|  | Predicted | Actual | Difference |
|---|---|---|---|
| Lighting Annual Energy Use kWh/m² | 14 | 43 | −29 |
| Installed Load W/m² | 9 | 19 | −10 |
| Effective hours/year | 1500 | 3600 | −2100 |
| Light level x 100 lux | 3.5 | 4 | −0.5 |
| Efficiency (w/m²)/100 lux | 2.5 | 3 | −0.5 |
| Occupied house/year | 3000 | 4000 | −1000 |
| Control/management factor (Per Cent) | 50 | 90 | −40 |

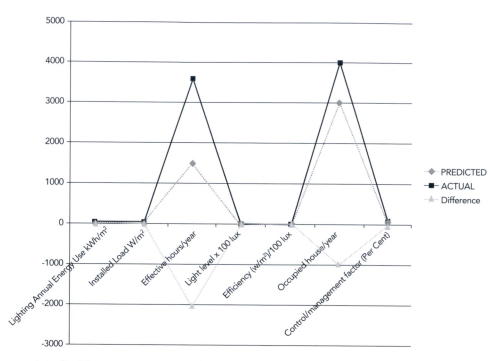

**5.4 Tree diagram analysis of building energy consumption and service provision: Comparison of predicted and actual energy use**

C), expected occupation hours (box G) and management/ control factors (box H). For occupied buildings, the installed power densities (box C) can be assessed onsite, while operating hours (box G) and control factors (box H) can be assessed by considering control schedules, observations and discussions with operators and occupants as in the approach used in the 'Plant' module of TM22 Option C.

2  How well-run buildings can inform the virtuous circle of good building energy management and satisfied users: A high standard of energy efficiency is a good indicator of high management standards. Efficiently run buildings tend to have design and operational arrangements which produce good staff relations and satisfied occupants. The assessment process can help to improve not just energy management but building design and management, and in turn the investigations and actions required to improve energy efficiency also tend to improve building design, management and occupant satisfaction.

The CIBSE TM22 assessment procedure offers three main options to assess energy performance and contribute to the virtuous circle of good building energy management and satisfied users or occupants (Field & CIBSE 2006). Option 1 involves a simple building assessment of the actual $CO_2$ emissions per unit floor area based on the metered energy use of a building of a single type with no more than two energy supplies – for example, electricity and fossil fuel. Option 2 entails a general building assessment of the actual $CO_2$ emissions per unit floor area based on the metered energy use of a building or site which can have zones of different types and non-standard occupancy and energy uses. Option 3 is a systems assessment against benchmarks for the building systems (Figure 5.5).

Energy assessors can use these options to provide assessments for designers, managers, operators and occupants of buildings. Designers can compare assessments at the design stages against benchmarks to make predictions about actual building performance,

Table 5.10 Fossil fuel and electricity benchmarks for hospitals (source: CIBSE Guide F)

| Hospitals | Energy consumption benchmarks for existing buildings (kWhm²) per year (unless otherwise stated) | | | | Basis of the benchmark |
|---|---|---|---|---|---|
| | Good practice | | Typical practice | | |
| | Fossil fuel | Electricity | Fossil fuel | Electricity | Heated floor area |
| Teaching and Specialist | 339 | 86 | 411 | 122 | Heated floor area |
| Acute and Maternity | 422 | 74 | 510 | 108 | Heated floor area |
| Cottage | 443 | 55 | 492 | 78 | Heated floor area |
| Long Stay | 401 | 48 | 518 | 72 | Heated floor area |

while energy management specialists can use the assessments to rate the design or buildings to determine the energy-saving measures required. Facilities or resource managers can use the assessments to reduce operating costs by identifying poorly performing buildings and systems, establishing reasons for poor performance as well as determining measures required to improve performance. The assessments may provide authoritative evidence of good performance and higher management standards while allowing prioritisation of remedial actions or areas in need of investment. By providing feedback on how buildings and systems perform, the assessments can aid building design, commissioning and operational management.

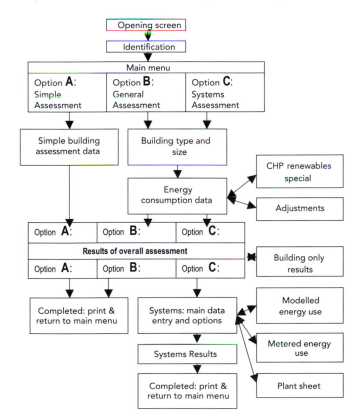

5.5 Flowchart: CIBSE TM22 assessment procedure offers three main options to assess energy performance (source: Field and CIBSE 2006)

To develop the CIBSE TM22 assessment procedure, nine considerations were used to provide underlying principles:

1 Provide clear description of the objectives of the energy assessment procedure.
2 Provide guidance to users on the appropriate type of energy analysis applicable to their purposes.
3 Avoid ambiguity and duplication; allow for easy comparison by keeping definitions of significant terms in keeping within the overall structure for building and energy data.
4 Record all data without adjustment.
5 Record separate consumption data relating to different fuel types.
6 Recorded quantitative data should be accompanied by descriptive data.
7 State or assess the accuracy requirements for critical data.
8 Ensure calculation procedures are appropriate to the accuracy of the required result and are designed to request no more information than necessary.
9 Where possible, adopt a layered approach of increasing complexity for data collection and input so that more information only needs to be sought where it is required.

A further nine considerations were used as underlying principles for the generalised assessment procedure:

1 Collect appropriate data on building design, construction, systems, occupancy and management.
2 Collect appropriate data on energy use and building extent such as floor area or volume.
3 Produce simple indices of energy use as a ratio of delivered energy to the measure of extent (e.g. kWh of annual energy use per m² of floor area). Normally there will be one index per fuel because the costs and environmental impacts of different fuels vary greatly. Overall indices of cost or $CO_2$ can generally be obtained simply from individual fuel indices if required.
4 Categorise the building to facilitate comparison of performance with buildings of a similar type and

obtain energy consumption yardsticks for the type of building. Overall cost or $CO_2$ yardsticks may be available or can generally be obtained from fuel yardsticks if required.
5 Consider unusual aspects of the building and its use to allow or adjust for their effects.
6 Compare the performance indices of the building with the performance yardsticks to obtain an assessment of the building; for example, the assessment may be low/medium/high consumption, good/typical practice or pass/fail.
7 Relate the building assessment to the observed building fabric, plant and usage.
8 Present building indices, yardsticks and assessment with critical descriptive and category information.
9 Consider restarting from step 1 with more detailed observation, analysis of records or goal-directed measurements to further explain building performance if significant aspects of the building performance remain unexplained. If appropriate, use more detailed performance indices and yardsticks, such as for individual end-use categories (e.g. heating and lighting).

3 Spreadsheet Use and Compatibility: This workbook is designed for a screen resolution of at least 800x600 (SVGA). If lower, one should reduce the zoom to 75%. More spreadsheet compatibility notes are provided in the sheet with tab label 'Technical compatibility', but one should not need to read these notes if using Excel 7 (1995) or later versions, or any spreadsheet compatible with these. However, we suggest users disable auto-completion (Tools, Options, Edit and uncheck the box labelled 'Enable auto completion') as we consider this to be good general practice for reducing errors during data entry.
4 Evidence base and further development of CIBSE TM22: The CIBSE TM22 procedure undertakes a detailed analysis of the overall energy use and performance of heating, ventilation and other systems. It requires and relies on the adoption of a metering strategy and mechanisms for capturing information to provide baseline data, against which building-in-use and other

information can be benchmarked or measured to assess the extent of changes. In practice, therefore, the installation of meters, sensors and measuring devices or real-time tracking technologies is of vital importance to ensure the capture of the relevant information or data. Establishing the discrepancies between predicted and actual data provides decision-makers with a mechanism to implement suitable actions to ensure sustainability targets are continuously met.

The CIBSE TM22 energy analysis tool provides a systematic framework for undertaking an energy survey and reporting and benchmarking the results. The 2012 version of CIBSE TM22 allows a building's energy use to be calculated in greater detail than before, with more scope for using sub-meter data and different benchmarks. Since its 2006 release, with the 2012 version partially driven by the Technology Strategy Board's (TSB) £8 million programme for building performance evaluations of domestic and non-domestic buildings, the tool has undergone significant development by the CIBSE to make energy analysis simple, unambiguous and robust, and to provide a useful aid to generate operational feedback.

Key changes for the CIBSE TM22 2012 version include the fact that the building types are now aligned with the 237 options for a Display Energy Certificate (DEC) from CIBSE TM46: Energy Benchmarking, compared to the original tool which was developed for offices but then expanded to include hotels, mixed-use industrial buildings and high street banks and agencies. As many non-domestic buildings seldom have one particular function, the 2012 version allows up to five different building functions to be modelled, thereby providing a mixed-use building benchmark that is also area-weighted. The energy benchmarks in TM22 now cover all types of non-domestic building. Users can therefore choose one of three reference benchmarks: those from a Display Energy Certificate (DEC), from CIBSE TM46: Energy Benchmarks, or benchmarks specified by the user (Figures 5.6 to 5.8).

The DEC benchmarks for electricity and heating are building-specific, accounting for location, degree days, typical hours of use and any mixed use. If a DEC is not available, benchmarks from CIBSE TM46 can be used. However, these are median benchmarks that need to be modified to suit the study building. User-specified benchmark data can be derived from a property portfolio of energy studies.

For the CIBSE TM22 2012 a simple assessment is confined to one worksheet, which gathers basic information for the building including floor area, energy use, input and output energy of CHP or renewables, separables and metered data – i.e. all that is required to benchmark the energy consumption and $CO_2$ emissions, with and without separables. Furthermore, it begins to provide an understanding of the building's energy efficiency, as the contribution of renewable sources is included in the section on building energy use.

Consistent with information found on DECs, with renewables charted as a negative value for total $CO_2$ emissions, CIBSE TM22 2012 also looks at the building energy use to gauge efficiency, which is the sum of delivered energy plus onsite renewables. Provision of CHP or renewables can certainly offset energy use, but can potentially mask the true building efficiency or energy use. For example, a large photovoltaic array that provides all the electricity in a building won't mean its electricity systems are efficient.

During the next stage of detailed analysis involving capturing information from electrical sub-metering and any gas sub-meters, such as for catering kitchens, a reasonable starting point is to gather a list of all sub-meters and records of energy use. Twelve months is a common period of appraisal, but analysis can be adjusted for any period. Starting at a basic level and building up the picture with more detail as one becomes confident with the method and the accuracy of data ensures the best possible approach. All energy consumption is then assigned against 20 end-use categories. Fifteen of these are pre-defined and five are user specified, including the six official DEC separable energy uses. There is a maximum of 30 items that can be assigned to each of the 20 categories, and each item is referenced to the appropriate sub-meter. CIBSE TM22 2012 allows for 50 sub-meters. However, where a building has more than 50 sub-meters the user will have to aggregate loads

Building & metered data ▸ Simple Assessment ▸ Sub-meters ▸ Profiles ▸ Electrical End Uses ▸ Electrical Reconcillation ▸ Prediction of Potential ▸ Fuel/Thermal Breakdown ▸ Detailed Assessment

## PROFILES

Use this sheet to define up to 15 operational profiles for equipment use. This is done by setting start and end times for weekdays, Saturdays and Sundays in the table below.

Daytime or overnight profiles can be used.

The profiles describe the hours that the equipment is available for use – e.g. for office PC's this would likely be the opening times of that area, or for a server room the operational profile would likely be 24 hours a day.

The user can also define the proportion of the year assigned to each sessional period, winter, summer and spring: these three factors should total 1.

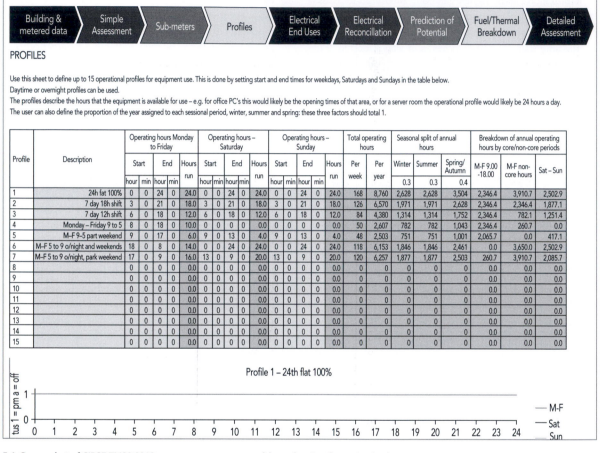

| Profile | Description | Operating hours Monday to Friday | | | | | Operating hours – Saturday | | | | | Operating hours – Sunday | | | | | Total operating hours | | Seasonal split of annual hours | | | Breakdown of annual operating hours by core/non-core periods | | |
|---|---|---|---|---|---|---|---|---|---|---|---|---|---|---|---|---|---|---|---|---|---|---|---|---|
| | | Start | | End | | Hours run | Start | | End | | Hours run | Start | | End | | Hours run | Per week | Per year | Winter | Summer | Spring/Autumn | M-F 9.00-18.00 | M-F non-core hours | Sat – Sun |
| | | hour | min | hour | min | | hour | min | hour | min | | hour | min | hour | min | | | | 0.3 | 0.3 | 0.4 | | | |
| 1 | 24h flat 100% | 0 | 0 | 24 | 0 | 24.0 | 0 | 0 | 24 | 0 | 24.0 | 0 | 0 | 24 | 0 | 24.0 | 168 | 8,760 | 2,628 | 2,628 | 3,504 | 2,346.4 | 3,910.7 | 2,502.9 |
| 2 | 7 day 18h shift | 3 | 0 | 21 | 0 | 18.0 | 3 | 0 | 21 | 0 | 18.0 | 3 | 0 | 21 | 0 | 18.0 | 126 | 6,570 | 1,971 | 1,971 | 2,628 | 2,346.4 | 2,346.4 | 1,877.1 |
| 3 | 7 day 12h shift | 6 | 0 | 18 | 0 | 12.0 | 6 | 0 | 18 | 0 | 12.0 | 6 | 0 | 18 | 0 | 12.0 | 84 | 4,380 | 1,314 | 1,314 | 1,752 | 2,346.4 | 782.1 | 1,251.4 |
| 4 | Monday – Friday 9 to 5 | 8 | 0 | 18 | 0 | 10.0 | 0 | 0 | 0 | 0 | 0.0 | 0 | 0 | 0 | 0 | 0.0 | 50 | 2,607 | 782 | 782 | 1,043 | 2,346.4 | 260.7 | 0.0 |
| 5 | M–F 9–5 part weekend | 9 | 0 | 17 | 0 | 6.0 | 9 | 0 | 13 | 0 | 4.0 | 9 | 0 | 13 | 0 | 4.0 | 48 | 2,503 | 751 | 751 | 1,001 | 2,065.7 | 0.0 | 417.1 |
| 6 | M–F 5 to 9 o/night and weekends | 18 | 0 | 8 | 0 | 14.0 | 0 | 0 | 24 | 0 | 24.0 | 0 | 0 | 24 | 0 | 24.0 | 118 | 6,153 | 1,846 | 1,846 | 2,461 | 2,346.4 | 3,650.0 | 2,502.9 |
| 7 | M–F 5 to 9 o/night, park weekend | 17 | 0 | 9 | 0 | 16.0 | 13 | 0 | 9 | 0 | 20.0 | 13 | 0 | 9 | 0 | 20.0 | 120 | 6,257 | 1,877 | 1,877 | 2,503 | 260.7 | 3,910.7 | 2,085.7 |
| 8 | | 0 | 0 | 0 | 0 | 0.0 | 0 | 0 | 0 | 0 | 0.0 | 0 | 0 | 0 | 0 | 0.0 | 0 | 0 | 0 | 0 | 0 | 0.0 | 0.0 | 0.0 |
| 9 | | 0 | 0 | 0 | 0 | 0.0 | 0 | 0 | 0 | 0 | 0.0 | 0 | 0 | 0 | 0 | 0.0 | 0 | 0 | 0 | 0 | 0 | 0.0 | 0.0 | 0.0 |
| 10 | | 0 | 0 | 0 | 0 | 0.0 | 0 | 0 | 0 | 0 | 0.0 | 0 | 0 | 0 | 0 | 0.0 | 0 | 0 | 0 | 0 | 0 | 0.0 | 0.0 | 0.0 |
| 11 | | 0 | 0 | 0 | 0 | 0.0 | 0 | 0 | 0 | 0 | 0.0 | 0 | 0 | 0 | 0 | 0.0 | 0 | 0 | 0 | 0 | 0 | 0.0 | 0.0 | 0.0 |
| 12 | | 0 | 0 | 0 | 0 | 0.0 | 0 | 0 | 0 | 0 | 0.0 | 0 | 0 | 0 | 0 | 0.0 | 0 | 0 | 0 | 0 | 0 | 0.0 | 0.0 | 0.0 |
| 13 | | 0 | 0 | 0 | 0 | 0.0 | 0 | 0 | 0 | 0 | 0.0 | 0 | 0 | 0 | 0 | 0.0 | 0 | 0 | 0 | 0 | 0 | 0.0 | 0.0 | 0.0 |
| 14 | | 0 | 0 | 0 | 0 | 0.0 | 0 | 0 | 0 | 0 | 0.0 | 0 | 0 | 0 | 0 | 0.0 | 0 | 0 | 0 | 0 | 0 | 0.0 | 0.0 | 0.0 |
| 15 | | 0 | 0 | 0 | 0 | 0.0 | 0 | 0 | 0 | 0 | 0.0 | 0 | 0 | 0 | 0 | 0.0 | 0 | 0 | 0 | 0 | 0 | 0.0 | 0.0 | 0.0 |

Profile 1 – 24th flat 100%

status 1 = pm a = off — M-F, Sat, Sun — (x-axis 0 to 24)

**5.6 Screen shot of CIBSE TM22 2012 energy assessment spreadsheet showing the navigation bars**

**Electrical sub-metering summary**

| Elecricity Usage Type | Annual consumption (kWh) | |
|---|---|---|
| General Elecricity | 208,000 | This is the building's electricity use including renewable electricity supplied and CHP.Separable energy uses are not included. |
| Total assigned to non-separable sub-meters | 200,000 | |
| General – not assigned to sub-meter | 8,000 | Red indicates that sub-metered total is greater than metered supply – check all entries |
| Total separable electricity | 18,000 | |
| Total separable electricity assigned to sub-meters | 18,000 | |
| Separable – not assigned to sub-meter | 0 | This value should be zero once sub-meter entry is complete. |

**Electrical Sub-meters list**

| Sub-meter | Reference | Description | Location | Meter type | Electricity usage type | Annual consumption (kWh) | H/H total kWh | Energy consumption breakdown | | |
|---|---|---|---|---|---|---|---|---|---|---|
| | | | | | | | | M-F 0900 - 18.00 | M-F non-core hours | Sat-Sun |
| No sub-meter | | No sub-meter | | | Electricity | 8,000 | | | | |
| E1 | sub 1 | Floors 1 to 2 | Switch Room | Manual readings | Electricity | 50,000 | | | | |
| E2 | sub 2 | Fans | Switch Room | Half hourly | Electricity | 42,000 | | | | |
| E3 | sub 3 | Controls | Switch Room | Half hourly | Electricity | 5,000 | | | | |
| E4 | sub 4 | Pumps | Switch Room | Manual readings | Electricity | 13,000 | | | | |
| E5 | sub 5 | Humidification | Switch Room | Manual readings | Electricity | 18,000 | | | | |
| E6 | sub 6 | cooling | Switch Room | Quarter hourly | Electricity | 31,000 | | | | |
| E7 | sub 7 | outdoor lighting | Switch Room | Manual readings | Electricity | 4,000 | | | | |
| E8 | sub 8 | floors 3 to 4 | Switch Room | Manual readings | Electricity | 31,000 | | | | |
| E9 | sub 9 | catering | Switch Room | AMR data | Electricity | 6,000 | | | | |
| E10 | sub 10 | regional server | Switch Room | BMS logs | Regional Server Room | 18,000 | | | | |
| E11 | | | | Click to select | | | | | | |
| E12 | | | | Click to select | | | | | | |
| E13 | | | | Click to select | | | | | | |

**5.7** Electrical sub-meter data is used in CIBSE TM22 2012 to reconcile against known loads and run times

of a similar nature. A certain degree of judgement is required, especially if the aggregated load turns out to be a significant fraction of the total.

CIBSE TM22 2012 allows the user to account for energy in three distinct periods: 1. core hours based on occupied period; 2. out of hours (normally weekday nights); and 3. weekends. This can provide a valuable insight into the building's energy consumption during occupied and non-occupied hours, helping to identify base load consumption and wastage.

Fifteen operational profiles for equipment use can be defined, which allow the on and off times to be set for equipment and provide total annual running hours. Some profiles are prefilled but able to be edited, while the remainder are totally user-defined. Seasonal use is

considered within each profile, with a proportion of the year assigned to each seasonal period – winter, summer and spring/autumn. For example, buildings in colder climates may spend a greater proportion of the year running in winter conditions, with significant heating and lighting demands and minimal cooling (Figure 5.9).

As with earlier versions of the tool, CIBSE TM22 2012 requires a value for intensity of equipment use. For example, equipment may only be used 80% of that time. The load factor is another requirement, which is the difference between the rating of the equipment and the actual power use. For instance, a pump can be rated at 1 kW, but where it is supplied by a variable speed drive it may consume 500 W, thus providing a load factor of 0.5.

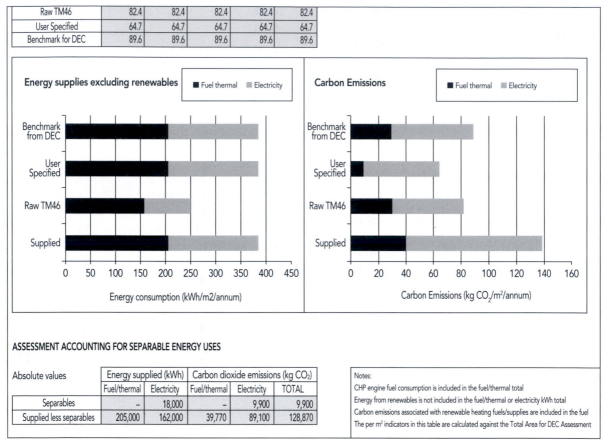

| | | | | | |
|---|---|---|---|---|---|
| Raw TM46 | 82.4 | 82.4 | 82.4 | 82.4 | 82.4 |
| User Specified | 64.7 | 64.7 | 64.7 | 64.7 | 64.7 |
| Benchmark for DEC | 89.6 | 89.6 | 89.6 | 89.6 | 89.6 |

**ASSESSMENT ACCOUNTING FOR SEPARABLE ENERGY USES**

| Absolute values | Energy supplied (kWh) | | Carbon dioxide emissions (kg CO₂) | | |
|---|---|---|---|---|---|
| | Fuel/thermal | Electricity | Fuel/thermal | Electricity | TOTAL |
| Separables | – | 18,000 | – | 9,900 | 9,900 |
| Supplied less separables | 205,000 | 162,000 | 39,770 | 89,100 | 128,870 |

Notes:
CHP engine fuel consumption is included in the fuel/thermal total
Energy from renewables is not included in the fuel/thermal or electricity kWh total
Carbon emissions associated with renewable heating fuels/supplies are included in the fuel
The per m² indicators in this table are calculated against the Total Area for DEC Assessment

5.8 CIBSE TM22 2012 automatically generates a graphical breakdown of the building's energy use by kilowatt hours and CO₂ emissions per annum

Once a detailed level analysis has been completed, CIBSE TM22 2012 sorts the data and completes a reconciliation of the energy use against each of the sub-meters, and the total energy use recorded by the utility meters. If half-hourly or quarter-hourly data is imported, the model can compare the amount of energy that it thinks is being consumed at different times of the day with the actual energy consumption being recorded. Half-hourly data only becomes important when trying to understand an energy consumption profile where wastage or sub-optimal running needs to be identified. At the early stages, half-hourly data is not as critical as submitter totals. Usually it is normal when undertaking a building survey to find sub-meters that are incorrectly calibrated or not even functioning. In a new

building this is a defect that needs to be rectified under warranty. However, if failings in meters are not resolved, there is an option to assign energy use to a 'no meter' option. Inevitably this adds a level of ambiguity to the results, and it should be considered only as a last resort.

Detailed analysis can deliver a breakdown for the 20 categories of electrical end use. This is presented as both electrical demand and equivalent electrical carbon emissions. When this information is integrated with heating loads, CIBSE TM22 2012 provides whole-building fossil fuel (equivalent) carbon emissions. An additional feature allows the user to calculate savings for any improvement measures, by changing ratings or the use of equipment. For example, a pump might be replaced by a more efficient item which draws less power. The results are graphically represented in end-use breakdown charts showing comparative before and after totals. This worksheet can be used in a variety of ways, including a review of in-use performance before and after a refurbishment or a comparison of design predictions with actual measured values.

CIBSE TM22 2012 has the potential to be a powerful tool for analysis, providing a common reference point for designers and operators alike throughout a health care project. The tool can be helpful in aligning expectations and providing a check mechanism for regulatory tools.

## Case studies of applying design for sustainability tools in health care

The case study of the Great Ormond Street Children's Hospital Phase 2A Morgan Stanley Building development shows how tools such as BREEAM Healthcare 2008 help enhance compliance with NHS requirements and aid the meeting of Department of Health targets for sustainability.

Championed by the Technology Strategy Board under its Building Performance Evaluation Programme of domestic and non-domestic buildings, CIBSE TM22 2012 can improve energy performance in health care facilities. "The fundamental purpose of detailed analysis using CIBSE's TM22 energy assessment tool is to enable users to reconcile the total energy use against various end uses. Designers can use the tool with the client at the briefing stage of a project to discuss a building's likely load profile and then use that information to set realistic performance targets" (Peter Tse, Senior Design Consultant with BSRIA).

Designers can use the CIBSE TM22 tool with the client at the briefing stage of a project to discuss a building's likely load profile, and use that information to set realistic but ambitious performance targets. After handover, facilities managers can use it to identify poorly performing systems and wasteful practices. For energy assessors there are clear ties to labelling and energy assessments for owners, operators and designers. Owners can benchmark their study buildings against typical benchmarks or estate-derived benchmarks.

## Great Ormond Street Children's Hospital, London

The development aspires to be one of the greenest hospitals in the UK, achieving a 20% reduction in carbon emissions through renewable sources (BREEAM[1] rating 77%) while meeting the targets set for the City of London. The Development Control Plan's aims relate to the initial plan for: GSHPs – Ground Source Heat Pumps (hot water supplement and thermal plan for heat rejection in summer months); PV – Photovoltaics (electrical generation and improved fabric insulation); and Solar Thermal (supplement LTHW – Low Temperature Hot Water, 80/70°C).

With GSHP not recognised under the London Plan, the development's focus is complying with the 2004 mayor's energy strategy for a reduction of energy usage (i.e. Be Lean!), increased use of renewable energy sources (i.e. Be Green!) and achieving efficiency of energy usage (i.e. Be Clean!), while acknowledging that a separate drive to include CHP negates gains from solar thermal collectors. Also, the strategy incorporates HV electrical generation with exports to the local electricity grid, MTHW (Medium Temperature Hot Water – 95/71°C) heat generation and the formation of Centralised Energy Centre (EnPOD 2), and tri-generation (CCHP – Combined Cooling Heating and Power) with CHW linkages to adjacent buildings and energy efficiency, plus decentralisation with priority over renewables. The carbon story, which was informed by the zero carbon hierarchy (measures allowing for the reduction of emissions that are difficult to achieve on-site – on-site energy generation – good building fabric performance), highlights primarily gas-fired systems based on future bio-gas/bio-oil fuels, a reduction in circulating temperature (i.e. 156 – 95°C), the provision of a mixed-mode ventilation to in-patient and canteen areas, and the installation of LED lighting and lighting control systems with energy efficiency and CCHP that exceed targets for carbon dioxide emissions by 20% (Figures 5.9 to 5.14).

Natural daylight penetration has been maximised in key areas of the building with full height glazing at the 'cranked' building footprint. Mixed mode ventilation is provided to all

---

[1] BRE Environmental Assessment Method

Table 5.11 **Minimum levels set for all the five BREEAM classified ratings from a 'pass' to 'outstanding' show the onus increasing as the rating rises**

| Categories | Design tools |
|---|---|
| 1. Improving Compliance with Statutory and Other Requirements | **P**remises **A**ssurance **M**odel (PAM): "A system-wide, nationally consistent approach to providing organisation board-level assurance of the quality and safety of premises in which NHS clinical services are delivered. The rigorous self-assessment methodology uses robust evidence, metrics and measurements to demonstrate that a health care provider's premises achieve the required statutory and nationally agreed standards on safety, efficiency, effectiveness and staff/patient (user) experience". |
| | **A**ctivity **D**ata**B**ase (ADB): "Relates uniquely to health care and is well-regarded in the industry. Contractors in the health care sector point out that ADB data is used on 95% of all health care projects". |
| 2. Design Quality Improvement | **A**chieving **D**esign **E**xcellence **E**valuation **T**ool **K**it (AEDET): "A sector-specific version of the industry standard Design Quality Indicator (DQI) widely adopted in the UK to establish a shared set of terms and concepts through which all those involved in the design process can map its quality". <br> **A S**taff & **P**atient **E**nvironment **C**alibration **T**ool (ASPECT): A plug-in for AEDET Evolution – "Can help communicate and allow sharing of values, clarify design strengths to build on, weaknesses to be overcome while identifying opportunities for improvement of the architectural health care environment". |
| | **D**esign **Q**uality **I**ndicator (DQI): "A method of evaluating the design quality and construction of new buildings as well as the refurbishment of existing ones, including police stations, office buildings, college and university buildings, libraries, and many other civic and private building projects. The process involves a wide group of people responsible for the design and construction, those who will use the building or are affected by it". <br> DQI for Health launched in March 2013 to succeed AEDET Evolution (above). |
| | **D**esign **A**nd **R**isk **T**ool (DART): "Estimates and manages the risks involved in a design under ProCure21 NHS Building Procurement; aids the client to make informed decisions when evaluating the inherent risks for specific design proposals". |
| | **I**nspiring **D**esign **E**xcellence and **A**chievements (IDEAs): "Initiates the design of health care places through considerations of people (patients, staff and visitors), medical equipment and furniture to respond to emotional and functional requirements of health and social care delivery". |
| 3. Enhancing Efficiency and Effectiveness | **S**trategic **H**ealth **A**sset **P**lanning and **E**valuation (SHAPE): "A web-enabled evidence-based application which informs and supports the strategic planning of services across a whole health geographical economy in order to deliver health and social care more efficiently and effectively while enabling decisions to be made closer to the patients (and all those people) that will be affected by them". |
| 4. Achieving Sustainability in the Architectural Health Care Estate | **B**uilding **R**esearch **E**stablishment's **E**nvironmental **A**ssessment **M**ethod (BREEAM): "Sets the standard for best practice in sustainable building and construction design and has been widely acknowledged as the measure to describe a building's environmental performance. Credits are awarded in nine categories according to performance which are then aggregated or added together to produce a single overall score on a scale equivalent to 'Pass', 'Good', 'Very Good', 'Excellent' and 'Outstanding' rating". |
| | **C**hartered **I**nstitution of **B**uilding **S**ervices **E**ngineers (CIBSE) TM22 (**E**nergy **A**ssessment & **R**eporting **M**ethodology [EARM™]): "a method for assessing a building's energy and services performance that can be handled by using a spreadsheet approach to consider feedback and operational performance and therefore allows building owners, facilities managers and designers to reconcile, for example, the total electrical use against various end uses". |

**Table 5.12 BREEAM Healthcare 2008 'excellent' mandatory credits**

|  | Credits | Description |
|---|---|---|
| Management – weighting 12.5% (Encouraging the sustainable commissioning of the building, environmental management systems, staff education and training and purchasing). | Man 2 | Considerate Constructors: Aim to recognise and encourage construction sites which are managed in an environmentally and socially considerate and accountable manner.<br>1 Credit: Where evidence provided demonstrates that there is a commitment to comply with best practice site management principles.<br>2 Credits: Where evidence provided demonstrates that there is a commitment to go beyond best practice site management principles (See Schedule of Evidence + Validation Statement). |
|  | Man 4 | Building User Guide: Aim to recognise and encourage the provision of guidance for the non-technical building user so they can understand and operate the building efficiently.<br>1 Credit: Where evidence provided demonstrates the provision of a simple guide that covers information relevant to the tenant/occupants and non-technical building manager on the operation and environmental performance of the building (See Schedule of Evidence + Validation Statement). |

Health & Well-being - 15.0% (Linking and consulting the community, sharing facilities, staff and patient empowerment).

| Energy – weighting 19.0% (Reducing carbon emissions, providing heating and lighting controls, energy monitoring and usage reduction facilities, use of daylight and alternative electricity tariffs). | Ene 1 | Reduction of $CO_2$ Emissions: Aim to recognise and encourage buildings that are designed to minimise the $CO_2$ emissions associated with their operational energy consumption.<br>15 Credits: Where evidence provided demonstrates an improvement in the energy efficiency of the building's fabric and services and therefore achieves lower building operational related $CO_2$ emissions (See Schedule of Evidence + Validation Statement). |
|---|---|---|
|  | Ene 5 | Low or Zero Carbon Technologies: Aim to reduce carbon emissions and atmospheric pollution by encouraging local energy generation from renewable sources to supply a significant proportion of the energy demand.<br>1 Credit: Where evidence provided demonstrates that a feasibility study considering local (on-site and/or near site) low or zero carbon (LZC) technologies has been carried out and the results implemented.<br>2 Credits: Where evidence provided demonstrates that the first credit has been achieved and there is a 10% reduction in the building's $CO_2$ emissions as a result of the installation of a feasible local LZC technology.<br>3 Credits: Where evidence provided demonstrates that the first credit has been achieved and there is a 15% reduction in the building's $CO_2$ emissions as a result of the installation of a feasible local LZC technology.<br>Alternatively 1 Credit: Where evidence provided demonstrates that a contract with an energy supplier is in place to provide sufficient electricity used within the assessed building/development to meet the above criteria from a 100% renewable energy source. (Note: a standard Green Tariff will not comply) (See Schedule of Evidence + Validation Statement). |

Transport – 8.0% (Reducing carbon emissions via provision of car parking, cyclist facilities, proximity to public transport facilities, distance to local amenities, green transport plan and compliance with controls assurance)

Water – 6.0% (Minimising water consumption through leak detection, water use monitoring, low flush toilets and grey water recycling).

Materials – 12.5% (Using materials from sustainable sources, prohibition of hazardous substances) BRE's Green Book Live + Green Guide to Specification provide useful information which make it more likely to achieve these credits (and the environmental benefit).

| Waste – 7.5% (Reducing waste, recycling and waste stream analysis). | Wst 3 | Recyclable Waste Storage: Aim to recognise the provision of dedicated storage facilities for a building's operational-related recyclable waste streams, so that such waste is diverted from landfill or incineration.<br>1 Credit: Where a central, dedicated space is provided for the storage of the building's recyclable waste streams (Schedule of Evidence + Validation Statement). |
|---|---|---|

Land Use + Ecology – 10.0% (Protecting ecological features and introducing natural habitats, re-use of sites and ecological enhancement)

Pollution –10.0% (Monitoring and addressing pollution, $NO_x$ emissions, ozone depleting substances, noise pollution and incineration practices)

Innovation – 9.0% (Providing additional recognition for a procurement strategy, design feature, management process or technological development that innovates sustainability, above and beyond the level that is currently recognised and rewarded within standard BREEAM issues)

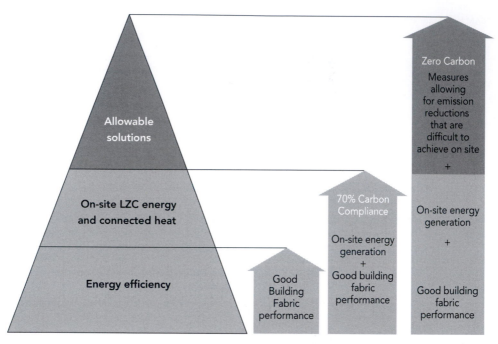

5.9  Great Ormond Street Children's Hospital redevelopment – the zero carbon hierarchy (source: WSP Group 2011)

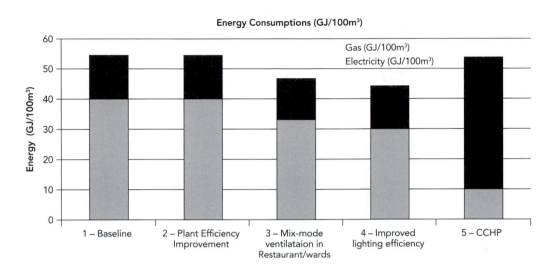

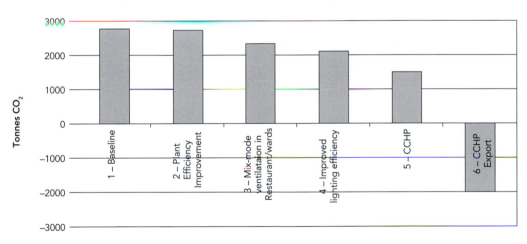

**5.10 Great Ormond Street Children's Hospital redevelopment – Energy Consumptions and carbon reductions (source: WSP Group 2011)**

ward bedrooms, giving patients and parents control of their environment when the external conditions allow. Mixed mode natural ventilation to the level 2 public and staff restaurants is achieved with cross-ventilation and a glazed thermal flue integrated into the Guilford Street façade. The thermal flue, expressed on the only public façade, makes a statement about the building and the Trust's aspirations towards sustainability. Extensive, semi-intensive and intensive green

roofs have been specified to increase biodiversity on a dense urban site to reduce both storm water run-off and the heat island effect at the hospital by increasing thermal performance. A post-tension concrete floor slab minimises the structural zone and concrete content in the building, and where possible its thermal mass is used to stabilise peak temperatures with all finishes selected to reduce embodied energy and enhance the internal healing environment.

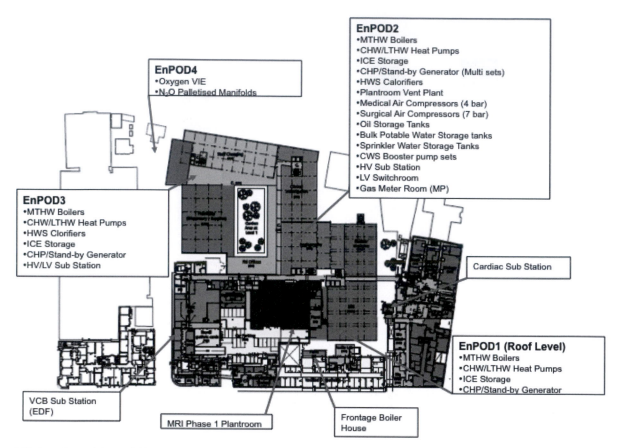

**EnPOD2**
- MTHW Boilers
- CHW/LTHW Heat Pumps
- ICE Storage
- CHP/Stand-by Generator (Multi sets)
- HWS Calorifiers
- Plantroom Vent Plant
- Medical Air Compressors (4 bar)
- Surgical Air Compressors (7 bar)
- Oil Storage Tanks
- Bulk Potable Water Storage tanks
- Sprinkler Water Storage Tanks
- CWS Booster pump sets
- HV Sub Station
- LV Switchroom
- Gas Meter Room (MP)

**EnPOD4**
- Oxygen VIE
- N$_2$O Palletised Manifolds

**EnPOD3**
- MTHW Boilers
- CHW/LTHW Heat Pumps
- HWS Clorifiers
- ICE Storage
- CHP/Stand-by Generator
- HV/LV Sub Station

Cardiac Sub Station

**EnPOD1 (Roof Level)**
- MTHW Boilers
- CHW/LTHW Heat Pumps
- ICE Storage
- CHP/Stand-by Generator

VCB Sub Station (EDF)

MRI Phase 1 Plantroom

Frontage Boiler House

5.11 Great Ormond Street Children's Hospital redevelopment (source: Llewellyn Davies 2011)

**5.12 Great Ormond Street Children's Hospital redevelopment (WSP Group) 2005 development control plan aims to reduce both carbon emissions and distribution temperature for the system while de-centralising the boiler plant**

# References

Capper G, Holmes J, Hudson G, and Currie JI (2005) The use of an environmental assessment tool in healthcare buildings. The 2005 World Sustainable Building Conference, Tokyo, 27–29 September 2005 (SB05Tokyo) www.irbnet.de/daten/iconda/CIB3738.pdf [Accessed 1 July 2012].

CIBSE TM22 and Field J, Soper J, Jones P, Bordass W, and Grigg P (1997) Energy performance of occupied non-domestic buildings assessment by analysing end-use energy consumptions. *Building Services Engineering Research and Technology* 18(1), 39–46.

CIBSE (2010) *Energy Assessment and Reporting Methodology* 2nd Edition (inc. CD-ROM). London, UK.

Darzi L (2008) Our NHS Our Future. Retrieved April 2008. http://www.ournhs.nhs.uk/ [Accessed May 2012].

Fisk WJ (2000) Health and productivity gains from better indoor environments and their relationship with building energy efficiency. Indoor Environment Department, Environmental Energy Technologies Division, Lawrence Berkeley National Laboratory, Berkeley, California, *Annual Review of Energy and the Environment* 25, 2000: 537–566.

Field J, and CIBSE TM22 (2006) *Energy Assessment and Reporting Method*. The Chartered Institution of Building Services Engineers Publications, London UK, ISBN-10: 1-903287-60-X and ISBN-13: 978-1-903287-60-6.

Lee W, and Burnett J (2007) Benchmarking energy use assessment of HK-BEAM, BREEAM and LEED. *Building and Environment,* 43 (11), 2008, 1882–1891.

Matthiessen LF, and Morris P (2004) *Costing Green: A Comprehensive Cost Database and Budgeting Methodology*. Los Angeles: Davis Langdon.

National Audit Office, (2007) *Building for the Future: Sustainable Construction and refurbishment on the Government Estate*. Report by the Comptroller and Auditor General, HC324, April 2007.

New Buildings Institute (ed.) (2003) Integrated energy systems – productivity and building science. Program final report, prepared for California Energy Commission, Public Interest Energy Research Program.

NHS Information Centre for Health and Social Care (2010) Hospital Episode Statistics: HES User Guide. http://www.hesonline.nhs.uk [Accessed August 2012] .

Nicklas MH, and Bailey GB (1996) Analyses of the performance of students in daylit schools. *Innovative Design*, Raleigh, NC.

Reed T, Clouston P, Hoque S, and Fisette P, (2010) An analysis of LEED and BREEAM Assessment Methods for Educational Institutions. *Journal of Green Building*, 5 (1), 2010, 132–154.

Roodman DM, and Lenssen N (1995) A building revolution: How ecology and health concerns are transforming construction. *Worldwatch Paper* #124. Washington, DC: Worldwatch Institute.

Sleeuw M (2011) A comparison of BREEAM and LEED environmental Assessment Methods. Report to the University of East Anglia Estates and Building Division, November 2011.

Tse P (2012) Assets and targets: Making sense of energy use has got a bit easier with a major revamp of CIBSE's TM22 energy assessment tool. *Delta T Magazine*, February 2012, 12–14.

Yates A (2001) Quantifying the business benefits of sustainable buildings: Summary of existing research findings. *Project Report* # 203995, Watford, UK: Building Research Establishment, Centre for Sustainable Construction.

# Appendix

**Table 5.13 BREEAM credits on which schedule of evidence + validation statement to be provided**

| | Credits | Description |
|---|---|---|
| Management – 12.5%<br><br>(Encouraging the sustainable commissioning of the building, environmental management systems, staff education and training and purchasing). | Man 1 – | **Commissioning:** Aim to recognise and encourage an appropriate level of building services commissioning that is carried out in a co-ordinated and comprehensive manner, thus ensuring optimum performance under actual occupancy conditions.<br>1 Credit: Where evidence provided demonstrates that an appropriate project team member has been appointed to monitor commissioning on behalf of the client to ensure commissioning will be carried out in line with current best practice.<br>2 Credits: Where, in addition to the above, evidence provided demonstrates that seasonal commissioning will be carried out during the first year of occupation, post-construction (or post-fit out). |
| | Man 2 – | **Considerate Constructors:** Aim to recognise and encourage construction sites which are managed in an environmentally and socially considerate and accountable manner.<br>1 Credit: Where evidence provided demonstrates that there is a commitment to comply with best practice site management principles.<br>2 Credit: Where evidence provided demonstrates that there is a commitment to go beyond best practice site management principles |
| | Man 3 – | **Construction Site Impacts:** Aim to recognise and encourage construction sites managed in an environmentally sound manner in terms of resource use, energy consumption and pollution.<br>3 Credits: Where evidence provided demonstrates that six or more of items a–g are achieved:<br>a  Monitor report and set targets for $CO_2$ or energy arising from site activities.<br>b  Monitor report and set targets for $CO_2$ or energy arising from transport to and from site.<br>c  Monitor report and set targets for water consumption arising from site activities.<br>d  Implement best practice policies in respect of air (dust) pollution arising from the site.<br>e  Implement best practice policies in respect of water (ground and surface) pollution occurring on the site.<br>f  Main contractor has an environmental materials Policy, used for sourcing of construction materials to be utilised on site.<br>g  Main contractor operates an Environmental Management System. |
| | Man 4 – | **Building User Guide:** Aim to recognise and encourage the provision of guidance for the non technical building user so they can understand and operate the building efficiently.<br>1 Credit: Where evidence provided demonstrates the provision of a simple guide that covers information relevant to the tenant/occupants and non-technical building manager on the operation and environmental performance of the building. |
| | Man 5 – | |
| | Man 6 – | **Consultation:** Aim to involve the relevant stakeholders (including building users, business, residents and local government) in the design process in order to provide buildings fit for purpose and to increase local "ownership".<br>1 Credit: Where evidence provided demonstrates that consultation has been, or is being, undertaken and feedback given to the local community and building users. In addition, advice should also have been sought from any relevant national and local history, archaeological bodies or military history groups regarding the heritage value of the building/site/surroundings.<br>2 Credits: Where, in addition to the above, evidence provided demonstrates that changes to the design and/or action has been taken as a result of the above consultation process. This should include the protection of any parts of the building (or site) having historic or heritage value in accordance with independent advice from the *relevant body*. |

**Table 5.13 continued**

| | Credits | Description |
|---|---|---|
| | Man 7 – | Shared Facilities: Aim to recognise and encourage flexible buildings designed to cater for shared use with the local community.<br>1 Credit: Where evidence provided demonstrates that shared facilities have been provided as a consequence of consultation feedback.<br>2 Credits: Where, in addition to the above, evidence provided demonstrates that these facilities can be accessed without compromising the safety and security of the building and its occupants. |
| | Man 8 – | Security: Aim to recognise and encourage the implementation of effective design measures that will reduce the opportunity for and fear of crime on the new development.<br>1 Credit: Where evidence provided demonstrates that an *Architectural Liaison Officer* (ALO) or *Crime Prevention Design Advisor* (CPDA) from the local police force has been consulted at the design stage and their recommendations incorporated into the design of the building and its parking facilities (if relevant). |
| | Man 9 – | |
| | Man 10 – | The Development as a Learning Resource: |
| | Man 11 – | Ease of Maintenance: Aim to recognise and encourage the specification of a building and building services that can be easily maintained during their lifecycle.<br>1 Credit: Where evidence provided demonstrates that specifications for the building and the building services/systems and landscaping have considered ease and efficiency of maintenance in line with best practice. |
| | Man 12 – | Life Cycle Costing: Aim to recognise and encourage the development of a Life Cycle Cost (LCC) analysis model for the project to improve design, specification and through-life maintenance and operation.<br>1 Credit: Where evidence provided demonstrates that a Life Cycle Cost (LCC) analysis based on the feasibility study proposals has been undertaken on the building design at a strategic and system level.<br>2 Credits: Where evidence provided demonstrates that the results of the feasibility study and consideration of LCC have been implemented. |
| | Man 13 – | Good Corporate Citizen: Aim to encourage the sustainable development of the NHS through the improvement of daily corporate activities.<br>1 Credit: Where evidence provided demonstrates that the Good Corporate Citizen model has been used to assess the development and that there is a commitment to continue to use the model to re-assess the development regularly. |
| Health & Wellbeing -15.0%<br><br>(Linking and consulting the community, encouraging sharing of facilities, staff and patient empowerment, access for the disabled, provision of views out of the building, budget for green plants, high frequency ballasts on lighting, signage and artwork). | Hea 1 – | Daylighting: Aim to give building users sufficient access to daylight.<br>2 Credits: Where at least 80% by floor area of occupied *staff* and *public areas* have an average daylight factor of 2% or more. **AND** Where at least 80% by floor area of occupied *patient areas* (dayrooms, wards) and consulting rooms have an average daylight factor of 3% or more. |
| | Hea 2 – | View Out: Aim to allow occupants to refocus their eyes from close work and enjoy an external view, thus reducing the risk of eyestrain and breaking the monotony of the indoor environment.<br>1 Credit: Where evidence provided demonstrates that all workstations/benches and desks and at least 80% by floor area of public areas have an adequate view out. |
| | Hea 3 – | Glare Control: Aim to reduce problems associated with glare in occupied areas through the provision of adequate controls.<br>1 Credit: Where evidence provided demonstrates that an occupant-controlled shading system (e.g. internal or external blinds) is fitted in *relevant building areas*. |
| | Hea 4 – | High Frequency Lighting: Aim to reduce the risk of health problems related to the flicker of fluorescent lighting.<br>1 Credit: Where evidence provided demonstrates that high frequency ballasts are installed on all fluorescent and compact fluorescent lamps (See Schedule of Evidence + Validation Statement). |
| | Hea 5 – | Internal + External Lighting Levels: Aim to ensure lighting has been designed in line with best practice for visual performance and comfort.<br>1 Credit: Where evidence provided demonstrates that all internal and external lighting, where relevant, is specified in accordance with the appropriate maintained illuminance levels (in lux) recommended by CIBSE. |

Hea 6 – **Lighting Zones + Controls**: Aim to ensure occupants have easy and accessible control over lighting within each *relevant building area*.
1 Credit: Where evidence provided demonstrates that, in all relevant building areas, lighting is appropriately zoned and occupant controllable.

Hea 7 – **Potential for Natural Ventilation**: Aim to recognise and encourage adequate cross flow of air in naturally ventilated buildings and flexibility in air-conditioned/mechanically ventilated buildings for future conversion to a natural ventilation strategy.
1 Credit: Where evidence provided demonstrates that fresh air is capable of being delivered to the *occupied spaces* of the building via a natural ventilation strategy, and there is sufficient user-control of the supply of fresh air.

Hea 8 – **Indoor Air Quality**: Aim to reduce the risk to health associated with poor indoor air quality.
1 Credit: Where air intakes serving occupied areas avoid major sources of external pollution and recirculation of exhaust air.

Hea 9 – **Volatile Organic Compounds**: Aim to recognise and encourage a healthy internal environment through the specification of internal finishes and fittings with low emissions of volatile organic compounds (VOCs).
1 Credit: Where evidence provided demonstrates that the emissions of VOCs and other substances from key internal finishes and fittings comply with best practice levels.

Hea 10 – **Thermal Comfort**: Aim to ensure, with the use of design tools, that appropriate thermal comfort levels are achieved.
1 Credit: Where evidence provided demonstrates that thermal comfort levels in *occupied spaces* of the building are assessed at the design stage to evaluate appropriate servicing options, ensuring appropriate thermal comfort levels are achieved.

Hea 11 – **Thermal Zoning**: Aim to recognise and encourage the provision of user controls which allow independent adjustment of heating/cooling systems within the building.
1 Credit: Where evidence provided demonstrates that local occupant control is available for temperature adjustment in each *occupied space* to reflect differing user demands.

Hea 12 – **Microbial Contamination**: Aim to ensure the building services are designed to reduce the risk of *legionellosis* in operation.
1 Credit: Where evidence provided demonstrates that the risk of waterborne and airborne *Legionella* contamination has been minimised (See Schedule of Evidence + Validation Statement).

Hea 13 – **Acoustic Performance**: Aim to ensure the acoustic performance of the building meets the appropriate standards for its purpose.
1 Credit: Where evidence provided demonstrates that indoor ambient noise levels and airborne and impact sound insulation levels achieve the recommended performance benchmarks outlined in Health Technical Memorandum (HTM) 08–01 Part A.
2 Credits: Where evidence provided demonstrates that reverberation times are compliant with the recommended performance benchmarks outlined in HTM 08–01 Part A.

Hea 14 – **Outdoor Space**: Aim to recognise and encourage the provision of external amenity space for building users.
1 Credit: Where evidence provided demonstrates the provision of an adequate outdoor amenity space accessible for use by the building's occupants.

Hea 15 –

Hea 16 –

Hea 17 – **Specification of Laboratory Fume Cupboards:**

Hea 18 – **Containment Level 2 & 3 Laboratory Areas:**

Hea 19 – **Arts in Health**: Aim to recognise and encourage the installation of artwork that enhances the healthcare environment for patients, staff and visitors.
1 Credit: Where evidence provided demonstrates that an art co-ordinator has been appointed or an art strategy and policy have been prepared for the development.

**Table 5.13 continued**

| | Credits | Description |
|---|---|---|
| Energy – 19.0%<br><br>(Reducing carbon emissions, providing heating and lighting controls, energy monitoring and usage reduction facilities, use of daylight and alternative electricity tariffs). | Ene 1 – | Reduction of $CO_2$ Emissions: Aim to recognise and encourage buildings that are designed to minimise the $CO_2$ emissions associated with their operational energy consumption.<br>15 Credits: Where evidence provided demonstrates an improvement in the energy efficiency of the building's fabric and services and therefore achieves lower building operational related $CO_2$ emissions. |
| | Ene 2 – | Sub-metering of Substantial Energy Uses: Aim to recognise and encourage the installation of energy sub-metering that facilitates the monitoring of in-use energy consumption.<br>1 Credit: Where evidence provided demonstrates the provision of direct sub-metering of energy uses within the building.<br>2 Credits: Where, in addition to the above, evidence provided demonstrates that sub-meters are connected to a BMS or other type of automated control device. |
| | Ene 3 – | Sub-metering of High Energy Load & Tenancy Areas: Aim to recognise and encourage the installation of energy sub-metering that facilitates the monitoring of in-use energy consumption by tenant or end user.<br>1 Credit: Where evidence provided demonstrates sub-metering of energy consumption by tenancy/ building function area is installed within the building. |
| | Ene 4 – | External Lighting: Aim to recognise and encourage the specification of energy-efficient light fittings for external areas of the development.<br>1 Credit: Where energy-efficient external lighting is specified and all light fittings are controlled for the presence of daylight. |
| | Ene 5 – | Low or Zero Carbon Technologies: Aim to reduce carbon emissions and atmospheric pollution by encouraging local energy generation from renewable sources to supply a significant proportion of the energy demand.<br>1 Credit: Where evidence provided demonstrates that a feasibility study considering local (*on-site* and/or *near site*) low or zero carbon (LZC) technologies has been carried out and the results implemented.<br>2 Credits: Where evidence provided demonstrates that the first credit has been achieved and there is a 10% reduction in the building's $CO_2$ emissions as a result of the installation of a feasible local LZC technology.<br>3 Credit: Where evidence provided demonstrates that the first credit has been achieved and there is a 15% reduction in the building's $CO_2$ emissions as a result of the installation of a feasible local LZC technology.<br>Alternatively 1 Credit: Where evidence provided demonstrates that a contract with an energy supplier is in place to provide sufficient electricity used within the assessed building/development to meet the above criteria from a 100% renewable energy source. (Note: a standard Green Tariff will not comply) |
| | Ene 6 – | Lifts: Aim to recognise and encourage the specification of energy-efficient transportation systems.<br>2 Creditss: Up to two credits are available where evidence provided demonstrates the installation of energy-efficient lift(s). |
| | Ene 7 – | Provision of Energy-Efficient Equipment: Aim to recognise and encourage procurement and commissioning of energy-efficient equipment to ensure optimum performance and energy savings.<br>1 Credit: Where evidence provided demonstrates procurement of office and domestic scale equipment on the basis of energy-efficient performance over the product life cycle. |
| | Ene 8 – | Lifts: |
| | Ene 9 – | Escalators and Travelling Walkways: |
| | Ene 10 – | Free Coding: |
| | Ene 11 – | Energy Efficient Fume Cupboards: |
| | Ene 12 – | Swimming Pool Ventilation and Heat Loss: |
| | Ene 13 – | Labelled Lighting Controls: |
| | Ene 14 – | BMS (Building Management System): |
| | Ene 15 – | Provision of Energy-Efficient Equipment: |

| | | |
|---|---|---|
| | Ene 16 – | **Community Combined Heat + Power (CHP)**: Aim to recognise and encourage CHP community energy schemes.<br>1 Credit: Where evidence provided demonstrates that a feasibility study has been carried out on the potential for the building to set up, contribute to or benefit from a local CHP community energy scheme. |
| | Ene 17 – | **Residential Areas – Energy Consumption:** |
| | Ene 18 – | |
| | Ene 19 – | **Energy Efficient Laboratories:** |
| | Ene 20 – | **Energy Efficient IT Solutions** |
| **Transport – 8.0%**<br><br>(Reducing carbon emissions via provision of car parking (e.g. 'Park+Ride'), cyclist facilities, proximity to public transport facilities, distance to local amenities, green transport plan and compliance with controls assurance). | Tra 1 – | **Provision of Public Transport**: Aim to recognise and encourage development in proximity to good public transport networks, thereby helping to reduce transport-related emissions and traffic congestion.<br>5 Credits: Awarded on a sliding scale based on the assessed buildings' accessibility to the public transport network. |
| | Tra 2 – | **Proximities to Amenities**: Aim to encourage and reward a building that is located in proximity to local amenities, thereby reducing the need for extended travel or multiple trips.<br>1 Credit: Where evidence provided demonstrates that the building is located within 500m of *accessible local amenities* appropriate to the building type and its users. |
| | Tra 3 – | **Cyclist Facilities**: Aim to encourage building users to cycle by ensuring adequate provision of cyclist facilities.<br>1 Credit: Where evidence provided demonstrates that covered, secure and well-lit cycle storage facilities are provided for all *building users*.<br>2 Credits: Where, in addition to the above, adequate changing facilities are provided for staff use. |
| | Tra 4 – | **Pedestrian and Cyclist Safety**: Aim to recognise and encourage the provision of safe and secure pedestrian and cycle access routes on the development.<br>1 Credit: Where evidence provided demonstrates that the site layout has been designed in accordance with best practice to ensure safe and adequate pedestrian and cycle access. |
| | Tra 5 – | **Travel Plan**: Aim to recognise the consideration given to accommodating a range of travel options for building users, thereby encouraging the reduction of user reliance on forms of travel that have the highest environmental impact.<br>1 Credit: Where evidence provided demonstrates that a travel plan has been developed and tailored to the specific needs of the *building users*. |
| | Tra 6 – | **Maximum Car Parking**: Aim to encourage the use of alternative means of transport to the building other than the private car, thereby helping to reduce transport related emissions and traffic congestion.<br>1 Credit: Where evidence provided demonstrates that the number of parking spaces provided for the building has been limited. |
| | Tra 7 – | **Travel Information Point**: Aim to ensure the building has the capacity to provide users with up-to-date information on local public transport routes and timetables.<br>1 Credit: Where evidence provided demonstrates there is a dedicated space within the development for the provision of real-time public transport information. |
| | Tra 8 – | **Deliveries + Manoeuvring**: Aim To ensure that safety is maintained and disruption due to delivery vehicles minimised through well-planned layout and access to the site.<br>1 Credit: Where evidence provided demonstrates that vehicle access areas have been designed to ensure adequate space for manoeuvring delivery vehicles and provide space away from manoeuvring area for storage of refuse skips and pallets. |

**Table 5.13 continued**

| | Credits | Description |
|---|---|---|
| Water – 6.0%<br><br>(Minimising water consumption through leak detection, water use monitoring, low flush toilets and grey water recycling). | Wat 1 – | Water Consumption: Aim to minimise the consumption of potable water in sanitary applications by encouraging the use of low water use fittings.<br>3 Credits: Where evidence provided demonstrates that the specification includes taps, urinals, WCs and showers that consume less potable water in use than standard specifications for the same type of fittings. |
| | Wat 2 – | Water Meter: Aim to ensure water consumption can be monitored and managed and therefore encourage reductions in water consumption.<br>1 Credit: Where evidence provided demonstrates that a water meter with a pulsed output will be installed on the mains supply to each building/unit. |
| | Wat 3 – | Major Leak Detection: Aim to reduce the impact of major water leaks that may otherwise go undetected.<br>1 Credit: Where evidence provided demonstrates that a leak detection system is specified or installed on the building's water supply. |
| | Wat 4 – | Sanitary Supply Shut-off: Aim to reduce the risk of minor leaks in toilet facilities.<br>1 Credit: Where evidence provided demonstrates that proximity detection shut-off is provided to the water supply to all toilet areas. |
| | Wat 5 – | Water Recycling: Aim to encourage the collection and re-use of waste water or rainwater to meet toilet flushing needs and reduce the demand for potable fresh water.<br>1 Credit: Where evidence provided demonstrates the specification of systems that collect, store and, where necessary treat, rainwater or grey water for WC and urinal flushing purposes. |
| | Wat 6 – | Irrigation Systems: Aim to reduce the consumption of potable water for ornamental planting and landscape irrigation.<br>1 Credit: Where evidence provided demonstrates that a low-water irrigation strategy/system has been installed, or where planting and landscaping is irrigated via rainwater or reclaimed water. |
| Materials – 12.5%<br><br>(Using materials from sustainable sources, prohibition of hazardous substances). | Mat 1 – | Material Specification: Aim to recognise and encourage the use of construction materials with a low environmental impact over the full life cycle of the building.<br>6 Credits: The credits are determined using the *Green Guide to Specification* ratings for the major building elements. |
| | Mat 2 – | Hard Landscaping + Boundary Protection: Aim to recognise and encourage the specification of materials for boundary protection and external hard surfaces that have a low environmental impact, taking account of the full life cycle of materials used.<br>1 Credit: Where evidence provided demonstrates that at least 80% of the combined area of external hard landscaping and boundary protection specifications achieve an A or A+ rating, as defined by the *Green Guide to Specification*. |
| | Mat 3 – | Re-use of Building Façade: Aim to recognise and encourage the in-situ reuse of existing building façades.<br>1 Credit: Where evidence provided demonstrates that at least 50% of the total final façade (by area) is reused in-situ and at least 80% of the reused façade (by mass) comprises in-situ reused material. |
| | Mat 4 – | Reuse of Building Structure: Aim to recognise and encourage the reuse of existing structures that previously occupied the site.<br>1 Credit: Where evidence provided demonstrates that a design reuses at least 80% of an existing primary structure and, for part refurbishment and part new build, the volume of the reused structure comprises at least 50% of the final structure's volume. |

Mat 5 – Responsible Sourcing of Materials: Aim to recognise and encourage the specification of responsibly sourced materials for key building elements.

3 Credits: Up to 3 credits are available where evidence provided demonstrates that 80% of the assessed materials in the following building elements are responsibly sourced:

Structural Frame
Ground floor
Upper floors (including separating floors)
Roof
External walls
Internal walls
Foundation/substructure
Staircase

Additionally 100% of any timber must be legally sourced.

Mat 6 – Insulation: Aim to recognise and encourage the use of thermal insulation which has a low embodied environmental performance relative to its thermal properties and has been responsibly sourced.

1 Credit: Where evidence provided demonstrates that thermal insulation products used in the building have a low embodied impact relative to their thermal properties, determined by the *Green Guide to Specification* ratings.

1 Credit: Where evidence provided demonstrates that thermal insulation products used in the building have been responsibly sourced.

Mat 7 – Designing for Robustness: Aim to recognise and encourage adequate protection of exposed parts of the building and landscape, therefore minimising the frequency of use of replacement materials.

1 Credit: Where protection is given to vulnerable parts of the building such as areas exposed to high pedestrian traffic, vehicular and trolley movements.

Waste –
7.5%

(Reducing waste by providing recycling facilities and waste stream analysis, staff waste interviews, storage for recycling).

Wst 1 – Construction Site Waste Management: Aim to promote resource efficiency via the effective and appropriate management of construction site waste.

3 Credits: Up to three credits are available where evidence provided demonstrates that the amount of non-hazardous construction waste ($m^3$/100m$^2$ or tonnes/100m$^2$) generated on site by the development is the same as or better than good or best practice levels.

1 Credit: Where evidence provided demonstrates that a significant majority of non-hazardous construction waste generated by the development will be diverted from landfill and reused or recycled.

Wst 2 – Recycled Aggregates: Aim to recognise and encourage the use of recycled and secondary aggregates in construction, thereby reducing the demand for virgin material.

1 Credit: Where evidence provided demonstrates the significant use of recycled or secondary aggregates in 'high-grade' building aggregate uses.

Wst 3 – Recyclable Waste Storage: Aim to recognise the provision of dedicated storage facilities for a building's operational-related recyclable waste streams, so that such waste is diverted from landfill or incineration.

1 Credit: Where a central, dedicated space is provided for the storage of the building's recyclable waste streams.

**Table 5.13 continued**

| | Credits | Description |
|---|---|---|
| **Land Use + Ecology 10.0%**<br><br>(Protecting ecological features and introducing natural habitats, re-use of sites and ecological enhancement). | LE 1 – | Reuse of Land: Aim to encourage the reuse of land that has been previously developed, and discourage the use of previously undeveloped land for building.<br>1 Credit: Where evidence is provided to demonstrate that the majority of the footprint of the proposed development falls within the boundary of previously developed land. |
| | LE 2 – | Contaminated Land: Aim to encourage positive action to use contaminated land that otherwise would not have been remediated and developed.<br>1 Credit: Where evidence is provided to demonstrate that the land used for the new development has, prior to development, been defined as contaminated and adequate remedial steps have been taken to decontaminate the site prior to construction. |
| | LE 3 – | Ecological Value of Site + Protection of Ecological Features: Aim to encourage development on land that already has limited value to wildlife and to protect existing ecological features from substantial damage during site preparation and completion of construction works.<br>1 Credit: Where evidence provided demonstrates that the site's construction zone is defined as land of low ecological value and all existing features of ecological value will be fully protected from damage during site preparation and construction works. |
| | LE 4 – | Mitigating Ecological Impact: Aim to minimise the impact of a building development on existing site ecology.<br>1 Credit: Where evidence provided demonstrates that the change in the site's existing ecological value, as a result of development, is *minimal*.<br>2 Credits: Where evidence provided demonstrates that there is *no negative change* in the site's existing ecological value as a result of development. |
| | LE 5 – | Enhancing Site Ecology: Aim to recognise and encourage actions taken to maintain and enhance the ecological value of the site as a result of development.<br>1 Credit: Where the design team (or client) has appointed a suitably qualified ecologist to advise and report on enhancing and protecting the ecological value of the site; and implemented the professional's recommendations for general enhancement and protection of site ecology.<br>2 Credits: Where there is a positive increase in the ecological value of the site of up to (but not including) six species.<br>3 Credits: Where there is a positive increase in the ecological value of the site of six species or greater. |
| | LE 6 – | Long-term Impact on Biodiversity: Aim to minimise the long-term impact of the development on the site's, and surrounding area's biodiversity.<br>1 Credit: The client has committed to achieving the mandatory requirements listed below and at least two of the additional requirements.<br>2 Credits: The client has committed to achieving the mandatory requirements listed below and at least four of the additional requirements. |
| **Pollution – 10.0%**<br><br>(Monitoring and reducing pollution, $NO_x$ emissions, ozone depleting substances, and noise pollution and incineration practices). | Pol 1 – | Refrigerant Global Warming Potential (GWP) Building Services: Aim to reduce the contribution to climate change from refrigerants with a high global warming potential.<br>1 Credit: Where evidence provided demonstrates the use of refrigerants with a global warming potential of less than five or where there are no refrigerants specified for use in building services. |
| | Pol 2 – | Preventing Refrigerant Leaks: Aim to reduce the emissions of refrigerants to the atmosphere arising from leakages in cooling plant.<br>1 Credit: Where evidence provided demonstrates that refrigerant leaks can be detected or where there are no refrigerants specified for the development.<br>1 Credit: Where evidence provided demonstrates that the provision of automatic refrigerant pump down is made to a heat exchanger (or dedicated storage tanks) with isolation valves **OR** Where there are no refrigerants specified for the development. |
| | Pol 3 – | |

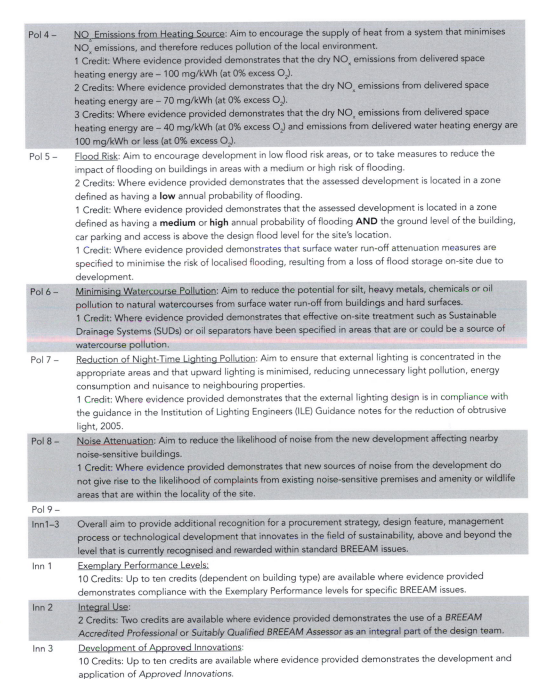

Pol 4 – **NO$_x$ Emissions from Heating Source**: Aim to encourage the supply of heat from a system that minimises NO$_x$ emissions, and therefore reduces pollution of the local environment.
1 Credit: Where evidence provided demonstrates that the dry NO$_x$ emissions from delivered space heating energy are – 100 mg/kWh (at 0% excess O$_2$).
2 Credits: Where evidence provided demonstrates that the dry NO$_x$ emissions from delivered space heating energy are – 70 mg/kWh (at 0% excess O$_2$).
3 Credits: Where evidence provided demonstrates that the dry NO$_x$ emissions from delivered space heating energy are – 40 mg/kWh (at 0% excess O$_2$) and emissions from delivered water heating energy are 100 mg/kWh or less (at 0% excess O$_2$).

Pol 5 – **Flood Risk**: Aim to encourage development in low flood risk areas, or to take measures to reduce the impact of flooding on buildings in areas with a medium or high risk of flooding.
2 Credits: Where evidence provided demonstrates that the assessed development is located in a zone defined as having a **low** annual probability of flooding.
1 Credit: Where evidence provided demonstrates that the assessed development is located in a zone defined as having a **medium** or **high** annual probability of flooding **AND** the ground level of the building, car parking and access is above the design flood level for the site's location.
1 Credit: Where evidence provided demonstrates that surface water run-off attenuation measures are specified to minimise the risk of localised flooding, resulting from a loss of flood storage on-site due to development.

Pol 6 – **Minimising Watercourse Pollution**: Aim to reduce the potential for silt, heavy metals, chemicals or oil pollution to natural watercourses from surface water run-off from buildings and hard surfaces.
1 Credit: Where evidence provided demonstrates that effective on-site treatment such as Sustainable Drainage Systems (SUDs) or oil separators have been specified in areas that are or could be a source of watercourse pollution.

Pol 7 – **Reduction of Night-Time Lighting Pollution**: Aim to ensure that external lighting is concentrated in the appropriate areas and that upward lighting is minimised, reducing unnecessary light pollution, energy consumption and nuisance to neighbouring properties.
1 Credit: Where evidence provided demonstrates that the external lighting design is in compliance with the guidance in the Institution of Lighting Engineers (ILE) Guidance notes for the reduction of obtrusive light, 2005.

Pol 8 – **Noise Attenuation**: Aim to reduce the likelihood of noise from the new development affecting nearby noise-sensitive buildings.
1 Credit: Where evidence provided demonstrates that new sources of noise from the development do not give rise to the likelihood of complaints from existing noise-sensitive premises and amenity or wildlife areas that are within the locality of the site.

Pol 9 –

Innovation – 9.0% (Providing additional recognition for a procurement strategy, design feature, management process or technological development)

Inn1–3 Overall aim to provide additional recognition for a procurement strategy, design feature, management process or technological development that innovates in the field of sustainability, above and beyond the level that is currently recognised and rewarded within standard BREEAM issues.

Inn 1 **Exemplary Performance Levels**:
10 Credits: Up to ten credits (dependent on building type) are available where evidence provided demonstrates compliance with the Exemplary Performance levels for specific BREEAM issues.

Inn 2 **Integral Use**:
2 Credits: Two credits are available where evidence provided demonstrates the use of a *BREEAM Accredited Professional* or *Suitably Qualified BREEAM Assessor* as an integral part of the design team.

Inn 3 **Development of Approved Innovations**:
10 Credits: Up to ten credits are available where evidence provided demonstrates the development and application of *Approved Innovations*.

# 6 What next for the development of design tools for evidence-based design?

This book highlights the relevance and the place of complementary design tools, underpinned by a robust and rigorous evidence base and supported by an evidence-based approach or process. For clarity and to enhance our understanding, these tools have been categorised into four main headings according to their aims and primary objectives – specifically improving compliance with statutory or regulatory requirements, design quality improvement, enhancing efficiency and effectiveness, and achieving sustainability – all of which are fundamental essentials for measuring the success of the health care estate. The underlying evidence-based approach is important because it allows the application of the evidence-based design to demonstrate objectively the improvement of hospitals and other health care facilities by applying the scientific method and its emphasis on the explicit and judicious use of current best evidence in making decisions in three key ways:

1   Enhancing patient well-being and safety by reducing infection, risk, injuries from falls, medical and medication errors. Effective patient care cannot be achieved without a safe, secure, technically sound, clean, available and controlled building environment. Key elements in such an environment are the building, heating/cooling levels, lighting, ventilation, hot and cold water and air conditioning of sensitive areas. Ineffective control of the environment via ventilation, air conditioning, filtration or positive pressures in operating theatres, intensive therapy units and isolation rooms puts patients at risk. Similarly, so do water temperatures, flow and storage patterns and the quality of water supply if not controlled effectively.
2   Eliminating environmental stressors, such as noise, lack of natural lighting, that negatively affect patient outcomes and staff performance.
3   Reducing stress and promoting healing by making hospital environments more pleasant, comfortable, and supportive for patients and staff alike (Rollins 2004).

However, to successfully implement evidence-based design principles, health care design teams must continually adopt approaches to create an environment of care that incorporates streamlined processes, new technologies, and nurtures innovative design elements.

Of importance to the development of evidence-based design tools is an appropriate evidence base to provide the essential research evidence. Learning from evidence-based medicine, external evidence invalidates previously accepted diagnostic tests and treatments and replaces them with new ones that are more powerful, more accurate, more efficacious and safer, and without current best evidence practice risks becoming rapidly out of date, to the detriment of patients (Sackett et al. July 1996).

**Table 6.1 Four categories of evidence-based design tools and challenges for further development**

### OUTCOMES from the implementation of the SHAPE Application by Kent County Council

Outcome 1 Workplace Planning and Evalation
- Mapping of physical social care asset interests and providers across Kent to enable a whole-system view for service design planning and evaluation. This was used to support workplace planning, joint commissioning plans, and other intelligence for commissioning of services. In this case, Kent County Council mapped 280 asset and service delivery/access points, tested and geocoded, worked on categorising asset type and service descriptions to provide a common health and social care description.
- The Council identified next stage mapping to include key partner providers such as clinics from Age UK. SHAPE was used to support the development of workplace strategies as part of the Health and Social Care Integration Programme.

Outcome 2 Integrated Emergency Planning
- Asset and service mapping enables Kent County Council to plan a more holistic approach to business continuity and emergency preparedness for extreme events, resilience and climate change adaptation work. A pan-service and cross-sector approach is essential for the development and delivery of effective adaptation and resilience strategies across the health and social care system.
- Work is progressing as part of a multi-agency approach in resilience planning, including identifying vulnerable communities in flood planning and other high risk areas for Kent so that these are considered as part of core plans and organisational risk management and business continuity functions.

Outcome 3 Strategic Commissioning
- The application supported Commissioning Managers, Performance Managers, and Service Improvement Managers. Strategic commissioners used SHAPE as a county level interactive mapping resource, allowing current and future planned services to be presented along with other relevant social care and health activities, and current and projected demographic profiling. This provides Kent County Council with the ability to select relevant data and match it with demographic trends for better strategic planning and market shaping.
- Modelling future planned housing developments and projected client numbers will inform joint service and asset planning with Health and other strategic partners across Adult and Children's Social Care.
- SHAPE was used to support the Good Day Programme, Kent's strategy for improving days for people with learning disabilities. As part of Community Services, Kent County Council mapped specialist community facilities such as Changing Places and Gateway to support plans in meeting the needs of people with a range of disabilities and their carers.
- SHAPE application is to be developed further to include Voluntary Organisations Services, Catchment Areas and the Services Available, Local Population Needs, Demographic Profiling, Risk stratification, and consideration of the impact of Adult and Children's Social Care transformation in Kent.

## Comparison of AEDET Evolution and ASPECT correlations

| AEDET Evolution statement | Correlation | ASPECT Section | Correlation |
|---|---|---|---|
| C1 The building respects the dignity of patients and allows for appropriate levels of privacy and dignity. | 0.5 | C1 | 0.9 |
| C2 There are good views inside and out of the building. | 1.0 | C2 | 0.7 |
| C3 Patients and staff have access to outdoors. | 0.5 | C3 | 0.9 |
| C4 There are high levels of both comfort and control of comfort. | 0.9 | C4 | 0.8 |
| C5 The building is clearly understandable. | −0.2 | C5 | 0.6 |
| C6 The interior of the building is attractive in appearance. | 0.2 | C6 | 0.5 |
| C7 There are good bath/toilet and other facilities for patients. | 0.7 | C7 | 0.7 |
| C8 There are good facilities for staff, including convenient places to work and relax without being on demand. | 0.9 | C8 | 0.8 |
| Overall | 0.5 | | 0.7 |

Working with an 'evidence base' therefore means applying the scientific principles of transparency, validity and reproducibility when assessing and evaluating the evidence. The evidence-based process is often referred to as comprising of five stages: 1. defining the health problem; 2. searching for evidence; 3. assessing the quality of the evidence; 4. implementing the evidence; and 5. monitoring and evaluation.

Similarly for evidence-based design, research evidence deriving from both empirical studies and systematic reviews is invaluable in underpinning the guidance and tools giving them authority, especially when designers are challenged by clinicians whose background and experience is in pure science, where full disclosure is the norm and researchers are expected to document, archive, share all data and the methodology of their studies so that these are available for careful scrutiny by other scientists, giving them the opportunity to verify or validate results by attempting to reproduce them. Conducting original empirical investigations such as Lawson and Phiri (2000), Stigsdotter and Grahn (2002) and Lawson and Phiri (2003) is essential to replenish or increase the number of well-designed scientific studies which indicate the importance of the physical environment on staff and patient health care outcomes. Stigsdotter and Grahn's (2002) study of the outcomes on healing gardens in Scandinavian countries is a useful example of gathering local knowledge. Collating, reviewing, structuring knowledge (Phiri 2006) or compiling/building up electronic databases – for example, the Sheffield Health Care Environment Database – concerns the adoption

of criteria and rigorous standards of hard science: a) rigorous, in that use is made of appropriate research methods that allow reasonable comparisons, and discard alternative hypotheses (the research studies are therefore assessed on their rigour, the quality of the research design and methods, the sample sizes and the degree of control); and b) high impact, in that the outcomes explored are of importance to health care decision-makers, patients, clinicians and society.

In 1992 the Cochrane Collaboration was established with the aim of making up-to-date, accurate information about the effects of health care readily available worldwide. Building up a library of systematic reviews of research evidence has been its greatest achievement. However, in architectural health care design, which lacks centres such as the UK's Cochrane Collaboration and Centre for Review and Dissemination which provide systematic reviews of the effects of health care, it is always going to be a challenge and a daunting task to keep the research evidence up to date. In response to this challenge, the University of Sheffield Health Care Research Group has for sometime promoted itself and sought to develop this role through its three main activities:

1 Conducting original empirical investigations such as Lawson and Phiri (2000, 2003), including carrying out post-project evaluations (incorporating post-occupancy evaluations) of hospitals and other health care facilities – for example, the Evaluation of Evelina Children's Hospital, Guy's and St Thomas' NHS Foundation Trust.

2  Collating, reviewing, structuring knowledge (Phiri 2006), disseminating such knowledge of the crucial role of the physical architectural environment in improving staff and patients outcomes (Lawson & Phiri 2003, Lawson & Wells-Thorpe 2002), and compiling electronic databases – for example, the Sheffield Health Care Environment Database currently under development as 'Healthcare Environment Architectural Resource' (acronym **HEAR**) http://hear.group.shef.ac.uk. This will also eventually be published on the Department of Health website www.spaceforhealth.nhs.uk (accessed 20 August 2012).

3  Developing standards guidance and design tools (such as ASPECT {A Staff/Patient Environment Calibration Tool}/AEDET {Achieving Excellence Design Evaluation Toolkit} Evolution/IDEAs {Inspiring Design Excellence and Achievements}) to aid the design process (Lawson 2007) and support the UK Department of Health Design Quality Improvement agenda.

A review of literature reviews – for example, Reizenstein 1982, Williams 1988, Winkel and Holahan 1985, Olds and Daniel 1987, Shepley, Fournier and McDougall 1998, Shepley and Quan 2003, Devlin and Arneill 2003, Ulrich et al. 2004, Phiri 2006, Dijkstra, Pieterse and Pruyn 2006, Velarde, Fry and Tveit 2007, Rechel, Buchan and McKee 2009, Gulwadi, Joseph and Keller 2009 – are needed to provide evidence of the impact of the physical environment on patient and staff outcomes.

Research is also needed to ensure information is assembled in a format and style that facilitates retrieval, use and updating by practitioners so that it is always relevant to the latest clinical practice and continually responding to changes including technological developments. In 1966 Donabedian introduced concepts of structure, process and outcome, and these remain the dominant paradigm for the evaluation of the quality of health care today. He identified the need in health care to look at quality improvement essentials, i.e. STRUCTURE (which includes the human, physical and financial resources of an organisation), PROCESS (which includes the set of activities and discrete steps in a process), and OUTCOME (the end result of care and service, e.g. length of hospital stay, health state, satisfaction, mortality and morbidity rates etc.). Research is

justified because of the need to link structural and process measures of the health care estate and patient and staff outcomes if there are to be quality improvements in health care (Donabedian 1988).

The growing challenges for all these design tools is that of development work, feedback and redevelopment in the changing wider and broader context. This includes addressing growing concerns about existing standards guidance in health care systems stifling innovation, as well as associated difficulties and inability to raise and sustain both quality and safety in health care facilities. Evidently, we see the existing ensemble of systems and standards guidance being described as incomplete, out-of-date and not adapted to today's National Health Service, and most importantly not appropriate to guide innovation in the future development of the service (Moss et al. 2001).

The greatest need is for a supportive context, framework, model or incentive similar to that provided by national hospital building programmes in which there is development work, feedback and redevelopment of both standards guidance and tools – for example, aiding a large continuous and centrally financed national hospital building programme such as the 1962 'Hospital Plan' initiated by the Bonham Carter Report, which produced the famous Hospital (Health) Building Notes (Ministry of Health 1961), the world's first point of reference in the field of hospital planning. Health Building Notes (HBNs), Health Equipment Notes (HENs), Health Technical Memoranda (HTMs) and Capricode began publication in the 1960s in support of the ten-year programme of hospital building. The Activity DataBase (ADB) and Room Layouts were also developed in the 1960s for the rapid computation of equipment schedules, department plans and whole hospital layouts in support of the hospital building programme set out in the 1962 'Hospital Plan'. Since the 1960s these systems and standards have built up into a 'big-system' of elaborate comprehensive health facility planning information, which requires and relies on heavy and continuous investment in professional work – something which has been lacking in recent years during the age of austerity and times of reducing health care expenditure.

An ageing population, with associated increases in long-term health conditions and disability, is one of the greatest challenges facing the developed world. With people living longer than ever before there has been a dramatic rise in the incidence of chronic diseases, which contribute up to 80% of the total UK health care spending due to declining numbers of economically active people contributing to health and social care finances. The NHS annual expenditure of £136.4 billion in 2009 increased more than tenfold from £11.4 billion in 1948 when the NHS was founded (Office for National Statistics 2012).

To address this, the UK Department of Health's Quality Innovation, Productivity and Prevention (QIPP) initiated and implemented a transformational programme with targets for £20 billion cost savings by 2015. Even with this, the urgent need is for integrated web-enabled, evidence-based health care resource planning tools that are easily accessed via a single domain website, with an integration of all government websites aimed at making public services easier to use. This will provide the necessary justification for investing in the development of tools to help meet the challenges of delivering 'value-for-money' at a time of austerity, dwindling resources and in line with the Government drive for efficiency, effectiveness and innovation. Within the context provided by the prototype single domain alphagov, launched on 11 May 2011 by the Cabinet Office, design tools can build on existing infrastructure and technologies that support mobile working, capitalise on the latest developments in the 'Cloud-Based Information Revolution' and facilitate service data comparisons in an open transparent platform for a variety of audiences.

Tools must also be developed that are rooted in the entire design–build–occupy cycle to acknowledge modelling and measurement of health care service demand and supply, selection of appropriate procurement methods, development of space/costing briefs, design/build and post-project evaluations to aid resource planning, facilities management and maintenance. Ultimately, all this must inevitably be evidenced in improved patients' well-being and health outcomes as well as in enhanced staff productivity.

Clearly when considering evidence-based tools, a key driver is the issue of how the costs of conducting the essential development work, testing and validations associated with the production of relevant up-to-date industry standards and guidance/norms are to be allocated

between the public and private sector. Of importance is addressing the collaboration, communication and coordination necessary because of the demands which arise as a result of the different perceptions and management of responsibilities and risk. Also, the role of certification and assurance systems needs to be clarified, identifying measures to support and incentivise design teams in capturing and sharing evidence, or in knowledge transfer from learning lessons from past projects for the application of new technologies and innovations.

Another driver when looking at tools in health care is the nature of organisational structures and their regulatory health care framework, including whether such a framework monitors and manages change either actively or passively. A smart regulatory framework that recognises and acknowledges the rapid ongoing application of new technologies and innovations while fostering the evidence-based approach is necessarily advocated here to provide adequate safeguards against breaches to safety and poor design solutions, while also offering opportunities for achieving the objectives of the four categories of the design tools.

To better understand and aid individuals with the responsibility of initiating, funding and maintaining health care design tools, four models for the continuous development of smart tools in health care are indicated here. These mirror the models for technical standards guidance or planning and building regulations.

1 Funding and support from public sector organisations (health care providers, national and local authorities), e.g. UK Department of Health, via implementation of Health Policies and Election Manifestos including Hospital Building Programmes (e.g. ASPECT/AEDET, IDEAs, DART, and NEAT) and Local Authorities on Care Homes.

2 Funding and support from private sector organisations (health care providers and other enterprises for profit not controlled by the State), e.g. the BRE (BREEAM) and the Construction Industry Council (e.g. DQI).

3 Funding and support via international institutions and organisations (e.g. the International Standards Organisation, the British Standards Institution – BSI – such as British Standards Online, which facilitates access

to some 55,000 British Standards, self-assessment tools – SATS – on quality, energy, health and safety, data protection and business continuity). Typically an ISO Standard is developed by a panel of experts within a technical committee representing industry, governments and other stakeholders.

4  Various combinations of all of the above.

Decisions as to which model to adopt may not be made consciously or rationally due to consideration with suitable strategic justifications, but often out of political expedience such as the reaction to the 2008 financial crisis and the need to curtail rising health care expenditure.

The UK Department of Health has produced health care guidance and design tools as mechanisms to ensure compliance with health policy requirements and directives. This model has been relatively successful throughout various hospital building programmes which the UK has undertaken, from the hospital plan of the 1960s to the PFI programme of the 2000s. The consequences of abandoning this model are usefully indicated by a Swedish study (Lindahl, Phiri et al. 2010). In Sweden the Healthcare and Social Welfare Planning and Rationalisation Institute (SPRI) was instrumental in this development, producing documents, reports and tools as well as guidelines for health care facility planning. SPRI 1968 to 1995 aimed to support health care planners with quality development, economy and informatics. Although this was a core competence centre for development, effectiveness and processes, it was closed when decentralisation became a more general rule for governing health care planning, with criteria for specific designs left to the individual hospitals. With the abolition of SPRI, national guidelines for health care facilities are no longer produced. Instead, what apply are general guidelines for all buildings and quality standards for health and safety. The absence of tools funded, sponsored or developed by the decentralised Swedish Healthcare System now means a reliance on those that are developed abroad, as opposed to bespoke ones based and derived from the Nordic situation. Hence, for example, statements from the project team: "The New Karolinska Solna will be designed to meet three main environmental assessment certifications: ISO 14001, LEED® and Green Building" (Lindahl, Phiri et al. 2010).

The crucial role of design tools within the context of Hospital Planning Information and Guidance has been acknowledged as a mechanism to facilitate the development or implementation of the design project goals of the Danish Hospital Building Programme 2008–20 for 38 hospital projects. This approach recognises the need for learning lessons and for feedback as well as sharing knowledge while also being able to develop new shared innovative solutions. With this in mind, in 2010 the Danish Regions launched a project to share knowledge with the ultimate goal of strengthening the regions' systematic shared knowledge base of central elements in hospital construction. Where appropriate, the regions would also join together to develop shared solutions for the construction projects.

Benefits and advantages for any individual country developing its own dedicated tools include the ability to relate these to that country's legislation, health care policies, cultural practices, published guides or benchmarks and particular circumstances. It avoids external dependence. However, a decision for the country to develop and maintain its own guidance system and tools can be costly, requiring sustained investment and intellectual expertise. An alternative to this is developing tools via international organisations and aspect, which allows the pooling of financial and intellectual resources to produce guidance/ norms and tools that remain current and technically sound and which can be carried by utilising Standards Organisations. This is often a viable option to avoid duplication, but it also introduces other challenges such as incorporating an evidence base and monitoring regimes from other countries. Wholesale importing of tools without the appropriate infrastructure in terms of monitoring and inspections for compliance in place to enforce them, especially if they are breached or not adhered to, may also result in inappropriate design solutions – for example, USA ASHARE guidance may lead to the creation of deep plan buildings in places where they may not be suitable, while CIBSE guides may contradict local building regulations.

Yet another alternative to public sector funding and sponsorship to develop design tools is that provided by the private sector organisations, for example the Environment Assessment Methods such as BREEAM, LEED™ and others

**Table 6.2 Hospital planning information and guidance underpinning the Danish Hospital Building Programme 2008–20 for 38 hospital projects (source: Office for Health and Social Politics, Danish Regions 2012)**

| Adjustment of the Dimensioning of the individual projects: |
| --- |

| Area: | • Gross/netto factor = 2.0 for Somatik, 1.8 for Psychiatry.<br>• Norm for floor area in patient single rooms (33–35m²). |
| --- | --- |
| Capacity: | • Projection of Need = Reduction in beds -> 20% and increase in number of outpatients visits with 50% in the period from 2007-2020. |

| General Adaption of the Area by 20%: |
| --- |

- Enhanced requirements for capacity utilisation (e.g. time for operating the hospital 245 days/7 hours).
- Building flexibly rather than building large.

| The economy of the project is to be adapted to Permanent Standards: |
| --- |

- New construction of university hospitals on green field 29.000 d.kr./m² (incl. 25% for information technology, scanners, and equipment).
- Other new construction and extension 27.000 d.kr./m² (incl. 20% for information technology, scanners, and equipment).
- Psychiatric building projects 22.000 d.kr./m².
- Conversion projects – reduced by 20%.

| Locked total Frames: |
| --- |

- The total frame for the building projects is locked.
- The regions are not allowed to put any further money into the building projects.
- Have to build exactly the number of square metres that is indicated in the commitment from the government.
- Allowed to build more than m² – but not fewer.
- Square metre price is fixed.
- 20–25% to IT, apparatus and equipment is tied to a specific definition.
- 70% of this frame has to be used on Patient-Centred Equipment.

| Eight focus areas for developing content for the new hospitals: |
| --- |

- Organisational structure with the patients' needs in the centre.
- New forms of management.
- Boundaries and interaction with the other parts of the healthcare sector.
- Emergency Departments and organising acute treatment/care.
- Easy and quick access to Diagnostics in hospitals.
- Workflows in Operating Rooms.
- Workflows in Day clinics/Outpatient clinics.
- Offices and mobile working stations.

incorporating registration and certification. Registration and certification bring with them assurance by another party that a certain process (e.g. evidence of sustainability considerations, quality assurance and expert audition) has been followed to achieve the outcomes. However, to ensure rigour and verification, the training of health care assessors and technical support regimes are established with registration fees levied from users to recover costs. Fees, registration and access via assessors are an obstacle which means that the tools (methodologies, data and evaluations) are not freely available to potential users. Furthermore, unlike in the public sector, the drive for private sector organisations to make a profit means that they may be unwilling to share knowledge, and they may be more likely to adopt practices and act to protect their intellectual property as a way to maintain an advantage over their competitors. Nonetheless, the system of registration and building certification offers advantages in terms of a level of continuous renting, income from renting, and selling price aspects which facilitate private sector involvement. In turn this allows continuous development of the tool using the funds obtained from fees for managing the tool, for registration and training of assessors, and from proceeds from marketing.

Adopting an approach which involves collaborations between both public and private sector organisations is far more attractive and is likely to yield or achieve more benefits while overcoming the individual shortcomings of either a public or private sector focus. Public sector involvement ensures relevance to government health policies despite risks from the fragility of health policies, while the private sector can bring private capital or investment and be seen as more efficient and better in delivering services than the public sector. Such an arrangement still requires the introduction of safeguards to avoid situations where tools are developed as mechanisms to generate profits without delivering their objectives – for example, design quality improvement or reduction in waste and $CO_2$ emissions.

All these issues and considerations represent important areas for further research studies from which to develop a suitable roadmap towards achieving success in the health care estate. Well-designed longitudinal studies are needed under all the four categories, namely Compliance with Statutory or Regulatory Requirements, Design Quality Improvement, Enhancing Efficiency and Effectiveness, and Achieving Sustainability in the health facility design. Specifically, it is essential to demonstrate in each case the changes that can be or have been achieved, the extent of improvement and to answer long-term questions about the delivery of their aims and objectives. The mandatory status afforded tools such as ASPECT/AEDET Evolution and BREEAM Healthcare 2008 within the UK procurement system has yet to be justified despite the 2000s PFI hospital building programme involving over 75 health care projects. AEDET data or results for these projects as they underwent the NHS Design Reviews before sign off by the Department of Health can be collated, analysed and interrogated to provide a baseline to examine the impact of AEDET. Therefore, unless we can demonstrate that these tools are achieving their intended goal it is difficult to justify their continued support and funding or investment.

# References

Devlin AS, and Arneill AB (2003) Healthcare environments and patient outcomes, a review of literature. *Environment and Behavior*, 35, 665–694.

Dijkstra K, Pieterse M, and Pruyn A (2006) Physical environment stimuli that turn healthcare facilities into healing environments through psychologically mediated effects: A systematic review. *Journal of Advanced Nursing*, 56, 166–181.

Donabedian A (1966) Evaluating the quality of medical care. *Milbank Quarterly*, 44, 166–206.

Donabedian A (1988) The quality of care: How can it be assessed? *JAMA*, September 23, 260 (12), 1743–1748.

Gulwadi GB, Joseph A, and Keller AB (2009) Exploring the impact of the physical environment of patients' outcomes in Ambulatory Care Settings. *Health Environmental Research & Design Journal (HERD)*, 2 (2 – Winter), 21–41.

Lawson BR (2007) Design indicators. In Stark D, *UK Healthcare Design Review*. Glasgow, Keppie Design, 88–95.

Lawson BR, and Phiri M (2000) Room for improvement. *Health Service Journal*, 110, 24–27.

Lawson BR, and Phiri M (2003) *The Architectural Healthcare Environment and its Effects on Patient Health Outcomes*. London TSO ISBN 0-11-322480-X.

Lawson BR, and Wells-Thorpe J (2002) The effect of the hospital environment on the patient experience and health outcomes. *The Journal of Healthcare Design and Development*, March, 27–32.

Lindhal G, Phiri M, Mills G, Fröst P, Strid M, and Price ADF (2010) *Quality Innovation and Evidence in Healthcare Physical Environments in England & Sweden – Establishing a Collaborative Roadmap*. 3rd Annual Conference of the Health and Care Infrastructure Research and Innovation Centre (HaCIRIC10): *Better healthcare through better infrastructure* – 22–24 September 2010 Edinburgh, Scotland pp. 6–16.

Moss R et al. (2001) *Rationalising Health Building Design: A Feasibility Study*. NHS Estates 2001.

Phiri M (2006) *Does the Physical Environment Affect Staff and Patient Health Outcomes? A Review of Studies and Articles 1965–2006*. London, TSO.

Office for National Statistics (2012) Expenditure on Healthcare in the UK – 1997–2010 http://www.ons.gov.

uk/ons/search/index.html?pageSize=50&sortBy=none &sortDirection=none&newquery (Accessed 15 August 2012).

Olds A, and Daniel P (1987) *Child Health Care Facilities: Design Guidelines – Literature Outline*. Bethesda, MD: Association for the Care of Children's Health.

Rechel B, Buchan J, and McKee M (2009) The impact of health facilities on healthcare workers' wellbeing and performance. *International Journal of Nursing Studies* 46, 1025–1034.

Reizenstein JE (1982) Hospital design and human behaviour: A review of the recent literature. In Baum A, and Singer JE (eds) *Advances in Environmental Psychology, Vol. 4, Environment and Health*. Hillsdale, NJ: Lawrence Erlbaum Associates.

Rollins JA (2004) Evidence-based hospital design improves healthcare outcomes for patients, families and staff. *Pediatric Nursing*, 30 (4), 338–339.

Rubin HR, Owens AJ, and Golden G (1998) Status Report: An investigation to determine whether the built environment affects patients' medical outcomes. Martinez CA: The Center for Health Design.

Sackett DL, Rosenberg WMC, Gray JAM, Haynes RB, and Richardson WS (1996) Evidence Based Medicine. *British Medical Journal*, 313 (7050), 170–171.

Shepley MM, and Quan X (2003) Health design research literature review: 1998–2002. Unpublished paper, Texas A&M University College Station TX.

Shepley MM, Fournier M-A, and McDougall K (1998) *Healthcare Environments for Children and their Families*. Dubuque: IO Kendal Hunt.

Stigsdotter UA, and Grahn P (2002) What makes a garden a healing garden? *Journal of Therapeutic Horticulture*, 8, 60–69.

Ulrich RS, Zimring C, Quan X, and Joseph A (2004) The Role of the Physical Environment in the Hospital of the 21st Century: A Once-in-a-lifetime Opportunity. Concord CA: The Center for Health Design.

Ulrich RS, Zimring CM, Zhu X, DuBose J, Seo H, Choi Y-S, Quan X, and Joseph A (2008) A review of the research literature on evidence-based healthcare design. *Health Environments Research and Design Journal*, 1 (3 – Spring), 61–125.

Velarde MD, Fry G, and Tveit M (2007) Health effects of viewing landscapes – landscapes in environmental psychology. *Urban Forestry & Greening*, 6, 199–212.

Williams MA (1988) The physical environment and patient care. *Annual Review of Nursing Research*, 6, 61–84

Williams MA (1989) Physical environment of the intensive care unit and elderly patients. *Critical Care Nursing Quarterly* 12 (1), 52–60.

Winkel GH, and Holahan CJ (1985) The environmental psychology of the hospital: Is the cure worse than the illness? *Prevention in Human Services*, 4, 11–13.

# Appendix

**Table 7.1** Reviews of literature reviews on the effects of the architectural environment on staff and patient health outcomes

|  | Outcome measures | Author's Conclusions |
|---|---|---|
| Devlin & Arneill 2003 | Depression, delirium, passivity, stress, elevated blood pressure, reduced immune system functioning, staff and patient satisfaction, pain, heart rate, level of functioning for patients and other outcome measures associated with 1. Patient involvement with healthcare (e.g. the role of patient control to increase their freedom of choice of daily rituals and to allow them access to education and information), 2.The impact of ambient environment (e.g. sound, light and art), 3. The emergence of specialised building types for defined or special populations (e.g. Alzheimer's patients) | Devlin and Arneill 2003 explored the literature on healthcare environments and their impact on patient outcomes. The review concluded that the body of literature is diverse in terms of focus and findings. Although the early research focused on the hospital environment, more recent research has examined a range of health facilities from ambulatory care centres, outpatient, elderly care facilities to Alzheimer's units. Researchers have examined the influence of such topics as ambient stressors (e.g. noise) nature and patient control. The research has been done by leaders in many fields including architecture, consulting, healthcare and psychology. Despite the progress that is being made, with some foundations supporting the process, the research is still accumulating and gaps do exist – some of them related to the difficult of conducting this research. |
| Dijkstra, Pieterse & Pruyn 2006 | Health- and behaviour-related outcome measures and those regarding appraisal of the physical environment of entire wards. Outcome measures relating to appraisal of the physical environment and patient's rating of their physician of treatment areas. Positive effects of waiting rooms; Effects on the length of stay, mortality rate, perceived stress and pain of ambient features (sunlight, sound, odour); of architectural features (windows, spatial layout) and of interior design features (nature, television, seating arrangements) | Dijkstra, Pieterse & Pruyn 2006 identified over500 potentially relevant studies and 30 met all criteria; 11 appeared to study a simultaneous manipulation of multiple environmental stimuli such as colour, art, plants, gardens, carpeting and room size. The systematic review to determine the effects of physical stimuli in healthcare settings on health and well-being of patients concluded that studies that manipulate several environmental stimuli simultaneously clearly support the general notion that the physical healthcare environment affects the well-being of patients. However, when scrutinizing the effects of specific environmental stimuli, conclusive evidence was still very limited and difficult to generalise. The field was in urgent need of well-conducted clinical trials. On the basis of the available research the review concluded that it would be premature to formulate evidence-based guidelines for designing healthcare environments. |

| | Outcome measures | Author's Conclusions |
|---|---|---|
| Gulwadi Joseph & Keller 2009 | Patient experience<br>Improved access and wayfinding<br>Enhanced waiting experience<br>Enhanced privacy<br>Enhanced physician/staff-patient communication<br>Reduced patient anxiety and<br>Reduced risk of infection | Given the range of Ambulatory Care Centres (surgery, community health, family planning, emergency and outpatient, outpatient clinics etc.) and population types and the paucity of literature focused on any one of these settings, the literature search process was broad-based to include not only peer-reviewed literature, but also "gray literature" on Ambulatory Care Centres design. The primary focus was on research studies and reports that centred on some aspect of the physical environment in Ambulatory Care Centres and their relationship to the physical environment in these settings. An initial set of key words was used to obtain the first round of articles from the Centre for Health Design databases and other common online databases (e.g. PubMed, Scirus, and Medline). Key words used alone and in various combinations include: ambulatory care, outpatient, clinic, community health centers, design, staff outcomes, patient outcomes, pain, anxiety, satisfaction, distress, waiting areas, medical home model and Health Insurance Portability and Accountability Act. The review identified physical design features of Ambulatory Care Centres that can promote favourable patient outcomes. However, most literature reviewed adheres to a physician-centred model of episodic illness in which care ends with the experience in the examination room of the Ambulatory Care Centre. A more patient-centred approach has not been explored fully in literature. The results indicate that there are many opportunities for future enquiry. |
| Olds & Daniel 1987 | The impact, i.e. positive contributions of :- Site, building exterior, external circulation and parking, approach and entry; Reception/ registration /admission; corridors & circulation; waiting, transition; spiritual support; patient units; bedrooms; bathrooms; critical & neonatal intensive care; isolation; outdoor play; classrooms Walls, ceilings, floors, windows; Light and lighting, acoustics and thermal; Colour; Heat and ventilation; Signage and graphics; Furnishings and equipment; Storage and display | Olds & Daniel 1987 sought reference which dealt primarily with children the physical environment and healthcare settings. The manual and computerised searches found that the majority of published work is observations, beliefs, suggestions, anecdotal evidence, best practice and other writings, which are not based on properly, conducted empirical research. These include descriptive articles, guidelines deriving from the author's professional experience, historical or futuristic resources, in which the author takes a backward or forward look at the subject matter in order to document historical trends or predict future changes and theoretical approach. Descriptive papers are the most prevalent, and simply "show and tell" claiming positive features of the design although in most cases without and supporting empirical evidence for the claims or conclusions. |

| | Outcome measures | Author's Conclusions |
|---|---|---|
| Phiri 2006 | Infection<br>Accidents (slips, trips and falls)<br>Medical errors, medication errors and adverse events<br>Violence and damage to property<br>Views, nature and outdoors | Phiri 2006 review sought evidence which address the UK NHS situation. The review identified the main pertinent issues and key dimensions: the physical environment is taken as given and often considered an irrelevance; there is an urgent need to lobby for and to increase awareness of, the importance of physical environment in healthcare; accessibility of the evidence from research findings is limited; and there are some methodological issues associated with studies. The evidence is the result of many different and often conflicting agendas, the result of different and varying funding priorities by funding agencies. There are problems with obtaining independent verification of findings from studies and experiments. The need is to continuously update the evidence to make it more relevant and responsive to changing technological developments. |
| Rechel, Buchan & McKee 2009 | Three broad categories<br>1. The impact of design on staff well-being<br>2. The impact of design on staff performance<br>3. Involvement of healthcare workers in the design of new facilities | As part of a larger study on investing in hospitals of the future, Rechel, Buchan & McKee 2009 reviewed published literature, identified through PubMed and Google as well as through searches of websites of relevant organisations such as World Health Organisation and International Council of Nurses. The initial PubMed search yielded 1058 hits. Titles and abstracts were reviewed and studies included when they met criteria of: - being published between 1985 and March 2008; English language; relating to the impact of facility design on healthcare workforce, and original research articles, literature reviews or conceptual or case studies. The review identified 33 studies from which 6 design factors emerge that impact on staff working in health facilities:- Location; 2. Hospital experience; 3. Access to personal space; 4. Choice of materials; 5. Creation of a safe environment and 6. Recognizing that many staff has family commitments. Better health facilities are therefore located near where staff live, provide sufficient daylight and ventilation and minimise walking distances. Studies identified in this paper often draw on single case studies, small, non-representative surveys of healthcare workers or before-after comparisons. What is lacking are more rigorous evaluations of the impact of health facilities on healthcare workers. |
| Reizenstein 1982 | The effects of hospital design on human behaviour | Reizenstein 1982 summarised the characteristics of literature on hospital design and human behaviour and concluded that those who make decisions in healthcare facilities tend to not to use the research that exists. The research was scattered widely, creating problems of utilisation and more came from the UK than USA. It contained more empirical work on non-acute hospitals, especially psychiatric ones, than on acute-care hospitals. The papers were divided equally between empirical and non-empirical studies and were varying quality, many anecdotal. Empirical included a variety of variables but potentially important ones remain unexamined. |

| | Outcome measures | Author's Conclusions |
|---|---|---|
| Rubin Owen & Golden 1998 | Impact of the physical environment on patient and staff outcomes | Rubin Owen & Golden 1998 reviewed 78,761 articles and based on their inclusion criteria for good design methodology found that only 84 met with the rigorous standards of hard science. Even the two well-known studies those by Ulrich 1984 about the positive effect of views of nature from patients recovering from surgery and Miller et al 1995 about premature babies who gained weight when their hospital stay used light cycled on diurnal patterns were subject to criticism. Studies with less rigorous methodology tended to show more positive results than more rigorously controlled studies. |
| Shepley & Quan 2003 | Impact on infants (developmental issues) and staff (stress issues) of environmental dimensions (light, noise, music, visual and spatial environment, and colour) | Shepley & Quan 2003 conducted a broader review similar to that of Rubin and her associates for 1998 and 2002 in which the search was expanded to include a variety of nursing, engineering and medical journals. The review examined 2000 papers and 35 were identified as being appropriate for inclusion using criteria similar to that of Rubin/Owen literature review. |
| Shepley, Fournier & McDougall 1998 | Impact on infants and staff of environmental dimensions (light, noise, music, visual and spatial environment, and colour); Family experience (e.g. parental role alteration), staff experience (e.g. satisfaction due the quality of family-infant and staff relations, sense of success etc.), visiting and Infection control | Shepley, Fournier & McDougall 1998 reviewed literature on children's facilities and found 277 studies focusing on paediatric healthcare facilities by identifying those publications that were descriptive (77), guidelines (7), literature reviews(13) and 'scientific studies' based on genuine qualitative and quantitative studies (50). The qualitative and quantitative studies represented only 18% of all publications. Of this total, 32 out of 277 studies (11.5%) addressed paediatric (PICU) and neonatal intensive care (NICU) units. |
| Ulrich et al 2004 | Patient falls\nHealthcare-acquired infections\nMedical errors\nNoise levels | A commission by the Robert Wood Foundation allowed Ulrich & Zimring 2004 to carry out an in-depth literature review similar to that conducted by Rubin and her associates in 1998. The review identified 650 scientific studies relating to how the design of hospital physical environments affects outcomes. The report summarise the strong evidence indicating that hospital design can promote healing by reducing patient falls, healthcare-acquired infections, medical errors and noise levels among other variables. |
| Ulrich Zimring et al 2008 | Patient safety issues (infections, medical errors and falls); Other patient outcomes (pain, sleep, stress, depression, length of stay, spatial orientation, privacy, communication, social support and overall patient satisfaction); Staff outcomes (injuries, stress, work effectiveness and satisfaction) | Overall, this review confirms the importance of improving the healthcare outcomes associated with a range of design characteristics or interventions such as single-bed rooms rather than multi-bed rooms, effective ventilation systems, a good acoustic environment, appropriate lighting, better ergonomic design and improved floor layouts and work settings.\nCompared to 2004 the body of evidence has grown rapidly and substantially. |

| | Outcome measures | Author's Conclusions |
|---|---|---|
| Velarde, Fry & Tveit 2007 | Three main kinds of health effects: 1. Short-term recovery from stress or mental fatigue (e.g. reduced stress, improved attentional capacity); 2. Faster physical recovery from illness, 3. Long-term overall improvement on people's health and well-being (e.g. ameliorating physical well-being in the elderly and behavioural changes that improve mood and general well-being) Addressed by means of viewing natural landscapes during a walk, view from a window, looking at a picture or a video or experiencing vegetation around residential or work environments. | Velarde, Fry & Tveit 2007 conducted a literature review of publications linking landscapes and health effects and identified 31 studies. The review found that the landscapes used studies were described loosely and in coarse categories mainly reflecting a broad "nature" versus "urban" dichotomy. Much less information was provided regarding specific landscape elements, structures and patterns within the urban and natural categories. Most studies (74%) do not report measurements on respondents from before the exposure to the landscape stimuli and therefore produce only relative values. These studies indicate that viewing a natural scene produces a positive health effect compared with viewing an urban scene, but fail to confirm the magnitude of the change or whether the effect of viewing the urban scene is negative or merely negative. Despite major advances in our understanding of the relationship between landscapes and human health one key question remains- What are the particular qualities of restorative landscapes? |
| Williams 1988 | The effects of physical environment on patient care<br>Patient recovery<br>Stress<br>Sleep | Williams 1988 found that the literature from which relevant research could be drawn is voluminous because the topical areas (such as hospital and unit design, sound light, colour, temperature and weather) are all part of the broad field of environment and behaviour. A typical research approach involves isolating an environmental variable, such as sound, and examining it to see if it negatively or positively affects certain aspects of patients' outcomes. The author concludes the review of the research linking the physical environmental factors and patient care by suggesting that the physical environment has commanded little attention from nurse researchers mainly because the physical environment has been incorporated minimally into main stream of Behavioural Science where much of the nursing literature is drawn from. Also there is limited empirical research by nurses. |
| Winkel & Holahan 1985 | Psychological and social problems encountered by patients in acute care and psychiatric institutions | Winkel & Holahan 1986 summarised the evidence bearing on the critical role that the physical environment plays in the prevention and reduction of psychological and social problems encountered by patients in acute care and psychiatric institutions They concluded that all too often the physical environment represents one of the most neglected and hidden components of prevention and care. The factors that prevent greater attention to environmental quality must be sought in organisational, structural and philosophical orientations to illness and injury. |

# Acronyms

| | |
|---|---|
| ADB | **A**ctivity **D**ata**B**ase |
| AEDET | **A**chieving **E**xcellence **D**esign **E**valuation **T**oolkit |
| ASPECT | **A S**taff/**P**atient **E**nvironment **C**alibration **T**ool |
| BOT | **B**uild **O**perate Transfer |
| BREEAM | **B**ritish **R**esearch **E**stablishment **E**nvironmental **A**ssessment **M**ethod |
| CABE | Commission for Architecture and the Built Environment |
| CEEQUAL | Civil Engineering Environmental Quality Assessment and Award Scheme |
| CIAMS | Commissioners' Investment and Asset Management Strategy |
| CIBSE TM22 | Chartered Institution of Building Services Engineers **E**nergy **A**ssessment & **R**eporting **M**ethodology (EARM™) |
| CIC | Construction Industry Council |
| DBO | Design Build Operate |
| DBOT | Design Build Operate Transfer |
| DEEP | **D**esign **E**xcellence **E**valuation **P**rocess (Ministry of Defence) |
| DQI | **D**esign **Q**uality **I**ndicator |
| EBD | Evidence-Based Design |
| ERIC | Estates Return Information Collection |
| HBN | Health Building Notes |
| HES | Hospital Episode Statistics |
| HRG | Healthcare Research Group |
| HTM | Health Technical Memoranda |
| IDEAs | **I**nspiring **D**esign **E**xcellence **A**chievements |
| KPI | Key Performance Indicators |
| LEED® | **L**eadership in **E**nergy and **E**nvironmental **D**esign |
| LIFT | Local Improvement Finance Trust |
| NEAT | **N**HS **E**nvironmental **A**ssessment **T**ool |
| NHS | National Health Service UK |
| ODS | Organisation Data Service |

| | |
|---|---|
| OGC | Office of Government Commerce |
| ONS | Office of National Statistics |
| PAM | **P**remises **A**ssurance **M**odel |
| PFI | Private Finance Initiative |
| PPP | Public Private Partnership |
| QIPP | Quality, Innovation, Productivity, Prevention |
| RIBA | Royal Institute of British Architects |
| SHAPE | **S**trategic **H**ealth **A**sset **P**lanning and **E**valuation |

# Bibliography

Alexander C, Ishikawa S, Silverstein M, with Jacobson M, Fiksdahl-King I, and Angel S (1977) *A Pattern Language: Towns, Buildings, Construction.* Oxford University Press, New York.

Baird CL, and Bell PA (1995) Place Attachment, Isolation and the Power of a Window in a Hospital Environment: A Case Study. *Psychological Reports,* 76, 847–850.

Beauchemin KM and Hays P (1996) Sunny hospital rooms expedite recovery from severe and refractory depressions. *Journal of Affective Disorders,* 40, 49–51.

Bernaldez FG, Gallardo D, and Abello RP (1987) Children's landscape preferences: From rejection to attraction. *Journal of Environmental Psychology,* 7, 169–176.

Berry LL, Parker D, Coile RC Jr., Kirk-Hamilton D, O'Neill DD, and Sadler BL (2004) The Business Case for Better Buildings. *Frontiers of Health Services Management,* 21(1), 3–24.

Blankson EJ and Green BH (1991) Use of landscape classification as an essential prerequisite to landscape evaluation. *Landscape and Planning,* 21, 149–176.

BMJ Editorial (1976) Nucleus Hospitals. *British Medical Journal,* 31 January 1976, 245–246

Campbell MI (1984) *Hospital patient room: A design and planning study.* Unpublished graduate research project at Syracuse University, US, p. 100.

Capper G, Holmes J, Hudson G, and Currie JI (2005) The use of an environmental assessment tool in healthcare buildings. The 2005 World Sustainable Building Conference, Tokyo, 27-29 September 2005 (SB05Tokyo) www.irbnet.de/daten/iconda/CIB3738.pdf [Accessed 1 July 2012].

CIBSE (2010) *Energy Assessment and Reporting Methodology* 2nd Edition (inc. CD-ROM). London, UK.

CIBSE TM22, and Field J, Soper J, Jones P, Bordass W, and Grigg P (1997) Energy performance of occupied non-domestic buildings assessment by analysing end-use energy consumptions. *Building Services Engineering Research and Technology,* 18 (1), 39–46.

Cox A, and Groves P (1990) *Design for Health Care.* Butterworth-Heinemann Ltd, London, ISBN-10: 0408003898.

Darzi L (2008) Our NHS Our Future. http://www.ournhs.nhs.uk/ [Accessed May 2012].

Department of Health/NHS Finance, Performance & Operations (2009) *The Operating Framework in NHS in England 2010/11.*

Department of Trade and Industry (DTI) (2001) *Better Public Buildings.* London, UK.

Devlin AS, and Arneill AB (2003) Healthcare environments and patient outcomes: A review of literature. *Environment and Behavior* 35, 665–694.

Dijkstra K, Pieterse M, and Pruyn A (2006) Physical environment stimuli that turn healthcare facilities into healing environments through psychologically mediated effects: A systematic review. *Journal of Advanced Nursing,* 56, 166–181.

Donabedian A, (1966) Evaluating the quality of medical care. *Milbank Quarterly,* 44, 166–206.

Donabedian A (1978) The Quality of Medical Care. *Science,* 200 (4344), 856–864.

Donabedian A (1988) The quality of care: How it can be assessed? *JAMA,* September 23, 260 (12), 1743–1748.

Egan J (1998) *Rethinking Construction.* Department of the Environment, Transport and the Regions (DETR), London.

Falk SA, and Woods NF (1973) Hospital noise-levels and potential health hazards. *New England Journal of Medicine,* 289 (15), 774–781.

Field J, and CIBSE TM22 (2006) *Energy Assessment and Reporting Method.* The Chartered Institution of Building Services Engineers Publications, London UK, ISBN-10: 1-903287-60-X and ISBN-13: 978-1-903287-60-6.

Fisk WJ (2000) Health and productivity gains from better indoor environments and their relationship with building energy efficiency. Indoor Environment Department, Environmental Energy Technologies Division, Lawrence Berkeley National Laboratory, Berkeley, California, *Annual Review of Energy and the Environment,* 25 (2000), 537–66.

Gann DW, Slater AJ, and Whyte JK (2003) Design Quality Indicators: Tools for thinking. *Building Research & Information,* 31 (5), 318–333.

Gesler W, Bell M, Curtis S, Hubbard P & Francis S (2004) Therapy by Design: Evaluating the UK hospital building program. *Health and Place,* 10, 117–128.

Gimblett HR (1990) Environmental cognition: The prediction of preference in rural Indiana. *Journal of Architectural and Planning Research,* 7 (3), 222–234.

Great Britain, Ministry of Health, National Health Service (1962) *A Hospital Plan.* HMSO, London.

Great Britain, Ministry of Health, National Health Service (1966) *The Hospital Building Programme.* HMSO, London.

Gulwadi GB, Joseph A, and Keller AB (2009) Exploring the impact of the physical environment of patients' outcomes in Ambulatory Care Settings. *Health Environmental Research & Design Journal (HERD),* 2 (2 – Winter), 21–41.

Hamilton KD (2003) The Four Levels of Evidence-Based Practice. *Healthcare Design,* 3 (4), 18–26.

Hamilton KD (2008) Evidence is found in many domains. *HERD: Health Environments Research & Design Journal,* 1 (3), 5–6.

Herzog TR (1985) A cognitive analysis of preference for waterscapes. *Journal of Environmental Psychology,* 5, 225–241.

Herzog TR (1989) A cognitive analysis of preference for urban nature. *Journal of Environmental Psychology,* 9, 27–43.

Hignett S and Lu J (2009) An investigation of the use of Health Building Notes by UK healthcare building designers. *Applied Ergonomics,* 40 (4), 608–616 (http://www.sciencedirect.com/science/journal/00036870/40/4 [Accessed May 2012]).

Hodgson RW, and Thayer RL (1980) Implied human influence reduces landscape beauty. *Landscape Planning,* 7, 171–179.

Hosking S, and Haggard L (1999) *Healing the Hospital Environment: Design, Maintenance and Management of Healthcare Premises.* E & FN Spon, London, ISBN 0419231706.

Hull RB, and Revell GR (1989) Cross-cultural comparison of landscape scenic beauty evaluations: A study in Bali. *Journal of Environmental Psychology,* 9, 177–191.

Jesinghaus J (2000) On the Art of Aggregating Apples and Oranges. Working Paper, Fondazione Eni Enrico Mattei, Milan, Italy.

Kaplan A (1964) *The Conduct of Inquiry: Methodology for Behavioral Science.* Chandler, New York.

Kaplan S, and Kaplan R (1989) *The Experience of Nature: A Psychological Perspective.* New York: Cambridge University Press.

LaFratta A (2006) An investigation into multi-activity generic spaces in the design of healthcare facilities. Unpublished MSc Dissertation, Loughborough University.

Lawson BR (2001) *A Language of Space*. The Architectural Press, Oxford, UK.

Lawson BR (2002) Healing Architecture. *The Architectural Review* CCXI (1261), 72–75.

Lawson BR (2005) Evidence-Based Design for Healthcare. In *Hospital Engineering and Facilities Management 2005*, W. Swaby, London, International Federation of Hospital Engineering, 25–27.

Lawson BR (2007) Design indicators. In Stark D, *UK Healthcare Design Review*. Keppie Design, Glasgow, 88–95.

Lawson BR and Phiri M (2000) Room for improvement. *Health Service Journal,* 110 (5688), 24–27.

Lawson BR and Phiri M (2003) *The Architectural Healthcare Environment and its Effects on Patient Health Outcomes*. TSO, London, ISBN 0-11-322480-X (reprinted January 2004).

Lawson BR and Phiri M (2004) AEDET Evolution: Learning from the evidence base of NHS design. Report by the University of Sheffield School of Architecture, UK.

Lawson BR, Bassanino M, Phiri M et al. (2003) Intentions, practices and aspirations: Understanding learning in design. *Design Studies,* 24 (4), 327–339.

Lawson BR, Bassanino M, Phiri M et al. (2003) Intentions, practices and aspirations. *Design Studies* 24 (4), 327–339.

Lawson BR and Phiri M, in collaboration with Wells-Thorpe J (2003) The Architectural Healthcare Environment and its Effect on Patient Health Outcomes: A Report on an NHS Estates Funded Research Project. The Stationery Office, London, 2003, 1–22, ISBN 0-11-322480-X.

Lawson BR, Phiri M, and Wells-Thorpe J (2003) *The Architectural Health Care Environment and its Effects on Patient Health Outcomes*. London TSO ISBN 978 0113 224 807 (Reprinted January 2004).

Lawson BR, and Wells-Thorpe J (2002) The effect of the hospital environment on the patient experience and health outcomes. *The Journal of Healthcare Design and Development*, March, 27–32.

Lee W, and Burnett J (2007) Benchmarking energy use assessment of HK-BEAM, BREEAM and LEED. *Building and Environment* 43 (11), 1882–1891.

Lindhal G, Phiri M, Mills G, Fröst P, Strid M, and Price ADF (2010) *Quality Innovation and Evidence in Healthcare*

*Physical Environments in England & Sweden – Establishing a Collaborative Roadmap.* 3rd Annual Conference of the Health and Care Infrastructure Research and Innovation Centre (HaCIRIC10): *Better healthcare through better infrastructure* . 22–24 September 2010 Edinburgh, Scotland pp. 6–16.

Martin C (2000) Putting patients first: Integrating hospital design and care. *The Lancet*, 356 (August), 518.

Matthiessen LF, and Morris P (2004) Costing Green: A Comprehensive Cost Database and Budgeting methodology. Los Angeles: Davis Langdon.

McCormick M and Shepley MM (2003) How can consumers benefit from therapeutic environments? *Journal of Architectural and Planning Research*, 20 (1), 4–15.

Moss R et al. (2001) *Rationalising Health Building Design: A Feasibility Study*. NHS Estates 2001.

National Audit Office (2005) *Improving Public Services Through Better Construction*. http://www.nao/org.uk/wp-content/uploads/2005/03/0405364es.pdf) [Accessed 10 August 2014].

National Audit Office (2007) *Building for the Future: Sustainable Construction and Refurbishment on the Government Estate*. Report by the Comptroller and Auditor General, HC324, April 2007.

New Buildings Institute (ed.) (2003) *Integrated energy systems – productivity and building science*. Final report prepared for California Energy Commission, Public Interest Energy Research Program.

NHS Estates (1994) *Better by Design: Pursuit of Excellence in Healthcare Buildings*. Leeds, UK.

NHS Estates (2002) Achieving Excellence Design Evaluation Toolkit – AEDET. Leeds, UK.

NHS Estates (2002) *Improving the Patient Experience: The Art of Good Health: A Practical Handbook*. The Stationery Office, London, UK.

NHS Estates, Department of Trade and Industry (DTI), Department of Health (DH) (2002) NEAT (NHS Environmental Assessment Tool). London, UK.

NHS Estates Design Brief Working Group (Chairman: Richard Burton) (2002) Advice to Trusts on the main components of the design brief for healthcare buildings. Leeds, UK.

NHS Information Centre for Health and Social Care (2010) Hospital Episode Statistics: HES User Guide (http://www.hesonline.nhs.uk) [Accessed August 2012].

NHS Premises Assurance Model Website: http://www.dh.gov.uk/en/Publicationsandstatistics/Publications/Publications PolicyAndGuidance/DH_128702 [Accessed May 2012].

Nicklas MH, and Bailey GB (1996) Analyses of the performance of students in day lit schools. *Innovative Design*, Raleigh, NC.

Nordh H, Hartig T, Hagerhall CM, and Fry G (2009) Components of small urban parks that predict the possibility for restoration. *Urban Forestry & Urban Greening*, 8, 225–235.

Office for National Statistics (2012) Expenditure on Healthcare in the UK – 1997–2010 http://www.ons.gov.uk/ons/search/index.tml?pageSize=50&sortBy=none&sortDirection=none&newquery [Accessed 15 August 2012].

O'Keeffe DJ (2008) Facilitating the design quality of hospitals by using AEDET (Achieving Excellence Design Evaluation Toolkit). Unpublished MBA Dissertation, College of Estate Management/University of Reading.

Olds A, and Daniel P (1987) *Child Health Care Facilities: Design Guidelines – Literature Outline*. Bethesda, MD: Association for the Care of Children's Health.

Patsfall MR, Feimer NR, Buyhoff GJ, and Wellman JD (1984) The prediction of scenic beauty from landscape content and composition. *Journal of Environmental Psychology*, 4, 7–26.

Phiri M (2002) *Sheffield Architectural Environment and Patient Outcomes Database: Design and User Manual*. School of Architecture, University of Sheffield, UK.

Phiri M (2006) *Does the Physical Environment Affect Staff and Patient Health Outcomes? A Review of Studies and Articles 1965–2006*. London, UK: TSO.

Phiri M, Mills GR, Chang C-L, and Price ADF (2011) *Evidence-Based Design: Refurbishment & Reconfiguration of the Healthcare Estate to Enhance Compliance with Standards and Tools to Optimise Innovation*. IBEA Innovation and the Built Environment Academy 1st Annual Conference – Innovation & Integration: Science, Technology and Policy in the Built Environment: 7, 8 & 9 October 2011, London South Bank University, UK, pp 341–360 IBSN 978-1-898523-02-4 (available online at www.lsbu.ac.uk/w2/ibeaconference) [Accessed 10 August 2014].

Phiri M, Mills GR, Chang C-L, Price ADF, and Austin SA (2011) *Evidence-Based Design at a Time of Austerity: Do Building Standards and Tools Reflect the Reality of Designing for Dementia, the Elderly, Children and Refurbishment or Reconfiguration?* 4th Annual Conference of the Health and Care Infrastructure Research and Innovation Centre (HaCIRIC11): Global health infrastructure – challenges for the next decade: Delivering innovation, demonstrating the benefits, 26–28 September 2011, Manchester, UK, 2011: pp. 190–208 (available online at http://www.haciric.org/static/doc/events/HaCIRIC_11_conference_proceedings.pdf) [Accessed 10 August 2014].

Phiri M, in association with Worthington J, and Leaman A (1998) Briefing a Continuous Building programme – factors for success: 35 years of design and construction at the University of York. Institute of Advanced Architectural Studies, University of York, UK.

Quan X, Joseph A, Malone E, and Pati D (November 2011) Healthcare Environmental Terms and Outcome Measures: An Evidence-based Design Glossary Phase 1 Report. Concord CA, USA: The Center for Health Design.

Rechel B, Buchan J, and McKee M (2009) The impact of health facilities on healthcare workers' wellbeing and performance. *International Journal of Nursing Studies* 46, 1025–1034.

Reed T, Clouston P, Hoque S, and Fisette P (2010) An analysis of LEED and BREEAM Assessment Methods for Educational Institutions. *Journal of Green Building*, 5 (1), 132–154.

Reizenstein JE (1982) Hospital design and human behaviour: A review of the recent literature. In Baum A, and Singer JE (eds) *Advances in Environmental Psychology*, *Vol. 4*, *Environment and Health*. Hillsdale, NJ: Lawrence Erlbaum Associates.

Rollins JA (2004) Evidence-based hospital design improves healthcare outcomes for patients, families and staff. *Pediatric Nursing*, 30 (4), 338–339

Roodman DM, and Lenssen N (1995) A building revolution: How ecology and health concerns are transforming construction. *Worldwatch Paper* #124. Washington, DC: Worldwatch Institute.

Royal College of Physicians (2003) *The Healing Environment: Without and Within*. London, UK.

Royal College of Psychiatrists (2000) *More than Bricks and Mortar*. London, UK.

Rubin HR, Owens AJ, and Golden G (1998) *Status Report: An Investigation to Determine Whether the Built Environment Affects Patients' Medical Outcomes*. Concord CA: The Center for Health Design.

Ruddell EJ, Gramann JH, Rudis VA, and Westphal JM (1989) The psychological utility of visual penetration in near view forest scenic beauty models. *Environment and Behavior*, 21 (4), 393–412.

Sackett DL, Rosenberg WMC, Gray JAM, Haynes RB, and Richardson WS (1996) Evidence Based Medicine. *British Medical Journal*, 313 (7050), 170–171.

Sadler BL, Berry LL, Guenther R, Hamilton KD, Hessler FA, Merritt C, and Parker D (2011) Fable hospital 2.0: The business case for building better health care facilities. *Hastings Center Report* Vol. 41, 1 (January/February), 13–23.

Sadler BL, Dubose J, and Zimring C (2008) The business case for building better hospitals through evidence-based design. *HERD: Health Environments Research & Design Journal*, 1 (3), 22–30.

Scott MJ, and Canter DV (1997) Picture or place? A multiple sorting study of landscape. *Journal of Environmental Psychology*, 17, 263–281.

Shepley MM, and Quan X (2003) Health design research literature review: 1998–2002. Unpublished paper, Texas A&M University College Station, TX.

Shepley MM, Fournier M-A, and McDougall K (1998) *Healthcare Environments for Children and their Families*. Dubuque: IO Kendal Hunt.

Sherman SA, Varni JW, Ulrich RS, and Malcarne VL (2005) Post occupancy evaluation of healing gardens in a paediatric cancer centre. *Landscape and Urban Planning*, 73 (2–3), 167–183.

Sleeuw M (2011) A comparison of BREEAM and LEED environmental Assessment Methods: A report to the University of East Anglia Estates and Building Division, November 2011.

Stigsdotter UA, and Grahn P (2002) What makes a garden a healing garden? *Journal of Therapeutic Horticulture*, 8, 60–9.

Taylor AF, Kuo FE, and Sullivan WC (2001) Growing up in the inner city: Green places to grow. *Environment and Behavior*, 33, 54–77.

Taylor AF, Kuo FE, and Sullivan WC (2002) Views of nature and self-discipline: Evidence from inner-city children. *Journal of Environmental Psychology*, 22, 49–64.

Tétreault M-H, and Passini R (2003) Architects' use of information in designing therapeutic environments. *Journal of Architectural and Planning Research*, 20 (1), 48–56.

Torbett R, Slater AJ, Gann DM, and Hobday M (2001) Design Performance Measurement in the Construction Sector: A Pilot Study. SPRU (Science and Technology Policy Research Unit) Submission to IEEE Transactions of Engineering Management, April 2001.

Tse P (2012) Assets and targets: Making sense of energy use has got a bit easier with a major revamp of CIBSE's TM22 energy assessment tool. *Delta T Magazine*, February, 12-14.

Tufte E (1997) *Visual Explanations: Images and Quantities, Evidence and Narrative*. Graphics Press, Cheshire, CT.

Ulrich RS (1977) Visual landscape preference: a model and application, *Man-Environment Systems*, 7, 279– 293.

Ulrich RS (1984) View through a window may influence recovery from surgery. *Science*, 224, 420–421.

Ulrich RS (1991) Effects of interior design on wellness: Theory and recent scientific research. *Journal of Health Care Interior Design*, 3, 97–109. [Reprinted in Marberry SO (Ed.) (1995) *Innovations in Healthcare Design*. New York: Van Nostrand Reinhold, 88–104.]

Ulrich RS (2000) Environmental research and critical care. In Hamilton DK (Ed.) *ICU 2010: Design for the Future*. Houston: Center for Innovation in Health Facilities, 195–207.

Ulrich RS, Zimring C, Quan X, and Joseph A (2004) *The role of the Physical Environment in the Hospital of the 21st Century: A Once-in-a-lifetime Opportunity*. Concord CA: The Center for Health Design.

Ulrich RS, Zimring CM, Zhu X, DuBose J, Seo H, Choi Y-S, Quan X, and Joseph A (2008) A review of the research literature on evidence-based healthcare design. *Health Environments Research and Design Journal*, 1 (3), 61–125.

Uzzell DL, and Lewand K, (1990) The psychology of landscape. *Landscape Design*, 1990, 34–35.

Van den Berg AE, Hartig T, and Staats H (2007) Preference for nature in urbanized societies: Stress, restoration, and the pursuit of sustainability. *Journal of Social Issues*, 63, 79–96 (doi:10.1111/j.1540-4560.2007.00497.x).

Varni JW, Burwinkle TM, Dickinson P, Sherman SA, Dixon P, Ervice JA, Leyden PA, and Sadler BL (2004) Evaluation of the built environment at a children's convalescent hospital: Development of the paediatric quality of life inventory™ parent and staff satisfaction measures for paediatric healthcare facilities. *Journal of Developmental & Behavioral Pediatrics*, 25, 1, 10–20.

Velarde MD, Fry G, and Tveit M (2007) Health effects of viewing landscapes – landscapes in environmental psychology. *Urban Forestry & Greening*, 6, 199–212.

Williams MA (1988) The physical environment and patient care. *Annual Review of Nursing Research*, 6, 61–84 (cited in Williams MA (1989) Physical environment of the intensive care unit and elderly patients. *Critical Care Nursing Quarterly* 12 (1), 52–60).

Winkel GH, and Holahan CJ (1985) The environmental psychology of the hospital: Is the cure worse than the illness? *Prevention in Human Services*, 4, 11–13.

Wotton H (1624/2011) *The Elements of Architecture*. John Bill, London. Architecture Revived, 28 September 2011.

Yates A (2001) Quantifying the business benefits of sustainable buildings: Summary of existing research findings. *Project Report* # 203995, Watford, UK: Building Research Establishment, Centre for Sustainable Construction.

Zeisel J (1981) *Inquiry by Design: Tools for environment-behavior research.* Brooks/Cole, Monterrey, California.

Zube EH (1973) Rating everyday rural landscapes of the Northeastern US. *Landscape Architecture*, 1973, 370–375.

Zube EH (1984) Themes in landscape assessment theory. *Landscape Journal*, 3 (2), 104–110.

Zube EH, Pitt DG, and Evans GW (1983) A lifespan development study of landscape assessment. *Journal of Environmental Psychology*, 3, 115–128.

Zube EH, Simcox DE, and Law CS (1987) Perceptual landscape simulations: History and prospect, *Landscape Journal,* 6 (1), 62–81.

## Websites

InformeDesign, http://www.informedesign.org/ developed at the University of Minnesota, USA with a difference in that they provide an analysis of the research studies (Accessed 20 August 2013).

http://shape.dh.gov.uk – website to access SHAPE (free-of-charge to NHS professionals) by formal registration and licence agreement with the SHAPE help desk (shape@nepho.org.uk), which also offers a number of regionally-based training events for all new and existing SHAPE users and includes organisation-based bespoke training sessions on a cost recovery basis.

# Index

Views: Children's Hospital, UK 107–8; Vienna North
    Hospital 97, 99
visitor facilities 112, 114
visualisation *see* graphical representation
Vitruvian principles 2, 55

waiting places 83, 141–2
wards, Vienna North Hospital 96
waste reduction 191
water use 191
wayfinding 31, 94–6
web-based databases 162–70

websites: IDEAs 75, 77–9; SHAPE dementia atlas 131;
    Sheffield database 161
weighting mechanism: AEDET Evolution 44; BREEAM 191;
    DQI 60, 63–4
well-being 190, 223
working areas, AEDET/ASPECT study 141–2
workplace planning/evaluation, SHAPE 136
workshops: DART 87; DQI 56, 62–3

year search, Sheffield database 157–8

zero carbon hierarchy 208

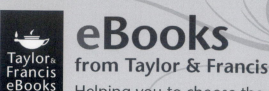